Staredown

Books by Thomas Hauser

General Non-Fiction

Missing

The Trial of Patrolman Thomas Shea

For Our Children
(with Frank Macchiarola)

The Family Legal Companion

Final Warning: The Legacy of Chernobyl
(with Dr. Robert Gale)

Arnold Palmer: A Personal Journey

Confronting America's Moral Crisis
(with Frank Macchiarola)

Healing: A Journal of Tolerance
and Understanding

With This Ring (with Frank Macchiarola)

Thomas Hauser on Sports

Reflections

Boxing Non-Fiction

The Black Lights: Inside the World
of Professional Boxing

Muhammad Ali: His Life and Times

Muhammad Ali: Memories

Muhammad Ali: In Perspective

Muhammad Ali & Company

A Beautiful Sickness

A Year At The Fights

Brutal Artistry

The View From Ringside

Chaos, Corruption, Courage, and Glory

I Don't Believe It, But It's True

Knockout (with Vikki LaMotta)

The Greatest Sport of All

The Boxing Scene

An Unforgiving Sport

Boxing Is . . .

Box: The Face of Boxing

The Legend of Muhammad Ali
(with Bart Barry)

Winks and Daggers

And the New . . .

Straight Writes and Jabs

Thomas Hauser on Boxing

A Hurting Sport

A Hard World

Muhammad Ali: A Tribute to the Greatest

There Will Always Be Boxing

Protect Yourself At All Times

A Dangerous Journey

Staredown

Fiction

Ashworth & Palmer

Agatha's Friends

The Beethoven Conspiracy

Hanneman's War

The Fantasy

Dear Hannah

The Hawthorne Group

Mark Twain Remembers

Finding The Princess

Waiting for Carver Boyd

The Final Recollections of
Charles Dickens

The Baker's Tale

For Children

Martin Bear & Friends

Staredown

Another Year Inside Boxing

Thomas Hauser

The University of Arkansas Press
Fayetteville
2020

ISBN: 978-1-68226-150-7
eISBN: 978-1-61075-732-4

Manufactured in the United States of America

24 23 22 21 20   5 4 3 2 1

⊗ The paper used in this publication meets the minimum requirements
of the American National Standard for Permanence of Paper for Printed
Library Materials Z39.48–1984.

Library of Congress Cataloging-in-Publication Data
Names: Hauser, Thomas, author.
Title: Staredown: another year inside boxing.
Description: Fayetteville: The University of Arkansas Press, 2020. | Summary:
    "Thomas Hauser's latest collection of articles about the contemporary boxing
    scene"—Provided by publisher.
Identifiers: LCCN 2020010934 (print) | LCCN 2020010935 (ebook) |
    ISBN 9781682261507 (paperback) | ISBN 9781610757324 (ebook)
Subjects: LCSH: Boxing—United States. | Boxers (Sports)—United States.
Classification: LCC GV1125.H2934 2020 (print) | LCC GV1125 (ebook) |
    DDC 796.83—dc23
LC record available at https://lccn.loc.gov/2020010934
LC ebook record available at https://lccn.loc.gov/2020010935

The following articles included in this book were originally published by *Sporting
News* (www.sportingnews.com): "Anthony Joshua vs. Andy Ruiz: There Are No
Sure Things in Boxing"; "Manny Pacquiao vs. Adrien Broner: 'AB' Punks Out";
"Errol Spence vs. Mikey Garcia: What Did You Expect?"; "Crawford–Khan and
the State of Boxing"; "History in the Making: Behind the Scenes at Canelo–
Jacobs"; "Wilder–Breazeale and the Heavyweight Puzzle"; "Gennady Golovkin
vs. Steve Rolls: As Expected"; "Manny Pacquiao Turns Back the Clock"; "*Smokin'
Joe*"; "Dempsey–Willard at 100"; "Street Fights"; "Smartphones on Fight Night";
"Fight Night Music"; "Before Video Games, There Was All-Star Baseball"; "Going
Home for a High School Football Game"; "When Red Corner vs. Blue Corner
Is Unfair"; "Fighter of the Decade"; "Saying Goodbye to Harold Lederman."

As a journalist, I rely heavily on sources, particularly in the area of investigative reporting. This book is dedicated to all of the people in boxing who have shared information with me over the years, sometimes under threat of severe retaliation.

Thank you. You know who you are.

Contents

Fighters and Fights

Curiosities

Issues and Answers

Author's Note

Staredown contains the articles about professional boxing that I authored in 2019 and also a few pieces written about other sports.

The articles I wrote about the sweet science prior to 2019 have been published in *Muhammad Ali & Company*; *A Beautiful Sickness*; *A Year at the Fights*; *The View From Ringside*; *Chaos, Corruption, Courage, and Glory*; *I Don't Believe It, But It's True*; *The Greatest Sport of All*; *The Boxing Scene*; *An Unforgiving Sport*; *Boxing Is*; *Winks and Daggers*; *And the New*; *Straight Writes and Jabs*; *Thomas Hauser on Boxing*; *A Hurting Sport*; *A Hard World*; *Muhammad Ali: A Tribute to the Greatest*; *There Will Always Be Boxing*; *Protect Yourself at All Times*; and *A Dangerous Journey*.

Fighters and Fights

Two days before fighting Andy Ruiz at Madison Square Garden, Anthony Joshua told a small group of reporters, "Mistakes make fights exciting."

Anthony Joshua vs. Andy Ruiz: There Are No Sure Things in Boxing

On June 1, 2019, Anthony Joshua fought outside the United Kingdom as a professional boxer for the first time and made his American ring debut at Madison Square Garden. As expected, the British heavyweight sensation made quick work of Andy Ruiz, stopping his hopelessly outclassed opponent in [note to editor: insert proper round here].

[Second note to editor: Oops! Sorry about that. I thought this sort of thing only happened in old sports comedy movies starring John Belushi. Here's the rewrite.]

Anthony Joshua has enjoyed rock-star popularity in his native England. He's charismatic, articulate, gracious, charming, and might have the prettiest smile ever for a heavyweight champion not named Muhammad Ali. After a ragged adolescence, he found purpose in the sweet science. Now twenty-nine years old, he looks back on his early days and says, "I realized I was getting in trouble for fighting in the streets and getting patted on the back for boxing. So I started boxing."

AJ, as he is often called, won a gold medal as a super-heavyweight at the 2012 Olympics, turned pro the following year, and had compiled a 22–0, (21 KOs) ring record as of Saturday morning, June 1. He captured the IBF heavyweight belt with a second-round stoppage of Charles Martin in 2016 and, two months later, knocked out Dominic Breazeale. Then, after a breather against Eric Molina, he prevailed in a thriller over Wladimir Klitschko to annex the WBA crown in front of ninety thousand screaming fans at Wembley Stadium. But he'd looked less impressive since then in beating Carlos Takam, Joseph Parker (thereby adding the WBO title to his inventory), and Alexander Povetkin.

Originally, Joshua was scheduled to fight Jarrell Miller on June 1. Big Baby, as the thirty-year-old Miller is known, stands six feet, four inches tall. His last three fights were fought at 305, 317, and 315 pounds. He carries his weight well, but there's too much of it.

To date, Jarrell's size and persona have outweighed his ring accomplishments. A Big Mac would have been more competitive than some of his opponents. But he had moved steadily up the ranks in a thin heavyweight division en route to a 23–0–1 (20 KOs) ring record.

"People say I don't deserve a title shot," Miller acknowledged after Joshua–Miller was announced. "But who did Joshua fight to get a title shot? Who did Wilder fight to get a title shot? Who did Fury fight to get a title shot? The guys I've fought have been just as good as the guys they fought. Being big is a privilege, and I love it so don't hate on it. Anthony Joshua ain't going to walk me down. Deontay Wilder ain't gonna walk me down. Ain't nobody gonna walk me down."

Once Joshua–Miller was announced, Jarrell followed with a flood of attention-grabbing statements:

* "AJ is making a huge mistake coming over to fight me in my own backyard. All he's doing is delivering me those belts by hand. He'll be leaving New York empty-handed."
* "That punk AJ is standing in the way of my dreams, and on June first he's getting run the hell over. He's a lion, sort of. He's a giant pussy. He'll get his knickers in a twist when I go at him."
* "He can be the pretty boy. All that humble crap and being nice is full of shit. The more that you understand what boxing is; all that humble, that fake shit he puts on. Boxing isn't a humble sport."
* "He's a privileged spoiled brat, and I'm from the grit of the street. He can keep his gold medal. I got street medals. He wants to win. I want to hurt him. I want to tear his head off his fucking body."

Then, at the February 19 kickoff press conference at Madison Square Garden, Miller stepped over the line of propriety. Earlier in the day, he'd attacked Joshua's character at a sit-down with a group of writers, saying, "There's a difference between being a role model and a real model. He's not genuine. He's a UK Uncle Tom."

Once the press conference began, Joshua and Miller strode by prearrangement to stage center for a staredown. And Jarrell departed from the script, giving AJ a hard two-handed shove.

Things degenerated from there with an obstreperous Miller inter-rupting Joshua whenever he tried to speak. Then, seeking to advance his own narrative, Jarrell told the assembled media, "I see my mother go through some stuff that none of you would survive. I see my family starving with no shoes on their feet. We are from the dirt, from the gutter. There were many years that I didn't know what I was doing with my life. I've always had this anger and drive in my stomach, though, that would keep me going. I knew that I must be fighting for something. God has a plan for everybody."

Joshua, who by then had had his fill of Miller, responded, "I got a tear in my eye, Big Baby. Get the violins."

But Miller persisted with insults, leading Joshua to proclaim, "He's stupid and ignorant. I'm going to throw this jab down his throat. I'm going to knock him the fuck out. Come out and watch this one, New York."

Later, after comparable comments from Miller at a press conference in London, Joshua added, "All this spirit this boy has in him, talking shit, I'm going to strip it from him. I'm going to strip him of his soul in that ring. I'm really looking forward to the challenge."

As Eddie Hearn (Joshua's promoter) noted, "It helps the promotion to have a good guy and a bad guy." Tickets were selling well. A strong 300-pound opponent with a big mouth is marketable. Joshua was a 5-to-1 betting favorite. But Miller is a powerful man and could not be taken lightly. It was likely that he would try to turn the fight into a street brawl and rely on an iron will that, to his way of thinking, couldn't be broken.

"He's never been in with nobody like me before," Miller declared. "I'm 300 pounds of lean mean fighting machine. I always get the job done. That's my mentality. There's a lot of things Joshua does well. He gets hit pretty well too."

Joshua, for his part, called Miller "easy work" and dismissed his trash-talking as "a sign of weakness."

"He's slow," AJ said of his opponent. "He's not a puncher. His stamina isn't that good. He'd probably do better in the NFL. He isn't the end of the rainbow. He's just another stepping stone, someone else in my way. On June second, Jarrell Miller will be irrelevant."

The fight promised to be fun while it lasted. Miller is durable. He takes a good punch but he's also relatively easy to hit. It was understood that he'd have to take a lot of punches to beat Joshua. And he'd have to be in peak condition to pressure AJ for twelve rounds. The widespread assumption was that Jarrell would lose, but he was expected to lose in an exciting way. Joshua–Miller would have energized the crowd and been an entertaining scrap.

Then everything fell apart.

On April 16, it was revealed that a urine sample the Voluntary Anti-Doping Association (VADA) took from Miller on March 20 had tested positive for GW1516 (a banned substance also known as Cardarine and Endurobol). On April 18, VADA notified the New York State Athletic Commission, promoter Eddie Hearn, and both the Joshua and Miller camps that a blood sample taken from Jarrell on March 31 had tested positive for human growth hormone, another banned substance. One day later, on April 19, Miller hit the trifecta when it was announced that a urine sample VADA took from him on March 31 had come back positive for EPO (Erythropoietin), a banned performance-enhancing drug that stimulates the production of red blood cells.

At that point, the New York State Athletic Commission refused to license Miller to fight in New York. Earlier in the year, Jarrell had observed, "There's only a short time to get something done in boxing. You get old quick in this game." Now he had lost out on the lion's share of a $6.5 million purse.

With Miller out of the picture, Team Joshua began looking for a new opponent. It says something about the sad state of boxing today that several ranked fighters turned down an opportunity to fight for the heavyweight championship of the world. Foremost among them were Luis Ortiz and Adam Kownacki (both of whom are in the Premier Boxing Champions universe and have been promised fights against WBC titleholder Deontay Wilder). Ortiz, it appears, will fight Wilder this fall. Kownacki's future is more speculative since Wilder announced on social media in late May that he'll be fighting Tyson Fury in early 2020. In theory, Wilder–Kownacki could be sandwiched in between these two Wilder fights. But a short time can change so much in boxing. In turning down multimillion-dollar offers to fight Joshua on June 1, Ortiz and Kownacki put their financial futures at risk.

Then, on May 1, twenty-nine-year-old Andy Ruiz was formally announced as Joshua's opponent.

Ruiz, who is Mexican American, was born and lives in California. He turned pro in 2009 and had compiled a 32–1 (21 KOs) ring record. Over the years, he had picked at the carcasses of Joe Hanks, Ray Austin, Franklin Lawrence, Kevin Johnson, and Alexander Dimitrenko. In 2016, he lost by majority decision in an IBF title bout against Joseph Parker.

Jarrell Miller has the physical attributes of an NFL lineman. The heavily tattooed Ruiz looks like an overweight biker gang member who has been eating six donuts a day and drinking copious amounts of beer for the past ten years.

Ruiz has a good amateur pedigree. But he fought his first pro fight in 2009 at 297 pounds. Top Rank (which promoted him for much of his career) became so disgusted with Ruiz over lifestyle issues that it let him buy his way out of his contract. Prior to fighting Joshua, Andy's most memorable moment in the sweet science had come after a ten-round decision over Siarhei Liakhovich in 2014 when he told the media, "I fucked up my hand really bad in the second round. Thankfully, it's just fractured and not broken."

Introducing Ruiz to the media at a May 4 press conference in Las Vegas, Eddie Hearn acknowledged, "It's been a shitty ten days." He then segued into promoter mode, declaring, "Andy Ruiz will be coming to win. He doesn't look intimidating, but he can really fight. Ruiz has been watching Joshua for years, thinking of ways to beat him. But Joshua hasn't been watching Ruiz. The guys in boxing all say, 'Wow! This is a really tough fight.' This guy can fight. This guy has fast hands. This guy has a high boxing IQ. This guy has a big heart. This guy has all of Mexico behind him."

Manny Robles (who trained Dominic Breazeale for his 2016 challenge to Joshua and now trains Ruiz) admonished, "A lot of people doubt Andy because of the way he looks. But looks can be deceiving."

Ruiz, who is unpretentious and seems affable enough, began his remarks with the warning, "Everyone underestimates me because of the way I look. I'm in this to win it." He then advised the assembled media that he eats a Snickers bar in his dressing room to give him energy before every fight and expressed the hope that he could parlay fighting Joshua into an endorsement deal with Snickers.

Asked if he had a message for AJ, Ruiz warned in his high-pitched singsong voice, "Anthony, don't underestimate this little fat boy. I'm coming for you."

Hah-hah-hah. Virtually no one believed any of it.

But—

Mark Twain famously opined, "Wagner's music is better than it sounds." In that vein, Ruiz is a better fighter than he looks. He was more formidable than Tom Schwarz (who will be fighting Tyson Fury on June 15). And his credentials were on a par with, if not better than, those of Dominic Breazeale (Deontay Wilder's most recent highlight-reel victim).

But Ruiz didn't look the part of a championship contender. In visual terms, Joshua–Ruiz was one of the worst mismatches in boxing history. AJ is six feet, six inches tall, a magnificently sculpted 245 pounds, and conjures up images of Michelangelo's statue of David. Ruiz claims to be six-foot-two but falls well short of that mark unless, perhaps, he's measured around the waist. On June 1, he would weigh in at 262 pounds.

Joshua was a 20-to-1 betting favorite. One week before the fight, Ruiz told Gareth Davies of the *Telegraph* that he was studying early Mike Tyson fights for moves he could unleash against AJ. That, people reasoned, was a little like Gareth studying videos of Michael Jordan for moves he could use against LeBron James. Even if he knew what to do, he couldn't do it.

And realistically speaking, Ruiz's portly appearance said something about the condition he was in. Didn't it?

Fight week was marked by far more talk about the possibility of Joshua fighting Deontay Wilder than about Joshua–Ruiz. At a sit-down with reporters just prior to the final pre-fight press conference, AJ acknowledged, "A fighter is supposed to say that he's focusing completely on the fighter in front of him. But I won't lie. I'm looking at the big picture."

At the same sit-down, Ruiz spoke of going to a boxing gym at age six at the urging of his father.

"My first amateur fight," he recalled, "I was seven years old. There was no kid my weight in my age group, so I had to fight an older kid. I was self-conscious about my weight when I was young, but I got used to it."

Ruiz also referenced having had some skirmishes with the law when he was an adolescent but added, "Boxing kept me away from getting in major trouble."

There was the usual fight week talk.

"Whatever he tries to do," Ruiz offered, "I'll make it difficult for him. . . . It only takes one punch to change a fight. . . . I come forward and throw combinations that Joshua hasn't seen. . . . I'm chubby and short but I'm as fast as lightning. . . . I'm willing to die in the ring to get this victory."

A fighter can visualize what he wants to do in the ring. But he still has to make it happen. The assumption was that Joshua would walk through Ruiz's power (or lack thereof). After all, fighters as pedestrian as Raphael Zumbano and Joell Godfrey had gone the distance with Andy.

The final pre-fight press conference was marked by expressions of mutual respect.

"I don't have nothing bad to say about Anthony Joshua," Ruiz proclaimed. "He's a champion. I respect him. I'm a fan of his. But in the ring, there are no fans."

Joshua responded in kind, saying, "Andy has the mentality and the heart. If it's all about aesthetics, you might as well go to a body-building gym and pick one out and say, 'We've got the next world champion on our hands.' It's not about that."

Still, it was clear that Jarrell Miller's banishment had taken the air out of the promotion. Eddie Hearn conceded that fight week "would have been less flat with Miller." And jokes about Ruiz's physique were the order of the day:

* "Ruiz looks like a circus clown without make-up."
* "Ruiz is a Mexican American version of Butterbean."
* "The only thing Ruiz is going to test positive for is pizza."

"Ruiz will do badly," one veteran scribe predicted.

"He won't do that well," another countered.

There was a time when the world stopped for a heavyweight championship fight at Madison Square Garden, and the heavyweight crown was the most coveted prize in sports. Those days are gone. In some respects, Joshua–Ruiz was as much about the positioning of economic assets as it was about history and glory.

Madison Square Garden came to life on June 1 when Irish Olympic gold medalist Katie Taylor entered the ring to defend her WBA, WBO, and IBF 135-pound women's titles against Delfine Persoon of Belgium (who brought the WBC strap to the table). An exceptionally good fight followed.

Taylor was the better boxer and landed the sharper cleaner punches. Persoon was stronger and kept forcing the action. As the rounds passed,

Persoon kept fighting, and Taylor kept boxing. But Taylor was tiring and not hitting hard enough to keep Persoon off.

The fight devolved into a bloody slugfest. Each fighter's face became more bruised and swollen. Persoon kept moving inexorably forward, throwing artless, clubbing right hands. And an exhausted Taylor kept firing back. Katie's power was gone. Her strength was gone. All she had left were the remnants of her conditioning and her will to survive.

In recent years, the New York State Athletic Commission has become known for bad decisions, most of which favor "the money fighter." Earlier in the evening, England's Josh Kelly (who's being groomed for bigger and better things) had gotten a gift draw against Ray Robinson (from Philadelphia). If the judges were unkind to a fighter from Philadelphia, it was unlikely that a fighter from Belgium would fare any better.

The consensus at ringside was that Persoon had forced the action effectively enough to deserve the nod. But the decision went to Taylor by a 96–94, 96–94, 95–95 margin.

Afterward, Belfast native Carl Frampton (the 2016 Boxing Writers Association of America Fighter of the Year) told BBC Radio 5, "The judges have got it wrong, and it is heartbreaking to see Delfine Persoon in tears. I thought she won that fight by miles. That was a disgraceful decision." Former WBA heavyweight beltholder David Haye added, "That is not the sight you want to see where someone has given everything, but they do not get the decision because of the political power."

Even Eddie Hearn (Taylor's promoter) acknowledged that he'd scored the fight a draw and conceded, "Quite a few people had Persoon winning." He also quoted Katie as saying, "We've got to fight her again, straightaway."

In women's boxing today, world championships are dispensed like trinkets from a gumball machine. That said; on Saturday night, both Taylor and Persoon earned the right to be called a champion.

As for Joshua–Ruiz; predictions, speculation, and hype no longer matter once the bell rings.

Prior to the fight, trainer Manny Robles had told his charge, "Show him early that you belong in the ring with him."

Ruiz did just that. In round one, he backed Joshua up with his jab and was elusive when AJ tried to find him with jabs of his own. Round two was more of the same. The little fat boy could box. The little fat boy had fast hands. Joshua wasn't making the statement that he'd hoped to make against the little fat boy. One had the sense that each passing round would be like a parking meter clicking away at AJ's reputation.

Forty seconds into round three, order was restored. Joshua landed a right uppercut followed by a thudding left hook up top that dropped Ruiz to the canvas. It was the first time in Ruiz's pro career that he'd been knocked down.

The little fat boy rose at the count of five. Joshua followed with a solid right hand. Then AJ got sloppy, and Ruiz staggered him with a counter left to the temple followed by a barrage of his own. Suddenly, Joshua was on the canvas with 1:45 left in the round. He rose. Ruiz went after him. Joshua fired back but he was on unsteady legs. Ruiz took his time, measured his foe, and dropped him again with an accumulation of blows. Joshua rose even more unsteadily than before and was saved by the bell.

The little fat boy could punch. The little fat boy could take a punch. The little fat boy could fight.

"Getting hit on top of the head; it dazed me a bit," Joshua said afterward. "I don't think I recovered. I can remember it, but there was so much going on."

During fight week, AJ had declared, "I'm a fighter; a serious fighter." Now, robbed of his full senses, his default instinct was to not fight.

In round four, Joshua was in survival mode. He gathered himself together to win round five with his jab but seemed tentative, even a bit gun-shy and befuddled.

Round six was all Ruiz as he scored heavily to the head and body.

By round seven, the fight had been beaten out of Joshua. Ruiz dropped him twice more. AJ beat the count, barely, after the final knockdown. But a fighter who rises has to be ready to fight, not just standing. Referee Michael Griffin appropriately halted the contest at the 1:27 mark.

"I don't think Anthony knew where he was," Eddie Hearn said afterward. "You know, he spat his gumshield out on the floor to try and probably get a little more time or just didn't know where he was. He's trying to stand up. He could hardly stand up, so he was looking at the ref. He didn't say, 'I don't want to continue.' The ref said, 'Are you okay?' And he sort of said, 'Yes, I'm okay.' But the fight was done."

"And the new. . . . " A heavyweight champion hopes to hear those words from inside the ring on the night that he wins the title. And never again. On Saturday night, Joshua heard them.

In a sour footnote to the proceedings, it became clear yet again after the fight that judging in New York is a troubling issue. Michael Alexander and Julie Lederman had Ruiz ahead by a meager one point at the time of the stoppage. Shockingly, Pasquale Procopio had Joshua in the lead by a 57–56 margin.

Ruiz was ebullient at the post-fight press conference. "I'm still pinching myself to see if this is real," he said. "That was followed by, "Mom, I love you, and our lives is gonna change. We don't have to struggle no more."

Joshua was gracious in defeat. A bit too gracious for some people.

Long after midnight—well after Ruiz and most media had left Madison Square Garden—AJ met with members of the fourth estate who had remained on site. In the ring after the fight, he'd told Sky Sports, "Boxing's a tough sport. I just got beat by a good fighter. This is all part of the story and the journey. This is the risk we take, isn't it?" Later, he'd told the BBC, "I'm a soldier. You take the good with the bad. Ruiz was the better man tonight."

"It's an upset, isn't it?" AJ asked rhetorically, "One shot on top of the dome rattled me a bit. I tried to stay in there a few more rounds. But respect to Andy. I move forward now and see who's next and what's next."

Who's next? What's next? That's not what boxing fans expect to hear under circumstances like this. What we expect is, "I can't wait for the rematch so I can get my title back."

There's a rematch clause in the fight contracts. Presumably, Joshua will exercise it.

Meanwhile, Joshua now hopes to emulate the success of Lennox Lewis who became the standard bearer for British boxing and, despite crushing defeats at the hands of Oliver McCall and Hasim Rahman, retired as King of the World. So let's give the final word to Lewis, who has observed, "Every time you lose in boxing, people think you're done. That's preposterous. They don't think that in other sports."

Fighters pay for mistakes that they make in the ring with the bill coming due immediately in the form of a punch in the face. Mistakes made outside the ring are often overlooked or rewarded.

Manny Pacquiao vs. Adrien Broner: "AB" Punks Out

When Premier Boxing Champions entered into long-term contracts last year with Fox and Showtime, the reaction among boxing fans was, "This is great!" The assumption was that these contracts, coupled with the alliance between Top Rank and ESPN, guaranteed that there would be lots of high-quality "free" boxing on television.

But it turns out that "free" television isn't so free. Nor does paying a monthly fee for Showtime or ESPN+ ensure that fans won't be charged an additional $74.99 to watch a fight. Exhibit A for this reality was the January 19, 2019, matchup on Showtime PPV between Manny Pacquiao (60–7–2, 39 KOs) and Adrien Broner (33–3–1, 24 KOs) at the MGM Grand in Las Vegas.

Pacquiao has been fighting professionally for twenty-four years and has been fixed in the consciousness of fight fans since 2001 when he destroyed Lehlo Ledwaba on HBO. He became an international feel-good icon and, at his peak, demolished strong opponents like Oscar De La Hoya, Ricky Hatton, and Miguel Cotto. An entire generation of boxing writers found it essential to learn how to spell "Pacquiao." He was the most electrifying force in boxing

But Pacquiao is forty now. Going into the Broner fight, he'd compiled a 6-and-4 record over the preceding seven years. Also, as a Filipino senator, Pacquiao has supported the authoritarian regime of president Rodrigo Duterte and called gay people "worse than animals." The feel-good story no longer feels so good.

On October 22, 2018, Pacquiao announced that he had entered into an agreement with Al Haymon. Pursuant to this alignment, MP Promotions (Pacquiao's promotional company) will promote or co-promote Manny's fights, some of which will be contested under the

PBC banner with Haymon's guidance. The deal also brings other fighters signed with MP Promotions into the PBC fold.

Broner, age twenty-nine, is a classic case of squandered talent. The "four-weight-division world champion" won his belts against Vicente Rodríguez, Antonio DeMarco, Paulie Malignaggi, and Khabib Allakhverdiev, all of whom were well past their prime when Adrien fought them or not very good to begin with.

Broner is a safety-first fighter. When fighting smaller, less talented opponents early in his career, he'd lay back until he broke his opponent down and was sure it was safe. Then he'd go for the kill. Against more formidable opposition, his primary concern has seemed to be going twelve rounds. He hasn't won a fight since edging Adrián Granados on a split decision twenty-three months ago.

The phrase "model citizen" is rarely associated with Broner unless it's preceded by the word "not." He fancies himself an icon in the hood and has made himself relevant in boxing circles by being obnoxious.

A 2016 video posted online shows Broner throwing his change (bills, not coins) in the air as he leaves a Walmart checkout counter and declaring, "He [the cashier] must not know; I'm AB. I don't need no change." This was one of Broner's more socially acceptable postings. Previous postings included (1) Broner having intercourse with two women and no condom, and (2) Broner half-dressed while purportedly defecating into a toilet at a Popeyes and then wiping himself with United States currency. That video was posted on YouTube with the title "Adrien Broner takes a shit in Popeyes."

In addition to a string of juvenile arrests, Broner has been charged with robbery, aggravated robbery, felonious assault, battery, sexual battery, illegal possession of a weapon, domestic violence, and intimidation of a witness.

In recent years, TMZ has served as a bad-news clearinghouse for Broner. Among its revelations are:

* As of April 2017, Broner had fathered seven children with six different women.
* Shortly before Christmas 2018, Pristine Jewelers NY (a Floyd Mayweather shopping stop) filed a lawsuit against Broner claiming an unpaid balance of $1,152,000 on multiple jewelry orders.

* Broner had criminal court appearances scheduled on the same day (January 7, 2019) in two different states in conjunction with charges of sexual misconduct. He was arrested in February 2018 after allegedly groping a woman against her will in an Atlanta shopping mall. Four months later, he was arrested after he allegedly molested a woman in a Cleveland nightclub and forced her to kiss him. That resulted in charges of gross sexual imposition. Broner was represented by counsel at the same-day hearings and not required to attend.

* Broner was arrested in Florida on December 23, 2018, in conjunction with his failure to appear in court on several earlier occasions to answer charges of speeding and driving without a license or registration.

The adoration that many boxing fans once had for Pacquiao has waned, even in his native Philippines. Fighting Broner allowed Manny to be cast as the good guy one more time in a boxing morality tale.

During a January 10 media conference call, Pacquiao assured the media, "I still have that killer instinct, and the fire in my eyes is still there. That aggressiveness, the speed, the power are still there."

Meanwhile, Broner remained true to form with utterances like, "This win makes me an icon. It makes me what I always wanted to be and what everybody always thought I would be. A win here and I'm a legend overnight. I'm already a star. After this victory, I will be taking over the sport of boxing. Adrien Broner will be the biggest name in boxing."

At the final pre-fight press conference, Broner refused to answer a question from Showtime commentator Al Bernstein (one of the most knowledgeable, well-liked people in boxing) and called him a "bitch-ass nigga." Then he told several Pacquiao supporters, "I've got a cat for you for dinner. I've got a sautéed German shepherd for you in the back." For those who wanted more, Adrien mocked Pacquiao's trainer, Freddie Roach (who suffers from Parkinson's syndrome).

"I'm happy he [Pacquiao] bringing Freddie back," Broner told Showtime's Jim Gray.

Gray asked why and Broner responded, "Shit. So we can get this thing shakin'."

But that's one of the reasons Showtime televises Broner's fights. The network made its accommodation long ago with Floyd Mayweather's misogynist behavior and used misogynist and homophobic statements by Mayweather and Conor McGregor as a marketing tool to engender pay-per-view buys for their 2017 fight.

When asked about Broner's conduct, Stephen Espinoza (president of Showtime Sports) responded, "People who are Adrien Broner fans tend to say similar things about him. It all revolves around his authenticity. He's not going to say the right thing because that's what's expected of him. He's not going to always do the right thing because he feels compelled to do so. He is authentic to himself; good, bad, or ugly. And he doesn't try to be anyone he's not. To some people, that's a negative and they would like a little bit more restraint in his actions and statements. But to a whole different part of the audience, they admire that authenticity, that realness, and the ability to say, 'Look, this is who I am. I'm not going to try to be anyone that I'm not. You can accept or reject me as I am.'"

In keeping with that spirit, Broner was joined on the January 19 pay-per-view telecast by Marcus Browne, another fighter with issues involving violence against women.

Browne, who lost in the first round of the 2012 Olympics while representing the United States, had compiled a 22–0 (16 KOs) professional record.

On December 28, 2017, an order of protection was issued against Browne at the request of his former girlfriend (and the mother of his child), who alleged that he'd assaulted her twelve days earlier. On March 30, 2018, Browne allegedly violated the order of protection. Thereafter, he was charged with criminal contempt, criminal mischief, and harassment. The two cases were consolidated, and he pled guilty to disorderly conduct. Spared time in jail, he was ordered to complete a course on domestic violence. Then, following yet another incident involving the same woman (who told police that, on September 27, 2018, Browne tried to choke her) he was arrested again and charged with criminal contempt, criminal obstruction of breathing and circulation, criminal mischief, and harassment.

Asked about the incidents, Brown declared, "I don't think that should worry any of you guys [the media] because it's my personal life. I don't worry about what goes on in your life. I mean, I might know some things in your life that you don't want anybody to know. I don't know why you guys focus on that and worry about it so much. At the end of the day, I am who I am. It's life and it happens."

Browne vs. Badou Jack (who's promoted by Mayweather and had compiled a 22–1–3, 13 KOs record) was the semifinal bout on the Pacquiao–Broner pay-per-view telecast.

Browne has talent, but his staying power and heart have been questioned. A decision in his favor over Radivoje Kalajdzic at Barclays Center in 2016 was aided by some questionable refereeing and scoring. And Marcus has evinced the unfortunate habit of hitting opponents when they're on the canvas, which should have resulted in disqualifications against both Kalajdzic and Thomas Williams a year later.

Jack, now thirty-five, was knocked out in the first round by Derek Edwards in 2014. Thereafter, he added victories over Andre Dirrell and George Groves to his résumé and fought to a draw against both James Gale and an aging Adonis Stevenson. But his only victory in the thirty-three months prior to facing Browne had been against Nathan Cleverly.

Against Browne, Jack looked sluggish from the start. He allowed Marcus to get off first and dictate the pace of the fight. When Jack got in close (where he'd hoped to fight effectively), Browne simply tied him up. Marcus's holding (augmented by low blows) was sufficiently egregious that referee Tony Weeks deducted a point in round seven.

Round seven was also when the fight turned ugly. Midway through the stanza, an accidental clash of heads opened a horrific gash on Jack's forehead. From that point on, he looked like a man fighting with a grotesque Halloween mask on his face. Blood gushed from the wound for the rest of the bout.

In round eleven, Weeks (whose shirt was drenched in blood) stopped the action and asked ring doctor Al Capanna to examine the cut. Capanna allowed the action to continue, which was moronic.

There was no good reason for the fight to continue. Browne had been dominant from round one on. Jack had zero chance of winning and, in addition to taking repeated blows to the head, was at risk of being disfigured for life. The gash was deep, wide, and opening wider with every punch that landed on it. The fight should have been stopped with the outcome determined by going to the judges' scorecards (standard operating procedure when a fight is terminated because of a cut caused by an accidental head butt). Instead, Capanna, Weeks, and Lou Del Valle (Jack's trainer) allowed the butchery to continue. Browne cruised to a 119–108, 117–110, 116–111 triumph, with 119–108 being the most accurate of the judges' scorecards.

As for Pacquiao–Broner, Manny entered the ring as a slightly-better-than-2-to-1 favorite. But the fight wasn't that close. Pacquiao spent twelve rounds trying to force the action, and Broner spent twelve rounds trying to avoid it. Adrien's lack of aggression meant that Manny was allowed to fight at the pace he chose, so his age was less of a factor than might otherwise have been the case.

Pacquiao worked well off his jab. His best moments came in rounds seven and nine when he drove Broner to the ropes and landed punches in bunches. But Adrien has a pretty good chin and weathered each storm, holding on to Manny like they were slow dancing together.

Broner was clearly behind as the bout progressed. But he never looked like he was trying to win. Indeed, he spent the last two rounds circling away and avoiding combat to the greatest extent possible. All told, Adrien landed a meager fifty punches over the course of twelve rounds. Then, at the final bell, he raised both arms in the air and jumped onto the ring ropes in an outlandish gesture of triumph.

The unanimous verdict in Pacquiao's favor was a foregone conclusion. After the judges' decision was announced, Broner told Jim Gray, "I beat him. Everybody out there knows I beat him. I controlled the fight. He was missing. I hit him clean more times. You know I beat that boy."

Later, at the post-fight press conference, Broner added, "My performance tonight talked for me."

It certainly did.

Boxers are held to a high standard of courage because thousands of courageous fighters who boxed before them have set that standard. On Saturday night, Adrien Broner fell short of that standard. He punked out.

On March 16, 2019, Premier Boxing Champions and Fox charged boxing fans $74.95 for yet another unsatisfying night.

Errol Spence vs. Mikey Garcia: What Did You Expect?

On Saturday night, March 16, 2019, Errol Spence dominated Mikey Garcia from start to finish before an announced crowd of 47,525 at The Jerry Jones Pleasure Palace a.k.a. AT&T Stadium (home of the Dallas Cowboys) in Arlington, Texas.

Spence, age twenty-nine, has now fashioned a 25-and-0 (21 KOs) ring record. He won the IBF 147-pound crown with an eleventh-round stoppage of Kell Brook in 2017 and successfully defended it against a faded Lamont Peterson and no-hoper Carlos Ocampo last year. As Tris Dixon wrote recently, "He is meticulous yet aggressive, clinical but watchable. He's patient but forceful. He remembers to work the body and also dazzles with shots upstairs. As with any true talent, the exciting part is seeing what happens when they match up against someone of similar ability."

The thirty-one-year-old Garcia (who entered the ring to face Spence with a 39–0, 30 KOs ledger) won the WBO 126 pound title by technical decision over Orlando Salido in 2013. Next, he seized the 130-pound WBO belt with an eighth-round stoppage of Román Martinez. Two more belts, courtesy of Sergey Lipinets (IBF 140) and Robert Easter (IBF 135) followed. A unanimous-decision triumph over Adrien Broner at a contract weight of 140 pounds was also in the mix.

Given the disparity in size between them, Spence was a curious choice of opponents for Garcia. Mikey began the year as a contractual free agent. He was free to work with any promoter. "If Mikey wants to be bold and prove how he's a fighter for all time," Frank Lotierzo wrote, "he'd holler from the mountaintop for Lomachenko, stating how he wants to be remembered for beating him when Vasyl was at his best. But no, he seeks a fight where he'll be praised for just showing up."

Even Spence seemed dubious about engaging with Garcia, acknowledging during a March 8 teleconference call. "At first, I didn't really care too much for fighting him. But it got to a point where he started talking a lot more and a lot of other welterweights like Shawn Porter, Keith Thurman, and Danny Garcia, they all had their dates. Manny Pacquiao too. Then, when I found that I could be fighting at AT&T Stadium, it just made sense."

Asked for more regarding the merits of the matchup against Garcia, Spence sounded almost apologetic, saying, "I'm not the bully here. Mikey really pushed for the fight. People who say that he doesn't stand a chance; I feel like they don't really know anything about boxing or don't know the history of boxing. He does have a lot of skills and he's fundamentally sound. So he definitely has a chance. I mean, everybody has a chance."

The promotion was built on platitudes like "dare to be great." Garcia took the lead, telling various media outlets, "I need this fight. I need a marquee name. I want to beat great champions . . . He's the best right now in the division. I want to make a statement. I want to make a mark . . . I want to be the best fighter on the planet, the pound-for-pound number one. I want people to talk about the things that I did inside a boxing ring long after my career is over. Taking on Errol Spence gives me the chance to get everything I ever wanted in one night."

Promoter Richard Schaefer predicted that the fight could do as many as one million pay-per-view buys, which everyone (including Schaefer) understood was multiples over the mark.

Bart Barry summed up the reality of the situation with a pre-fight analysis that read, "Garcia now shoots at the moon, bounding up a couple of weight classes and fighting one of the world's two best welterweights. What will happen in Arlington? What we think will happen. Two of this generation's best fighters in an unsatisfying handicap match."

The betting public made Spence an almost 4-to-1 favorite.

Garcia talked the talk before the fight:

* "People say Errol is bigger. That's just obvious. But there's a lot more that goes into this sport and who's going to win this particular fight."

* "It's the subtle little moves that make the difference inside the ring. I'm always one step ahead. Opponents don't see that on video. When they get in the ring, they realize it's a whole different experience. I don't have any doubts. I know I'll win."

★ "I have all the tools and all the skills needed to beat Errol Spence. When it comes to timing, speed, reflexes and defense; you name it, I'm better. Saturday night, Errol is going to find out why I picked this fight. I've always said I'm better than him. Not by a lot, but just enough to beat him."

Garcia's partisans evoked images ranging from Manny Pacquiao vs. the larger Oscar De La Hoya to the biblical David vs. Goliath. But De La Hoya was an old man in boxing terms when Pacquiao fought him whereas Spence is in his prime. And David brought a sling onto the battlefield when he fought Goliath. No smooth stones would be allowed at AT&T Stadium.

Size matters in boxing. That's why they have weight divisions. No matter how much Garcia built up his body, the five-foot-ten Spence would be four inches taller than Mikey on fight night and the naturally bigger man. Indeed, Garcia had never before been in a fight where either combatant tipped the scales at 140 pounds or more.

The biggest question regarding Spence as a fighter is whether he can take a bigtime punch. Throughout his career, his management team has steered him clear of punchers. But few knowledgeable observers expected Garcia, who seems to have left his power behind as he moved up in weight, to make a serious inquiry regarding Errol's chin.

"I can't worry about what Mikey sees in me," Spence said at the final pre-fight press conference. Everyone thinks they see something looking on the outside, but it's a lot harder once you're in the ring. Skill for skill and talent for talent, I'm more dominant than him in every aspect. I'll beat him at anything he wants to do."

Bottom line: If Garcia were to win, the headlines would trumpet that Mikey had taken a step toward greatness. If, as expected, Spence prevailed, the storyline would be, "Errol beat up a little guy he was supposed to beat."

Spence–Garcia was the inaugural pay-per-view telecast for the union between Premier Boxing Champions (which controls rights to Spence) and Fox. The network pulled out all the stops in promoting the event, including an hour-long press conference that was televised on the Fox broadcast network one month before the fight card as well as extensive shoulder programming on Fox and FS1.

When fight night arrived, there was an eight-person commentating team consisting of Kenny Albert, Chris Myers, Joe Goossen, Lennox Lewis, Ray Mancini, Shawn Porter, Heidi Androl, and Kate Abdo. Eight was too many.

The camera work was good but there was too much hype. Viewers were told throughout the telecast that Spence–Garcia was "a fight for the ages" and the winner of every undercard fight looked "great."

Thirty-eight-year-old Chris Arreola didn't look great.

Arreola, who'd won just three of eight fights over the preceding eight years, entered the ring for the first pay-per-view fight of the evening with a 37–5–1 (32 KOs) record. His opponent, Jean Pierre Augustin, had a manufactured 17–0–1 (12 KOs) ledger and had last fought in 2017 against a 334-pound club fighter.

Arreola's timing, reflexes, and balance were off. One had to push memory a bit to remember that he was once a world-class fighter. But Augustin seemed intimidated from the start and tired visibly in the second round. Arreola wobbled him with a jab in round three and stopped him at the 2:03 mark. The Fox announcing team said that it was "an amazing win." In reality, all it did was set Chris up to lose to another Premier Boxing Champions heavyweight like Adam Kownacki.

Next up, former WBC 118-pound champion Luis Nery (28–0, 22 KOs), who lost his title on the scales last year, faced light-punching McJoe Arroyo (who last scored a knockout five years ago). Nery–Arroyo was a dreary beatdown that the latter's corner mercifully halted after four knockdowns in four rounds.

Then, to fill dead-air time, Fox inserted a mismatch that saw Lindolfo Delgado brutally demolish a no-hope opponent named James Roach in the first stanza.

The final bout before the main event matched twenty-two-year-old former WBC 168-pound beltholder David Benavidez (20–0, 17 KOs) against J'Leon Love (who'd scored one win in three fights since 2016). Benavidez, who was stripped of his title in September of 2018 after testing positive for cocaine, scored a predictable second-round knockout.

As for the main event; the assumption was that Garcia would fight to win, at least at the start. But once the bell rang, Mikey didn't dare to be great.

Spence controlled an uneventful round one with his jab. Rounds two and three were more of the same. Then Errol opened up, and Mikey fought a tactical survival fight for the rest of the bout.

Neither man gave the other much to work with. But as the fight progressed, Spence took what he wanted. He was bigger and stronger. He completely outboxed Garcia, dictating the distance between them with his reach, footwork, and jab. Mikey never made adjustments. He rarely got close enough to counter effectively and didn't seem anxious to try.

In round nine, Lennox Lewis said of Garcia, "He has to take chances. I haven't seen him take one chance." But by then Spence had stepped up the pace, digging effectively to the body, and Mikey was doing all that he could to simply survive.

The CompuBox numbers were a lopsided 345-to-75 in Spence's favor. The judges' scorecards were just as lopsided: 120–107, 120–108, 120–108.

Before fighting Mikey Garcia, Errol Spence said, "This win makes me pound-for-pound number one."

No! If Errol Spence wants to be #1 pound-for-pound, he should fight Terence Crawford.

Vasyl Lomachenko fights like he's trying to win a sporting event. Terence Crawford fights like he's trying to beat a guy up.

Crawford–Khan
and the State of Boxing

Omaha, Nebraska is famous for its stockyards, where millions of cattle, hogs, and sheep are slaughtered annually to feed a nation. On Saturday night, April 20, 2019, Omaha native Terence Crawford displayed his talent as a butcher when he brutalized Amir Khan en route to a sixth-round stoppage at Madison Square Garden.

Crawford, age thirty-one, is a complete fighter. He now has a 35–0 (26 KOs) ring record and holds the WBO title in boxing's talent-laden 147-pound division. Prior to moving up in weight, he'd simultaneously held all four major 140-pound belts.

Crawford dishes out what writer Jimmy Tobin calls "the type of lingering abuse that ages fighters overnight. There is something Mayweather-like about Crawford in the way he first studies, then disarms his opponents," Tobin states. "But unlike Mayweather, Crawford goes beyond merely establishing dominance. Crawford is as good a finisher as you will find. Patient, accurate, creative. You do not hang around with 'Bud'."

Frank Lotierzo elaborates on this theme, noting, "Crawford has no stylistic weaknesses. He can do everything a fighter can be asked to do in a boxing ring. His fundamentals are very good. He has a great boxing mind. His boxing aptitude is off the charts. He fights with heightened concentration and sees everything, whether it's on offense or defense. And he has the strength, power, and technique to execute what his mind tells him. Defensively, going by the way he looks after his bouts, Crawford must be hard to hit because his face is seldom marked. Offensively, Crawford has more gears than any fighter in boxing and he's quicker and a little bit of a bigger puncher than he is given credit for. Terence has more resources physically and processes information faster than any fighter we've seen in a long time. He's a natural fighter with a mean streak a mile wide."

About that mean streak . . . Writing after Crawford's ninth-round demolition of Jeff Horn last year, Bart Barry observed, "Crawford enjoyed Horn's diminishment. He felt Horn relenting and smiled. This is what makes men like Crawford exceptional. Where something like empathy for a man being stripped publicly of his dignity begins to drain others, such a stripping makes the purest fighters euphoric. It transcends professionalism: I'm not doing this because it's my job. No, I'm doing this because I like hurting you."

Crawford is also a hard worker. "Camp is never easy," he says. "If camp is ever easy, then your trainer is doing something wrong."

Amir Khan (now 33–5, 20 KOs, 4 KOs by) began his ring career with high expectations as a seventeen-year-old prodigy who'd won a silver medal on behalf of England at the 2004 Olympics. A 2008 knockout loss to Breidis Prescott deflated his bubble. But Khan rebounded with victories over Paulie Malignaggi, Marcos Maidana, and Zab Judah to claim the WBA and IBF titles at 140 pounds before losing a questionable split decision to Lamont Peterson in Washington, DC (a jurisdiction notorious for poor officiating and also Peterson's hometown). Then, on July 14, 2012, Danny Garcia knocked Amir out in the fourth round.

Since then, Khan has been better known for talking than fighting. To his credit, he has at times shown a willingness to go in tough. Three years ago, he embarked on a quixotic quest against Canelo Alvarez, who rendered him unconscious in the sixth round. But Amir has passed the point of relevance in elite boxing circles except as an opponent. There was a time when he was a better fighter than anyone currently on Crawford's résumé. He isn't anymore.

Asked at a January 17 press conference why he was fighting Khan, Crawford referenced the protective wall that Premier Boxing Champions has built around its 147-pound fighters and stated, "I'm just rolling with the tide. He was the best welterweight to choose from, being that everyone else has fights. I can't make them fight me."

Khan didn't see himself as an opponent. But that's what he was. "People are expecting me to get beat," he acknowledged. The early odds favored Crawford by a 7-to-1 margin and rose significantly higher as fight night approached.

The fighters were respectful toward one another during the pre-fight buildup.

At the final pre-fight press conference, promoter Bob Arum analogized Crawford-Khan to Sugar Ray Leonard's initial encounters against Roberto Duran and Thomas Hearns and assured the media that, years from now, fans who bought the pay-per-view would be talking reverentially about the bout with their children and grandchildren.

Hyperbole aside, it was clear that Khan had far more to gain from the fight than Crawford did. A win would go a long way toward fulfilling his early promise and elevating his legacy. "It's a fight that can redeem my whole career," he said.

Crawford, on the other hand, didn't stand to win much by winning. But a loss would seriously undermine his status.

Big arenas are quiet places on fight night when the first fight begins. Several hundred spectators were scattered around Madison Square Garden, most of them in the cheap seats, when Lawrence Newton squared off against Jonathan Garza on April 20 at 6:00 p.m. The building filled up as the night wore on.

The pay-per-view telecast started at 9:00 p.m. with three showcase bouts for Top Rank fighters.

Lightweight Felix Verdejo (24–1, 16 KOs) is a flashy boxer with charisma who was being hyped as Puerto Rico's next ring icon until Antonio Lozado exposed his shortcomings and knocked him out at Madison Square Garden last year. Bryan Vásquez (37–3, 20 KOs) is a gatekeeper who had lost to Raymundo Beltran, Javier Fortuna, and Takashi Uchiyama. Against Vásquez, Verdejo cruised to an uninspired unanimous decision triumph.

Next up, twenty-one-year-old Shakur Stevenson (10–0, 6 KOs), who won a silver medal in the bantamweight division at the 2016 Olympics, took on Christopher Diaz (24–1, 16 KOs).

There was a blip on the radar screen earlier this month when an online video surfaced showing—graphically showing—Stevenson administering a vicious beating to a defenseless man who had been knocked down on the concrete floor of a Miami Beach parking garage. Shakur, it turned out, is currently under indictment on charges of felony battery in conjunction with the incident, which occurred in July of 2018. Diaz represented a step up in caliber over Stevenson's previous ring and garage opposition. But Christopher's plodding, one-dimensional style was made-to-order for Shakur, who thoroughly outboxed him in a dreary fight that occasioned boos and jeers at the final bell.

In the final undercard fight of the evening, Teofimo Lopez (12–0, 10 KOs), also twenty-one, fought Edis Tatli (31–2, 10 KOs) of Finland. Lopez has all the earmarks of a rising star in the lightweight division. Tatli was in over his head, and everyone knew it. The open questions were: (1) How would the defensive-minded Tatli react when Lopez caught up to him and whacked him with a solid punch?; and (2) How long would it take for that to happen? The answers were (1) poorly and (2) four-and-a-half rounds. Midway through round five, Teofimo landed a body-shot for a one-punch knockout.

Then it was time for Crawford–Khan.

Crawford tends to start cautiously while figuring out his opponents. Then, once he has learned what he wants to know, he shifts into high gear. Against Khan, that didn't take long. A little more than two minutes into round one, a chopping right hand over a Khan jab staggered Amir and a follow-up left hook put him on the canvas.

There's a surgical quality to the way Crawford breaks down and carves up his opponents. He's always looking to make something happen. Opponents have zero time off. And as Terence's "man strength" has increased, he has become a significantly harder puncher.

In round three, Crawford transitioned from an orthodox to a southpaw stance. Brutal bodywork followed.

Prior to fighting Crawford, Khan had claimed confidence with the observation, "As you get older, you get wiser as a fighter."

But as fighters age, they also get slower and the punches hurt more.

The beating that Crawford inflicted on Khan worsened. Then, two minutes into round six as Terence was throwing a hook to the body, Amir pushed down hard with his upper arm on the back of Crawford's head causing the punch to stray low. Very low. Khan was hurt by the blow. There's no doubt about that. But rather than take the five minutes allowed to recover, he and his corner chose to not continue, giving Crawford a sixth-round knockout triumph.

"He was looking for a way out," Terence said afterward. "I saw him shaking his head and talking to his trainer and I thought, 'Oh hell, I know he's going to quit.' I don't like to win a fight like that."

So . . . What does Crawford–Khan mean for boxing? Crawford is establishing himself as a major talent. But in the larger scheme of things, that doesn't necessarily equate to cause for celebration.

For starters, indications are that, despite rhetoric to the contrary, ESPN (which televises all of Top Rank's fights) regards boxing as a niche sport. To find the boxing portal on the ESPN website, one has to move past a list of major sports to "other" and then scroll down. Boxing is the twelfth "other" sport listed (after entries such as Little League World Series and cricket).

When Sergey Kovalev fought Eleider Alvarez on ESPN+ on February 2, the bell for round one rang at 1:00 a.m. eastern time. Vasyl Lomachenko vs. Anthony Crolla, televised on ESPN+ on April 12, didn't start until 12:20 a.m. This is not the mainstream exposure that fans were promised when ESPN returned to boxing.

Crawford–Khan was the first pay-per-view fight card televised pursuant to ESPN's alliance with Top Rank. At the January 15 kickoff press conference, ESPN executive vice president for programming and scheduling Burke Magnus praised the bout as "truly a cause for celebration" and "a perfect example of the vision that we had when we teamed up with Top Rank."

So much for free fights on ESPN or capping the monthly bill for fight fans at $4.99 for ESPN+. One of the more eloquent statements in opposition came from writer Paul Magno, who opined, "To see the mighty ESPN, which invested tens of millions into establishing a real boxing presence, passing the hat to consumers is downright insulting. The outrage over this should come from fans who, despite new business models popping up and deep pockets swooping in to 'rescue' the sport, are still being asked to pay twice and thrice for being loyal to the sport. If a promoter or network can't make a buck with a fight, then they need to explore the real reasons behind why they can't make that buck."

Bob Arum has defended putting Crawford-Khan on pay-per-view. During a March 26, 2019, media conference call, the promoter declared, "This is professional boxing. The fighters have to be compensated. And you cannot rely on a network to constantly come up with big, big money as a rights fee. So if the fight is big enough, you have to go to the public and say to the public, 'Hey, this is a terrific fight. You have to support the fight.' Now, sometimes the public says 'no.' But we can stop playing the games of whether a fight should be pay-per-view or shouldn't be pay-per-view. The first question is, 'Is it a really good matchup?' And then, 'Is it affordable on regular television? Can a rights fee support the fight?' That is the mindset. Everything else is noise."

But—and this is a big "but"—to reach a point where networks are willing to finance putting boxing's biggest fights on free television rather than pay-per-view, advertisers have to be willing to pay big dollars for commercials. How does boxing get to that point? By putting fights like Crawford–Khan on free TV.

Saying that boxing doesn't have enough fans to generate advertising revenue to cover the purse guarantees for big fights becomes a self-defeating prophecy. Boxing and boxing's best fighters will never become magnets for big advertising dollars unless the public is exposed on a large scale to the best that boxing has to offer.

Here again, Magno is on point, writing, "If ESPN's investment in boxing was all about snatching up an underachieving, underperforming niche sport and creating something new, dynamic, and profitable with it, then the goal had to be long-term growth, building towards real payoffs. Sticking your marquee star behind a PPV paywall in the second fight after you sign him to a major deal is pure stupidity."

Meanwhile, Top Rank is using its ties to ESPN and ESPN's checkbook to renew its bond with fighters already under contract and sign new talent. Dan Rafael of ESPN.com says that Terence Crawford is now guaranteed a minimum of $3 million for fights on ESPN, $3.5 million for fights on ESPN+, and $4 million for pay-per-view bouts. For Crawford–Khan, Rafael reports, Terence was guaranteed a minimum of $5.5 million.

More strikingly, on February 18, 2019, ESPN, Top Rank, and Queensberry Promotions (which promotes Tyson Fury) announced a multiyear agreement that calls for Fury to fight at least twice annually in the United States. All of Tyson's fights will be televised in the United States on an ESPN platform and in the United Kingdom on BT Sport. According to press reports, the deal is for five Fury fights, has a price tag of $103 million, and includes all of Queensberry's other fighters as part of the package.

Fury's first fight under the contract is scheduled for June 15 in Las

Vegas against Tom Schwarz and will be streamed on ESPN+. Schwarz is as prohibitive as an underdog can get.

It's no secret that crazy money is pouring into boxing these days. In some instances—such as Canelo Alvarez vs. Danny Jacobs slated for DAZN on May 4—the money has led to the best fighting the best. But matchups of this nature are few and far between.

Contrary to logic, most of the powers that be in boxing now seem wedded to a business model that discourages megafights. Premier Boxing Champions proudly declares that, starting with Errol Spence, it controls most of the top welterweights in the world today; Keith Thurman, Shawn Porter, Danny Garcia, and Manny Pacquiao among them. But it has used an oversized lightweight (Mikey Garcia) as its primary tool to build Spence.

Anthony Joshua (DAZN–Matchroom), Deontay Wilder (PBC–Showtime), and Tyson Fury (ESPN–Queensberry–Top Rank) seem to be competing in separate leagues that are largely closed off from one another.

Vasyl Lomachenko—at or near the top of most pound-for-pound lists—was refreshingly candid when asked about fighting Anthony Crolla instead of a more imposing opponent on ESPN+ on April 12.

"Of course, I don't like it," Lomachenko responded. "It's not good for me. But it is what it is."

Even Bob Arum acknowledged that there were better fights to be made but pointed to Crolla's status as the mandatory challenger for Lomachenko's WBA title and declared, "The fight got shoved up our ass with the mandatory, and that's what you're gonna see on Friday night. It's certainly not the fight, given our druthers, that we would have made."

When HBO entered the boxing business four decades ago, it payed what was considered an outlandish amount of money to lure elite fighters away from broadcast television. But it paid that money to make big fights, not avoid them.

That brings us back to Terence Crawford.

"Where we watch fights has changed," Jimmy Tobin writes. "So has how we watch them. But the reasons we watch remain the same. Crawford is one of those reasons. There are scant few stronger."

Some fighters need protecting. Crawford neither needs nor wants it. He means it when he says, "Anything I do, I want to be the best. I feel I'm the number one guy. Spence feels he's the number one guy. If everybody in the division wants to fight each other and they're serious about it, it will happen. If not, it won't. If you look at my history, I never turned down any fight."

Crawford–Spence (or Spence–Crawford, if you prefer) wouldn't be hard to make. Terence tells Top Rank, "Make the fucking fight." Errol tells PBC, "Make the fucking fight." It would be a joint pay-per-view venture between ESPN and the network of PBC's choosing (similar to HBO and Showtime working together on Lennox Lewis vs. Mike Tyson and Floyd Mayweather vs. Manny Pacquiao). Revenue and promotional expenses would be split fifty-fifty between the two camps. The Spence camp would advocate for AT&T Stadium in Texas (Errol's home state) as the site. But Las Vegas would come up with enough money to warrant putting the fight on neutral ground. There. That was easy, wasn't it.

With or without Spence as an opponent, Crawford will be well paid for the foreseeable future. So will most of today's other elite fighters. But in terms of being able to prove their greatness, they're victims of the current system. And as boxing fans, so are we.

Terence Crawford has never fought an elite fighter. That's the hole in his résumé. Here, the thoughts of Carlos Acevedo are instructive: "A fighter such as Crawford, no matter how much money he makes, is, in a sense, cheating himself. Which is a shame because Crawford—the switch-hitting stylist with a mean streak and a killer instinct—resembles, in nearly every aspect, the ideal fighter except where it counts most: in the record books. All fighters have had the same dreams for as long as boxing has been in the mainstream. Is it possible that these dreams are smaller now than ever?"

Canelo Alvarez has evolved from a child prodigy to an elite fighter.

History in the Making:
Behind the Scenes at Canelo–Jacobs

On May 4, 2019, Saul "Canelo" Alvarez successfully defended his WBC, WBA, and *Ring Magazine* titles against Danny Jacobs in Las Vegas and added Jacobs's IBF belt to his wardrobe. With that victory, Canelo continued to build his legacy the way a fighter's legacy should be built. Not by self-aggrandizing talk but by deeds in the ring, one fight at a time.

Elite fighters have self-belief. Alvarez believes in himself and radiates quiet confidence without the loud bravado often associated with boxing. He chooses his words carefully when speaking in public and keeps his guard up during interviews as he does in the ring.

Canelo has the mindset of a fighter. He's goal-oriented and fundamentally sound with speed, power, and a solid chin. Now 28, he began boxing professionally at age fifteen and has compiled a 51–1-2 ring ledger. One of the draws came when he was fifteen years old. The other was against Gennady Golovkin. The loss was to Floyd Mayweather when Mayweather was at his peak and Canelo had yet to mature as a fighter.

Alvarez didn't rest on his early success. He has worked hard to get better and tested himself at every level. He's willing to fight quality opponents who are good enough to beat him. Three of his last four bouts have been against Golovkin (twice) and Jacobs. He embraces challenges.

There was a blip on the radar screen in February 2018 when urine samples that Alvarez provided to the Voluntary Anti-Doping Association tested positive for Clenbuterol, a banned substance. The amount of the drug in his system was consistent with the ingestion of tainted beef. But a boxer is responsible for what goes into his body. Canelo agreed to a six-month suspension and paid $50,000 out of his own pocket for year-round VADA testing. Since then, he has been tested more thoroughly by VADA than any boxer ever, always without complaint and never with an adverse test result.

"There will always be critics," Canelo says. "It comes with success.

But I love what I do. I truly love boxing. When I started as a young kid, I always dreamed of becoming a world champion. As I learned with experience, I started challenging myself more and saying, 'Why one championship? I can go on and win more.' I'm still growing and seeing this process. That's what motivates me, to continue writing history and to continue reaching those goals. I want to be remembered as one the greats in boxing. That's why I continue to work hard and continue taking on these type of fights, so I can continue writing history."

Danny Jacobs came into the ring against Canelo with 35 victories and 2 defeats. But despite being the IBF 160-pound champion and having held a WBA belt in the past, he'd never been The Man in the middleweight division. Early in his career, he suffered a fifth-round demolition at the hands of Dmitriy Pirog. Two years ago, he was on the short end of a close decision against Golovkin.

"I'm more of a threat than a superstar," Jacobs says. "So sometimes, when they talk about big fights, I get left out of the equation. Controversy sells, but that's not who I am. That's not where I came from. I'm not sure if that's why I'm not a household name, but I can't concentrate on that. I stay true to who I am and how I was raised. I'll always keep that integrity and try to be a stand-up guy. Also, by having a son, I know he watches everything that I do, and I can't be acting up and being goofy to get more ratings."

Jacobs is a good representative for boxing. He also takes pride in being a symbol of hope for cancer survivors, having overcome a harrowing illness to get to where he is today.

Canelo–Jacobs was streamed live by DAZN, which hopes to become the Netflix of sports. There was skepticism when it was announced in May 2018 that DAZN would invest at least a billion dollars in boxing over its first eight years in the United States. That number now appears to be accurate in light of the $365 million contract that the streaming service has entered into with Canelo and Golden Boy and its recent three-year, six-fight deal with Golovkin.

DAZN's entry into boxing sparked a bidding war with ESPN and Premier Boxing Champions that has seen purses for a handful of fighters rise to extraordinary levels. One would expect this to result in the best fighting the best. But overall, that hasn't been the case. Instead, fans have been subjected to a plethora of one-sided fights and boring matchups. Within that milieu, Canelo–Jacobs was a welcome relief. Unlike the other powers that be in boxing, DAZN wasn't protecting its franchise fighter. It was putting him in tough. And Canelo was a willing participant.

The early buildup to Canelo–Jacobs was dominated by talk of whether Danny could get a fair shake from the judges in Las Vegas. Canelo had fought Golovkin twice in Sin City en route to a controversial draw in their first encounter and a majority-decision victory in the rematch. Jacobs offered the opinion that "the second fight was closer, but I thought Golovkin beat Canelo both times." Then he added, "It's a little annoying to have to keep talking about the judges and Canelo getting favoritism. But it's also a fact in most people's mind, so that's why it comes up so much."

Ultimately, the same three judges who worked the Canelo–Golovkin rematch—Dave Moretti, Steve Weisfeld, and Glenn Feldman—were chosen for Canelo–Jacobs. Moretti had scored Canelo–Golovkin I for Gennady and the rematch for Canelo. Weisfeld scored the rematch for Canelo, while Feldman had it even.

The Canelo–Jacobs promotion was marked by good will and mutual respect between the camps.

"He's a complete fighter," Canelo said of Danny. "He can box, punch. He's tall, agile. It's going to be a very difficult fight, especially in the first few rounds until I start adapting and imposing my style. In boxing, anything can happen. That's why today I train harder than ever, so that it doesn't happen."

"It has never been my intention in the lead-up to any fight to create animosity to sell the fight or to bash my opponent," Jacobs responded in kind. "Never have I ever wanted to do that. It has never been in my nature. So for me, this has been one of the best promotions that I've been a part of because I share the same ideas with my opponent, which is being professional and let our skills and what we bring to the table speak for itself. I'm grateful for that; that we don't have to go out there and be goofy or go out there and be someone who we aren't. That's a breath of fresh air for me."

But when fight week arrived, the promotion was struggling a bit.

Canelo–Jacobs was part of a nine-day feast on DAZN that saw a super-flyweight championship rematch between Srisaket Sor Rungvisai and Juan Francisco Estrada, two World Boxing Super Series semifinal bouts, and Alvarez (the most bankable fighter in the world) against a dangerous challenger. As DAZN executive vice president for North America Joseph Markowski noted, "The only thing missing is the pay-per-view price tag."

However, the days when Las Vegas stopped for a big fight are pretty much gone. The MGM Grand was the host hotel for Canelo–Jacobs, but the Billboard Music Awards were a higher priority. The fight week media center, traditionally in Studios A and B, was relocated to the Premier Ballroom on the third floor of the adjacent MGM Grand Conference Center, a twenty-minute walk from the heart of the hotel.

Another problem the promotion faced was that, while DAZN has some excellent public relations personnel, the subscription service isn't wired into the minds of boxing fans the way HBO was and Showtime is, nor does it have the benefit of a promotional platform like ESPN or Fox.

Canelo had fought four times at the T-Mobile Arena—against Golovkin (twice), Julio Cesar Chavez Jr, and Amir Khan—generating almost $70 million in ticket sales. Overall, he'd headlined nine fight cards in Las Vegas, grossing more than $115 million in ticket revenue. But despite Canelo–Jacobs being on Cinco de Mayo weekend, ticket sales were falling short of expectations. Final numbers released by the Nevada State Athletic Commission later revealed 15,730 tickets sold, 1,388 comps, and a live gate of $8,685,750.

The nights get longer for most fighters during the week of a fight. More than anyone else, they understand and feel the risks involved and the weight upon their shoulders. They sleep more fitfully as the big night approaches.

Canelo seemed immune to that. Throughout fight week, he seemed comfortable with who and where he was. The only irritation he showed was a residue of resentment toward Golovkin and trainer Abel Sanchez as a consequence of comments they'd made last year regarding performance-enhancing drugs and, in the case of Sanchez, Canelo's Mexican heritage. But when asked for his thoughts about Golovkin's recent dismissal of Sanchez as his trainer, Canelo answered simply, "I have no comment on that. To each his own."

Jacobs, perhaps in an effort to lobby the judges, took advantage of several media sit-downs to voice the theme, "Canelo fights for thirty seconds a round. I'll be much more active than that on Saturday night. Canelo likes to fight in spurts. I'll be fighting for three minutes of every round."

Taking stock of where he was in his ring career, Danny proclaimed, "I'm having a great time. This is what you dream of when you put the gloves on for the first time. Right now, Canelo is the face of boxing. I want that to be me."

Then, at the weigh-in on Friday, the cordial relations came to an end.

Jacobs tipped the scale at the middleweight limit of 160 pounds, Alvarez at 159.6. The fighters were brought together for the staredown—boxing's most idiotic ritual. And Danny stepped out of character, pushing his head forward into Canelo's space. Maybe he was trying to intimidate Canelo. Maybe he was trying to send a message to the judges: "I'm a warrior; I'm coming to fight." Canelo shoved him. They exchanged uncomplimentary words having to do with sexual intercourse and their respective mothers (with Jacobs again taking the lead). And the era of good feeling was over.

By the day of the fight, the odds (which had opened at 3-to-1) were approaching 4-to-1 in Alvarez's favor.

"Jacobs can pose problems for anyone," Canelo acknowledged. "He's a strong fighter, a big fighter. That's why I prepare for the fight."

When it was pointed out that Jacobs was known for being strong-willed, Canelo responded, "He's strong-minded. I'm strong-minded too. That's only part of boxing."

Canelo had the support of an entire country. Jacobs had the support of a relatively small boxing community in New York. But the fans can't fight, and the outcome of the bout was by no means a foregone conclusion.

Mentally and physically, Jacobs is a better fighter now than he was in 2010 when he was knocked out by Pirog. And in some ways, the Golovkin fight (which Danny also lost) was a plus for him. He'd fought Gennady as competitively as Alvarez had.

Canelo has had trouble with slick boxers like Floyd Mayweather, Erislandy Lara, and Austin Trout. Even Amir Khan posed problems until he tired after four rounds. Jacobs was planning to outbox Canelo; the fewer firefights, the better. Canelo, he hoped, would have trouble finding him. And when he did find him, Danny can punch.

"Canelo isn't going to dictate the pace of the fight. I will," Jacobs posited. "For me, it's about establishing my style early. I'm a versatile fighter. I can do a lot of different things in the ring. Box, punch, go forward, go back. I go southpaw from time to time. As a fighter, you have to build. You have to get experience. This isn't my first rodeo. In terms of my physical abilities and what I know, I'm a better fighter now than I ever was. I'm in my prime. I'm super confident. This is my chance at greatness."

And there was another factor that weighed in Jacob's favor—size. At six feet tall, he had a four-inch height advantage over Canelo, a comparable advantage in reach, and was expected to enter the ring with a ten-pound cushion in weight.

The contract for Canelo–Jacobs included a rehydration clause that required each fighter to weigh in a second time at 8:00 a.m. on the morning of the fight with neither fighter allowed to exceed 170 pounds (ten pounds over the official middleweight limit). The penalty for missing weight was $250,000 per pound or any portion thereof.

Canelo weighed 169 pounds at the same-day weigh-in. Jacobs registered 173.6. That seemed like more than an innocent mistake.

The "official" purses for Canelo–Jacobs were $35 million for Canelo and $2.5 million for Jacobs. But ESPN.com reported that Danny was guaranteed a minimum of $10 million for the fight. Coming in 3.6 pounds over the contractual weight limit—and with the likelihood that he'd gain at least five pounds more before the opening bell—gave Jacobs a significant advantage. If he'd won on Saturday night, it would have been a good investment. But he lost, which left him lighter in the wallet and with a bit of tarnish on his reputation.

★ ★ ★

Wearing a white tracksuit with gold trim, Canelo Alvarez arrived at T-Mobile Arena on Saturday night at 6:00 p.m. The partition between dressing rooms #7 and #8 had been removed, leaving ample space for the substantial entourage that accompanied him. Black sofas, folding black-cushioned chairs, and four long tables covered with black cloth ringed the room.

Chepo and Eddy Reynoso (Canelo's manager and trainer respectively) unpacked their bags, laying out the tools of their trade on two of the tables. Canelo sat on a sofa at one end of the room beneath a large Mexican flag, took out a smartphone, and began texting. From time to time, he looked at a large wall-mounted TV monitor that was displaying the DAZN telecast.

There were seventy people in the room. Crews from several Mexican television networks conducted interviews. Canelo's personal camera crew and a team from DAZN were also there. Ten more photographers took still photos. Chepo Reynoso watched it all with the look of a man who wished the interviews would end so the team could get down to business.

IBF supervisor Randy Neumann came in to get Canelo's signature on the sanctioning body's bout agreement. Neumann was wearing a tie emblazoned with images of John L. Sullivan.

"Who is that?" Canelo queried.

"John L. Sullivan," Neumann answered. "He was a great champion."

"Oh. I think it is Pancho Villa."

Canelo's longtime girlfriend brought their daughter, Maria Fernanda Alvarez, into the room. This was Maria's third pre-fight dressing room experience with her father. Her first appearance had been at Canelo–Golovkin II when she wasn't old enough to walk. Now she was able to navigate on her own and made her way to her father.

Canelo was handed a pink balloon and blew it up. Maria backed away in fear. Canelo let the air out slowly and she returned. The process was repeated several times. Finally, Canelo knotted the end of the balloon and handed it to Maria who embraced it.

Golden Boy matchmaker Roberto Diaz, who monitors Canelo's dressing room on fight nights, addressed the multitude.

"Guys, can we wrap it up with the cameras now?"

There was partial compliance.

"Cameras, please," Diaz urged.

Maria and her mother left. Thirty people remained, most of them wearing Team Alvarez tracksuits.

At 6:45 p.m., Canelo took off his shoes, socks, and tracksuit and pulled a latex sheath over his left knee. Then he put on the socks, shoes, and trunks he would wear into the ring and tied a red weave bracelet over his left sock just above the shoe top. Ramiro Gonzalez (a Golden Boy publicist and friend) had brought the bracelet to a priest to be blessed, a ritual that he and Canelo follow before each fight.

Mike Bazzell (one of Danny Jacobs's cornermen) came in to watch Canelo's hands being wrapped. Eddy Reynoso worked quickly, right hand first. While the wrapping was underway, Nevada State Athletic Commission executive director Bob Bennett entered with assorted dignitaries, sanctioning body officials, and referee Tony Weeks.

Weeks gave Canelo his pre-fight instructions with NSAC chief inspector Francisco Soto translating into Spanish. Then it was Soto's turn to address the room.

"Ladies and gentlemen," he said authoritatively, "I now need all of you to exit."

Canelo hugged a dozen entourage members as they left.

"Okay," Soto said to those who had stayed behind, "I need everybody to start moving. Please!"

Foremost among the departing were singers Usher and Maluma.

Eddy applied Vaseline to Canelo's face and arms.

A DAZN technician wired Eddy and Chepo for sound.

Andre Rozier (Jacobs's trainer) came in to watch Canelo being gloved up.

The final preliminary fight—Vergil Ortiz vs. Mauricio Herrera—came on the TV monitor.

Canelo's emotions rarely vary in the dressing room before a fight. He's always calm and low-key. Now he shadowboxed a bit and paced back and forth, looking at the fight on the monitor from time to time.

DAZN production coordinator Tami Cotel came in and announced, "After this fight ends, it will be twenty minutes before you walk."

Ortiz bludgeoned Herrera into submission in the third round.

Canelo sat on a sofa, alone with his thoughts.

"How do you feel?" Ramiro asked.

"I'm happy," Canelo answered.

Gennady Golovkin appeared on the TV monitor.

"He looks old," Ramiro noted.

"He is old," Canelo said.

At 8:15 p.m., Canelo began hitting the pads with Eddy Reynoso, the first in a series of exercises designed to ready him for combat.

Cotel reappeared.

"The anthems are next," she announced.

Canelo stood at attention, watching the TV screen as the Mexican and American anthems sounded.

Chepo draped a white-and-gold serape over his shoulders.

In a matter of minutes, Canelo would climb into a small enclosure that was both a stage and a cage. Seventeen thousand people in the arena would be focused on his every move. Millions more would be watching on electronic platforms around the world. Most would be rooting for him to succeed. Some would hope that he'd be beaten into unconsciousness. Only a handful would see or feel the humanity in him. He'd be a symbol, a commodity, an action video game figure come to life. That's all.

If Canelo were to be knocked flat on his back, he'd find himself staring up at the cupola of the video board suspended above the ring. The inside of the cupola is black, as dark as the nighttime sky when the moon and stars are in hiding. The referee would flash fingers in his face. Optimally, he'd recognize the numbers from the start of the count. If the first number he heard was "seven," he'd be in trouble. As he rose, the black above would give way to a swirling image of the crowd. The roar would be deafening.

He wouldn't think about whether or not he was fit to continue. It wasn't his job to assess that. Maybe he'd be hurt. Hurt as in physical pain. Or worse, hurt as in being unable to fully control the movement of his body. If the referee asked, "Are you all right? Do you want to continue?" he'd answer yes even though some part of his mind and body—his instinct for self-preservation—might be shouting "No!"

If the fight continued, the same man who'd knocked him down would try to destroy him. The roar of the crowd wouldn't stop. Canelo would be in the fire. And when it was over, the people who'd been watching would go on with their lives. They might talk about the fight, but they wouldn't have bumps and bruises and swelling and pain. If their thoughts were fuzzy, it would be from too many beers, not punches they'd taken.

Canelo had never been knocked down in his ring career. But he knew what he'd done to Amir Khan, James Kirkland, and so many other fighters. Could it happen to him? Of course, it could.

★ ★ ★

At a sit-down with a small group of reporters just before the final pre-fight press conference, Danny Jacobs had said, "I want this to be one of those fights that people talk about for years to come." For weeks, he'd repeated the mantra, "Canelo only fights for thirty seconds a round. I'll be active for all three minutes." Jacobs had talked the talk and gotten in Canelo's face at the weigh-in. He'd waxed eloquent about being the bigger stronger fighter.

But when the moment of reckoning came, Jacobs fought a safety-first fight. Canelo might not have wanted the victory more, but he fought like he did.

Round one was a feeling out stanza. Canelo moved forward, looking to engage while Jacobs moved away, right hand held defensively by his chin rather than cocked to fire. As the bout progressed, Canelo began closing the distance between them. Jacobs transitioned to southpaw from time to time, but it wasn't a particularly effective maneuver. Canelo's head movement kept Danny from establishing his jab, and Jacobs didn't do anything to take Canelo out of his rhythm.

It's easy to say that a fighter should fight more aggressively. But that only works if he can hit his opponent and not get hit harder in return. Canelo is hard to hit and one of the best counterpunchers in boxing. The rounds were close, but Canelo was winning most of them. After eight rounds, he led by four points on each judge's scorecard.

Two minutes into round nine, Jacobs landed his best punch of the fight—a straight left up top from a southpaw stance. Canelo took it well. Thereafter, Danny held his ground more and fought more aggressively. But it was too little too late. The 116–112, 115–113, 115–113 decision in Canelo's favor was on the mark.

The big "if" from Jacobs's perspective was what would have happened had he fought more aggressively from the start. But he didn't, and that was that. He gave away the early rounds, and Canelo wouldn't give them back.

After the bout, there was the usual bedlam in Canelo's post-fight dressing room. Family and friends exchanged hugs and kisses amid laughter and cheers.

Chepo and Eddy Reynoso stood quietly to the side, each with a satisfied look on his face. The odds are overwhelmingly against a young man journeying from poverty to international acclaim with his fists. But by definition, a chosen few will succeed where others fail. Years ago, the Reynosos took charge of a boy. No matter how much natural ability Canelo has been blessed with, someone had to teach him to box.

Meanwhile, Maria Fernanda Alvarez was toddling around the room when she spied four championship belts spread out on a sofa. Colorful, shiny, better than a balloon. The WBC championship belt captured her attention first. But the WBA belt had more gold, and the Ring belt was the most colorful. She moved joyfully from one to the next.

Canelo—his face a bit swollen beneath his right eye but otherwise unmarked—joined her.

Maria pressed her hand against one of the belts and uttered one of the first words a child learns regardless of language.

"Mia" (mine).

"No," Canelo said with a smile, "Es de Papa."

After knocking out Dominic Breazeale, Deontay Wilder proclaimed, "These trainers, especially the old-school trainers, have the old mindset. If you do it this way, this is what it takes because they've seen former champions accomplish so many things following these rules. But it's a different time and era. We have so many different things, technology, that can take us to the next step that they didn't have in the past. And for me, I'm just a rare kind. I'm a different species."

Wilder–Breazeale and the Heavyweight Puzzle

On Saturday night, May 18, 2019, Deontay Wilder knocked out Dominic Breazeale in the first round at Barclays Center in Brooklyn. Their fight marked the start of a four-week span in which all three claimants to the heavyweight throne—Wilder, Anthony Joshua, and Tyson Fury—will see action, although not against the opponents that boxing fans want to see them fight (which is each other).

Wilder (now 41–0–1, 40 KOs) won the WBC heavyweight title in 2015. His most recent fight was contested last December when he rallied in the final round to earn a draw against Fury. He's largely a one-dimensional fighter, but that dimension is massive power. For every second of every round, he's looking to end matters with one punch. He's strong-willed and has a fervent belief in himself.

Breazeale, like Wilder, is thirty-three years old and stands six feet, seven inches tall. At the Friday weigh-in, he tipped the scales at 255 pounds, 32 pounds heavier than Deontay. Dominic's most notable previous outing came on June 25, 2016, when he challenged Anthony Joshua for the IBF heavyweight crown and was stopped in the seventh round. Prior to taking up boxing, he'd played football at the University of Northern Colorado.

"You're talking to a quarterback who usually takes all the damage," Breazeale noted during a pre-fight media conference call. "The tables are turned. I'm the aggressor now."

In a vacuum, Wilder–Breazeale would have been an easy fight to make. Breazeale was the mandatory challenger for Wilder's WBC belt, and each man fights under the Premier Boxing Champions banner. But almost everything that happens in boxing these days is complicated by the ongoing war between three competing factions (1) PBC–Showtime–Fox; (2) Top Rank–Queensberry–ESPN; and (3) Matchroom–Golden Boy–DAZN.

Initially, it was assumed that Wilder and Fury would engage in a rematch. Their first fight had generated a modest live gate of $3,515,122 with an estimated 315,000 buys on Showtime PPV in the United States and 420,000 more with BT Sport in the United Kingdom. However, the rematch was expected to put up stronger numbers. Fury was offered a fifty-fifty split to fight Wilder at Barclays Center on May 18 with Showtime PPV and BT Sport reprising their roles

Then things got complicated.

On February 18, 2019, ESPN, Top Rank, and Queensberry (Fury's promoter) announced a multiyear agreement that calls for Fury to fight at least twice annually in the United States. All of his fights will be televised in the US on an ESPN platform.

Wilder was then offered a multifight deal that would have seen him fight this spring on ESPN or ESPN+ against a relatively easy opponent for a purse of $12.5 million before moving to a Fury rematch for a minimum guarantee of $20 million. However, Wilder's management team (guided by PBC impresario Al Haymon and Shelly Finkel with input from Jay Deas) preferred that Deontay remain with Showtime for the time being. And Haymon didn't want to work with Top Rank CEO Bob Arum. Thus, the offer was turned down. But by then, DAZN had entered the fray.

Multiple sources say that Lou DiBella (the promoter of record for many of Wilder's earlier fights) urged Deontay to hear DAZN out before making a final decision. On March 12, Wilder, Haymon, and Finkel met with DAZN executive chairman John Skipper in New York and were offered two alternative packages: (1) three fights for $100 million ($20 million to fight Breazeale; $40 million to fight Joshua in the fall; and $40 million for an immediate rematch with Joshua) or (2) the same package with a $20 million fight thrown in between the two Joshua fights. The first fight with Joshua would have been in the United States and the second in the UK.

Oddly, when the media arrived at Barclays Center on March 19 for the kickoff press conference for Wilder–Breazeale, it still hadn't been announced whether the fight would be on DAZN, ESPN, or Showtime. It wasn't until several Showtime personnel were spotted that it could be said with certainty that Wilder would be making his twelfth appearance on a Showtime platform.

Details of the contract have been shrouded in secrecy. Showtime Sports president Stephen Espinoza said at the press conference that Wilder had made "a decision that guarantees financial success for a long time." He later told Keith Idec of BoxingScene.com that Wilder's purse for fighting Breazeale would be less than $20 million but that the path Deontay had chosen left him "generally in the same neighborhood with the financial opportunities."

Showtime is said to have paid a license fee of $5 million to $6 million for Wilder–Breazeale but that number is speculative at best. Estimates as to Wilder's purse range from $12.5 million to $18 million. Other components of the deal are also unclear, although multiple sources say that Wilder is not locked into Showtime for future fights.

Sources also say that Wilder's management and promotional team wanted the fight on Showtime—not Showtime PPV—because if a Wilder–Breazeale pay-per-view promotion had gone poorly in terms of buys, it would have hurt Deontay's bargaining position down the line against Fury and Joshua.

What is known with certainty is that the competition from DAZN increased Wilder's paycheck for the Breazeale fight. And it reportedly left DiBella (whose counseling Wilder led to the increase) persona non grata with Showtime, Haymon, and Finkel for throwing a temporary speed bump in front of their plans. We also know that someone (most likely PBC) will take a significant short-term loss to make good on Wilder's guarantee for the Breazeale fight. In return, that party expects to share in bigger paydays down the road.

Wilder explained his decision in terms of self-empowerment.

"I move as I please," he said. "Those guys [Joshua and Fury], they have to do as they're told. I make commands and demands. They take them. I move where I want. Soon, I will be the highest paid athlete in the world. You'll see. I'm betting on myself. I look at the bigger picture. You sell me a number, and I know there's going to be a bigger number than that. They saw a guy they thought they could throw some money at and that would be it. But they found out the hard way."

Wilder later elaborated on this theme, telling writer Greg Leon, "ESPN and DAZN, they wanted a long term on me. I like to dictate my own career and I like to see where it's going for myself. When you're giving these guys so many years, you're giving them too much control. I don't like people to have too much control over me and my career because I know what it is, and I know where it's going. They put out a big number. And being human, you see that, and you automatically think 'Oh My God!' But you need to know what's going on behind the details of that number. I'm not no fool. I know the cards that I hold in this division. I bet on myself because I know that I hold all the keys and I possess the power. I'm a living walking icon. I am the best heavyweight in the world. I am the most dangerous and exciting heavyweight in the game, period. Everyone is going to want somebody like me. So why would I give that all away when I can bet it on myself?"

But there's a difference between opportunities and guarantees. Hasim Rahman thought that he held all the cards when he "bet on himself" after knocking out Lennox Lewis in 2001 to become the undisputed heavyweight champion of the world. HBO offered Rahman a multifight deal that began with a rematch against Lewis and would have guaranteed him a lifetime of wealth. But Don King played to Hasim's ego, assuring him that he was The Man. Rahman passed on HBO's offer and then, to his chagrin, found out that being The Man can end with one punch.

The buildup to Wilder–Breazeale was ugly. There were the usual prefight rituals and promotional activities. But the dialogue was dominated by intense animosity between Deontay and Dominic that was very personal and very real.

The bad blood dated to an incident that occurred on February 2, 2017, after Wilder and Breazeale fought in separate bouts on the same card in Birmingham, Alabama. There had been an argument at ringside between Breazeale and Deontay's younger brother, Marsellos. Later that night, the hostilities resumed in more heated fashion in the lobby of The Westin Birmingham Hotel. Marsellos is believed to have been the primary instigator, but Deontay was a participant. The police were called. No arrests were made.

The following day, Breazeale posted a statement on Instagram that read, "I want to address the fact that Deontay Wilder and a mob of about 20 people unprovokedly attacked my team and my family in the lobby last night. My coach and I were blindsided by sucker punches and my team was assaulted as well all in front my wife and kids. This cowardly attack has no place in boxing and believe me it will not go unpunished."

The animosity between the fighters was on display at the March 19 kickoff press conference.

"Payback is a motherfucker," Wilder proclaimed. "Pain is the name of the game. We all know who does that best, and it's legal. He's fucking with the wrong person. I got gold on the tip of my tongue. When I speak, my words come true. This is gonna be a massacre. I expect him to make some funeral arrangements."

Breazeale isn't given to trash-talking, but on this occasion, he responded: "I'm sick of seeing this bum walk around with his belt. I'm going to put him on his ass."

Asked for more details about the hotel lobby incident, Dominic said, "I didn't have an urban dictionary with me, so I couldn't understand what he was saying."

Then Wilder took things to another level. Deontay has an aura of menace about him. And he likes to hear himself talk. In mid-April as the war of words escalated, he was asked by a reporter for the *Daily Mail* if he'd feel remorse if Breazeale died from fight-inflicted injuries.

"Not one bit of remorse," Wilder answered. "This is boxing. This is what we do. This is what we sign up for. Anything can happen. Your head is not meant to be hit in the first place. You talk about me killing the guy. If it happens, it happens. When you are dealing with a situation like this and it's personal, I don't mean well for him nor do he mean well for me. I'm a realist and I speak how it is. I don't like him. At all."

On a May 9 media conference call, Wilder elaborated on this theme, saying, "I don't mean no good for him. All bad intentions. If you're a first-time viewer of boxing, it depends on how you feel about seeing a body on the ground or seeing blood come from somebody. A lot of these guys wanna speak kind and soft and wanna be politically correct and wanna talk proper. Nah! I tell you how you I feel. It's punishment time. It's judgment time. And I am the judge."

During the same conference call, Wilder challenged Breazeale's version of events in the hotel lobby and maintained, "I put him on my card. He didn't have to be on my card. But you come to my hometown and cause this mess? You want to start this drama and act like you were the victim and your wife was the victim? He's an opportunist. A man comes to my city and starts chaos like that and then telling a bogus story. He's like one of these guys that will come into your establishment and waste water on the floor and slip on it just to sue you."

Five days later, during a media workout at Gleason's Gym, Wilder went further, saying, "His life is on the line for this fight, and I do mean his life. I'm still trying to get me a body on my record. You can ask any doctor around the world, and he'll tell you a head is not meant to be hit. This is the only sport where you can kill a man and get paid for it at the same time. It's legal. So why not use my right to do so?"

Asked later by BBC Sport if he wanted to walk back that comment, Wilder doubled down, stating, "I don't regret nothing that I say. I've always been real. I don't worry about being politically correct."

Breazeale responded in more dignified fashion, saying, "You never want to hear an individual—and I don't care what sport it is but especially in the sport of boxing—who has the ability to put someone else in a bad state of mind or hurt them physically [talk like that]. Both he and I have knocked out individuals with shots where I'm like, 'Oh God, I hope he's going to be okay from this.' There is no way you can get behind a heavyweight champ who wants to put harm on another individual or take another man's life or put him in a coma. That's not the barbaric state of mind that any champion should be in."

Carlos Acevedo put the matter in perspective, writing, "When Wilder was charged with domestic battery a few years ago, that was something to hush up. But now we have the new homicidal Wilder, a man whose recent talk is both debased and debasing and, more to the point, as loud as various mixed media platforms of the day allow him to be. His lectures to schoolchildren, his talk of his Christian faith, his fairy tale rise from working at IHOP and Red Lobster to becoming a multimillionaire, his sob story about his daughter [who suffers from spina bifida]—all of that is now overshadowed by a noisy loathsomeness likely to continue in the future."

At the final pre-fight press conference on May 16, Breazeale's initial comments were innocuous. Then, when it was Wilder's turn to speak, a Wilder aide dropped an urban dictionary on the dais in front of Breazeale so, in Deontay's words, "he can understand the urbanology of what I'm about to say to him."

Wilder then called Breazeale "a uppity Negro" and said "he don't have enough bass in his voice" before adding, "Guys understand, when they get in the ring with Deontay Wilder, it's more than just a boxing match. This is not a game. We don't play games. We know that, when I speak, I speak truth. I'm not in this business to make no friends. There's so many things I've said, and I mean every word I've said. This has been a long time coming for him. He asked for this, and he shall receive. I'm gonna fade him out, baby. I can't wait. Come Saturday night, I can do whatever I want to do. If anybody thinks this is a game, you better close your eyes when the TV comes on. Or if you're there, you better bring your blindfold because this is gonna be a tragedy. It's gonna be a tragedy. The least I can do, I can pay for the funeral."

Then Wilder put an even more ominous spin on things, saying, "Dominic Breazeale almost lost his life that night [in the Alabama hotel]. He don't know how close he came. I had guys apologizing to me because they had stuff known that they was gonna take him out. I begged them off."

And speaking to Breazeale, Wilder warned, "You better gather around your loved ones tonight, because Saturday night they might not be able to talk to you. Trust me. You know I don't play no games. It's gonna be good. When you close your eyes in the hospital room, you're gonna see my face over and over and over again."

"A win for myself is a win for the world," Breazeale said afterward. "He's a disgrace to boxing and worse."

Wilder was a 7-to-1 betting favorite. In the face of those odds, Breazeale was upbeat. The knockout loss to Joshua, he maintained, was a plus. "An eye opener," he called it.

"I learned that I had a lot to learn," Dominic reasoned. "The loss and the experience of losing opened my eyes. There was a bigger, stronger, more athletic man across the ring that night. I was standing there and taking some damage that I didn't need to take because of the big guy that I am. My way of bouncing back from that was to study the film day in and day out. I watched it round after round, minute after minute. I watched it in silence. I watched it with people. I watched it without people. And the quarterback background in me was studying. I wanted to see everything that I did wrong. I learned a lot more from that one loss than I learned from all my wins in my whole boxing career."

As for Wilder, Breazeale declared, "I don't see any fundamental skills. He hasn't grown. He hasn't changed. He looks the same as he did in the amateurs. Yes, he's got a big right hand, but don't we all in the heavyweight division? In boxing, it's the shots you don't see coming. But that shot he throws, man, it's from way back. I don't plan on getting hit a lot on May 18. And if I do, I've been there. I've done that. If the right hand comes, so be it. I'll deal with it."

Still, most boxing insiders agreed with the odds. An opponent can't stand in front of Wilder at long range and let him dictate the terms of engagement. If that happens, Deontay will keep throwing his right hand until he lands it. It's essential to keep him turning so he can't set his feet to punch. Among other things, that requires nimble footwork.

Breazeale was the perfect opponent for Wilder. Words like ponderous, wooden, and slow come to mind when describing Dominic's ring style. He takes a good punch but gets hit a lot. Wilder is a poor choice as an opponent for a fighter who's easy to hit. It was doubtful that Breazeale could survive Wilder's power.

"Breazeale don't belong in the ring with me," Wilder said. "I don't see this fight going no more than five rounds, and I'm probably going to cut him down in three. Nobody he could work with could get him prepared for Deontay Wilder. It's like I told Tyson Fury. You have to be perfect for all twelve rounds. I only have to be perfect for two seconds."

When fight night came, one could be forgiven for feeling that an ugly haze hung over the ring at Barclays Center. The announced attendance was 13,181. But the promotion had struggled to sell tickets and thousands of comps were given away in the days before the fight.

The crowd, which had been silent for much of the evening, came to life as Wilder made his way to the ring. When referee Harvey Dock gave the fighters their final instructions, Wilder looked eager to get the fight started. Breazeale seemed anxious to get it over.

They fought on even terms until the opening bell. Eighty seconds after the bout began, Wilder staggered Breazeale with a straight right hand. Dominic fought back. Wilder got separation, jabbed, and fired an explosive, crushing, highlight-reel right hand that landed flush on the side of Breazeale's head just beneath his left ear. Dominic plummeted to the canvas, struggled to rise, and just missed beating the count. But even if he'd made it to his feet in time, he was in no condition to continue. The time of the knockout was 2 minutes 17 seconds of the first round.

At the post-fight press conference, Wilder addressed the negativity that had preceded the fight. First, he referenced speaking with Breazeale in the ring immediately after the bout.

"After doing what I did," Wilder recounted, "I just wanted to come over and say, 'Man, it's over with. We got in the ring. We fought it out. It shouldn't be no more animosity against each other. What happened, happened in the past. We're gonna keep it in the past.'" But Deontay went on to say, "All the negative energy I had towards him, everything that was built up inside of me, I had the opportunity to release. That's why boxing is very important for me, because it gives me the opportunity to release negative energy even if it have to be on another human being. And I love it."

Then, talking about the vulnerability of fighters, Wilder noted, "No man wants to get humiliated on national TV and their body drops like that. You never know what it's gonna do after you get hit from a devastating punch. You can fall on your face. You can ball up. Your legs can bend. You can fall out of the ring. Many different things. And no one wants the highlight on them because the way the Internet is set up right now, it's undefeated."

Breazeale chose to not attend the post-fight press conference. That was understandable. At its core, there's something visceral and primal about a prize fight. Combine that with smoldering hatred and being knocked out in the first round, and it hurts. The fight was a bitter pill for Dominic to swallow. In many ways, the psychological pain was worse than the physical. Now he has to say to himself, "Hey, it happened. I came out of it healthy. I made good money that I can put toward providing for my family. What happened wasn't as bad as a life-altering car crash or a doctor telling me that someone I love has a malignant tumor."

Meanwhile, one has to ask, "What does Wilder–Breazeale mean for boxing?" The answer is that, at present, "The pieces of the heavyweight jigsaw puzzle that boxing is trying to put together don't fit."

Despite an enormous amount of money pouring into the sport from DAZN, ESPN, and Fox, the sweet science isn't making new converts in the United States. In fact, today's diluted product is turning off once loyal fans.

A handful of fighters are being paid purses far beyond the revenue that they're generating. And a few promoters are reaping substantial rewards. The hope among the powers that be is that this will lead to big pay-per-view scores, increased subscription buys, and more advertising dollars in the future. But to be successful, marketers have to energize their base.

Boxing is failing to energize its base. And it's competing year round with sports that give fans what they want: the best against the best.

The SEC has a contract for its football games with CBS. Alabama and Georgia are in the SEC. The Big Ten has contracts for its football games with ESPN and Fox. Ohio State, Michigan, and Penn State are in the Big Ten. And Notre Dame has a contract with NBC. These teams don't hide behind their TV contracts. When championships are on the line, they play each other.

On April 14, Tiger Woods thrilled the sports world by winning the Masters for his fifteenth major triumph. That weekend, boxing fans had to settle for a mismatch between Vasyl Lomachenko and Anthony Crolla.

Now the NBA playoffs are underway. Great players and great teams are being tested nightly over a two-month period as they strive to reach the pinnacle of their sport. The heavyweight championship of the world is the pinnacle of boxing. Anthony Joshua, Tyson Fury, and Deontay Wilder should be fighting each other, not Andy Ruiz, Tom Schwarz, and Dominic Breazeale.

For a long time, Wilder was protected by his management team in their choice of opponents. He doesn't have to be protected anymore. It's too early to anoint him a great heavyweight. But he appears to be the equal of Joshua and Fury. And Wilder in the ring against any heavyweight ever would be compelling to watch. He's a formidable presence with a destructive aura about him. His right hand is an explosive weapon with a good delivery system. When he works behind his jab, he's very good.

He's quick and he's tough. Like the Klitschkos, he has learned to use his height and reach to stay out of harm's way.

So for the time being, let's give Wilder the final word with some thoughts that he expressed at the May 18 post-fight press conference:

* ★ "I'm finally getting my respect. It took a long time, but I'm very patient. I've tried to prove myself for a very long time."
* ★ "One second and you can be gone. I'm a dangerous guy. I can be lethal. I put fear in any man."
* ★ "People think, 'Oh, he just got a right hand, so you stay away from that. But when I settle myself down and use my intelligence in the ring, magic happens."

Gennady Golovkin vs. Steve Rolls: As Expected

On June 8, 2019, one week after Andy Ruiz's shocking upset of Anthony Joshua, Madison Square Garden played host to another presumably lopsided fight. This one ran true to form as Gennady Golovkin knocked out Steve Rolls in the fourth round.

Golovkin (now 39–1–1, 35 KOs) once reigned as middleweight champion of the world. He looked great in destroying a long line of competent but not outstanding opponents. It wasn't who he beat but how he beat them that was so impressive. Then he struggled but won a controversial decision against Danny Jacobs; fought to a draw against Canelo Alvarez in a fight that most observers thought Gennady won; pulverized an overmatched Vanes Martirosyan; and lost a close but legitimate decision in a rematch against Alvarez.

Rolls, who entered the ring on June 8 with a 19–0 (10 KOs) ledger, is a thirty-five-year-old Canadian who evoked images of the opponents that Roy Jones faced when RJ was on his "mailman tour." Rolls had never beaten a world-class fighter, nor had he fought one. He works as a personal trainer between fights.

Asked at the kickoff press conference in New York to name the toughest opponent he'd faced in the professional ranks, Rolls cited Demond Nicholson (who he defeated by split decision two years ago). He also noted that he'd gained experience by working as a sparring partner for Andy Lee, Adonis Stevenson, Billy Joe Saunders, David Lemieux, and Glen Johnson.

The template for most fighters in Rolls's position on Saturday night is one payday and a loss followed by a return to obscurity and low purses.

Golovkin–Rolls was Golovkin's first non-title fight since he fought Mikhail Makarov ten years and twenty-three fights ago. The contract weight was 164 pounds. That meant Gennady didn't have to sacrifice as much to make weight and allowed him to gauge what it might be like to fight for a 168-pound belt down the road.

It was a given that the promotion would try to capitalize on Andy Ruiz's upset of Anthony Joshua in the same ring one week earlier. And because Rolls is from Toronto, reference was made to the Toronto Raptors' success to date in the NBA Championship Finals. But in truth, Golovkin–Rolls was less like Joshua–Ruiz and more like Canelo Alvarez vs. Rocky Fielding (a gimme to jumpstart Canelo's ten-fight contract with DAZN). And basketball ain't boxing.

There was limited buzz for the promotion. Much of the media attention focused not on the fight but on Golovkin's decision to part ways with Abel Sanchez, who had been his trainer since Gennady fought Milton Nunez nine years ago.

Sanchez had been paid the standard ten percent trainer's share of Golovkin's purses. Then, on March 8, DAZN announced that it had signed Gennady to a three-year, six-fight deal with DAZN agreeing to stream two GGG Promotions fight cards annually as an add-on. On May 19, Golovkin and his attorney met with Sanchez and told him that they wanted to restructure the deal so that the trainer would be paid a flat fee for each fight. Sanchez later complained to the *Los Angeles Times* that this would have resulted in his getting "one-fifth of what I was earning before." Sanchez asked Golovkin for time to think about the offer and then sent a counterproposal. The response came on April 24, when Gennady met with him alone and said, "We'll be going somewhere else."

Later that day, Golovkin issued a press release that read, "I would like to announce that I have made a major decision for myself and for my career. I want to build on what I have already achieved and continue to better myself. Therefore, I will not be training with Abel Sanchez. This was not an easy decision for me, and it is not a reflection on Abel's professional abilities. He is a great trainer, a loyal trainer, and a Hall of Fame trainer. I will be announcing my new trainer at a later date. But today, I want to thank Abel for the lessons he taught me in boxing."

Sanchez took the firing poorly. "Greedy and ungrateful," he told ESPN. "He just signed a one hundred million dollar contract, and all of a sudden you have to make drastic steps because you don't have enough money? I feel for the morals and scruples of somebody like that.

I wouldn't take what they were trying to insult me with. It's very disappointing because I never would have guessed that this young man would do that. I thought this young man had more scruples, more morals, a better upbringing. I was blindsided, really. I think we accomplished a lot of great things. Unfortunately, money corrupts, and, in this case, money was more important than a relationship, a great legacy, and history."

Later, Sanchez elaborated on this theme, telling Greg Leon of *Boxing Talk*, "In this business, the one who spends the most time with the athlete is the only one on the team that isn't protected by a contract, and that's the coach. I was asking for a little less than half of what I was making before. And I was blindsided. It's hard to try to decipher, really. I've had a lot of fighters, but I would have never expected this from this kid. Never!"

Thereafter, Johnathon Banks was named as Golovkin's new trainer. "I'm looking for little things in this fight," Banks said. "Not big changes because we've had a very short time together. I'd like to see more head movement from Gennady, and we'll build from there."

Golovkin was a prohibitive favorite over Rolls with some betting lines running as high as 35-to-1. Gennady is thirty-seven years old now, and his years in boxing might be catching up with him. His face looks older and harder than it did when he first fought at Madison Square Garden six years ago. But he's still an elite fighter, probably the second-best middleweight in the world. By way of comparison, the BoxRec.com computer rankings list Rolls as the seventy-ninth-best middleweight in the world and the fifth-best middleweight in Canada.

Lou DiBella (who promotes Rolls) was passionate in defending his fighter at the kickoff press conference.

"Steve has no chance," DiBella proclaimed. "Keep thinking that. I hope Golovkin feels the same fucking way. If Golovkin thinks this is a walkover, he's in for a long fucking night. I'm not bringing a victim to Madison Square Garden. I don't believe Steve is a stepping stone for anybody. DAZN wants to get to the big fight, Triple-G against Canelo. I know that. Steve knows that. But this fight comes first. Steve is a real fighter. He's not going to roll over for Gennady Golovkin. Do we know if Steve is a top-five fighter? No. But he thinks he is. He has nineteen wins in nineteen fights. He's a grown man. He works his butt off. He's a winner. He's hungry. The future of his family changes in one night with a good night. I'd rather see a guy who steps up to the opportunity of a lifetime and has never tasted defeat than another old recycled fighter. Steve has done everything that he was supposed to do, and he's worked as hard as he can work for a long time. I know he's going to justify this opportunity."

Rolls was in accord, saying, "The opportunity came to me. I'm determined. This isn't a tune-up. I'm coming to fight. I'm going to have to do everything I can do and use everything I know to win this fight. After June 8, you won't forget me."

Rolls was as credible an opponent as Vanes Martirosyan, who Golovkin fought between his two fights against Canelo Alvarez. But Gennady likes to style his fights as "big drama show." And this one had the feel of an off-Broadway production. The final pre-fight press conference lasted 45 minutes. Promoter Tom Loeffler talked for 25 of them. The other nine participants combined talked for twenty.

Tickets were priced as low as fifty dollars, but the promotion still struggled. The announced crowd of 12,357 included quite a few fans who benefited from generosity on the part of the promoters. The undercard was highlighted by a spirited match that saw Brian Ceballo outpoint Bakhtiyar Eyubov in a battle of undefeated welterweights.

Golovkin–Rolls unfolded about as expected. Lou DiBella had asked that Rolls be assigned the same dressing room that Andy Ruiz had been in one week earlier. But once Rolls reached the ring, his hopes for an upset faded.

Golovkin's defense was more porous than it has been in the past. After a first round in which Rolls looked tentative, Steve realized that, if he threw punches, he could hit Gennady. But Golovkin was the stronger of the two and hit harder. Rolls could sting him but not hurt him. Midway through round four, a barrage of punches moved Rolls back against the ropes, at which point Gennady shifted to a southpaw stance and ended matters with a straight left to the jaw at the 2:09 mark.

Golovkin–Rolls was designed to set up a third fight between Gennady and Canelo Alvarez in Las Vegas on September 14 in conjunction with Mexican Independence Day. That's the fight Golovkin wants next. It's also the fight that DAZN (which has established a strong foothold in the middleweight division) would like to see happen. But Canelo will be in the driver's seat as negotiations progress. Nothing will come easily on that one.

Manny Pacquiao surprised a lot of people, including me, with his performance against Keith Thurman.

Manny Pacquiao
Turns Back the Clock

Writing about Manny Pacquiao, Bart Barry recently proclaimed, "There has been no one like him since his debut in 1995, and that phrase may hold up still in the year 2050."

On July 20, 2019, at age forty, Pacquiao added to his legend by out-pointing previously undefeated Keith Thurman in a dramatic fast-paced fight at the MGM Grand in Las Vegas.

Pacquiao has been a notable presence on the boxing scene since 2001, when he made his American television debut on HBO and obliterated Lehlo Ledwaba to claim the IBF 122-pound crown. Notable victories over Marco Antonio Barrera, Erik Morales, and Juan Manuel Marquez followed as Manny became boxing's most marketable feel-good story.

But Pacquiao is now ten years removed from the glorious twelve-month high point of his ring career when he pulverized Oscar De La Hoya, Ricky Hatton, and Miguel Cotto to become a global icon. The physical qualities that made him a great fighter have diminished. Although this assertion might appear to have been challenged by Pacquiao's performance against Thurman on Saturday night, Manny's reflexes, handspeed, footwork, and workrate have slowed. His power isn't what it once was. He has recorded one knockout victory in sixteen fights dating back to 2009. And his burgeoning political career—Pacquiao is a senator in his native Philippines—has engendered mixed reviews. His embrace of Filipino strong-man president Rodrigo Duterte coupled with several intemperate homophobic utterances have taken the luster off Manny Pacquiao.

Thurman was six years old when Pacquiao made his pro debut and twelve when Manny burst upon the scene against Ledwaba. Keith has yet to establish himself as a great fighter, but he's a good one. The signature wins on his résumé are a 115–113, 115–113, 115–113 decision over Shawn Porter to claim the 147-pound WBA title in 2016 and a 116–112, 115–113, 113–115 triumph against Danny Garcia one year later.

When Thurman beat Garcia, he unified the WBA and WBC titles and thus was elevated from "world champion" to "super world champion" status by the WBA. That paved the way in the convoluted world of boxing for Pacquiao to become the regular WBA world champion by beating Lucas Matthysse last year. The WBA might as well adopt the motto, "There can never be enough world champions."

After Thurman beat Garcia, he was sidelined by injuries for twenty-three months. "As a puncher, you can always find ways to hurt your hands," Keith says. "Hands were not made to punch each other in the skull. Hands were designed for something a little different."

Thurman also suffered an elbow injury that added to this period of inactivity.

"It's human nature that not every day is going to be our best day," Keith acknowledged earlier this month, "And for me, my thought process started to get a little morbid. I started to ask myself the question, 'Are you ever going to fight again? Is your career over at the age of twenty-eight, twenty-nine years old? Are you done?' It was quite depressing to start thinking like that. I had some depressing moments and some negative thought patterns at that time."

Meanwhile, the measured pace of Thurman's return and his talk of future fights (which pointedly brushed off Errol Spence as an opponent in the foreseeable future) led to questions regarding his commitment to boxing. Keith's only ring appearance since March 2017 had been a January 26, 2019, decision over Josesito Lopez. And the Lopez fight was problematic. Thurman won a decision. But Josesito is a relatively light puncher with eight defeats on his ring ledger. And he rocked Keith in the seventh round.

Thurman chose to put a positive spin on things, saying, "In the seventh round, I showed that Keith Thurman is not a punk. If you want to fight me, fight me. You want to hurt me, hurt me. If you drop me, you drop me. But you better stop me. As long as you don't stop me, I'm coming out the champion. I got caught. I was in danger. Then I got caught again. And then, after that, I got caught again. I got hit with three big shots that round. I said you better put your hands up. You better move your feet because only you know you're okay right now. The whole world thinks you're going to be knocked out. Just get out of this round and let's show them what kind of champion you really are."

"I tried to explain to you guys from the beginning of the year when the Josesito Lopez fight happened," Thurman advised the media during a July 10 conference call. "All of 2019 is just Keith Thurman getting back. This is still a get back year."

Pacquiao–Thurman was viewed as part of that get back process. The storyline to the fight was based in part on the presumption that neither man was the fighter he'd once been—Pacquiao because he's forty years old and Thurman because he might have lost a bit of the desire that once motivated him—but that their downward curves were intersecting at just the right time to make for an exciting competitive contest.

Pacquiao admitted that he had fallen prey to "womanizing, gambling, and drunkenness" in the past as his fame grew. But then, he said, God spoke to him in a dream. Properly counseled, Manny cleaned up his act, after which Juan Manuel Marquez planted him face first on the canvas and Floyd Mayweather embarrassed him over twelve lethargic rounds. But according to Pacquiao, "That was all part of God's plan."

"My time is not yet over," Manny cautioned Thurman. "It's easy to say things, but it's not easy to do it in the ring. Let's see who's tougher in the ring on July 20."

Thurman was his usual engaging self during the buildup to the fight. He disputed the notion that his desire had diminished. He voiced respect for Pacquiao, saying, "He's not the young Manny Pacquiao that he once was, but he still is a great world-class fighter." And he confirmed the intriguing nature of his own personality with thoughts like:

* "Keith Thurman is not a nine-to-five kind of guy. I was ten years old when I said nobody is going to be the boss of me. I shocked a lot of people with that statement. I was rebellious, I was a dreamer. I was very passionate. I'm still very passionate. I live off of passion."
* "I was not a boxing fan at a young age. I'm not a big fan of almost any sport because I'm not a spectator. I love participating in sports. I'm not one that sits down, watches games. I live too much of an active lifestyle. I want to be a part of the action. Put me in the game, coach. I started watching more professional boxing when I knew I was going to turn pro."
* "I love the sport of boxing. I want to have fun. This is my job. When you go to work, you should enjoy yourself. If you don't

enjoy your job, you should get a new job. I love my job. This is my entertainment. I'm living a dream. I'm happy. We're making money. We're making history in a sport that I've always wanted to make history in."

There were the usual pre-fight predictions.

Freddie Roach (who was once again Pacquiao's trainer after a brief absence) declared, "Thurman is definitely a good fighter. But if you look at his last three fights, he's faded a little bit. He's not doing quite as well. You study tapes on him and you can see the gradual slowdown. Manny's speed will overwhelm him. Manny is so unbelievably fast. He's much faster with his footwork and his hand speed. Thurman is slower than Heinz ketchup."

Thurman, of course, took a contrary view.

"He's forty; I'm thirty," Keith said. "He's the legend, but I have ten years of youth on my side. I'm doing to Manny Pacquiao what he did to Oscar De La Hoya. The hourglass is almost finished. He doesn't have much left. My prediction? Less than six rounds."

And what would Thurman do if Pacquiao beat him?

"I would bow down in the middle of the ring," Keith answered. "I'll say, 'Oh, senator! Oh, senator! Great is ye, oh, senator.'"

Would he retire if he lost?

"I'd think about it. I'd at least be like, 'Can I do some more commentating or something?' Momma said I look good in a suit. I don't think she wants to see her boy punched on TV, getting beat up by an old man."

Bottom line . . . Pacquiao was unlikely to get better at this stage of his ring career. The open issue regarding Manny was the slope of his decline. Not only is he forty years old; his body had been subjected to the wear and tear of sixty-eight professional fights, many of them against the best fighters of his era.

By contrast, Thurman had been plagued by injuries and the possible loss of motivation but was young enough to successfully rebound. The unanswered question regarding Keith was how far had he come back. His one fight in the preceding twenty-eight months (against Josesito Lopez) had left doubters.

"This is a once in a lifetime opportunity to destroy a legend and to create my own legacy," Thurman declared. "Manny Pacquiao has had an amazing career. It feels as if I'm facing Sugar Ray Robinson, as if I'm facing Roberto Duran."

But at age forty, Robinson had lost his magic (and twice to Paul Pender). Duran ushered in his fortieth birthday by losing to Pat Lawlor. Neither Robinson or Duran beat a world class fighter at age forty or after.

"Manny believes this is fate," Freddie Roach told Dylan Hernandez of the *Los Angeles Times*. But then Roach added a cautionary note: "I don't believe in fate. I don't think God is a good matchmaker."

Thurman had opened as a 7-to-5 betting favorite. By fight night, a flood of money from Pacquiao fans had moved the odds to 4-to-3 in Manny's favor.

Prior to the bout, Michael Rosenthal wrote, "I hope Pacquiao performs more like Bernard Hopkins than Roy Jones Jr. at this stage of their careers."

In truth, Pacquiao's performance was likely to lie somewhere in between. Jones's technique was flawed. He was great when he was young because of preternatural physical gifts. But once his physical decline began, he was a dangerously vulnerable fighter. Hopkins, on the other hand, was a precision textbook boxer whose conditioning and technique compensated for advancing age. Pacquiao had extraordinary physical gifts and was better technically than Jones. But there were holes in his ring modus operandi. And forty is forty.

Pacquiao–Thurman was a fast-paced entertaining fight. After a period of physical decline culminating in his loss to Jeff Horn in 2017, Manny appears to have grown faster and stronger again. Cynics will read into that what they will.

Two punches were crucial to outcome of Pacquiao–Thurman.

Late in round one, a straight left to the body followed by a right hook up top dropped Thurman to the canvas. That brought back memories of Pacquiao's first fight against Juan Manuel Marquez, when Marquez was dropped three times in the opening stanza after being caught off guard by Manny's speed and the ferocity of his attack. Unlike Marquez, Thurman rose quickly and wasn't seriously hurt. But the knockdown changed what likely would have been a 10–9 round in Thurman's favor to 10–8 for Pacquiao. Ultimately, that three-point swing was the difference between Pacquiao–Thurman being adjudicated a draw and a victory for Pacquiao. And the knockdown took the edge off Thurman's confidence.

Rounds two through five were vintage Pacquiao. He controlled the fight, bloodied Thurman's nose, and forced Keith into uncharted waters. Thoughts of Pacquiao–Marquez IV lingered in the mind. One wondered if Pacquiao might get reckless and run into something unfortunate as happened in his final outing against Marquez when, seemingly on the verge of victory, Manny regained consciousness while lying face first on the canvas.

That didn't happen here. But in round six against Thurman, Pacquiao's age began to show. He seemed to tire. The spring left his legs which took away his ability to move into position and punch with the angles in his favor.

Rounds six through nine belonged to Thurman. Then, in round ten, Pacquiao landed his second fight-altering blow. A straight left to the body at the 1:40 mark hurt Thurman badly, put him on his bike, and changed the momentum of the bout back in Manny's favor.

The judges were in agreement on nine of the twelve rounds. Each of them scored rounds 1, 2, 4, 5, and 10 for Pacquiao while giving the nod to Thurman in 6, 7, and 11. Dave Moretti and Tim Cheatham were on the mark, favoring Pacquiao by a 115–112 margin. Glenn Feldman (114–113 Thurman) has had better nights as a judge.

Thurman was gracious in defeat.

"Manny Pacquiao is a truly great, legendary champion," Keith said in an in-the-ring post-fight interview. "Oh, senator! Oh, senator! Great is ye, oh, senator! I promised I'd say that if he won tonight." The defeated fighter then added, "My conditioning, my output, was just behind Manny Pacquiao. Tonight was a blessing and a lesson. Thank you, everybody. And thank you, Manny Pacquiao."

The widespread assumption going into Pacquiao–Thurman was that Pacquiao's primary value as a fighter had trended toward his being a victim on someone else's ring ledger; that things in the ring will not end well for him because he'll keep fighting until he has suffered at least one bad beating too many, maybe more.

"It just a matter of time," people said.

Maybe so. But on Saturday night, Manny Pacquiao said, "Not this time."

Mike Lee was protected in his first twenty-one pro fights. But against Caleb Plant, he was the opponent.

Caleb Plant Is Making His Mark

The July 20, 2019, IBF 168-pound title fight between Caleb Plant and Mike Lee wasn't expected to be competitive. But it was a coming out party for one of boxing's more compelling personalities.

Plant was born and raised in Tennessee. As his ring career progressed, he moved to Henderson, Nevada on the outskirts of Las Vegas to hone his craft. On January 13 of this year, he scored an upset decision victory over Jose Uzcategui to claim the IBF belt and bring his record to 18–0 with 10 KOs. Prior to that, his hardscrabble origins had been scarred by tragedy.

Plant grew up in a home where alcohol and drug abuse were common. His own daughter, Alia, was born with severe brain damage.

"She had zero motor skills," Caleb recounted last year. "She couldn't sit up. She couldn't hold her head up. She couldn't lift her arm. She couldn't eat. She ate through a tube in her stomach. I didn't know if she was gonna know who I was. I didn't know if she knew that I loved her. She was never gonna stand and say, 'I love you, dad' or 'Merry Christmas, dad.' She's not gonna know what it's like to have friends. But what if I could just give her a nice life, a life that I didn't have. What if I could work so hard that I can give her a life and things that I never had as a kid. We won't be able to have the relationship that I had with my dad. But I'll give her my all, my best, no matter what. This is what I can try to give her. A roof over her head; food in her stomach, even if it's not through her mouth."

In 2015, at nineteen months of age, Alia was in the hospital on life support for the fifth and final time in her young life. Plant's words speak for themselves.

"The doctors were telling me, 'Mr. Plant, your daughter is gonna pass away.' That's a tough conversation to have. She was slowly going down and down and down and down. I went to her. It was just me, and I said, 'You know, this has been a long nineteen months, and I know you have to be tired. And if you are over this, then I'm okay with that. I'm not gonna be mad at you. I'm not gonna be disappointed in you. I'm not gonna be upset with you. If you're tired of this and you're done and you don't want to do this anymore, then your daddy supports you. And I'm gonna be right here.' And right after that conversation—a conversation that I had never had with her before because, every time before, it was 'No, this is not gonna happen'—she started going down. I said, 'I want you guys to take this stuff off of her because I don't want her to pass with these tubes down her throat and an EEG machine on her head and sticky and all that stuff.' They took all that stuff out. They cleaned her off and washed her hair. They took everything out. I got to sit there with her. She took her last breath at 10:55. And I just sat with her there for a long while."

Adding to the tragedy in Plant's life, his mother was shot and killed by a police officer in March of this year. According to the Tennessee Bureau of Investigation, Beth Plant was being taken to a hospital by ambulance when she became unruly and pulled a knife from her backpack. The driver pulled over to the side of the road and called for assistance from law enforcement. When a policeman arrived, Plant came toward him brandishing the knife and he shot her.

After Plant's mother died, Caleb posted a message on Facebook that read,

> Love you forever and always momma. You always said "work hard bubba" and I did. I know that we spent a lot of time wishing the relationship we had was different but you was still my momma. We both wished we could start from scratch so we could go back and you could have a fresh start with me and Maddie. Regardless you was one of the sweetest ladies I've ever come across. You had your demons but you'd give the shoes off your feet and your last dollar to someone who needed it less than you. I love you momma and I know you are up there with Alia now and her and grandma finally get to spend time together like we talked about way back. You are the first one out of all of us to see what Alia is really like so make the most of that and kiss her up and tell her that her daddy loves and misses her. I know in the end it's your demons we always talked about that got the best of you. Maybe you always told me because you knew I'd understand because we shared some of the same ones.

The saving grace in Plant's life has been boxing.

"I've been boxing since I was nine years old," Caleb says. "There ain't never been a Plan B. Not to go to college. Not to get a nine-to-five. Not to get a job. Not to be in the NFL. Not any of that. All I've ever had is boxing. I'm from the metho-heroin capital of the US where a mother will sell her child's last toy for one Xanax. Where a mother will lock her son and her daughter in a room for hours, not taking care of them, just so she can be locked away in her room doing her own stuff. I'm from where the Bethesda Center gives out-of-date canned food to you because you ain't got no food. There ain't no Plan B."

Elaborating on that theme during a July 1 media conference call, Plant declared, "Boxing has always been like a sanctuary for me. It's been a place that I could go and be somebody. As a kid, I was somebody that nobody would want to be, living in a place where nobody would want to be in. When I got to go to the gym, then I got to be somebody that everybody wanted to be. Grown men looking up to me, oohing and ahhing. And once I got back out of those doors, I had to go back to being that kid that nobody wanted to be. So that became like an addiction for me, to want to be there, want to be in the gym."

"Through everything that came and left in my life," Plant continued. "Through all the things that I've lost, through all the things I've been deprived of or haven't had, boxing has always stood by my side. Boxing has always been there for me through thick and thin. Boxing is like a woman. If you treat her right and you do good by her, then she'll stand by you and she'll do right by you. But she's a jealous woman. And the difference between me and my opponent is, I haven't glanced off of her. I haven't endeavored into other things."

Mike Lee comes from a world that Caleb Plant is unfamiliar with.

Lee went to high school at the Benet Academy in Lisle, Illinois. Virtually all of Benet's students go on to college. Lee spent a year at the University of Missouri before transferring to Notre Dame, where he graduated with a degree in finance. "I relax by watching CNBC," he told writer Kieran Mulvaney several years ago. "And I like reading the *Wall Street Journal*."

For most of Lee's ring career, he was well marketed and well protected by Top Rank. At one point, he parlayed his Notre Dame pedigree into a much-commented-upon Subway commercial. Recently, he left Top Rank to campaign under the Premier Boxing Champions banner. Now thirty-two (five years older than Plant), he came into Saturday night's fight with a 21–0 (11 KOs) record, having fought his entire career at light-heavyweight or a shade higher.

Plant's opposition had been suspect prior to his victory over Uzcategui. Lee's opposition had been worse. "The typical Mike Lee opponent," one matchmaker observed, "has had ten fights and won all but nine of them."

Kickoff press conferences are usually characterized by the lack of anything eloquent being said. The May 21 press conference for Plant–Lee was different. Lee spoke first, voicing the usual platitudes.

"Every single fight is different. I don't really care what his other opponents have done in or out of the ring. It doesn't matter. On fight night, the bell rings, it's just me and him. The best man will win. I've been in so many press conferences where opponents either talk shit or they're dismissive or they're respectful. I've beat them all. This is an incredible opportunity and I will make the most of it. I'm going to shock a lot of people."

Then it was Plant's turn.

"I've been boxing my whole life," Caleb said. "No college degree for me. No high school sports. No acting gigs. No Subway commercials. Just boxing, day in and day out, rain, sleet, or snow. He may have a financial degree. But in boxing I have a PhD and that's something he don't know anything about. Something else I have a PhD in is being cold and being hungry and being deprived, coming from very rock bottom. That's something he don't know anything about. So if this guy ever thought for one second that I would let him mess this up for me and send me back there; unlike him, I have everything to lose. This is how I keep a roof over my head and food in my belly. That's something he don't know anything about. So if he thinks he's going to mess this up for me, he's not half as educated as I thought he was."

At times, the dialogue seemed to verge on class warfare. And it continued in that vein through fight week.

"There are zoo lions and there are jungle lions," Plant said at the final pre-fight press conference two days before the bout. "The zoo lion will look at the jungle lion and think they're the same thing. And from a distance they look the same. Until it's time to eat or be eaten."

"The trash-talking goes back and forth," Lee responded. "That's as old as time. Nothing he's saying is new. It's all recycled stuff he's heard on TV or heard in movies. It's nothing new to me. It doesn't even bother me. I laugh at it."

Plant–Lee was broadcast live on Fox as a lead-in to the Pacquiao–Thurman pay-per-view card. Lee was a 15-to-1 underdog. The consensus was that he had as much chance of beating Plant in a boxing match as Yale would have of beating Notre Dame in football.

Nevada's choice of seventy-six-year-old referee Robert Byrd as third man in the ring was a bit of a surprise. Byrd was once a capable referee, but his performance in recent years has been erratic. The most egregious example of this was his mishandling of the June 15 World Boxing Super Series cruiserweight semifinal bout between Mairis Briedis and Krzysztof Glowacki.

Byrd is past the point where he can move nimbly around the ring and was out of position for much of Briedis–Glowacki. His judgment was also faulty. In round two, while the fighters were in a clinch, Glowacki hit Breidis in the back of the head with a rabbit punch. Briedis retaliated by flagrantly smashing an elbow into Glowacki's face, driving Krzysztof to the canvas. In a post-fight in-the-ring interview on DAZN, Briedis acknowledged the foul, saying, "I did a little bit dirty."

Glowacki, for his part, noted, "The elbow was really strong and clear to the chin. I did not know what happened. I do not remember a lot after that."

Byrd deducted a point from Briedis but didn't give Glowacki additional time to recover. Still hurt, Glowacki was knocked down fifteen seconds later by a two-punch combination that ended with a right hand to the back of the head. He rose. The bell rang to end the round. And Byrd didn't hear it.

"The bell's gone," DAZN blow-by-blow commentator Jim Rosenthal shouted. "They're carrying on. Come on, referee. I can hear it. Get in there."

But Byrd allowed the action to continue. With people at ringside waving their arms and screaming at him that the round had ended, he allowed Briedis to batter Glowacki for another eight seconds until Mairis scored another knockdown.

"He's gone down after the bell," Rosenthal proclaimed. "What is occurring in there? What is occurring? That bell was ringing for ages. It's farcical. He's saying he couldn't hear the bell. He must have been the only one in the arena."

A badly damaged Glowacki was allowed out of his corner for round three but was stopped twenty seconds later. In the same post-fight interview on DAZN, Briedis conceded that he'd heard the bell ending round two but kept punching.

As for Plant–Lee, the fight lived down to expectations. Lee tried to fight aggressively but didn't have the tools to do it. Plant was the faster, stronger, tougher, better-schooled fighter. He dropped Lee with a lead left hook late in round one, dug effectively to the body throughout, and put Lee on the canvas thrice more in the third stanza. After the final knockdown, Byrd stopped the mismatch. According to CompuBox, Lee landed just eight punches in the entire bout.

It will be interesting to see how Plant progresses from here, in and out of the ring. In that regard, it should be noted that writer Jeremy Herriges talked at length recently with Carman Jean Briscoe-Lee (Alia's mother, who was once Caleb's companion). Thereafter, Herriges wrote a thought-provoking article for *NY Fights* that calls portions of Plant's narrative into question.

Meanwhile, Caleb remains a work in progress.

"I'm not a grown man," he said during a July 1 media conference call. "I'm a growing man. So I'm going to continue to become better in the ring. I'm going to continue to become a better man outside the ring. Thus far, I think I've done a good job of handling that responsibility. If I just continue to follow what I've done, I think I'll be on the right path."

Let's see how the journey unfolds.

Chris Arreola has said, "Every punch that I got hit with was the most painful punch ever." On August 3, 2019, he got hit with a lot of them.

A Sad Night for Chris Arreola

The August 3, 2019, fight at Barclays Center between Chris Arreola and Adam Kownacki highlighted what's enthralling about boxing and also the sad side of the sport.

When Arreola turned pro in 2003, he seemed destined for success. He was a heavyweight with a good amateur pedigree, power, solid ring skills, and a crowd-pleasing, hit-me-and-I'll-hit-you-back style. He was media-friendly and likable with refreshing candor and a good sense of humor. His Mexican American heritage was a plus. And he was guided by boxing impresario Al Haymon at a time when *HBO Championship Boxing* and *HBO Boxing After Dark* were, in essence, programmed by Haymon.

There were times when Arreola trained less diligently than he should have. A fighter doesn't get more out of boxing than he puts into it, and Chris was rarely in top shape. Indeed, Henry Ramirez (who trained Arreola for most of his ring career) acknowledged, "Sometimes I don't think he gives us the best chance to win. Sometimes he comes in a little too far out of shape." But that was part of the package.

"Who gives a fuck if I'm fat?" Arreola asked rhetorically. "There's plenty of guys who look like Tarzan and fight like Jane."

Other "Arreolaisms" included:

★ "Boxing is two guys in the ring who hardly know each other beating the crap out of each other. The crowd oohs and aahs, and I want to get my oohs and aahs in. Then it's over and you shake hands and hug each other. Go figure."

★ "My defense has to get better. I'm ugly and I don't want to get any more uglier."

★ "I'm not big-headed. I'm one of the guys, a regular Joe Schmo. But it makes me angry when people think I'm dumb, when they talk down to me, when they think I'm a meathead because I'm a fighter."

Ten years ago, Arreola's record stood at 27–0 with only one opponent having gone the distance against him. Then, on September 26, 2009, he challenged Vitali Klitschko for the World Boxing Council heavyweight crown. Chris fought with honor but was outclassed from the opening bell. The outcome of the fight was never in doubt. Klitschko outlanded him 301 to 86 and turned him into a human bobblehead doll. Ramirez called a halt to the beating after ten one-sided rounds.

Arreola has been on a long downhill slide since then. Seven months after losing to Klitschko, he was outpointed by Tomasz Adamek. "He beat my ass," Chris said in a post-fight interview. "I look like fucking Shrek right now."

After being complimented on his "toughness" following a twelve-round decision loss to Bermane Stiverne in 2013, Arreola responded, "It doesn't matter how tough you are. I lost the fight."

Subsequent title opportunities against Stiverne (2014) and Deontay Wilder (2016) ended in knockout defeats.

Asked prior to fighting Wilder if he thought that, given his recent ring performances, he deserved another title opportunity, Arreola replied, "Let's be honest, man. Do I deserve it? Come on. No. But when a title shot comes knocking, you don't turn it down."

The gaping hole in Arreola's ring résumé is that he has never beaten a world-class opponent. His biggest win was a first round stoppage of former Michigan State linebacker Seth Mitchell (who was 26–1–1 at the time). "He better bring his helmet if he expects to beat me," Chris said before that fight. He also stopped a faded thirty-nine-year-old Jameel McCline short of the distance.

Readying to fight Kownacki, Arreola was thirty-eight years old with a 38–5 (33 KOs, 3 KOs by) ring record that wasn't as good as it looked.

At the June 18 kickoff press conference for Kownacki–Arreola, Chris had a pensive look in his eyes. He was born with a fighter's face that has been forged further in the fire of combat, adding scar tissue and a nose that has been ground every which way while being broken multiple times.

Once upon a time, Arreola was the A-side in main events. Not anymore. The thirty-year-old Kownacki had built a 19–0 (15 KOs) record against the same class of fighter that Chris used to beat. Adam is a big strong guy who throws punches with abandon, wears opponents down, has minimal defense, and is being groomed as an opponent for Deontay Wilder.

Arreola was seated on the B-side of the dais. His name was listed after Kownacki's on all promotional material. On fight night, he would be in the red (designated loser) corner. If the powers that be at Premier Boxing Champions thought he had a realistic chance of beating Adam, they wouldn't have made the fight.

"How did Arreola feel about being the B-side of the promotion?"

"I'm okay with it," Chris said. "It's part of the game. Once I was a young lion and now I'm the old veteran. Boxing humbles you. But I'm not a stepping stone for anyone."

How did he feel about Andy Ruiz upsetting Anthony Joshua to become boxing's first Mexican American heavyweight champion?

"I'm happy for Andy. The difference between Andy and me is, he made the best of his opportunities and I didn't. Good for him. The first time we sparred together, Andy was seventeen years old. Back then, he wanted to be like me. Now I want to be like him."

Kownacki's fortunes have also changed but he's going in a different direction. In 2015, Adam had made his Barclays Center debut in a swing bout on the undercard of Amir Khan versus Chris Algieri. Now he anticipated beating Arreola which, in his words, "would make me a top ten heavyweight on everyone's list."

"On paper, it's the perfect fight," Kownacki added. "Now it's in my hands to do what I gotta do, which is get a knockout and put on a great performance."

There were more sound bites from Arreola as the buildup to the fight progressed:

* (when asked to define himself): "I'm brash but respectful of other people. I'm kindhearted, old-school in a lot of ways. I'm at peace with myself. I'm me."
* (about being a role model): "People ask me, 'What do you say to kids?' And I tell them, 'I don't say shit to kids. I talk to their parents and tell them to be there for their children."
* (about his family): "My wife and I have two children, a

seventeen-year-old daughter and four-year-old son. That's thirteen years apart. But same father, same mother. Make sure you write that."

★ (about fighting Kownacki): "It's not personal. I like Adam and I think he likes me. But I'm going to try to punch him in the face and knock him out, and that's what he's going to try to do to me."

"How big a puncher is Adam?" Chris was asked.

"I'll find out on Saturday night," Arreola answered. "He's fought some good fighters, but I've fought better."

But the better fighters that Arreola had fought beat him.

The most pressing question in advance of the fight was, "How much did Chris have left?"

At a certain age, a fighter knows what to do in the ring better than he did before, but he can't do it anymore. And at thirty-eight, a fighter doesn't take punches as well as he did when he was young. Arreola used to hate the rigors of training but liked sparring. Now he acknowledged, "I don't mind training, but I hate sparring. My body isn't the same anymore. When I get hit now, it hurts more and the pain lasts longer."

Arreola's weight—an issue in the past—was down. He would enter the ring at 244 pounds, a better number than Kownacki's career high 266. But was Chris in fighting shape? And with what he had left as a fighter, would it matter?

"This is my last chance," Arreola said. "If I lose this fight, I'll retire, plain and simple. Not because of the media or anything like that. This is my last chance because I say so. If I lose, there's no reason for me to be in the sport of boxing. I'm in boxing to be a champion. If I lose, it brings me all the way back to the bottom, and I don't want to keep crawling back up and crawling back up again. I'm too old to be doing that. So it's a make or break kind of fight. If I lose, I go home. No matter if it's a great fight or it could have gone either way. Plain and simple; I lose it, I go home, I stay home. One and done, no more."

Old athletes are surpassed by young ones in every sport. But it's more painful to watch when the sport is boxing and the older competitor is getting beaten up.

There was a time when Arreola fought mostly in Southern California before crowds that were solidly behind him. Now he was in Brooklyn in a promotion aimed at Polish American fight fans. Kownacki, who had fought at Barclays Center on eight previous occasions, was the house fighter. The announced crowd of 8,790 booed when Chris entered the ring and cheered wildly for Adam.

It was an exciting fight with little subtlety about it. One of boxing's cardinal rules is, "Never give an opponent a free shot." That said; both men fought like they didn't understand that holding up their hands, slipping punches, and otherwise defending themselves is an integral part of the sweet science. They punched and mauled for twelve rounds in a nonstop slugfest that resembled two mastodons locked in battle for supremacy of the herd.

In the early rounds, it appeared as though Kownacki might walk through Arreola. He was a bit quicker, had a bit more on his punches, and seemed better able to absorb punishment. Then, in the middle rounds, Adam slowed a bit and one had to consider the fact that Chris had gone twelve rounds on four occasions and ten rounds three times while Kownacki had gone ten rounds once. In other words, Arreola had been down this road before and might be better able to navigate the terrain as it got increasingly more rugged.

Then, in round nine, Arreola tired noticeably. From that point on, it seemed as though he was fighting from memory. But he never stopped trying to win. On the few occasions when Kownacki tried to slow the pace, Chris forced the action. One can question Arreola's ring skills. One can question his judgment. His courage and heart aren't in doubt.

The judges were on the mark with scorecards that favored Kownacki by a 118–110, 117–111, 117–111 margin. His limitations as a boxer showed in the fight and he lacks the one-punch knockout power that might compensate for them at the elite level. But Kownacki–Arreola was a barnburner. According to CompuBox, the fighters threw 2,172 punches between them and landed 667, both of which exceeded previous CompuBox highs for a heavyweight fight.

"Adam is relentless," Arreola said in a post-fight interview. "He just keeps coming. I know I got him with some good punches, and he got me with some good ones. I was more than ready to go all twelve, but Adam came in and won the fight."

Then Chris went to the hospital to check on the status of his left hand and possibly more. Just before entering the ambulance, he acknowledged, "I'm a little dejected. I lost. This ain't the way I wanted to go out, but I gave my all. Much respect to Adam. We were in a proverbial phone booth beating the shit out of each other, and it was fun. It was fun for me and it was fun for him and I hope the fans enjoyed the fight."

Boxing is a form of theatre in the round.

Fight Notes

Friday night fights at Madison Square Garden were once boxing's most anticipated weekly event. On Friday, January 18, 2019, Matchroom USA and DAZN teamed up for the latest installment.

There were five fights of note.

Amanda Serrano (35–1, 28 KOs) is one of today's better women fighters and has made a career out of winning belts of questionable provenance against an assortment of opponents who've ranged from competent to inept. By last count, she'd won world championships at 130, 135, 126, 118, 122, and 140 pounds. Now she was dropping from 138½ pounds in her last outing to 115 pounds in effort to claim the WBO super-flyweight bauble (which would give her a world championship in a seventh weight division).

Eva Voraberger (24–5, 11 KOs), a 25-to-1 underdog, was the designated loser.

One day before the fight, Serrano weighed in at 115 pounds. On fight night, she weighed 133.

Serrano–Voraberger lasted all of 35 seconds. Voraberger had the look of a deer in the headlights from the moment the bell rang and was dropped for the count by the first body shot that Serrano landed.

For more than a century, the term "champion" was synonymous with glory and greatness in boxing. Now it's a devalued marketing ploy, particularly for women boxers.

John Sheppard, who oversees BoxRec.com, reported last year that boxing's world sanctioning bodies have created 110 different women's titles. This means that, assuming each title is available in 17 weight divisions, the sanctioning bodies have belts for 1,870 women's champions. Meanwhile, according to Sheppard, there were only 1,430 active women boxers in the world. Thus, there were approximately 1.3 titles available for each woman boxer.

In the fight immediately preceding Serrano–Voraberger, Reshat Mati knocked out Benjamin Borteye in 66 seconds. That meant, because of TV scheduling, there was a stretch lasting for an hour and five minutes during which fans saw 101 seconds of boxing.

When DAZN and Matchroom announced their alliance last spring, Eddie Hearn pledged to improve the onsite experience for boxing fans in the United States. One presumes this wasn't what he had in mind.

Serrano–Voraberger was followed by Chris Algieri (22–3, 8 KOs) vs. Daniel Gonzalez (17–1–1, 7 KOs).

Algieri, age thirty-four, is willing to go in tough. He showed skill, heart, and determination five years ago in rallying from two first-round knockdowns to decision Ruslan Provodnikov for the WBO 140-pound title. But since then, Algieri had lost three of five fights (to Manny Pacquiao, Amir Khan, and Errol Spence). Gonzalez was expected to pose a lesser challenge. The fight was made for Chris to win.

Algieri–Gonzalez was a much better fight than it should have been, largely because it appears as though Chris can't perform at a world-class level anymore. He started well, but his reflexes aren't what they once were. And for a fighter who has relied on quickness and speed throughout his career, that spells doom.

In round three, Algieri started getting hit with shots that Gonzalez wouldn't have hit him with several years ago. Then Chris tired, and the second half of the bout was an exercise in survival. In an effort to shorten the fight, Algieri circled away whenever possible and held when Gonzalez got inside. Meanwhile, Daniel started throwing more and was cutting off the ring well.

Algieri once said, "Empathy is bad for a fighter. When you win, you can't think about what you've just done to the other guy's life."

That said; everyone in the arena other than Gonzalez and his partisans must have felt empathy for Chris. It appears as though the judges did.

The consensus at ringside was that a draw would have been credible. The judges thought otherwise, giving Algieri a 98–92, 97–93, 96–94 triumph that was booed by the pro-Algieri crowd. The 98–92 scorecard was beyond the pale and was turned in by James Pierce who has a history of turning in horrid scorecards. One that comes to mind was Pierce's 78–74 verdict last year in favor of Heather Hardy over Iranda Paola Torres.

Next up; Irish-born T. J. Doheny (20–0, 14 KOs), now living in

Australia, defended his IBF super-bantamweight belt against Ryohei
Takahashi (16–3–1, 6 KOs) of Japan. Takahashi evinced the skill level of
a club fighter. Doheny wore him down en route to a stoppage at 2:18 of
round eleven.

In the semifinal bout of the evening, Jorge Linares (45–4, 28 KOs)
moved up to 140-pounds to pit his skills against Pablo Cesar Cano (31–7,
21 KOs).

Linares, age thirty-three, has held belts at 126, 130, and 135 pounds.
All of his defeats had come by way of knockout (against Juan Carlos
Salgado, Antonio DeMarco, Sergio Thompson, and Vasyl Lomachenko).
Cano had compiled a 5-and-6 record with one no contest during the
preceding six-and-a-half years.

Linares–Cano was bombs away from the start. Thirteen seconds into
round one, Cano dropped Linares to the canvas with an overhand right.
Jorge rose and seemed to be okay. But he wasn't. Cano dropped him again
with a left hook up top just past the midway point of round one and
again forty seconds later. A fourth knockdown seemed imminent when
referee Ricky Gonzalez stepped between the fighters and appropriately
stopped the bout at the 2:48 mark.

The ease with which Cano dispatched Linares might lead to a reeval-
uation of Vasyl Lomachenko's struggle against Linares at 135 pounds in
May of last year.

Then it was time for the main event: Demetrius Andrade (26–0, 16
KOs) vs. Artur Akavov (19–2, 8 KOs).

Andrade, who will turn thirty-one next month, represented the
United States as a welterweight at the 2008 Beijing Olympics and lost
in the third round to eventual bronze medalist Kim Jung-Joo of South
Korea. He won the WBO 154-pound title by split decision over Vanes
Martirosyan in a dreadfully dull fight in 2013; a WBA 154-pound belt via
split decision over Jack Culcay in a dreadfully dull fight in 2017, and the
vacant WBO 160-pound title by decision over Walter Kautondokwa last
year. He has never fought a top-tier opponent.

Evaluating Andrade as a fighter, trainer-commentator Teddy Atlas has
opined. "He's like a cake that comes out of the oven looking perfect. But
when you eat it, it tastes like something the cake needed was left out."

Akavov, born in Russia and now living in California, was a typical
Andrade opponent. A 20-to-1 underdog, he has limited ring skills, limited

power, and was outboxed in his one step-up fight (against Billy Joe Saunders in 2016).

Andrade–Akavov was a boring tactical fight. Andrade used his jab— it's a good one—as an offensive and defensive weapon to control the action. Akavov was outclassed. And if he didn't know it before the fight began, he knew it from round one on. After a few stanzas, he seemed interested primarily in going the distance.

It's hard to knock out a fighter who's trying simply to survive; particularly if you're not trying to knock him out (which Andrade didn't seem intent on doing). Demetrius fights with the urgency of a man who's in the gym, sparring. On this occasion, he seemed content to simply put rounds in the bank.

The crowd thinned noticeably as Andrade–Akavov dragged on. With 24 seconds left in round twelve, referee Arthur Mercante stepped between the fighters and, over Akavov's bitter protest, stopped the contest. It wasn't the worst stoppage in recent memory. But it wasn't the best either. Mercante has been justly criticized in the past for letting fights go on too long. Better too early than too late.

★ ★ ★

The January 26, 2019, Premier Boxing Champions fight card at Barclays Center offered fans a mixed bag. There were thirteen bouts live and on various viewing platforms. Fans onsite saw the predictable one-sided undercard bouts with one notable exception. In the second fight of the evening, Marsellos Wilder (Deontay's younger brother) fought a late replacement from Kearney, Nebraska, named—depending on which source one credits—William Deets or William Quintana.

Deets/Quintana came into the bout with 6 wins, 12 losses, and a meager two knockouts to his credit. Further tarnishing his résumé, he'd been out of action from mid-2013 through mid-2018 and, according to the *Lincoln Journal Star*, spent two years in prison after pleading no contest to charges that he sexually assaulted two women that he met online. Three additional women also came forward and made similar allegations against him. At his sentencing, the judge noted that Deets seemed to have "a low regard for women."

Wilder dominated the early going to the point where the fight was almost stopped after two rounds. Then, in the fourth stanza, Marsellos got tired. Deets/Quintana whacked him with a left-right combination, and Wilder went down. He rose on unsteady legs, fell into the ring ropes, and referee Al LoBianco properly stopped the contest with 25 seconds left in the bout.

That's why they fight the fights instead of just mailing in the results.

Three bouts were televised on the Fox broadcast network.

Mongolian-born Tugstsogt Nyambayar (10–0, 9 KOs), who fights out of Los Angeles, announced his presence on the boxing scene with a 116–111, 115–112, 114–113 verdict over Claudio Marrero (23–2, 17 KOs) in a WBC featherweight elimination bout. Boxing writers and fans who spent years learning how to spell "Pacquiao" will track Tugstsogt's career with trepidation.

Then it was time for Adam Kownacki (18–0, 14 KOs) vs. Gerald Washington (19–2–1, 12 KOs).

Kownacki looks as though his 260 pounds (give or take a few donuts) have been sculpted out of wet pancake mix. He's a big, strong, affable man whose heart is unquestioned and defensive skills are suspect. Washington is a big, strong, better-sculpted fighter whose chin and punching power are in doubt. That combination made Kownacki a 5-to-1 betting favorite in what promised to be an entertaining fight.

A large, vocal contingent of Polish American fans made its feelings known as the fighters entered the ring. During the pre-fight introductions, Kownacki seemed happy to be there; Washington, not.

Adam came to fight. Gerald came to box. But Washington's boxing wasn't good enough to keep Kownacki off. There's very little subtlety in the way Adam fights. It's full speed ahead, throwing punches (mostly right hands), hit, get hit, and punch some more.

Kownacki staggered Washington with a series of right hands in round one. Fighting aggressively at the start of round two, Gerald opened a cut over Adam's left eye. Then Kownacki dropped him with a right. Washington rose on wobbly legs, took a few more punches, and referee Harvey Dock stopped the bout at the 1:09 mark.

It was a statement win for Kownacki and his most impressive victory to date. Two years ago, Washington lasted into the fifth round against Deontay Wilder and the eighth round against Jarrell Miller. Comparisons will be made, although that's a bit like comparing apples and oranges.

Adam was able to walk through Washington's jab. He won't be able to do that against a world-class heavyweight.

The main event matched Keith Thurman (28–0, 22 KOs) against Josesito Lopez (36–7, 19 KOs).

Thurman, age thirty, turned pro in 2007 and established himself as a champion in the true sense of the word when he decisioned Shawn Porter and Danny Garcia to claim the WBA and WBC titles. But he has been plagued by injuries in recent years, needing elbow surgery after his March 4, 2017, victory over Garcia and then suffering a deep bone bruise on his left hand during training. Those injuries kept Keith on the shelf for almost twenty-three months and led some to question his commitment to boxing.

"I can care less what people say and what they think about Keith Thurman," Thurman noted during a February 24 media conference call. "'Oh, he's ducking guys. He's getting injured to avoid people.' There's a lot of people that don't understand what it means to be a world-class fighter. So a lot of opinions just really don't get to me. If anything, some of them were humorous. You know—I'm Keith 'One-Time' Thurman. I'm Keith 'Run-Time' Thurman, Keith 'Sometime' Thurman, Keith 'Once-Upon-a-Time' Thurman. That was pretty amusing."

"You always have to be a little worried about new injuries," Thurman added. "There's nothing wrong with your car until the day it decides to break down. So at the end of the day, it's always in the back of my mind. Athletes and their bodies go through a lot of things."

Thurman–Lopez was viewed in advance by many as a non-competitive showcase fight. Josesito is willing to go in tough. But when he does, the results tend to not be good. He was knocked out by Andre Berto, Marcos Maidana, and Canelo Alvarez, and had four other losses on his record.

When asked about being regarded as a low-level opponent, Lopez responded, "I wouldn't say it offends me. There's a lot of casuals that don't understand the ins and outs and don't realize what I bring to the table. You can't really judge a fighter by his wins and losses. I've had some tough defeats and some close defeats. Wins and losses aren't everything. I'm a better fighter than I've ever been. So it doesn't matter how many bumps on the road I might have had throughout my career. I'm not new to the game. I know exactly what I have to do. I've just got to go out there and execute. People are overlooking me. Does it bother me? Not at all. It motivates me."

But talk is cheap. Thurman was a prohibitive betting favorite with the odds running as high as 50-to-1 in some quarters.

It turned out to be an entertaining fight. Early in Thurman's career, observers focused on his power. But he's also a skilled defensive boxer— always moving and hard to hit—who transitions well from circling out of harm's way to quick-strike offense.

Against Lopez, Thurman traded blow-for-blow when he had to but preferred to punch and keep moving rather than wait for a receipt. He had an edge in speed, power, and basic ring skills. Lopez kept coming forward, but his efforts were largely ineffective, and his punches rarely found the mark the way they were intended to.

Late in round two, a textbook left hook up top deposited Josesito on the canvas.

Round seven saw one of those dramatic shifts that make boxing at its best the most compelling sport of all. Midway through the stanza, Lopez (who fought valiantly throughout the bout) shook Thurman with a straight right hand, then followed up with a left hook and another right.

Suddenly, Thurman was in trouble. "He had me buzzed and shaken up in the seventh round," Keith admitted afterward.

For the next minute-and-a-half, Thurman backed away as fast as he could, throwing next to nothing and struggling to survive. He stayed on his feet but was on the short end of a 10–8 calculation on each judge's scorecard.

Then, as suddenly as it had opened, Lopez's window of opportunity closed.

The overwhelming majority of people at ringside thought Thurman won by a comfortable margin. CompuBox statistics are sometimes wide of the mark. But here, they showed undeniable superiority for Thurman in the form of a 247-to-117 advantage in punches landed.

Inexplicably, ring judge Don Ackerman scored the bout even at 113–113. Order was restored by Tom Schreck (117–109) and Steve Weisfeld (115–111) who, unlike Ackerman, appeared to have watched the fight and understood what they were watching.

★ ★ ★

It's an old story. A man has three or four mistresses, spreads himself thin, and tells each of the women that he loves her. Despite evidence to the contrary, each of the women believes that the man loves her best.

Right now, Al Haymon is romancing Showtime, Fox, Barclays Center, several other venues around the United States, and more than a hundred fighters. It's an interesting balancing act that continued to unfold on the *Showtime Championship Boxing* card televised from Barclays Center on March 2, 2019.

In recent years, Barclays has established a credible boxing franchise, in large part by casting its lot with Haymon. On September 6, 2018, it announced that it had become "the official East Coast venue" for Premier Boxing Champions (Haymon's primary promotional vehicle) and the exclusive New York City venue for PBC fights. As part of the deal, Barclays is expected to host a minimum of eight PBC fight cards per year.

Meanwhile, on December 14, 2018, it was announced that Brett Yormark (CEO for BSE Global, which oversees Barclays Center) would head an advisory board devoted to "PBC marketing, branding, and growth initiatives."

But in recent months, Barclays hasn't hosted the kind of match-ups that boxing fans have come to expect. One year ago—on March 3, 2018—an excited crowd saw Luis Ortiz do battle against Deontay Wilder. On Saturday night, Ortiz fought Christian Hammer in a half-empty arena. It was the twentieth boxing telecast from Barclays Center for the Showtime–CBS–Haymon combine and one of the least attractive.

As expected, the fighters in the blue corner won all six undercard bouts.

Then Bryan De Gracia (24–1–1, 20 KOs) of Panama fought Eduardo Ramirez (21–1–3, 8 KOs) of Mexico for something called the WBA "gold featherweight championship." For eight rounds, Ramirez seemed more committed to, and adept at, evading punches than landing them. De Gracia wanted to engage, but Ramirez had enough skills to neutralize his clumsy, lunging assault.

Then De Gracia got sloppier. Maybe it was lack of respect for his opponent. After all, Ramirez had been running for most of the fight and had recorded only 8 KOs in 25 previous outings. Regardless, 1 minute 52 seconds into round nine, De Gracia lunged once too often and Ramirez landed a hellacious right uppercut that put him on wobbly legs. If De

Gracia had gone down, he might have had time to recover and regain control of his senses. But he stayed on his feet which enabled Ramirez to pound him some more.

With 54 seconds left in the stanza, De Gracia fell into the ropes with his butt landing on the bottom strand. At that point, referee Benjy Esteves could, and should, have called a knockdown. Instead, he let the action continue before halting the proceedings at the 2:10 mark.

Next up, Ortiz (30–1, 26 KOs), now thirty-nine years old, stepped into the ring to face Hammer (24–5, 14 KOs, 3 KOs by).

Ortiz is a product of the Cuban amateur system. His signature victories were knockouts of Bryant Jennings in 2015 and Tony Thompson one year later. Hammer, who was born in Romania and now lives in Germany, is a high-level club fighter. When a world class fighter meets a club fighter, the world class fighter can be expected to win.

Hammer fought bravely, gave a good account of himself, and landed more lead right hands than he should have. He also took Ortiz's punches well, but he took too many of them. And he was handicapped by the fact that he appeared to not know how to throw a jab.

Ortiz—a 12-to-1 betting favorite—was the more polished, stronger fighter. He fought sluggishly at times but moved inexorably forward. Both men tired down the stretch with Ortiz prevailing on the judges' scorecards by a 100–90, 99–91, 99–91 margin.

In the main event, Erislandy Lara (25–3–2, 14 KOs) challenged Argentina's Brian Castano (15–0, 11 KOs).

Lara, age thirty-five, was born in Cuba and now lives in Houston. Like Ortiz, he was a much-decorated amateur and is a world-class boxer. At one point, he held the WBA 154-pound title which he lost last year to Jarrett Hurd. But Lara was defeated by Paul Williams (an unjust decision) and Canelo Alvarez in addition to his loss to Hurd and was held to a draw by Carlos Molina and Vanes Martirosyan. The most impressive win on his résumé was a 2013 decision over Austin Trout.

Castano is the phony WBA 154-pound champion, having decisioned someone named Cedric Vitu for a belt in March 2018. Hurd is the real WBA 154-pound champion.

Lara has slowed in recent years. Castano was the aggressor throughout the bout and came on strong at the end to sweep the last three rounds on each judge's scorecard en route to a 115–113, 113–115, 114–114 draw.

"Branding," Charles Jay once wrote," goes beyond mere name recognition. Branding is a promise. It's something that the brand stands for, what the consumer can depend on."

Right now, PBC, Showtime, and Barclays have some decisions to make regarding the quality of their brand.

★ ★ ★

Boxing's three "major leagues" showed their respective wares this past weekend. On Friday night (March 15, 2019), DAZN presented a nine-bout card in conjunction with Matchroom USA. On Saturday, Fox and Premier Boxing champions teamed up for the Errol Spence vs. Mikey Garcia pay-per-view event. Then, on Sunday, ESPN and Top Rank had their turn in the form of a St. Patrick's Day card in The Hulu Theater at Madison Square Garden headed by Belfast native and former Olympian Michael Conlan.

The star of the show was St. Patrick, the fifth-century saint widely credited with bringing Christianity to Ireland. In his honor, there were three Irishmen on the card: Conlan, flyweight Paddy Barnes, and welterweight Lee Reeves. That said; there was a Hispanic flavor to the proceedings. The sixteen combatants included Eduardo Torres, Victor Rosas, Juan Tapia, Ricardo Maldonado, Adriano Ramirez, Oscar Mojica, Joseph Adorno, John Bauza, Luis Collazo, Ruben Garcia Hernandez, and two Vargases (Josue and Samuel).

Irish Americans have a record of supporting Irish fighters, particularly on St. Patrick's Day. This was no exception. The announced crowd of 3,712 arrived early. During the final pre-fight press conference, Top Rank president Todd duBoef had paid homage to the fans, although he did voice the view that, on St. Patrick's Day, "Their cognitive behavior is manipulated by the beer."

On fight night, the in-arena music was chosen accordingly. "What Shall We Do with a Drunken Sailor?" was played twice over the sound system.

Lee Reeves (2–0, 2 KOs) of Limerick, Ireland, opened the show with a four-round decision over Edward Torres.

In the third bout of the evening, Vladimir Nikitin (2–0, 0 KOs) won a majority decision over Juan Tapia. Nikitin defeated Conlan in the quarter-finals at the 2016 Olympics, Presumably, they'll fight again at a time of maximum opportunity for Conlan.

Flyweight Paddy Barnes (5–1, 1 KO) of Belfast was a teammate of Conlan's at the 2016 Olympics but lost in the first round to Spain's Samuel Carmona. On St. Patrick's Day, Barnes was matched against Oscar Mojica (12–5–1), who had one career knockout and had gone 3–5–1 in his previous nine outings.

Mojica broke Barnes's nose in round one and knocked him down with a body shot in the second stanza (although to the mystification of those in the press section, referee Danny Schiavone waved off the knockdown). It was a spirited outing in which both men were too easy to hit for their own good. Barnes rallied nicely in the second half of the bout and arguably did enough to win the decision. But two of the three judges thought otherwise, leading to a 58–56, 58–56, 56–58 verdict in Mojica's favor.

In the next-to-last fight of the evening, Luis Collazo (38–7, 20 KOs) took on Samuel Vargas (30–4–2, 14 KOs).

Collazo, now thirty-seven years old, reigned briefly as WBA welterweight champion twelve years ago. Since then, he had cobbled together twelve victories (an average of one per year) against six losses in eighteen fights. Vargas had one win in his previous three outings and has never gotten a "W" against a name opponent.

It was a phone booth fight which worked to Collazo's advantage because Luis's legs aren't what they once were. The decision could have gone either way. Two judges scored the bout 96–94; one for Collazo and the other for Vargas. Frank Lombardi turned in a wide-of-the-mark 98–92 scorecard in Collazo's favor.

Then it was time for the main event.

Conlan (10–0, 6 KOs) is best known to boxing fans for having given the finger (two middle fingers, actually) to the judges after coming out on the short end of a decision in the second round of the Rio de Janeiro Olympics. His skill set is better suited to the amateur than professional ranks. But his Irish heritage is a significant marketing plus. And Top Rank specializes in both savvy matchmaking and building narratives.

This was the third consecutive year that Conlan, now a featherweight, celebrated St. Patrick's Day weekend by fighting at Madison Square Garden. His ringwalk was marked by Irish-themed pageantry. And Ruben Garcia Hernandez, his opponent, was tailor-made for him.

Conlan controlled the fight with his jab. Nothing much else happened. "Mick" emerged victorious 100–90 on all three judges' scorecards. And the fans went home happy because their man won.

★ ★ ★

Boxing is accustomed to having a major fight in Las Vegas as the centerpiece of Mexican Independence Day Weekend. This year, Canelo Alvarez was penciled in as the star attraction. But Canelo and his presumed challenger, Gennady Golovkin, couldn't come to terms, and boxing's PPV-streaming-video king decided that he would enter the ring next against Sergey Kovalev on November 2. That left a holiday void to fill and three separate promotions vying to fill it.

The action began on Friday, September 13, at Madison Square Garden's Hulu Theater. Three bouts were billed as featured attractions on a Matchroom USA card streamed on DAZN.

First up, as expected, Michael Hunter (17–1, 12 KOs) outslicked Sergey Kuzmin (15–0, 11 KOs). Kuzmin has an extensive amateur background in the Russian amateur system but is a one-dimensional fighter. For most of the fight, he plodded forward while Hunter potshotted him at will in what looked like a spirited sparring session en route to a 117–110, 117–110, 117–110 triumph.

Next, Amanda Serrano (36–1–1, 27 KOs), who has won belts in weight classes ranging from 115 to 140 pounds, challenged WBO 126-pound beltholder Heather Hardy (22–0, 4 KOs). It was expected to be an ugly beatdown with Hardy on the receiving end. The only open issue for most fight fans was how long Heather would last.

Hardy only knows one way to fight: moving forward, which she has been able to do in the past against stationary opponents who had less of a punch than she did. All of her previous fights had been made for her to win. Questionable hometown judging carried her across the finish line on several occasions when it appeared as though she had fallen short.

At the final pre-fight press conference for Hardy–Serrano, Heather proclaimed, "I'm the toughest girl I know."

But tough alone doesn't win fights. Against Serrano, Hardy took a pounding in a lopsided first round that two of the judges correctly scored 10–8 in Amanda's favor. Round two was more of the same. Serrano was the more skilled, faster, stronger fighter and a sharper puncher. Heather hung tough. But she was hanging from a thread.

Over the next eight rounds, Hardy showed courage and heart. For the first time in her career, she was in the ring against an opponent who hadn't been chosen because it was presumed that Heather would beat her. She survived and legitimately won a few rounds in the process.

The final scorecards were 98–91, 98–91, 98–92 in Serrano's favor. Each woman received an $80,000 purse. Hardy earned every penny of it. And she earned respect for her effort in a way that none of the "W"s on her ring record had brought her.

The main event showcased lightweight Devin Haney (22–0, 14 KOs) against Zaur Abdullaev (11–0, 7 KOs). Haney is 20 years young and a hot prospect. Abdullaev, age twenty-five, is a solid fighter but in a different league than Haney.

Devin entered the ring as a 20-to-1 favorite. At this point in his career, he appears to be the whole package: speed, power, explosiveness, and good ring skills. Physically and mentally, he's mature beyond his years as a fighter but still has the enthusiasm of youth. Over the course of four rounds, he gave Abdullaev nothing to work with, broke the Russian down, and fractured Zaur's cheekbone. Abdullaev corner called a halt to the proceedings after the fourth stanza.

Haney has The Look that fighters like Shane Mosley and Roy Jones Jr. had when they were young. He and boxing are in their honeymoon years. As for the immediate future; Devin has been calling out Vasyl Lomachenko. But given the different promotional entities and networks involved, the chances of that fight happening anytime soon are nil.

Twenty years ago, fight fans could have looked forward to Haney being meaningfully challenged at each level as he moved forward in an attempt to prove how good he is. In today's fragmented boxing world, what happens next is anyone's guess.

On Saturday, the scene shifted to Dignity Health Sports Park in Carson, California, for another DAZN telecast. This one was promoted by Golden Boy and was supposed to showcase twenty-one-year-old lightweight Ryan Garcia (18–0, 15 KOs), who's being marketed as a heartthrob who can fight, against light-punching Avery Sparrow (10–1, 3 KOs). That match evaporated one day before its scheduled date when Sparrow was arrested and taken into custody on an outstanding arrest warrant issued after he allegedly brandished a handgun in a domestic dispute this past April.

The main event wasn't much of a contest either with Jaime Munguia (33–0, 26 KOs) defending his WBO 154-pound belt against Patrick Allotey (40–3, 30 KOs) of Ghana.

Munguia had nice wins last year against Sadam Ali and Liam Smith. Then, five months ago, he was undressed by Dennis Hogan (although the judges in Monterrey, Mexico, found a way to give Jaime a dubious home country majority decision). Allotey's record looked good until one checked the quality of his opponents on BoxRec.com. Munguia was a 30-to-1 favorite.

When the fight began, Allotey seemed most comfortable on his bicycle and decidedly uncomfortable when he was getting hit by the hooks that Munguia pounded repeatedly into his body. Two minutes into round three, one of those hooks put him on the canvas. A combination dropped him for the second time just before the bell. Patrick seemed disinclined to come out of his corner for round four but was nudged back into the conflict. Two minutes later, he took a knee after another hook to the body and his corner stopped the bout.

The third significant fight card of Mexican Independence Day weekend was the biggest of the three. Promoted by Top Rank and streamed on ESPN+, it featured Tyson Fury vs. Otto Wallin at T-Mobile Arena in Las Vegas.

Like the other two shows, this one disappointed at the gate. On Friday night, the Hulu Theater had been reconfigured so that the rear sections were curtained off. There were more empty seats than seats with people in them at Dignity Health Sports Park on Saturday.

When Fury fought Tom Schwarz at the MGM Grand in Las Vegas on June 15, Top Rank had announced a crowd of 9,012. But according to final receipts submitted to the Nevada State Athletic Commission, only

5,489 tickets were sold for that event with another 1,187 complimentary tickets being given away. The announced attendance for Fury–Wallin was 8,249. T-Mobile arena seats 20,000 for boxing.

ESPN+'s featured three-fight stream didn't begin until 11:00 p.m. eastern time. Jose Zepeda (30–2, 25 KOs) won a 97–93, 97–93, 97–93 decision over former beltholder Jose Pedraza (26–2, 13 KOs). Then WBO 122-pound titlist Emanuel Navarrete (28–1, 24 KOs) cruised to a fourth-round stoppage of Juan Miguel Elorde (28–1, 15 KOs). That set the stage for Fury–Wallin.

There are plenty of "world heavyweight championship" belts to go around these days. Claimants during the past four years have included Manuel Charr, Joseph Parker, Ruslan Chagaev, Lucas Browne, Charles Martin, and Bermane Stiverne. Fury (who entered the ring with a 28–0, 20 KOs record) is currently being marketed as the "lineal" heavyweight champion and can trace his lineal roots all the way back to Wladimir Klitschko (which falls short of going back to John L. Sullivan). The best things said about Wallin (20–0, 13 KOs) during fight week were that he was probably better than Tom Schwarz (Fury's most recent opponent) and that, as noted by Keith Idec of *Boxing Scene*, Wallin was "perfectly polite" during the fight-week festivities.

Bob Arum, who shares a promotional interest in Fury with Frank Warren, praised Fury as the second coming of The Greatest and advised the media, "People are seeing things that they haven't seen since Muhammad Ali. You're seeing a great fighter who can connect to the people and he's a real showman."

Fury (born, raised, and still living in the United Kingdom) got into the spirit of things and proclaimed, "I am going to change my name for the weekend to El Rey Gitano," which translates from Spanish to English as "The Gypsy King." And he further declared, "Isn't it a great thing that a total outsider is showing so much love, passion, and respect for the Mexican people. At the minute, they are being oppressed by the people here [in the United States]. Building a wall, chucking 'em all out, and treating them terrible. I don't know what is going on, but it is nice to see a total stranger, heavyweight champion of the world, coming here and respecting people and paying homage to their beliefs and special days. I've got the Mexican shorts, the Mexican gloves, the Mexican mask, the

Mexican music, the Mexican flag. I have Mexicans as part of my training team. There is a lot of honor and respect in fighting on this date."

That elicited a response from WBA–IBF–WBO heavyweight champion Andy Ruiz, who declared on social media, "Tyson Fury's talking shit. He's representing Mexico—he's not even Mexican, what kind of shit is that? A British fuckin, he ain't even Mexican, wearing the fucking Mexican flag, messed up man. Stay in your lane."

Meanwhile, with no existing World Boxing Council title at stake, WBC president Mauricio Sulaiman stepped in and announced that Fury–Wallin would be contested for a special "Mayan belt" that was also offered to the winner of Munguia–Allotey. Maybe someday boxing will have interim Mayan belts and Mayan belts in recess.

Fury was a 25-to-1 betting favorite. For two rounds, everything went according to plan. Then, in round three, a looping left by Wallin opened a horrible, deep gash along Tyson's right eyebrow. The cut gave the fight high drama. There was a real chance that it would worsen to the point where there was no alternative to stopping the bout. Despite the efforts of cutman Jorge Capetillo, blood streamed from the wound for the rest of the fight.

Knowing that he was in danger, Fury abandoned what he likes to think of as finesse boxing and began to brawl, coming forward and trying to impose his six-foot-nine, 254-pound bulk on his opponent. By round eight, Wallin was exhausted. Tyson was teeing off from a distance and, when he came inside, bullying Otto around.

Wallin fought as well as he could. But he was being pounded around the ring and getting beaten down. Then, remarkably, 38 seconds into round twelve, he whacked Fury with a good left hand and, suddenly—if only temporarily—Tyson was holding on.

The final scorecards read 118–110, 117–111, 116–112 in Fury's favor.

"I was happy that he was cut," Wallin said afterward. "But I wish I could of capitalized a little more on it."

And a final thought . . . When there are three heavyweight "world champions" (which is what boxing has now), there is no heavyweight champion at all.

★ ★ ★

The last boxing card of 2019 at Madison Square Garden had trouble gaining traction with ticket-buyers. Promoter Bob Arum conceded prior to the final pre-fight press conference that the main event between Terence Crawford and Egidijus Kavaliauskas was "a 10-to-1, 12-to-1 fight, so there's not much interest in it." But fans who made it to the Garden on December 14 (the announced attendance of 10,101 included some yeast) got their money's worth. There was a competitive undercard (a pleasant change from the norm in boxing these days) coupled with several storylines of note. When the night was done, Teofimo Lopez had stolen the show.

First, some introductory notes.

Edgar Berlanga, a twenty-two-year-old super-middleweight prospect, came into his fight against Cesar Nunez (16–1, 8 KOs) with twelve first-round knockout victories in twelve bouts. On one level, that's good. But Berlanga hasn't experienced what it's like to go back to his corner after the first round of a professional fight, have his trainer rinse out his mouthpiece, and get ready for more. He didn't know what it was like to get off his stool and hear someone saying, "Round five . . . Round six . . . Round seven."

Nunez had been knocked out in Germany four months ago by a gentleman named Vincent Feigenbutz. The assumption was that he would give Berlanga some rounds and then get knocked out. But Berlanga has heavy hands. He dropped Nunez early in round one, put a beating on him, dropped him again, and the fight was over . . . KO 1.

The first of three featured bouts of the evening matched 2016 Irish Olympian Michael Conlan (12–0, 7 KOs) against Vladimir Nikitin (3–0, 0 KOs), the man who defeated Conlan on a questionable decision in Rio de Janeiro.

Among the thoughts Conlan offered during fight week were:

* "When I got to the pros, I was a little surprised by how much of a business it is. Everything is business."
* "At first, when there were negative comments about me on social media, it bothered me. It gets to you a little. Then I realized there was no reason to give attention to it. I don't even read it anymore."
* "I'd love to be in a position someday where I can call the shots and demand long-term VADA testing for all of my fights."

Insofar as the professional-ranks version of Conlan–Nikitin was concerned, Conlan maintained, "This is straight business for me. There's no personal or emotional attachment to it. Vladimir, obviously he beat me in 2013 when I moved up to bantamweight. In 2016, he [just] got the decision. But he knows deep down he needs to prove something on Saturday night. I don't believe he will."

"I don't have to prove anything to anyone," Nikitin countered. "I won two bouts against him in the amateurs. This is just another big step in my professional career."

When the moment of reckoning came, Nikitin was the more aggressive fighter. But it was ineffective aggression. Conlan outboxed him throughout the fight and went to the body often enough that it was a factor. On those occasions when Nikitin managed to work his way inside, Mick got off first or tied him up en route to a 100–90, 99–91, 98–92 triumph.

Conlan has flaws as a fighter, including a notable lack of power. But he's a hard worker, articulate, and marketable with a solid Irish fan base. As long as he keeps doing what he's doing, Top Rank will move him well.

The most intriguing fight of the night—the one that fight fans most wanted to see—was Richard Commey (29–2, 26 KOs) vs. twenty-two-year-old Teofimo Lopez (14–0, 11 KOs).

Commey, a thirty-two-year-old Ghanaian now living in the Bronx, came up short against Robert Easter and Denis Shafikov in previous outings but captured the vacant IBF 135-pound belt earlier this year with a victory over unheralded Isa Chaniev before defending it successfully against Raymundo Beltran.

Lopez (a 2-to-1 betting favorite) has been groomed by Top Rank and was being tested at a world-class level for the first time. The feeling going in was that, if he couldn't hurt Commey early, things would get interesting. And if he did hurt Commey early—well, that would be interesting too.

Round one saw Commey throwing cautionary jabs. Lopez was the hunter. He wanted to make something happen. Forty seconds into the second stanza, he did. Both men threw right hands. Teofimo's landed explosively. Commey plummeted to one knee, pitched forward, and rolled onto his back. He rose through an act of Herculean will and was being battered against the ropes when referee David Fields stopped the slaughter at the 1:13 mark. It was a statement win for Lopez.

Next came the main event.

WBO welterweight champion Terence Crawford (35–0, 26 KOs) unified the four major 140-pound belts in 2017 before moving north to claim the WBO welterweight title. For several years, he has been in the thick of boxing's pound-for-pound conversation but says, "At the end of the day, it's just opinion."

Kavaliauskas (21–0–1, 17 KOs), a thirty-one-year-old Lithuanian, was a typical mandatory challenger.

At a media sit-down just prior to the final pre-fight press conference, Crawford bridled when asked if he was frustrated by not getting fights against boxing's other top welterweights because they're signed with Premier Boxing Champions (which seems intent on freezing him out).

"I'm not frustrated by nothing," Terence answered, "except I thought I'd get three fights this year and I only got two. I'm not focused on no other opponent besides the opponent that's in front of me. My goal is to make sure I get the victory come this weekend, and that's the only person I'm focused on now. Anyone else is talk. It goes in one ear and out the other."

Crawford also had words for media and fans who disparage fighters who box rather than slug.

"All those people that criticize boxers for boxing never been in the ring before. They never had the pleasure of getting knocked upside the head for twelve rounds. It's not fun. We do it because it's our job. But boxers go in the ring as one person and leave a different person. You go home; you eat your popcorn; and you say, 'Oh, that was a great fight.' It was a great fight for you to watch, but you don't think about the fighters that went through hell to entertain you."

Crawford–Kavaliauskas was an entertaining fight.

Crawford did what Crawford does best. He took his time, figured out what he needed to know, and broke Kavaliauskas down. But he was a bit sloppier and less surgical than usual.

Terence fights like he knows what he wants to do, while his opponents fight like, "Let me see if I can do something."

Midway through round three, Kavaliauskas did something. He nailed Crawford with a sharp right hand that likely would have dropped him to the ring mat had Terence not held on. Egidijus then fired a hook to the body that deposited Terence on the canvas, but referee Ricky Gonzalez ruled it a slip (which looked like the wrong call).

More than most boxers, Crawford appears to take it personally when someone punches him in the face. Thereafter, he and Kavaliauskas fired back and forth. But Terence had the faster hands, sharper punches, and more effective body attack. Late in round seven, he put Kavaliauskas down with a right behind the ear. From that point on, it was a question of when the end would come rather than what the end would be.

Early in round nine, Kavaliauskas visited the canvas for the second time courtesy of right uppercut. He rose and, seconds later, was felled by a right hook. End of fight.

Crawford has an arguable claim to the #1 slot in boxing's pound-for-pound rankings. But at age thirty-two, he has yet to fight an elite fighter, and it's unlikely that he will anytime soon. Meanwhile, it appears as though Teofimo Lopez, at age twenty-two, will have the opportunity to make his mark in a signature fight against Vasyl Lomachenko in 2020.

Lomachenko–Lopez could be an interesting fight. Very.

Joe Frazier once said of Muhammad Ali, "He ain't no fighter. He's a boxer. I'm a fighter."

Smokin' Joe

Hundreds of books have been written about Muhammad Ali. As Ali biographer Wilfrid Sheed noted, "He's one of those madonnas you want to paint at least once in your life." But surprisingly few books—and fewer good ones—have been written about the men who, with Ali, defined "the golden age of heavyweight boxing." Joe Frazier, George Foreman, and Larry Holmes lent their names to autobiographies. But none of these efforts did justice to their subject.

Smokin' Joe: The Life of Joe Frazier by Mark Kram Jr. (published by HarperCollins) does justice to its subject.

Frazier won a gold medal at the 1964 Olympics and engaged in memorable heavyweight championship fights against Jimmy Ellis and George Foreman. But he's best remembered for three fights that he fought against Muhammad Ali, historic encounters that are the pyramids of boxing.

At his best, Frazier fought with unrelenting savage fury. "His way was the hard way," Kram writes. "In the ring, he lived and died by the simple yet daring principle of engagement that, in order to deliver one bone-crunching blow, it was frequently necessary to absorb three in exchange. No one would ever have cause to question his heart or his courage under fire."

After fighting Frazier, George Chuvalo declared, "He fights six minutes of every round."

Frazier was born in Beaufort County in South Carolina on January 12, 1944. His parents, Rubin and Dolly Frazier, had eleven children (eight boys and three girls).

A lot has been written about growing up in the midst of ignorance, poverty, and disease in the poorest parts of rural America. Kram's treatment of the subject is well researched and evocatively written. He writes about Frazier's early years in a way that brings "Billy Boy" (as Joe was known then) and his surroundings to life.

It was a world where, in Kram's words, "Fifty percent of African American males [in Beaufort County] suffered from syphilis which rendered them ineligible for service in World War II. Whatever contrived harmony existed between the races hinged on the adherence by blacks to a wide range of humiliating inequities."

Frazier dropped out of school at an early age. His rural South Carolina vernacular left many with the false impression that he was "slow of mind"—an image that Ali later cruelly propagated. He took a bus north to New York where he stole cars and sold them to a junkyard no-questions-asked to make ends meet. Then he moved to Philadelphia, found work in a slaughterhouse, and took up boxing under the watchful eye of Yank Durham.

Frazier was short for a heavyweight and had a limited reach. But as Kram notes, "Beyond the raw power he spotted in Frazier, Durham ascertained that there was a big engine inside him. To counterbalance Joe's physical shortcomings, he was of the belief that Frazier only had one way to go and that was straight ahead into the chest of his opponent."

That was how Frazier fought.

Kram explores the Philadelphia gym culture and the ring wars that came with it. He chronicles Frazier's pro career from his first fight through the sad coda at the end of his fighting days; an undeserved draw against Floyd "Jumbo" Cummings. He details how, for much of his career, Joe fought with eye damage that severely limited his vision ("I'd rather be rich and blind than poor and blind," he said).

Frazier, of course, will be remembered forever in tandem with Ali and measured forever against him.

Muhammad Ali, who proclaimed, "I outshine the sun."

"The rivalry between Frazier and Ali," Kram writes, "was a cultural happening that exposed the deep fissures in American society. By an accident of circumstances, they ended up in the crosshairs of an argument far larger than themselves."

In this rivalry, Kram notes, Frazier "came face to face with black-on-black hate language in his exchanges with Ali. Whatever heights of athletic achievement they drove each other to inside the ring, they dragged each other down in a running feud outside of it."

Kram deftly chronicles the burgeoning war of words between Frazier and Ali; a war that verged on violence between the two men on several occasions during Ali's exile from boxing. As the book evolves, all three Ali–Frazier fights are well told.

In the dressing room before Ali–Frazier I, Durham told Frazier, "Win tonight and the road will be paved in gold."

Joe won. But even then, his dreams weren't fully realized. Ali had turned a substantial portion of black America against him. The now-undisputed heavyweight champion of the world wasn't able to fully enjoy his reign. He never received the respect he should have as a fighter or a man.

Smokin' Joe covers a wide range of subjects from the formation of Cloverlay (the Philadelphia syndicate that financially backed Frazier) to Joe's unfortunate relationship with Frank Rizzo (the Philadelphia cop who was elected mayor on a platform of not-so-subtle racism aimed at the black community).

It's infused with anecdotal material such as Frazier's effort to launch a singing career (his most notable moment as a singer came in 1970 when he slipped onstage while performing and broke his ankle).

One theme explored in depth is Frazier's profligate womanizing.

Joe had four children by two different women (Florence Smith and Rosetta Green) before his nineteenth birthday. He and Florence married on June 25, 1963, while she was pregnant with their third child. They were so poor that Joe borrowed his sister Mazie's wedding ring to use in the ceremony.

Kram describes Frazier as being "restless at home." That's an under-statement. Over the years, he fathered eleven children (six daughters and five sons) by six different women. Florence was the mother of five of these children. In addition to Rosetta, four other women—Joan Mahoney, Sharon Hatch, Janice Cotton, and Sheri Gibson—carried a child of Joe's to term.

"Frazier let the good times roll when it came to women," Kram writes. "He was prolific in his sexual adventures. Although he loved his children and took seriously his obligation to see to their welfare, he felt hemmed in by the sameness of domestic life. Occasionally, as the four walls began closing in on him, he would engage in quarrels at home late at night as a pretext to storm out of the house in search of action. He looked upon his dalliances as a prerogative due him once the [household] bills were paid."

Some of Frazier's children were raised in comfort. Others grew up in inner-city public housing. But he loved all of them. At one point, he took his 1964 Olympic gold medal to a jeweler with instructions to carve it into charms, one for each child.

In 1985, Joe and Florence began litigating a divorce. The proceeding (like a Dickensian tale out of *Bleak House*) took twelve years to resolve.

Kram also gives a detailed account of Frazier's long (1968 through 2011) relationship with Denise Menz, the most consistent of his extra-marital lovers. Over the years, Menz became, in Kram's words, Frazier's "confidante, lover, business partner, and, occasionally, indentured servant. Wherever Joe appeared, it seemed that she was never far away. Charged by Frazier with running his office, she kept the books, lined up caterers, helped him choose his wardrobe, decorated the gym and the upstairs living quarters, and even did loads of laundry."

Menz (who was one of Kram's sources in writing *Smokin' Joe*) said of her lover, "He would kneel at his bedside and say his prayers the way a small child would. He believed in all of the Ten Commandments except the ones dealing with adultery. He told me, 'The Lord don't care about that.'"

Denise also acknowledged what Kram calls "episodes of turbulence" between Joe and herself with regard to his relationships with other women. "It was the only thing we ever fought about," Menz said. "I knew I was the other woman but not that there were other women."

One twist in their relationship was that Denise is white.

"Given how society frowned upon interracial affairs in the 1960s," Kram states, "it would not have gone well for Joe if it became common knowledge that he was engaged in one. Beyond the certain havoc that it would have caused at home, it surely would have hurt his efforts to build a commercial brand."

The decades after Frazier retired as an active fighter are also well told in *Smokin' Joe*. He had always been a drinker. But he drank a lot more after his days in the ring came to an end.

Eventually, Frazier tried his hand at training fighters. In the late 1970s and 1980s, he worked with his oldest child, Marvis, who'd been born in

1960 when Joe and Florence were sixteen. Marvis was taller and a much lighter puncher than his famous father. He also had a not-particularly-good chin. Referencing Joe's deficiencies as a trainer, Kram observes, "When it came to passing down his know-how, he only knew the way he had done it. He was not adaptable to fighters' individual skill sets. When he worked with young fighters, it was as if he saw within them the potential to re-create himself."

Commenting on Frazier's my-way-or-the-highway approach to training, Eddie Futch declared, "You'll never be able to convince Joe that he was wrong. Anyone who disagrees with him on anything becomes the enemy."

, Marvis won 19 fights as a pro but suffered brutal knockout defeats when overmatched against Larry Holmes and Mike Tyson. He is now said to have cognitive issues.

One of Frazier's children is now an attorney. Another died in prison. Nine of Joe's eleven children are alive today. Kram interviewed four of them. Joseph Jordan Frazier (born to Sharon Hatch in the early 1980s) shared the thought, "My father loved the only way he knew how."

Late in life, his money gone, Frazier suffered from diabetes and hypertension. He underwent surgery for neck, back, and shoulder problems. While mowing the lawn—and possibly intoxicated—he accidentally cut off one of his toes. Worse, he developed cognitive issues of his own, presumably from the many blows to the head he took in boxing. The final blow was liver cancer. He died on November 7, 2011.

There are some nagging factual errors in *Smokin' Joe*. For example, Kram writes that Ali was allowed to fight Oscar Bonavena at Madison Square Garden (with Ali–Frazier I on the horizon) because "New York had relented and given him a license on the heels of his comeback in Atlanta." But New York didn't "relent." A federal judge ruled that the New York State Athletic Commission had violated Ali's constitutional rights and ordered the commission to give him a license.

There's also a questionable interpretation of events in the book's final three pages when Kram recounts what some say was a reconciliation that took place at a private dinner between Frazier and Ali during NBA All-Star weekend in 2002. The dinner did happen. And as recounted by

Kram, some kind words were spoken. But in truth, Frazier never let go of the bitterness and anger that he felt toward Ali.

Kram acknowledges as much when he begins his book by stating in the prologue, "As the years unfolded and Ali grew infirm, as his speech became slurred and his hands increasingly quivered, Frazier appeared to take cruel pleasure in the adversity that had befallen 'Clay.' 'Look at him, and now look at me,' he told me [Kram] and others. 'Who do you think came out the winner?' He had convinced himself that his signature was embossed on the physical wreck Ali had become. Even as friends reminded him that Ali was a sick man and implored him to back off, Frazier could not help himself from battering his erstwhile rival with verbal haymakers."

Near the end of *Smokin' Joe*, hedging on this acknowledgment, Kram writes, "People who knew him for years told me they were sure that Frazier carried his animus for Ali to the grave, that he had been wounded so deeply that he could never let it go. But others were certain that he had come to peace with Ali, particularly those who knew him from his boyhood days in South Carolina. Nearly all told me some variation of 'Billy never hated a soul in his life.'"

But those who knew Frazier "from his boyhood days in South Carolina" were wrong. It's beyond question that, at times in his life, Frazier did hate Ali. Thus, Kram would have done better to end *Smokin' Joe* with his own eloquently worded observation: "Any conclusion either way is perhaps clouded by your own thoughts of how forgiving you would be in the same circumstances. Perhaps some of it also has to do with your own belief in the power of reconciliation, how you define 'unforgivable,' and the enchantment of happy endings."

Boxing was once part of the cultural fabric of America. Jack Dempsey was one of the reasons why.

Dempsey–Willard at 100

One hundred years ago—on July 4, 1919—Jack Dempsey battered Jess Willard over three brutal rounds to claim the heavyweight championship of the world.

The world was very different then. Women were denied the right to vote in many states. Five months earlier, the Eighteenth Amendment to the Constitution had outlawed the production, importation, transportation, and sale of alcoholic beverages in the United States.

Putting matters in perspective for sports fans, Harvard finished in the top spot that year in five college football national championship polls. Babe Ruth led the major leagues with 29 home runs. His closest pursuer, Gavvy Cravath, had 12. Neither the National Football League nor its forerunner (the American Professional Football Conference) existed. Rocky Marciano had yet to be born.

Dempsey–Willard is an important milestone in the history of boxing and symbolizes the essence of the sport. It doesn't have the social and political significance of Jack Johnson vs. James Jeffries, the rematch between Joe Louis and Max Schmeling, or the first encounter between Muhammad Ali and Joe Frazier. But its one hundredth anniversary is an appropriate time for remembrance.

Dempsey was born in 1895 in Manassa, Colorado. For five years beginning at age sixteen, he was what he later described as a "wandering man."

Dempsey biographer Randy Roberts says of those years, "There was no romance in the life. He lived in mining camps and hobo jungles, rode the rods, and more than once begged for food. What separated him was his willingness, even eagerness, to work. He accepted any type of employment from washing dishes, cutting lawns, and scrubbing floors to the harder work of coal-mining, digging ditches, and picking fruit."

Dempsey later recalled, "On the banks of the railroad tracks, generally near a fresh-water stream, hobos, tramps, and others who had fallen on hard times would gather, bundled up in layers of old clothing and news-paper, warming themselves and whatever food they pooled over a fire. As long as you threw a donation in the pot, you were welcome to eat. Moving was part of the business of survival. When all the peaches had been picked in one town, we'd hear that the beets were coming in a hun-dred miles away. I was a dishwasher and a miner. I dug ditches, punched cattle, and shined shoes. I went hungry for days rather than steal. I begged for any kind of job to earn a flop and a meal."

During those years, Dempsey began fighting to make money. He later estimated that he had a hundred fights under the name "Kid Blackie" in Colorado, Utah, and Nevada between 1911 and mid-1914.

"There were days when fighting only got me a buck or two," he remembered. "I was knocked down plenty. I wanted to stay down; I couldn't. I had to collect that two dollars for winning or go hungry. I had one fight when I was knocked down eleven times before I got up to win. I had to get up. I was a hungry fighter. When you haven't eaten for two days, you'll understand."

Meanwhile, by virtue of his 1915 victory over Jack Johnson, Jess Willard had become one of the most famous men in America. But rather than stay active as a fighter, Willard transitioned to the vaudeville circuit and "Wild West" shows where he could make as much as $6,000 a week. He fought only once in the fifty-one months after beating Johnson, win-ning an unimpressive "newspaper decision" in 1916 over Frank Moran.

Finally, in 1919, Tex Rickard (America's premier boxing promoter) lured Willard back into the ring with a $100,000 guarantee to fight an opponent of Rickard's choosing. The promoter wanted a challenger who could beat Willard and would be a marketable champion. Dempsey was his man.

It was a time when the sweet science was emerging from the shadows in America. Religious reform movements were weakening. As the prohi-bition against boxing was lifted from state to state, fights were becoming cause for celebration and Fourth of July prizefights were common.

Tommy Burns had successfully defended the heavyweight champi-onship against Billy Squires in California on July 4, 1907. More famously, on July 4, 1910, Jack Johnson devastated James Jeffries in Reno, Nevada. Two years later, Johnson fought again on America's birthday, knocking out Fireman Jim Flynn in New Mexico.

BoxRec.com reports that, in addition to Dempsey–Willard, there were fights at sixty-two venues in the United States on July 4, 1919. Most notably, Sam Langford lost a decision to Harry Wills in St. Louis; Jack Britton decisioned Johnny Griffiths in Canton; and Harry Greb decisioned Bill Brennan in Tulsa.

Dempsey–Willard was contested in Toledo, Ohio, in a temporary arena constructed from unpolished pine boards replete with splinters and oozing sap. The temperature was 110 degrees when the bout began at 4:09 p.m.

Four years earlier, Willard had been thirty-three years old and weighed 238 pounds when he defeated Jack Johnson. Johnson, well past his prime by then, was four years older than Willard and had entered the ring at a career high 225 pounds, an indication that he wasn't in the best of shape.

Now Willard was thirty-seven years old and weighed 245 pounds. Dempsey was thirteen years younger and weighed 58 pounds less.

Dempsey–Willard was a brutal fight. One minute into round one, the challenger landed a series of blows to the champion's body followed by a left hook that all but caved in the right side of Willard's face. In 1919, a fighter who knocked an opponent down could stand over him and attack as soon as his opponent's knee left the canvas. Dempsey downed Willard seven times in the first round, smashing him to the canvas again and again while the champion was in the process of rising but not yet ready to defend himself. Willard suffered a horrible beating. His jaw and nose were broken. Six teeth were knocked out. There were cuts above and below both eyes. He was unable to answer the bell for round four.

Dempsey's victory over Willard heralded the dawn of a new era in sports and was a harbinger of things to come in boxing. His wild brawling fighting style captured the imagination of America.

In the ring, Dempsey attacked with unrelenting ferocity, moving forward, chin tucked in, throwing punches with all-out aggression with both hands from the opening bell. Every punch he threw had the power to hurt his opponent. If he was knocked down, he got up and started punching again. He was the ideal vehicle for the implementation of Tex Rickard's master plan.

"Rickard's goal," Randy Roberts explains, "was to make boxing a thoroughly respectable sport that would toss together wealthy heiresses, rich businessmen, members of the middle class, and strong-armed laborers in arenas." In pursuit of that goal, he was aided by a new media that fueled the commercialization of sports through more compelling sports writing, more sophisticated film techniques, and radio.

Prior to Dempsey–Willard, the record gate for a prizefight had been $270,755 (generated by Johnson–Jeffries). Dempsey–Willard drew $452,224 in gate receipts.

Then Dempsey and Rickard took boxing to new heights. Dempsey vs. Georges Carpentier was contested on July 2, 1921, in a temporary arena on the outskirts of Jersey City, New Jersey. More than eighty thousand spectators (the largest crowd in America to witness a sporting event until that time) attended. The aristocracy was represented at ringside by Vanderbilts, Rockefellers, Whitneys, Fords, Harrimans, Biddles, and Astors. The United States Senate and House of Representatives adjourned in anticipation of the event because twelve senators and ninety congressmen had tickets. The fight was also attended by a significant number of women. Ladies had been present at Dempsey–Willard but were confined to a special section. At Dempsey–Carpentier, they mingled freely with the men.

The live gate for Dempsey–Carpentier was $1,789,238 (equivalent to more than $25 million today). It was also the first world championship match to be broadcast blow-by-blow on radio.

Two years later—on September 14, 1923—more than eighty-eight thousand fans jammed into the Polo Grounds in New York to see Dempsey defend his championship against Luis Firpo. An estimated thirty-five thousand fans were turned away.

Then, like Jess Willard before him, Dempsey retreated from the ring in pursuit of an easier life. He moved to Los Angeles and signed a contract to star in ten feature films for a minimum guarantee of $1,000,000. Three years passed before he returned to combat, this time against Gene Tunney. On September 23, 1926, the extraordinary total of 120,757 spectators filled Sesquicentennial Stadium in Philadelphia to witness the end of The Manassa Mauler's reign. One year later, 104,943 fans crammed into Soldiers' Field in Chicago for the legendary Tunney–Dempsey "long count" rematch and Tunney prevailed on the scorecards again.

Most former heavyweight champions fade from view. Dempsey remained a public figure all his life and kept his dignity as he aged. Even today, memories of him defy the erosion of time. He is still vivid in the imagination of fight fans, an iconic figure and enduring symbol of boxing glory.

Years ago, I had a conversation with Andy Lee about Jermain Taylor and John Duddy. Taylor was middleweight champion at the time and Duddy was a popular Irish contender.

"John and Jermain are both nice guys," Lee told me. "I like them a lot. But you're always measuring each other when you're together because you know that someday you might be fighting each other. So it's a strange dynamic. There's always that edge between us."

Andy Lee: Fighter

Myriad books are published each year by and about fighters who've won minor championships. Many of these books are hagiographies and not particularly well written. One learns to approach them with a jaundiced eye. *Fighter*, written by Andy Lee with Niall Kelly and published by Gill Books, is worthy of note.

Lee represented Ireland at the 2004 Olympics. He turned pro in 2006 under the guidance of Emanuel Steward, backed by a group of investors who paid Lee a $250,000 signing bonus and a monthly stipend. Two years later, Andy was a 15-and-0 fighter on the rise. But on March 23, 2008, he was knocked out by Brian Vera in what was supposed to be his coming-out party on ESPN. That fed into the view of critics who said he was nothing more than an Emanuel Steward hype job.

Thirteen more victories followed, including a lopsided unanimous-decision triumph in a rematch against Vera. Then Lee challenged Julio Cesar Chavez Jr. in a WBC 160-pound title bout and failed to survive the seventh round. Four months later—on October 25, 2012—Steward died of cancer. Adam Booth oversaw the rest of Andy's career.

Lee was a supportive presence in Steward's final days, but they had a complicated relationship. Andy trained under Emanuel and lived in his home for years. *Fighter* scratches the surface of Steward's character, acknowledging his "flamboyant lifestyle" of "good food, sharp clothes, fast cars" and "the entourage that seems to attach itself to him everywhere he goes and expects him to open his wallet every time."

Lee also recreates the brotherhood at the Kronk Gym and what it meant to Emanuel, writing, "The Kronk is not just a talent factory to him. It's a community, a family. He knows that some people come through that door and they will never be the stars of the show. But they couldn't get by from day to day without his help, and they're as welcome as the best fighter in the world."

But Steward was often overextended. At any given time, he had commitments to dozens of fighters, a lucrative high-profile commentating job with HBO, and an active social life. Inevitably, Lee took a back seat to Emanuel's big-money fighters, most notably Wladimir Klitschko. That's boxing and that's life. But Andy was unhappy about it.

Writing of his loss to Vera, Lee recalls, "We didn't take the little things seriously at all in our preparations, and Emanuel was as responsible for that as anyone. He was doing a great job of promoting me and getting my name out there, but the nitty gritty of the work wasn't being done. When we got to fight night and I could sense that he was a bit worried, it annoyed me. There's no point in your being worried now, I thought to myself. The time for that has passed."

After Lee lost to Vera, Steward—by Andy's reckoning—became "a little bit disinterested." There was a comeback victory over Willie Gibbs. But Emanuel was less of a presence than before.

"I'm in the gym every day," Lee writes, recounting his preparation for the Gibbs bout. "But I can't get Emanuel's attention at all. He becomes less and less involved in my training until, by the end of the year, he's barely working with me. Emanuel does the pre-fight media. He's there in my corner on fight night. But none of that is any use to me if I don't have his undivided attention in the gym. Sugar Hill [a Steward protege] effectively takes over as my head trainer. I didn't turn pro to be trained by Sugar Hill. I turned pro to be trained by Emanuel."

Steward became active again during negotiations for a 2011 fight between Lee and Craig McEwan on HBO (which Lee won on a late KO). But by then, Emanuel no longer had his fighter's full trust.

"Once upon a time," Lee notes, "I would have taken Emanuel's word as gospel. But I know him now, and I know that he's more than capable of a few sleights of hand, a white lie or two, if it's in his interest."

Their last fight together was Lee's challenge to Julio Cesar Chavez Jr. For most of Lee's training camp, Steward was otherwise engaged, working with Wladimir Klitschko for a July 7 title defense against Tony Thompson.

"I remember how Emanuel promised me that I would be his world champion," Lee writes. "Now we're a few days away from that moment and he's on the other side of the world. This wasn't what we agreed. This wasn't the plan."

Lee won a belt in 2014 with Adam Booth in his corner when he knocked out Matt Korobov to claim the vacant WBO 160-pound title. But the real middleweight champion by then was Miguel Cotto (who'd dethroned Sergio Martinez). In two title defenses, Lee battled to a draw against Peter Quillin and then lost his belt when he was outpointed by Billy Joe Saunders. He fought once more before retiring from boxing. His final ring record was 35–3–1 with 24 KOs and 2 KOs by.

Fighter is a thoughtful, self-revelatory memoir. There's some interesting material about Lee's gypsy heritage and other aspects of his personal life. There are also places where it delves knowingly into the essence of boxing:

★ "You have to forget all of your best, most compassionate instincts. Abandon yourself to the transformation and be this entirely different person. Nasty, spiteful, brutal. There are times when I have been cruel. I don't regret anything I've ever done in the ring—no pain I've ever inflicted, no punch I've thrown that I wish I could take back. When we sign the contract [to fight], when we shake hands at the press conference, we both understand that I'm going to try to hurt you and you're going to try to hurt me, and we're both okay with that. I don't hate you. I probably don't even dislike you. But I'm there and this is my job. It's your job too."

★ "When you're in a fight, you are making huge life decisions every second with every punch you throw, with every move you make. One head movement, one punch, a moment too early or a moment too late, can change the course of your life."

★ "They live in a different world, the journeymen. They don't come to win. They come to survive. They know each other, united in the camaraderie of grim acceptance, bonded by the same bleak fate. Fed to a young prospect so he can get rounds under his belt and a win on his record. Or fed to each other by heartless promoters with no concern other than how they are going to pad out space on the card.

I hear them talking about the last fight. The last beating. I wonder if they loved it once, if this was their dream."

* "Once a fight happens, it exists forever. Every time you look at your professional boxing record from now until the day you die, the fight will be there. It will be a part of history and it will be a part of you. You have to live with the consequences tied to your name and tied to your identity in neat tidy numbers."

* "I see fighters who can lose a fight and brush it off like it means nothing to them. I don't know if I admire them or if I think they're idiots."

So where does Lee come out at the end of all this? In a pretty good place, I'd say.

"Memory should be a teacher," he writes, "not a torment. It should remind you of the mistakes that you've made so that you learn from them." And he puts things in perspective nicely, observing, "When you start out in life, when you're young, you have dreams. You look thirty or forty years down the road and project. You imagine the things that you will achieve, the type of person that you will be, and the life you will live. Some people dream of fame and fortune. Some people dream of family and friends. Those dreams, the possibility that they might someday come true, make you happy. As you grow up, your dreams move from tomorrow to today. They stop being ambitions that exist in the distant future and become more present, more urgent. They will either happen in the here and now or never. And if they don't happen, you slowly have to accept that you didn't make it. You settle into the life that you do have and make peace with it."

The only good thing about mismatches in boxing is that, on occasion, they lead to an extraordinary upset.

Kevin McBride:
"I've Been There"

On June 1, 2019—the night that Andy Ruiz shocked the world by beating Anthony Joshua—a large hulking man, casually dressed, with a pleasant demeanor made his way through the crowd at Madison Square Garden. He didn't exactly blend in. At six feet, six inches tall and weighing more than three hundred pounds, it's hard to blend. Those who saw him could have been forgiven for thinking that he was a retired National Football League lineman.

He's a nice man, amiable and easygoing, a bit reticent when meeting strangers. But the words flow when he feels comfortable. His name is Kevin McBride. On the night of June 11, 2005, he secured a place in boxing history. On that night at the MCI Center in Washington, DC, he became "The Conqueror of Mike Tyson."

"How long has it been?" McBride is asked.

"In ten days, it will be fourteen years to the day," he answers. "But who's counting."

McBride was born on May 10, 1973, in Clones, a small town just south of the border between the Irish Republic and Northern Ireland. He was eleven or twelve years old—he's not sure which—when he had his first fight. His opponent was also from Clones and stopped Kevin in 30 seconds. "But I won my next fight," McBride says. "And I fell in love with boxing."

At age nineteen, McBride represented Ireland in the super-heavyweight division at the 1992 Barcelona Olympics and lost in the second round after a first-round bye. He turned pro later that year and came to the United States in 1999 to pursue his ring career. By June 2005, his record stood 32 wins, 4 losses, and 1 draw with 28 knockouts. He was a club fighter with 4 KOs by on his résumé. One of those defeats came against Michael Murray, who lost 17 of his final 18 fights. Murray's sole win during that stretch was his knockout of McBride.

There was a time when fighting Mike Tyson was akin to being a Christian thrown to the lions at the Roman Colosseum. But by 2005, Tyson was stumbling toward the end of his ring career. McBride's most important qualification for being chosen to fight Iron Mike was that he had virtually no chance of winning. He was marketed to the public as the "Clones Colossus" and viewed as a sacrificial lamb.

When the fighters met for the first time at a press conference in Washington, DC, McBride was in awe of his opponent. "I was going to fight Mike Tyson," he later remembered. "He had the tattoo on his face like I'd seen on television. He looked larger than life to me. I said to myself, 'This is really Mike Tyson.'"

At the final pre-fight press conference, Tyson told McBride that he was going to fillet him like a fish, although the consensus was that he was more likely to club him to death like a baby seal.

On fight night, McBride was in a decidedly hostile environment. "Everything was about Tyson," he would recall. "The only people rooting for me were the people in my corner. The crowd was all for Mike. Even the commission was on his side."

Now, fourteen years later, McBride says, "You have to believe you can do it. But then you have to do it. That's the hard part. To be honest with you; waiting for the opening bell, I was asking myself, 'What the fuck did I get myself into?' But I was there. I had to fight."

Fortunately for McBride, Tyson was a lesser fighter that night than he had ever been before. His timing was off, his defense was nonexistent, and his punches lacked power. When the first round ended, the Clones Colossus was relieved to find himself on his feet. Then the sacrificial lamb rose up and slaughtered the butcher.

Early in the fight, Tyson tried to bite McBride's nipple, "That was the scariest thing that happened," Kevin later recounted. "And he was head-butting, throwing low blows. A couple of times, he tried to break my arm off at the elbow. But as the fight went on, I could see that he was getting tired and frustrated. Finally, I said to him, 'If that's all you've got, you're in trouble.' Near the end, I was cracking him with everything I had, and I could feel the energy going out of him."

In round six, Tyson was penalized two points for an intentional head butt, fouled some more, and fell to the canvas in exhaustion. He quit on his stool before the start of the seventh round.

After the fight, McBride needed seventeen stitches to close a cut over his left eye that had been caused by a head butt. His thighs were bruised for days from low blows.

Appearing at the post-fight press conference, Tyson told the media, "I don't have the guts to be in this sport anymore. I'd liked to have continued, but I saw that I was getting beat on. I just don't have this in my heart anymore. I'm not going to disrespect the sport by losing to this caliber of fighter. I'm not interested in fighting anymore. I hate the smell of a gym. I hate the boxing game. That guy in 1985, 1986; I don't know that guy anymore. I'm just not that person anymore. I believed that I was still a fighter, but I'm not. I'm washed up."

Rock Newman, who had promoted the fight, then told Tyson that he was going to applaud him for his career accomplishments and encouraged those in attendance to join him. But Tyson shut the tribute down, crying out, "No, no, no, no. Sit down. Sit down, please. People have given me enough applause in my life."

After the fight, McBride went back to Clones.

"It was wonderful," he later recalled. "The whole town stayed up for the fight. Because of the time difference, it started there around four o'clock in the morning. I don't think the pubs closed that night. I went back to the school that I went to when I was a boy. They had an assembly; all the kids were there. I told them what my father told me. 'If you work hard and believe in yourself, you can accomplish your dreams.' All the kids crowded around me, asking for my autograph like I was famous."

But McBride was unable to parlay his victory over Tyson into bigger and better things. Faced with a higher grade of opponent than he'd fought before, he lost six of his next eight fights and retired in 2011. He now lives with his wife, fourteen-year-old daughter, and eleven-year-old son in Dorchester, Massachusetts, where he works for a company called Horticare Tree Preservation, planting, pruning, and cutting down trees.

"The last time I saw Mike was at the Hall of Fame ceremonies last year," McBride recounts. "I didn't know if he recognized me, so I went over and said, 'Hi, Mike. I'm Kevin McBride.' He looked at me and said, 'I know who you are.' Then we shook hands, but that was all."

And what does McBride think of today's heavyweight scene?

"I wish I was ten years younger," he says. "That's for sure."

"It's such a great sport, boxing," McBride says in closing. "It's a sport where dreams can come true. I know what it's like to have dreams and be laughed at; to be a huge underdog and then pull off the upset like Andy Ruiz did against Anthony Joshua. I've been there. You know, Muhammad Ali was there the night I beat Tyson. I met him after the fight. So in one night, I beat a legend and I met the greatest legend of all time. It was the greatest night of my life. Sometimes, I still can't believe it happened."

What the F Is Paulie Malignaggi Thinking?

On June 22, 2019, Paulie Malignaggi and Artem Lobov will meet in a ring at the Florida State Fairgrounds Entertainment Hall in Tampa in what is being styled as a Bare Knuckle Fighting Championship (BKFC) grudge match. Under BKFC rules, fights are contested in a circular ring with a twenty-two-foot diameter. Combatants can throw punches in a clinch or while grabbing the back of an opponent's neck. No kneeing, elbowing, or kicking is allowed. The contract weight is 155 pounds.

Malignaggi is well known to boxing fans. He's thirty-eight years old and, when he enters the ring to face Lobov, it will have been twenty-seven months since he saw combat. His last ring foray ended poorly when he was knocked out by Sam Eggington in eight rounds.

Lobov, age thirty-two, is a mixed martial artist who has fought for various MMA promoters (most notably UFC) en route to a 16–15–1 record with one no contest. He has also had one fight in bare knuckle competition which he won by decision on April 6 of this year.

Lobov is friends with Conor McGregor and was a training partner with McGregor when the Irishman was preparing to fight Floyd Mayweather in 2017. During that time, Malignaggi was brought into camp to work briefly with McGregor as a sparring partner. Therein the story lies.

Malignaggi–Lobov moved onto the radar screen at a May 20 kickoff press conference in New York where Paulie was a poster boy for bad behavior. He spat on Lobov and tried to hit Artem on the head with a handheld microphone. At various times, he called Lobov "a pussy hypocrite fuck," "a hypocrite pussy fuck," "a bitch-ass pussy fuck," and "a piece of shit." Other thoughts he uttered included:

* "My hands are like razor blades. Get a good look at this guy's face right now because next month I'm gonna make it all look like a road map. Permanently, because these scars are not gonna go away."
* "You're a piece of shit and I'm gonna treat you like the dirtbag that you are. After I beat the shit out of you, I'm gonna spit on you. I might take out my dick and piss on you. I'm gonna take out my dick after I knock your teeth out and piss in that toothless mouth of yours. You got five weeks to live, motherfucker."
* "Next month, I'm gonna put this guy in a fucking coma."
* The following day, for good measure, Paulie referred to Lobov and the mixed martial arts community as "your piece of shit community and your piece of shit people."

Most of the reaction to Malignaggi's conduct at the press conference has ranged from disappointment to condemnation. There are concerns that he's acting in a self-destructive manner and adding to the ugliness that permeates public dialogue today. Others are worried that his actions might jeopardize his credibility as a Showtime and Sky Sports commentator.

There are two issues: (1) Paulie's decision to fight again, and (2) his conduct in the buildup to the fight. Let's start with his decision to fight.

On the surface, Paulie appears to have it made. He earned good money in boxing and kept a lot of it. He's one of the best expert analysts in the business with several lucrative commentating contracts. And he retired from boxing with his faculties intact (although one might argue that his foray into bare-knuckle fighting contradicts that assumption).

Bare-knuckle fighting is a huge step down in platform for a man who was at the center of the boxing world when he fought in main events at Madison Square Garden, Barclays Center, and the MGM Grand Garden Arena. So why is Paulie fighting Lobov?

One theory is that Paulie is a junkie for combat sports. That it's not enough for him to call the action from ringside; he has to be in the ring. But after his loss to Eggington, he could no longer compete at a high level in boxing, so he found a smaller pond where he's still a big fish.

I spoke with Paulie at length this week, and he disputed that notion. He was calm and rational throughout our conversation. His primary reason for fighting, he said, is money. He doesn't need it. But like most of us, he likes it.

"There's a price for everything where you calculate risk/reward," Paulie told me. "I'm making a lot of money for this fight. A lot of money. They came to me with a deal that was too good to turn down. There's a big guarantee and, if the pay-per-view goes well, it will be one of my biggest paydays ever."

"People say I shouldn't be boxing anymore," Paulie continued. "But at the end of my boxing career, my legs were the big issue. For short periods, my legs are still good. This fight is five two-minute rounds. I can go at an intense level for that. And maybe my reflexes aren't quite as sharp as they used to be. But I don't see me being at risk in this fight. If Lobov was a real boxer, I wouldn't be doing this. But he isn't. I think he'll go wild and crazy at the start. And then, when I stuff my jab in his face a couple of times and hit him with some body shots, either he'll just try to survive or fold completely. I look at this as a lot of money for an easy outing."

And what about Paulie's conduct at the kickoff press conference?

As noted above, Malignaggi sparred briefly with Conor McGregor two years ago. Thereafter, McGregor claimed to have gotten the better of him and released a snippet of video footage to bolster that apparently spurious claim. As time went by, Paulie felt more and more humiliated by the situation. Lobov, who piled on in support of McGregor, is a proxy for Conor and, in Paulie's mind, worthy of scorn in his own right.

"This is bringing out a side of me that I thought I'd left in my past," Malignaggi told me. "It's a response to the lies and humiliation and pain to me and my family and everything else that this guy and his piece-of-shit friend Conor McGregor caused to be dumped on me. It reminds me of why I became a fighter."

"I grew up in a not-very-nice place," Paulie elaborated. "And I'm not talking about the neighborhood. I'm talking about what my life was like and the abuse I took. I went into boxing to get away from that place and to deal with the anger that I had inside me in an acceptable way."

"You have to put the press conference in context," Paulie continued. "There's a whole backstory that people don't understand. I wish I'd never gone to spar with McGregor. They treated me like shit when I was there. Then they lied and dumped shit on my reputation afterward. But I did go spar with him and you can't undo the past. And I still have to deal with it. You should have seen the social media after I sparred with McGregor. His idiot fans calling me a faggot, a little dago, things they wouldn't have the courage to come up to me on the street and say to my face. And they don't just put it on their sites. They put it all over my social media pages. I can post a photo of me at the beach and, a day later, there's all sorts of ugly shit attached to it. I have a young niece and nephew who read this shit about me. My mother sees it. It's been two years since I sparred with that scumbag and this shit still follows me every day."

And the comment about putting Lobov in a coma?

"I don't usually wish anything bad for anybody," Paulie answered. "And I certainly don't want to see anybody hurt in that way. Usually. But this guy has been part of causing so much pain for me and my family. And he has talked so much shit about boxing. So do I actively want to put him in a coma? No. But if it happened, I wouldn't care."

I've been around boxing long enough now to have seen a lot of promising young fighters become champions and then grow old. I've followed the trajectory of Paulie's career from the beginning. I remember sitting opposite him at the Brooklyn Diner in Manhattan shortly before his 2001 pro debut against Thadeus Parker. I remember talking with him for hours in my apartment before his 2006 fight against Miguel Cotto. I've been in his dressing room before and after hard-fought victories and heartbreaking defeats. We've always been honest with each other and respect each other's point of view when our views differ.

There was a time when the stars were properly aligned and Paulie could command seven-figure purses. His last payday at that level came in 2015 when he fought Danny Garcia at Barclays Center. One year later, fighting in the same arena against Gabriel Bracero, his purse was $150,000.

I've been told in confidence what Paulie has been guaranteed and the per-view upside he can earn for fighting Lobov if the promotion does well. It's good money. But is it worth the cost? A source with knowledge of the inner workings at Showtime says that the network pays Paulie in excess of $10,000 per telecast to serve as an expert analyst. His Showtime earnings are supplemented by his work for Sky Sports. And Paulie saved money when he was fighting. He wasn't a profligate spender.

Years ago, Paulie told me, "I hope to get old someday, but it won't be in the ring."

But in the ring, Paulie is now old. He's confident that Lobov doesn't box well enough to find him or hit hard enough to hurt him. Don't forget; for sixteen years, Paulie fought skilled craftsmen like Miguel Cotto, Ricky Hatton, Shawn Porter, and Danny Garcia. Lobov isn't anywhere near their league as a boxer or a puncher.

But Paulie already has physical issues as a consequence of boxing—for example, nerve damage in his face—that will shadow him for the rest of his life. His hands have been a problem throughout his career. Now he'll be fighting with no handwraps and no gloves. He thinks he can slap Lobov silly, go to the body, and take something off his punches to the head. But Lobov is likely to be in his face all night. Paulie wants the money. Lobov needs it. There are those who think that Paulie is walking into this fight with his hands down and his chin up in the air.

I hope Paulie has a letter of credit for his guarantee. I hope the check clears for whatever upside on the pay-per-view he might be entitled to. And by the way; if an ironclad letter of credit isn't in place before the fight, what does Paulie do? He should pull out. But if he does, social media (which played a role in Paulie's decision to fight Lobov and also in his meltdown at the May 20 press conference) will be unkind to him.

Society today is plagued by an ugly lack of civility. We're living in an age when people hide behind the anonymity of social media and say things that they wouldn't dare say face-to-face to another person. Racism, misogyny, and homophobia are extolled as virtues in some quarters.

In theory, Paulie's hatred for McGregor and Lobov, and his reference to MMA fans as a "piece of shit community," will help engender PPV buys. But it will also further antagonize MMA fans against Paulie and ensure more social media attacks. It brings to mind the admonition of Charles Horton Cooley, who a century ago observed, "Hatred floods your mind with the idea of the one you hate. Your thoughts reflect his, and you act in his spirit. If you wish to be like your enemy, to be wholly his, hate him."

Paulie has lamented the fact that his niece, nephew, and mother have been exposed on an ongoing basis to the ugliness leveled against him on social media. But what will his niece, nephew, and mother think if they watch a video of Paulie at the May 20 press conference?

"After I beat the shit out of you," he said, "I'm gonna spit on you. I might take out my dick and piss on you. I'm gonna take out my dick after I knock your teeth out and piss in that toothless mouth of yours. You got five weeks to live, motherfucker."

Life is about choices. On January 30, 2008, Paulie and I went to a meeting at St. Francis College in Brooklyn. Frank Macchiarola (then the president of St. Francis) was there with two administrators. Paulie had won the IBF 140-pound title on a twelve-round decision over Lovemore Ndou the previous June and defended it successfully against Hermann Ngoudjo twenty-five days before the meeting.

Macchiarola saw untapped potential in Paulie. He offered to enroll him free of charge in a St. Francis College program that would help him earn a high school equivalency diploma. Then Paulie could work toward a college degree.

"All your life, there have been people in school who told you you're stupid," Macchiarola said to Paulie. "You're not. I know enough about you to know that you're a very smart guy. There's nothing you can't do in the classroom if you put your mind to it. An education will give you options in life that you might not otherwise have. And it will give you tools to make better choices."

It was a wide-ranging conversation. At one point, one of the administrators told Paulie, "You're a pretty important person. There aren't many world champions. At St. Francis, people will know who you are, but you'll be treated like everyone else."

Macchiarola also talked a bit about the philosophy behind the school's athletic program. "I call it bait and switch," he said with a twinkle in his eye. "Kids come here thinking they're coming to play basketball, and then we give them an education."

Paulie set up an appointment to take evaluation tests in English and math to determine what skills he needed to work on in preparation for his high school equivalency examination. Then a tutoring program consistent with the demands that being a fighter put upon him would be implemented.

But the planning ended. Paulie decided to go in a different direction, one that he felt was better for him.

Now Paulie has another choice to make. Like a lot of people, I feel that the best place for him in combat sports in 2019 is behind a microphone.

Certain people are of unique value. Harold Lederman was like that. He created a role—the unofficial ringside judge—and made it his own. There have been dozens of "unofficial scorers at ringside" on telecasts since then. In some instances, their scoring has been just as good as Harold's. But none of them have become an integral part of the boxing scene. Harold was special. He had a passion for boxing. He loved the fights—not just the main events, all fights. He was accessible, not just to the powers that be but to everyday boxing fans. He was a boxing feel-good story.

Paulie has qualities that could enable him to help fill the void left by Harold's passing. In some ways, Paulie and Harold are as different as night and day. Harold would not have threatened to knock out someone's teeth, spit on him, and urinate into his open mouth while his victim was unconscious.

But Paulie, like Harold, is exceptionally knowledgeable about boxing and communicates information well. He treats four-round preliminary fighters with the same respect that he evinces for pound-for-pound contenders. He loves talking about boxing, has a unique style, and has a wellspring of good qualities in him. He could have a huge positive impact on boxing as a ringside commentator. Instead, he's risking his health unnecessarily and becoming a poster boy for antisocial behavior. He's justifiably angry about the ugliness that has been heaped upon him. But now he's spewing more of the same into the public discourse. By giving vent to his anger in the way that he has, he has contributed to the ugliness. That's a shame. Paulie can't clean up the cesspool by himself. But he shouldn't contribute to it.

And a final thought: I can't say that my heart will be in Paulie's gloves on June 22 because he won't be wearing gloves, but I'll be rooting for him.

Author's Note: The fight was anticlimactic. Lobov fought less aggressively than he should have at first. When he did get inside, Malignaggi clinched and referee Bill Clancy separated the fighters even though Lobov sometimes had a hand free to punch.

Paulie clearly won rounds one and two but his reflexes were off. Then he tired. By the end of the bout, there was an ugly vertical gash that sliced through his left eyebrow, a horizontal cut on his right eyelid, and a third cut under his right eye by his nose. He just doesn't have what it takes to be a professional fighter anymore. Once upon a time, he was a very good one.

The pre-fight animosity was real but ephemeral. Paulie reached out to touch gloves after the third and fourth rounds. At the final bell, the fighters embraced. All three judges scored the bout 48–47 for Lobov.

Fighters who can write are few and far between.

Punching from the Shadows

McFarland & Company publishes books about boxing on a regular basis. Some of them are solid works that contribute to the historical record of the sport. Others have the feel of vanity publishing, although McFarland doesn't take payment from authors. On occasion, a particularly good book makes its way through the pipeline. *Punching from the Shadows* by Glen Sharp is a particularly good book.

Sharp has an undergraduate degree in economics and a master's degree in English. He has worked in state government for more than thirty years and is currently an analyst and editor at the California Energy Commission. Within that milieu, his most unique credential is that he boxed professionally for a year before retiring with a 1-and-2 ring record. His sojourn through the sweet science is realistically and evocatively written from the early roots of his journey to the end.

"I had major league dreams but not even minor league success and was haunted by my failure for years," Sharp writes in the preface to his book. "I thought telling my rise-and-fall story about a boxer that does not have much rise to it might be of help to me, too."

Sharp grew up in a reasonably comfortable middle-class environment in a small farm town in Illinois.

"A common social confusion is that economic impoverishment is what leads people into boxing," he notes. "But that is not the case. People are attracted to boxing or not, just as they are drawn to writing or acting or playing a musical instrument. But boxing is such difficult, painful, and dangerous work that the temptation to turn away from its call is difficult to ignore, and this is especially so when opportunities for an easier life are available elsewhere. Poverty does not force someone to begin boxing. There are billions of poor people in the world but not billions of boxers. But having some money in the bank, or even a chance to obtain cash any other way than by fighting, can lead someone to stop, which I would eventually discover for myself."

Sharp's introduction to boxing, his first sparring session, the Golden

Gloves, and other rites of passage are well told. He recreates the sights and sounds of gym life well. He had decent physical gifts (in his imagination, he fancied himself a smaller version of Joe Frazier) and recalls, "I had been gifted with the ability to punch, especially with my left hand, in the same way other guys can throw a ball ninety-five miles an hour or more. I might not have had the best location, so to speak, or any off-speed stuff to set up my power, but I could rear back and fire."

He also recreates an early amateur fight that saw a trainer named Alex Sherer in his corner.

"I had a difficult first round with the guy I was fighting," Sharp recounts. "He landed lot of punches on me, including one right hand that left my nose bleeding. My nose wasn't broken but the faucet was certainly on. As I sat on the stool in my corner after the round, Alex climbed into the ring and wiped my face with a towel. I was breathing heavily already and, with every exhalation, a fine mist of blood would float into the air between us. Alex, kneeling right in front of me, looked like he was in a state of shock. I thought he was worried about me but I was wrong. 'This is a brand new shirt, goddam it,' he yelled at me, pointing at his chest while the red cloud settled on him like fog upon the ground. 'This is the first day I've worn it.' He stood up and stepped back to look at the damage. 'Jesus Christ,' he kept yelling. 'A fucking brand new shirt and you're getting blood all over it.'"

Eventually, Sharp took his quest to the next level.

"A young person with decent athletic ability can be taught well enough to compete successfully at lower levels of boxing without having to discover how brave he is," he notes. "At some point, however, as he progressively fights stiffer competition, it will become apparent how much of a stomach he has for boxing."

Sharp had the stomach for it. At least, he thought he did. But his motivation was suspect. After graduating from college, in his words, "I began living like a lot of directionless college graduates, which is a lifestyle not much different than being in school except it's better because you don't have to attend classes. I worked out sporadically, getting in shape for a fight when drinking beer and having fun got boring. I stayed in decent condition, but the inconsistency of training did not allow for much in the way of skill development."

But reality was calling.

"The world expected me to become a contributing member of society," he recalls. "Going to school was never fun for me and could sometimes involve a lot of work, but at least it allowed me to partially avoid the responsibilities of life. It finally dawned on me to become a professional boxer. After graduating from college, I didn't see any other option for me. Some people might laugh at the idea of a guy fighting professionally because he is too lazy or egotistical to get a job, but it doesn't seem funny to me."

In late 1981, Sharp decided to turn pro and took a job as a service attendant on the night shift in a gas station to enable him to pursue his ring career. Joe Risso (a restaurant owner who knew virtually nothing about the business of boxing) became his manager. Former middleweight champion Bobo Olson (who might have had trouble training a fish to swim) was hired by Risso as Glen's trainer.

Sharp's relationship with Olson was doomed from the start. First, Bobo was disinterested in his new charge. And second, he insisted that Sharp fight "out of a shell." But Glen didn't have the physical gifts to implement that style.

"Each boxer," Sharp explains, "has a basic style of fighting which reflects his physical assets and limitations, his personality and temperament, how much punishment he is willing and able to endure, his experience, and who trained him and how. But all successful boxers develop their own particular style for the same root reason—to land punches while at the same time minimizing the number of punches the opponent lands in return. As an amateur, I had two main talents. I could punch hard and I could take a punch. I relied on that ability and accepted the consequences of my other shortcomings. I knew what I had to do to win, and I knew how I would lose if I could not impose myself on my opponent. Everything about my fights made sense to me, even when they were not going well. I needed to learn how to pace myself. How to throw decoy punches. How to set up big punches. How to counter more cleanly and strategically. How to make my counterpunching so smooth and effective that my offense and my defense were not clearly distinguishable. I needed to improve a lot. None of the teaching that I needed, however, would have conflicted with my intent to become a smart slugger. My intentions would have become more sophisticated, but not more confused."

"But Bobo's demands," Sharp continues, "were alien to me both physically and psychologically. Neither my body nor my mind was designed to fight like Bobo wanted, and I knew it. With Bobo's shell, I punched less often, less quickly, less powerfully, and less accurately. My defensive skills were reduced. I couldn't move my head as freely or as quickly. I couldn't follow my opponent's punches as well as I had before. I knew what Bobo wanted was wrong for me, and so I was at war with myself. Boxing is a difficult enough sport when you are comfortable with what you are trying to do in the ring. Trying to bring someone else contentment by parroting what he or she wants is suicidal."

Then Yaqui Lopez came into Sharp's life.

Lopez was a world class fighter who had fallen just short in championship outings against John Conteh, Victor Galindez, and Matthew Saad Muhammad. Like Sharp, he fought as a light-heavyweight.

In March 1982 (two months before Sharp's first pro fight), Joe Risso arranged for Glen to spar with Lopez several days a week. That meant training with Olson in Sacramento on some days and driving to Stockton to spar with Yaqui on others. Sharp's exposition of the year that he spent as Lopez's sparring partner is superb:

★ "This is what the first day with Yaqui felt like. I knew I was going to get the worst of it when I was in the middle of the ring, when I was at the end of his jab. I expected that. I didn't know exactly how bad the worst of it was going to be, but I knew it was going to be kind of bad. What I didn't expect was for it to be the same when I was inside his reach, boxing at close quarters. There was no place I could find to mount any kind of offense. There was no punch I could throw from any angle that seemed to bother Yaqui at all. In the three rounds we boxed that day, I don't think I landed a single punch. I got pieces of him, glancing blows off the top of his head or body punches that he did not completely block, but I did not land any clean shots. Worse than that, there was no place in the ring I found to be safe. Everywhere I moved, I was at Yaqui's mercy. He picked me apart with his jabs and rights from a distance. When I stepped closer, he would combine the right hands with left hooks. When I got on top of him, he would blast me with uppercuts along with the hooks. Yaqui was better than me in every phase of boxing.

He had an absolute advantage in everything we were doing in the ring, and I had never experienced that before."

★ "There was not much drama or art to be seen in my boxing with Yaqui. He quickly established that he was the hunter and I was the prey. Although I would occasionally challenge this hierarchy, my efforts always proved to be unsuccessful except for the briefest of moments. Until meeting Yaqui, I had something of an alpha male attitude about myself, always thinking I was the hunter in a boxing ring, and so my demotion was hurtful psychologically as well as physically. Every time I attempted to assert myself and temporarily reverse our roles, he would become even more assertive in response."

★ "In the short term, in the course of a fight, you can commit yourself to taking more punches than you world normally enjoy. You might make that commitment because you see it as your only chance to win. But in daily sparring, there is no competition to win a contest, and it becomes difficult to commit yourself to taking that level of punishment on a regular basis day after day. I would go home every day and stand under the shower for fifteen or twenty minutes, hoping the water pounding on my head would balance the throbbing coming from the other direction. I tried not to think about how it was going to happen all over again the next day. In the worst of the days with Yaqui, I did not feel much like someone who used his sparring with world class talent as a learning experience. I thought of myself as being more like the aging failed fighters who were just trying to make a few dollars by letting themselves be punched around."

★ "As physically demanding as boxing with Yaqui was, the most difficult part was emotional as I saw no light at the end of the tunnel. You develop a unique perspective on life when you rise at six in the morning to run a few miles and one of your first waking thoughts is that, later in the day, you are going to get beat up. Every day during the hour drive to Stockton, my stomach would tighten as I went over what would take place once I got there, knowing there was nothing I could do or change to stop what was going to happen, knowing the next day was going to be the same. I could not ask for relief, either.

Yaqui was not taking cheap shots at me, he was only doing his job, and I was the one who had put myself in the position of being his sparring partner. You cannot ask another man to lighten up on you. You can wish for pity. You can hope the guy kicking your butt begins to feel sorry for you, or at least his cornermen do and tell their guy to ease up a bit. You can even think about developing a religious life with the hope God might have mercy on your soul. But you cannot ask the guy you are boxing with to lighten up on you."

Sharp's first professional fight was contested in Stockton on May 5, 1982. The opponent was a novice with a record of 0-and-1 named Lamont Santanas.

"Besides boxing differently depending upon whether I was training in Stockton or Sacramento," Sharp writes, "I had two completely different training routines. I had Bobo's routine when he was in the gym, and I trained like Yaqui when I was with him and Bobo was not around. Not only were there differences in personalities and struggles for power, I was being taught two entirely different ways to fight. Every morning upon waking, I would remind myself what kind of fighter I was supposed to be that day."

Against Santanas, Sharp won a four-round decision but recalls, "I only won this fight because I regressed to my amateur style. Three months of training with Bobo, and I fought better by ignoring most of what he had taught me. I knew my amateur approach was not the ticket to long-term success, but Bobo was not taking me where I needed to go, either."

Eight weeks later, Sharp was in the ring again. His original opponent fell out. Glen was then required to weaken himself by dropping down to 165 pounds to face a 6-and-12 journeyman named Michael Hutchinson (the only opponent that Risso could get on short notice). Making matters worse, Hutchinson blew off the weight and came in at 174 pounds.

"This describes my relationship with Joe pretty well," Sharp writes. "He was a good decent person in most every way. He didn't know anything about boxing, though, and was even less aware of how little he knew. Joe wanted to be a deal maker. He thought having a manager's license made him a player in the world of boxing. What having a manager's license means in reality, though, is that the manager could afford the thirty dollars application fee for a license. It was his job to have said that his fighter who had barely eaten for the past week so he could lose an extra eight pounds was not going into the ring with someone who hadn't starved himself at all. The manager makes his money because he is supposed to protect his fighters from the promoters and matchmakers and other managers who have other priorities and interests. But that's not what Joe did."

Meanwhile, shortly before the bout, Olson called and told Glen that he had hurt his back and would be unable to work his corner for the fight.

"Bobo told me to box the way he had taught me," Sharp recalls. "I thanked him and hung up the phone. It was the last time we would speak."

Yaqui Lopez was in Sharp's corner for the fight against Hutchinson. Glen picks up the narrative after the first round.

"The next thing I remember, I am sitting on the stool in my corner as the bell rings. Thinking the next round had just begun, I stood and took a step toward the center of the ring, but Yaqui grabs my arm and tells me the fight is over."

"Who won?" Sharp asked.

Looking back on that moment, Glen observes, "A good general rule in boxing is that, if you have to ask who won the fight you were just in, the answer is probably the other guy. Hutchinson had dropped me with a right hand and, when I rose, he hit me with about a dozen more punches before the referee stopped the fight. This all happened in the first round, and I have no memory of it."

Thereafter, insult was added to injury.

"The morning after the fight," Sharp recounts, "I called one of the doctors employed by the California Athletic Commission as ringside physicians during fights and explained my nose had been broken in Stockton the night before. He asked about the swelling, and I told him it was substantial. He said I should make an appointment for the next week when the swelling had subsided, and I did. When I saw [him] a week later, I had no bruising or swelling, and the only evidence that my nose had been broken was that it was crooked and made noises when I inhaled. The doctor said the bone was already healing and that he could no longer treat me for a broken nose. 'You should have come here last week,' he said, 'before the bone began to set.'"

On November 27, 1982, Sharp entered the ring for the third and final time as a professional boxer. The opponent, Joe Dale Lewis, was making his pro debut and would finish his career with 2 wins, 9 losses, and 7 KOs by. Glen was stopped on cuts in the third round.

"My head was hanging in the air like a piñata," Sharp writes. "Lewis must have thought it was his birthday. I could not figure out how he was hitting me so easily. I have replayed this fight in my mind thousands of times. It's like watching a train wreck in slow motion over and over again. I could see the punches coming, but I could not get out of the way. I knew I was confused by what was happening, but I could not understand why what was happening was happening the way it was. It's called freezing. I stood in front of Lewis like a deer caught in headlights. I have not been shy about expressing how disappointed I was with those around me [with regard to the weight issue] when I lost my fight with Mike Hutchinson. But this loss rests squarely on my shoulders. This was all mine."

After the loss to Lewis, any thoughts that Sharp had of becoming a world-class fighter were in the past.

"I was a 1–2 fighter who had lost two fights in a row," he acknowledges. "And those two losses did not happen by accident. I still thought I could probably become a decent fighter, but the world is full of decent fighters. It is one thing to be a utility infielder on a major league baseball team. But it is something completely different to be a utility boxer, to be a club fighter. I had lost hope that I could become a really good fighter, good enough to make the kind of money that validated the decision to box in the first place. If I was going to end up sitting at a desk anyway, why would I want to spend the next ten years just making ends meet—getting beat, getting hurt, wearing my body and my mind out—to eventually need the same sort of job I had been desperately trying to avoid, only to be ten years behind in that race."

So Sharp retired. But something was eating away at his soul. In his words, "When Marlon Brando's character, Terry Malloy, said to his brother in *On the Waterfront*, 'I coulda been a contender. I coulda been somebody,' he is talking about being someone to himself. When he said he could have had class, he meant he could have had self-respect. He could have been proud of the character he played in his own story if he had only allowed himself to play that role. That is what he most wanted in life."

Sharp wasn't proud of himself. To the contrary, the more time passed, the more he became ashamed of how he had approached boxing.

"The idea of a professional boxer being someone who makes money from fighting is true only in the most literal sense," he writes. "One is a professional more as a function of attitude than a matter of compensation. My aim was to be a successful professional boxer so I didn't have to get a job, which means I was destined to fail. My attraction to boxing was legitimate, but the relationship I developed with it was not. Boxing is a skill sport more than it is an athletic contest, and I was athletic enough to have become skilled enough. But I had not done the work necessary. Then I ran away from it when the work became too demanding. It is not easy to see yourself being less honorable than you thought you were."

In 1987, Sharp started thinking about a comeback.

"I began training again," he writes, "to finally make the commitment that I had failed to do when younger and had led to the failure. I hoped it was not too late. I wanted the story of my life in boxing to be an honorable one, even if unsuccessful. It was an attempt to atone for squandering a gift I had taken for granted when young and not realized how much I loved."

Sharp trained for close to three years. Then reason prevailed in the form of advice from boxing minds wiser than his own. He never fought again.

Punching from the Shadows deserves a wide audience. Sharp brings a lot to the table. Unlike most writers, he has been in the ring. His journey through boxing was standard in some ways but unusual in others. And he writes well. Things that the reader thinks will happen don't. And things that the reader is sure will never happen do. There's a self-revelatory examination of Sharp's personal relationships—particularly with his father and some of the women he dated—but not so much that it becomes cumbersome.

There are short axiomatic observations:

* "Very little in life is as truthful as a fight."
* "Two contests are going on in a boxing ring, the boxer with his opponent and the boxer with himself."
* "The fight itself is often fun. Waiting for the fun to begin is not."

* "Getting concussions is probably not the best way to learn how to box."

At times, the book is an intelligent exploration of the psychology of boxing.

"For the boxer," Sharp explains, "two primal and perfectly natural responses—either fighting or taking flight—must find a way to live with each other. Being brave is not a matter of mindlessly throwing caution to the wind. Strength of character is required to hold both heroic intent and the desire to be safe in balanced tension with one another. A tremendous amount of work is required to strengthen oneself to hold that tension, to remain mindful, which is a state of awareness that strives to perform courageously but not unintelligently so."

In other places, *Punching from the Shadows* is an engaging primer on boxing fundamentals.

Sharp offers an exceptionally good explanation of Joe Frazier's fighting style and Frazier's strengths and weakness as a fighter. Other insights include:

* "All good fighters learn to regulate their breathing, inhaling and exhaling rhythmically, a pattern upon which everything else is based. Every punch, every feint, every defensive move, every step forward or backward or sideways is coordinated with breathing. This reminds me of the schoolyard maxim that, if you ever get into a fight with someone who breathes through his nose, you should probably turn around and run because that guy knows what he is doing."
* "The face is rubbed with Vaseline primarily so that, when it is hit with a punch, the leather gloves will slide off the skin more easily than otherwise would happen, reducing the chances of the facial skin being cut by a punch. The body is rubbed with Vaseline to make sure the opponent's gloves are in contact with grease as often as possible. Every time boxers are close together or punching to the body or in a clinch, the gloves are rubbing against Vaseline, becoming coated with grease."
* "Although hitting the speed bag can look impressive, I don't know that it provides much benefit. The idea is that it increases your

hand-eye coordination. But once you learn what you are doing and get a feel for the rhythm of the specific bag you are hitting, you can do it with your eyes closed. I would think that developing hand-eye coordination requires the eyes to at least be open. But I could be wrong because a guy with a 1–2 record obviously has a lot to learn about boxing."

In the preface to *Punching from the Shadows*, Sharp writes, "I hope that you find me to be a pretty good storyteller, because I sure wasn't much of a fighter."

Sharp is better than a pretty good storyteller. He's first-rate.

Most athletes believe they won't get hurt in competition. Boxers know they will.

Sergiy Derevyanchenko
and the Harsh Reality of Boxing

When Oscar De La Hoya was nearing the end of his storied ring career, he offered a stark assessment of the risks inherent in the trade he had chosen.

"I hate getting hit," De La Hoya said. "Getting hit hurts. It damages you. When a fighter trains his body and mind to fight, there's no room for fear. But I'm realistic enough to understand that there's no way to know what the effect of getting hit will be ten or fifteen years from now."

Boxers are not like ordinary people. They court danger and have a tolerance for pain that most of us think we can imagine but can't. That harsh reality was on display when Gennady Golovkin and Sergiy Derevyanchenko met in the ring at Madison Square Garden on October 5, 2019, in a fight that will be long remembered as a showcase for the brutal artistry of boxing.

Derevyanchenko, age thirty-three, was born in Ukraine and now lives in Brooklyn. He had roughly four hundred amateur fights in the Ukrainian amateur system, which gave him a wealth of experience but also put considerable wear and tear on his body. He turned pro in 2014 and, prior to facing Golovkin, had a record of 13 wins against 1 loss with 10 knockouts. The loss came in his one outing against a world-class opponent —a 115–112, 115–112, 113–114 split-decision defeat at the hands of Danny Jacobs at Madison Square Garden last year.

Derevyanchenko is soft-spoken with a brush haircut, often impassive face, and eyes that can be hard. He understands some English but prefers to have questions translated into Russian and answer in his native language.

"I don't like to talk about myself," Derevyanchenko says. "I'm a private person. The attention that comes with boxing is a double-edged sword. For the money it helps me make, the attention is good. But the loss of privacy sometimes, especially when I am out with my family, it is not so good."

Golovkin, age thirty-seven, is well known to boxing fans. Born in Kazakhstan, now living in Los Angeles. he brutalized a succession of pretty good fighters like Matthew Macklin and David Lemieux en route to becoming the best middleweight in the world. But thirty months ago, Gennady struggled to win a narrow decision on points over Danny Jacobs at Madison Square Garden. Thereafter, he'd had four fights: gimme knockouts of Vanes Martirosyan and Steve Rolls and two outings against Canelo Alvarez. The first Golovkin–Canelo fight (which most observers thought Gennady won) was declared a draw. The second ended with a credible 115–113, 115–113, 114–114 decision in Canelo's favor, the first loss of Golovkin's ring career.

Golovkin–Derevyanchenko crystalized how bizarre the business of boxing has become in recent years.

Last year, the IBF stripped Golovkin of its 160-pound belt for not fighting a mandatory defense against Derevyanchenko. Then Jacobs beat Derevyanchenko for the vacant IBF title but lost to Canelo Alvarez in his next outing. Thereafter, the IBF stripped Canelo for not fighting a mandatory defense against Derevyanchenko despite the fact that Sergiy's only win after losing to Jacobs was a decision over lightly regarded Jack Culcay. Thus, Golovkin was fighting Derevyanchenko for the same belt he was stripped of for not fighting Sergiy last year.

If that sounds strange, the money being thrown around was stranger.

Traditionally, a fighter had to win one or more big fights before getting a seven-figure purse. But DAZN, ESPN, Fox, and Showtime are locked in a bidding war that has led to huge license fees that often bear no correlation to revenue generated for a network by its fighters.

DAZN (which has a multifight deal with Golovkin) wanted Golovkin–Derevyanchenko as the launching pad for the final quarter of its 2019 season. The network was already locked into a deal that would pay Gennady a reported purse of $7.5 million in cash plus $7.5 million in stock in DAZN's parent company to fight on October 5. DAZN then leaned on promoter Eddie Hearn to contribute significantly to Derevyanchenko's purse to bring Sergiy into the fold.

Thus it was that Derevyanchenko (a largely unknown fighter with thirteen pro victories on his résumé, who had never beaten a world-class fighter) was rewarded with a purse totaling $5.2 million to fight Golovkin. Training expenses, manager Keith Connally's share, taxes, and whatever Premier Boxing Champions took (Derevyanchenko is a PBC fighter) came out of that total. Still, very few fighters in history have had a payday approaching that number. A marketable belt was at stake, but the fight wasn't even for "the" middleweight championship of the world (a title that presently resides with Canelo).

"I like the sport," Sergiy said when asked about boxing three days before fighting Golovkin. "I like the business. The business is crazy now."

It certainly is. And adding to the drama, there was no rematch clause. Win or lose, Derevyanchenko would be contractually free to fight any opponent on any network after fighting Golovkin.

There was no trash-talking by either side during the buildup to the fight. The only sour note came at a sit-down with reporters just prior to the final pre-fight press conference when Golovkin was asked one question too many about a possible third fight against Alvarez.

"All these questions about Canelo," Gennady answered. "It's your problem, not mine."

Golovkin was a 4-to-1 betting favorite over Derevyanchenko. He and Sergiy had each fought on even terms against Jacobs. But styles make fights. And the feeling was that while Gennady and Sergiy had similar styles, Golovkin did everything a little bit better. He hit harder, took a better punch, was a shade faster, and so on down the line. ESPN asked eleven of its boxing reporters to predict the outcome of the fight. Ten thought that Golovkin would win by knockout. The eleventh chose Gennady by decision.

But while few insiders predicted that Derevyanchenko would win, no one was counting him out either.

The question most often asked when the outcome of the fight was discussed was whether Golovkin had slipped with age. And if so, how far? Also, Derevyanchenko was in the best condition of his life, having spent six weeks in California preparing for the bout at Victor Conte's SNAC conditioning facility.

This was Sergiy's chance to prove that he belonged at the table with boxing's top-echelon middleweights.

"Gennady has been a great champion, but his time is coming to an end," Derevyanchenko prophesied. "I want to be the one who makes it come to an end."

Wearing a black Nike tracksuit with white trim, Derevyanchenko arrived in dressing room #3 at Madison Square Garden on Saturday night at 8:20 p.m.

The room was roughly thirty feet long and twenty feet wide with a linoleum floor styled to look like hardwood planks. Ten cushioned metal-frame folding chairs were set against the walls. A green two-seat imitation leather sofa fronted a large flat-screen television mounted on the wall opposite the door. A college football game—Oregon vs. California—was underway.

Some fighters like lots of action in their dressing room. Derevyanchenko prefers calm with no distractions. For the next two hours, he was quiet and self-contained. Except for manager Keith Connolly, no one even looked at a cell phone. From the moment Sergiy entered the room until he walked to the ring, everything was businesslike and low-key.

After leaving the room briefly for a pre-fight physical, Derevyanchenko returned, sat on a metal folding chair with his hands clasped behind his head, and stretched out his legs. Then he moved to the sofa and adopted a similar position.

A handful of people came and went—Sergiy's wife, Iryna, Pat Connolly (Keith's father), PBC representative Sam Watson.

Co-trainers Andre Rozier and Gary Stark, Sergiy Konchynsky (a friend of Derevyanchenko's since childhood), and cutman Mike Bazzel were a constant presence. Unlike Jacobs–Derevyanchenko, when Rozier (who trained both men) worked Danny's corner, Sergiy's team was now unified.

At 9:00 p.m., Sergiy rose from the sofa, walked over to a shrink-wrapped package that contained twenty-four bottles of Aquafina, opened a bottle, and took a sip. Then he began changing into his boxing gear, folding his street clothes neatly before putting them aside.

At 9:05 p.m., referee Harvey Dock came in and gave Sergiy his pre-fight instructions: "There is no three-knockdown rule . . . If your mouthpiece comes out . . . If you score a knockdown. . . ."

When Dock was done, Keith Connolly raised the issue of Golovkin hitting opponents on the back of the head and asked the referee to affirm that he would take strict action in the event of a foul. Dock promised to enforce the rules. Connolly repeated his point and got the same answer the second time around.

At 9:15 p.m., Stitch Duran (Golovkin's cutman) came in to watch Stark wrap Sergiy's hands.

Rozier fiddled with the TV remote until the DAZN undercard appeared on the screen.

At 9:34 p.m., the wrapping was done.

Sergiy began stretching on his own.

Connolly handed him a smartphone. Al Haymon was calling to wish Sergiy well. The conversation was short, a ten-second best-wishes for the fight.

Sergiy put a white towel on the floor and continued stretching. When that was done, he stood up and Stark led him through more stretching exercises.

Konchynsky approached Maggie Lange (the lead New York State Athletic Commission inspector in the room) and showed her a silver cannister labeled "Boost Oxygen."

"Is it all right if we use this?"

"What is it?," Lange countered.

"Oxygen."

"I don't know," Lange said. "Let's go for a ruling."

Konchynsky and the inspector left the room to consult with the NYSAC medical staff.

Derevyanchenko began shadowboxing.

"It's your night, bro," Rozier told him.

Konchynsky and Lange returned. The powers that be had said no to Boost Oxygen.

Stark gloved Derevyanchenko up.

Sergiy pounded his gloves together and hit the pads with the trainer.

Mike Bazzel greased him down.

Rozier led the group in a brief prayer.

Golovkin's image appeared on the TV monitor. If he and Sergiy weren't about to fight each other, one could imagine them sitting side-by-side in someone's living room watching the fight together on television. By virtue of their trade, they had more in common than most people in the arena.

Sergiy shadowboxed a bit more, then paced back and forth, deep in thought. He had followed these rituals many times before. But the stakes had never been this high. Glory and a possible eight-figure payday for his next fight if he won. And the very real possibility that he would be physically damaged before the night was done. This wasn't a movie about life. It was the real thing. More than anyone else, fighters know what's at stake every time they enter the ring.

Even name fighters have been struggling at the gate lately in the United States. Golovkin was no exception. In the days leading up to the fight, a large number of tickets had been given away by the promotion. Even so, the announced attendance of 12,577 was far short of capacity.

Golovkin had fought in the main arena at Madison Square Garden on four previous occasions and twice in MSG's smaller Hulu Theater. He was the crowd favorite.

Both men started cautiously. Then, two minutes into round one, Derevyanchenko ducked low as Golovkin threw a right hand. The punch landed just behind the top of Sergiy's head and put him down.

"He hit me in the back of the head," Derevyanchenko said later. "I didn't see the punch, but it didn't really affect me that much. I got up and I wasn't really hurt, so it was nothing too bad."

But the round had been up for grabs until that point. Now it was a two-point round for Golovkin. And the next stanza brought something very bad for Sergiy. A left hook landed cleanly and opened an ugly gash on his right eyelid.

Referee Harvey Dock mistakenly ruled that the cut had been caused by an accidental head butt. And because the New York State Athletic Commission doesn't allow for instant video review, that ruling stood. Be that as it may, Derevyanchenko was now at a distinct disadvantage.

Cutman Mike Bazzel swabbed adrenaline into the cut and applied pressure after every round. But he was never able to completely stop the flow of blood. The dripping was a distraction. And as the bout progressed, Sergiy had increasing difficulty seeing Golovkin's punches coming.

"The cut really changed the fight," Sergiy said afterward. "I couldn't see at times. And he was targeting the eye."

Now Derevyanchenko was in a hole. But a fighter can't let his mind wander to what happened the round before or several punches ago. He has to stay in the moment.

Sergiy's response to adversity was to fight more aggressively. "When

I started moving [in the first two rounds]," he explained later, "I felt like I was giving him room and I was getting hit with those shots that he threw. That's why I started taking the fight to him and getting closer and not giving him room to maneuver."

The strategy worked. Golovkin appeared to have the heavier hands. But Derevyanchenko began winning the war in the trenches. Several body shots hurt Gennady. He seemed to be tiring and losing his edge. One had the feeling that, if Sergiy's eye held up and he was able to take the fight into the late rounds, an upset was possible. Golovkin had a look about him that said, "Either I'm getting old or you're good."

Brutal warfare followed. Choose your metaphor. Two men walking through fire. A dogfight between pit bulls.

The crowd roared through it all.

Neither man shied away from confrontations. In round eleven, Sergiy's left eyelid (the one that hadn't been cut) noticeably puffed up. It round twelve, it looked like a balloon. Both men dug as deep as it was possible to dig. And then some.

Most ringside observers thought Derevyanchenko won the fight by a narrow margin. But before the decision was announced, DAZN blow-by-blow commentator Brian Kenny observed, "[The judges] come into the fight with a certain mindset. Golovkin is the favorite. You expect him to do better."

That mindset was reflected in the judges' verdicts: Frank Lombardi 115–112, Eric Marlinski 115–112, Kevin Morgan 114–113—all for Golovkin. The crowd booed when the decision was announced. They weren't booing Gennady, who had fought as heroically as Sergiy. They were booing the decision. A draw would have been equitable. One point in favor of Golovkin was within the realm of reason. 115–112 (7 rounds to 5 for Gennady) was bad judging.

Golovkin himself seemed to acknowledge the iffy nature of the decision when he said in the ring after the fight, "I want to say thank you so much to my opponent. He's a very tough guy. This is huge experience for me. This was a tough fight. I need to still get stronger in my camp. I need a little bit more focus. Right now, it's bad day for me. It's a huge day for Sergiy. Sergiy was ready. He showed me such a big heart. I told him, 'Sergiy, this is best fight for me.'"

That thought was echoed by Johnathon Banks (Golovkin's trainer), who later acknowledged, "I don't remember the exact scores, but I thought the fight was a lot closer than that."

After the fight, the skin around Derevyanchenko's eyes was swollen to the point that each eye was almost shut. His right eyelid was purple, bulging, and sliced open. There was a huge pocket of blood beneath his left eyelid.

Neither fighter attended the post-fight press conference. Sergey Konchynsky came into Derevyanchenko's dressing room, packed Sergiy's civilian clothes in a gym bag, and left. Then he went with Derevyanchenko to Bellevue Hospital where they were joined by Golovkin, who was brought in as a precautionary measure.

"It took forever at the hospital," Keith Connolly recalls. "Sergiy and Gennady might have been the only patients there who weren't hand-cuffed to a gurney."

Derevyanchenko was stitched up and released from the hospital around 5:00 a.m. Then he, Iryna, Konchynsky, and Connolly went to the Tick-Tock Diner on 34th Street where Sergiy ate blueberry pancakes before going back to his hotel to sleep.

The middleweight division has some quality fighters. Derevyanchenko can now be counted among them. The way he fought against Golovkin on Saturday night raised his profile. Big-money bouts that might be available to him in the near future include a rematch against Gennady or an even more lucrative outing against Canelo Alvarez. Alternatively, Al Haymon might come to manager Keith Connolly with an offer for Sergiy to fight WBC 160-pound beltholder Jermall Charlo.

But for now, let's celebrate the courage and fortitude that Sergiy Derevyanchenko and Gennady Golovkin showed in the ring while battling against one another. And remember: fighters are damaged every time they step into the ring; fights like this take a heavy toll on both fighters; and sometimes the winner is damaged more than the loser.

Canelo Alvarez:
Contemplating Greatness

On November 2, 2019, Canelo Alvarez and Sergey Kovalev met in the ring at the MGM Grand Garden Arena in Las Vegas and fought for the World Boxing Organization 175-pound title.

Alvarez is conscious of the image that he projects. He's generally quiet and reserved in public. A lengthy recitation of his ring exploits is unnecessary here. Suffice it to say that, since turning pro in 2005 at age fifteen, Canelo has compiled a record of 53 wins, 1 loss, and 2 draws with 36 knockouts. He's boxing's biggest star and only twenty-nine years old.

It's fashionable in some circles to demean Canelo because his power is sometimes overshadowed by his finesse. This, his critics say, is a betrayal of his Mexican roots. He's not a "Mexican-style" fighter.

Bart Barry rebutted that notion, writing, "Mexican prizefighters do not wish to get struck in the face any more than any other type of prize-fighter does."

Canelo speaks to the same point, noting, "In boxing, you have to take care of yourself. I haven't had as many wars as others have had. But there is no need for you to let yourself take a beating and to be bloody to be a great fighter. I am not going to stop what I'm doing to get all bloody and get knocked down all over the place if I have no need to."

Initially, it was expected that Canelo would fight Gennady Golovkin in Las Vegas on September 14 in conjunction with Mexican Independence Day weekend. But bad blood between the two camps led Canelo to seek another opponent. That left DAZN, which has invested a reported $465 million in multibout contracts with the two fighters, in a quandary. DAZN needed a marketable opponent for Canelo, who is its flagship attraction. The nod went to Kovalev.

Kovalev, now thirty-six years old, came into the fight with a 34–3–1 (29 KOs) record. Once, he was the best of boxing's 175-pound champions, having torn undefeated through the light-heavyweight division. He'd dominated an aging Bernard Hopkins en route to a unanimous shutout decision in Atlantic City and knocked out Jean Pascal twice before losing a controversial decision (114–113 on each judges' scorecard) to Andre Ward in 2016. Meanwhile, two months prior to Kovalev–Ward, Canelo had fought Liam Smith at 154 pounds.

The idea that Canelo and Kovalev might meet in the ring someday would have been derided as fanciful three years ago. But after Kovalev–Ward I, Sergey faltered. He was knocked out in a rematch against Ward and, subsequent to reclaiming the WBO belt by stoppage over Vyacheslav Shabranskyy, was KO'd by Eleider Alvarez. He rebounded to decision Eleider in February of this year but struggled to defeat Anthony Yarde this August.

Canelo, who has grown comfortable at 160 pounds during the past two years, would be moving up two weight classes to challenge Kovalev. To his credit, he did not demand a catchweight.

Asked about Canelo–Kovalev, Ward (who now works as commentator for ESPN) replied, "There are a lot of variables I'm trying to process right now. It is going to be a good fight. I know that."

The promotion was about Canelo. The storyline wasn't whether Kovalev could withstand the challenge from his younger opponent. Nor was it a defining fight for boxing's light-heavyweight division. But it would be a defining fight for Canelo.

Throughout fight week, Canelo was relaxed, confident, and comfortable. "I always imagine the best," he said. "But when I turned pro, I never imagined that I would fight at 175 pounds." Speaking of Chepo and Eddy Reynoso who have guided him in and out of the ring for fourteen years, he proclaimed, "It is beautiful to have a family like this. I am who I am because of them." And referencing the good will between Kovalev and himself, he declared, "We are to put on a fight, not to insult and be rude to each other."

Kovalev responded in kind, saying, "I like his boxing style. I like him as person. Boxers punch each other. But after fight, we will be friends again."

Then, recalling several days in 2011 when he and Canelo were in the same training camp, Sergey added, "He seemed like nice guy. We say hello. I never think we fight each other."

Canelo was a 7-to-2 betting favorite.

The case for an upset by Kovalev rested in large measure on the size differential between the fighters. Canelo was the naturally smaller man. He'd turned pro at 139 pounds. Three years ago, as previously noted, he was fighting at 154. Six months ago, he entered the ring to face Danny Jacobs after weighing in at 159½ pounds. Sergey had fought at light-heavyweight for his entire ring career.

Canelo is five-foot-eight. Sergey is four inches taller. Canelo would have to get inside Kovalev's jab to nullify Sergey's advantage in reach and work the body. It's a good jab. Kovalev hits harder than anyone Canelo had fought before with the possible exception of Golovkin. And how effective would Canelo's punches be against a man who was bigger than anyone he had previously fought?

"It's going to be a hard fight," Kovalev acknowledged. "Canelo is very dangerous. He is strong. He smashes you with body punches, hooks, uppercuts. He has good technique. He is great champion. But this is my division, not his. I am bigger. I am taller. I make the fight my way."

That said; Kovalev has been known to wilt when his body is effectively attacked. Canelo has "man strength" now, coupled with a ferocious body attack. And the 175-pound contract weight was a double-edged sword as revealed by the satellite tour interviews that the fighters engaged in two days before the fight.

Canelo looked hale and hearty. He hadn't put on weight to fight at 175 pounds. He had simply lost less weight while adding muscle in the process.

"Do you like fighting at a heavier weight?" he was asked.

"Si," Canelo answered. "More eat, more happy."

Kovalev, by contrast, looked tired and drawn. When asked about Canelo coming up in weight, he answered, "He is more dangerous now than ever because he does not have to lose energy to make weight. When you are losing weight, you are losing energy. He is saving energy. For me, it is more difficult now to make weight, but next division is very high for me. One-eighty-five would be best, but there is no title at 185. I will be very happy for the weigh-in."

When the weigh-in came, Canelo registered 174½ pounds; Kovalev 176. Sergey removed the crucifix from around his neck . . . 175½.

He took off his shorts . . . 175¼.

He excused himself, went to the restroom, vomited, and returned to the scale . . . 175.

★ ★ ★

Canelo Alvarez arrived in his dressing room at the MGM Grand Garden Arena on Saturday, November 2, at 6:35 p.m. Eighteen camp members wearing matching navy blue tracksuits trimmed in white and lime were with him.

The room had industrial carpet and cinderblock walls painted ivory white. Two black sofas and fourteen cushioned folding chairs were spread about. A large flat-screen television mounted on the far wall faced a six-by-twelve-foot Mexican flag.

Ryan Garcia, who would fight Romero Duno for a minor WBC title in the next-to-last bout of the evening, was already there. Garcia was sharing the dressing room with Canelo because Eddy Reynoso trained both men. The two fighters greeted each other warmly.

A rectangular table had been set perpendicular against the wall near one end of the room to create a small alcove in front of the television. Canelo settled in the alcove on a folding chair opposite the TV. Chepo Reynoso sat beside him.

Garcia turned off his music in deference to the champion. It was Canelo's room now.

At seven o'clock, Shane Mosley came in to wish Canelo well. Mosley turned pro in 1993 and blazed through the lightweight division before moving up in weight to conquer Oscar De La Hoya at 147 pounds. Then came the fall. In Shane's last twenty-one fights, he suffered ten losses—an all-too-common end game for a once great fighter. One of Mosley's losses was a lopsided decision defeat to Canelo.

Garcia started warming up.

Canelo watched as a bloody bout between Seniesa Estrada and Marlen Esparza unfolded on the television in front of him. In round five, Esparza suffered a horrible gash on her forehead from an accidental head butt. With each round, it worsened. The conventional wisdom in boxing is that a cut on the forehead shouldn't stop a fight. Here, the conventional wisdom was wrong. Esparza had been cut to the bone. But for reasons unknown, referee Robert Byrd, the ring doctor assigned to Esparza's corner, and Esparza's seconds let the fight continue. Canelo and Chepo shook their heads.

At 7:35 p.m., Nevada State Athletic Commission executive director Bob Bennett entered with referee Russell Mora and assorted dignitaries who listened as Mora gave Canelo pre-fight instructions.

The thud of Ryan Garcia hitting the pads with Eddy Reynoso resonated through the room.

The bloody mask that was Marlen Esparza's face grew bloodier.

Eddy began wrapping Canelo's hands.

Finally, after nine rounds, Estrada–Esparza was stopped. Canelo nodded approvingly. There was no reason for it to have gone on that long.

At 8:00 p.m., Dan Bilzerian (a professional poker player and internet personality) was escorted into the room to meet Canelo. The fighter rose to shake hands and, after Bilzerian left, returned to the chair he'd been sitting on for the past ninety minutes.

A cape was draped over Ryan Garcia's shoulders as he readied to leave for the ring.

"Looking good," Canelo exhorted.

Then Canelo's two-year-old daughter (Maria Fernanda) and infant son (Adiel) were brought into the room.

"Papa!" Maria Fernanda cried out as she rushed toward him.

Father and daughter embraced.

Then Maria Fernanda examined her father's hands and announced that she wanted her hands to look like papa's.

Canelo put a strip of tape on the back of her hand.

Maria Fernanda informed him that this was unsatisfactory. She wanted the real thing. So on a night when his place in boxing history hung in the balance, Canelo Alvarez took gauze and tape and elaborately wrapped his daughter's hands.

"This is not a distraction," he explained. "It is motivation. Having my children here reminds me of what I am fighting for."

Almost unnoticed, Ryan Garcia left the room with Eddy Reynoso at his side for what was expected to be the biggest challenge of his ring career.

Maria Fernanda, her hands now properly wrapped, began an impromptu dance recital for her father.

At 8:25 p.m., Canelo lay down on the floor for a series of stretching exercises, his first physical boxing-related activity of the evening. Maria Fernanda climbed on top of his chest and kissed him. Then, while physical conditioner Munir Somoya stretched Canelo's legs one at a time, she simultaneously tugged on the other.

A loud "OOOH!" resounded through the room. Ryan Garcia had scored a devastating first-round knockout.

Canelo stopped stretching and looked at the television to watch a video replay of the knockout: Jab, straight right, left hook. KO at 1:38 of round one.

Three minutes later, Eddy was back in the dressing room. Garcia was still being interviewed in the ring.

Eddy gloved Canelo up.

Garcia returned and Canelo embraced him. Minutes later, Duane Ford (president of the WBC North American Boxing Federation) came in and told Garcia that the belt he'd just won had to be returned to Duno.

"The WBC will mail you a new one next week," Ford explained. "This one belongs to him. If you want to present it to him personally, come with me."

Garcia left the room with Ford and returned alone minutes later.

"That was hard to see," Ryan said. "In the ring, you do what you do. But just now, Duno was crying. I felt bad for him."

Canelo paced back and forth, stopping occasionally to rotate his torso. Then absurdity set in.

It was 9:05 p.m. Team Canelo had been told to be ready to walk by 9:15 p.m. But earlier in the week, DAZN had made the decision to delay the start of Canelo–Kovalev until after the conclusion of a UFC pay-per-view card that was being contested in New York. Thus, there would be an unconscionably long delay between the end of Garcia–Duno and the start of Canelo–Kovalev which would ultimately begin at 10:18 p.m. (1:18 a.m. eastern time).

That was insulting to fans who had traveled to Las Vegas and bought tickets for Canelo–Kovalev. It was off-putting to DAZN's East Coast subscribers (Canelo–Kovalev didn't end until after 2:00 a.m. eastern time). And it was both disrespectful and grossly unfair to Canelo and Kovalev.

As one disgruntled media scribe noted afterward, "You can't spell 'fuck' without a U, an F, and a C."

The delay was more compatible with the rhythms of Canelo's dressing room than it would have been for most fighters. There's very little physical exertion on his part in the hours before a fight and his psychological makeup minimizes tension. If anything, during the next hour, he got a bit bored; that's all. He chatted with Chepo and Eddy, watched DAZN's filler content on the television, and rose occasionally to shadowbox.

Finally, at 9:52 p.m., DAZN production coordinator Tami Cotel came into the room and announced, "You walk in eleven minutes."

Canelo hit the pads with Eddy . . . Ferociously . . . With power . . . Now he looked like a fighter. A tattoo in English on the left side of his upper back reads, "Destiny is not a matter of chance. It's a matter of choice. Life is hard but never give up. Keep on trying and always believe in yourself to achieve your dreams."

Inside the arena, three national anthems—Russian, Mexican, and United States—were sung.

Eddy massaged Canelo's shoulders while the Mexican anthem sounded.

Chepo draped a serape over Canelo's shoulders.

At 10:08 p.m, Canelo left the sanctuary of his dressing room for war.

★ ★ ★

The live gate for Canelo–Kovalev had been hurt by the fact that Canelo's fans are used to traveling to Las Vegas to see him fight on Cinco de Mayo and Mexican Independence Day weekends, not in early November. The casino ticket buy had been smaller than usual.

The announced crowd of 14,490 was heavily pro-Canelo.

The notes I took as the fight progressed read as follows:

> Round 1—Kovalev throwing a probing jab with his right hand cocked. Canelo biding his time, processing Kovalev's timing and rhythm.

> Round 2—Kovalev busier, keeping Canelo at bay with his jab. Canelo has to find a way to pressure more effectively. He can't let Kovalev control the fight from the outside with his jab.

Round 3—Canelo advancing. Kovalev still dictating the terms of the fight with his jab. Sergey has won the first three rounds.

Round 4—Kovalev sticking to his fight plan. Canelo fighting a patient fight, starting to land to the body.

Round 5—Canelo the aggressor, looks like the more powerful fighter. Kovalev circling away, jabbing.

Round 6—Good body work by Canelo. The body shots are starting to break Kovalev down. Kovalev not throwing his right hand much because it will open him up to hooks to the body. Fight even after six.

Round 7—Kovalev looks to be tiring, throwing a stay-away-from-me jab. Holding when Canelo gets inside or pushing him off with his shoulder.

Round 8—Canelo backing away, going to the ropes, trying to lure Kovalev in. Poor strategic decision. Giving away the round.

Round 9—Kovalev seems rejuvenated by the last round

Round 10—Canelo more aggressive now. Kovalev still holding when Canelo gets inside or trying to push him off with his shoulder (and maybe break Canelo's nose). The fight is even after ten.

Round 11—Canelo in control again.

BOOM ! ! !

With 53 seconds left in round eleven, Canelo landed a chopping right hand that shook Kovalev; then followed with a left hook to the side of the head that put Sergey on spaghetti legs. Kovalev started to fall and a crushing right rendered him senseless with his upper body draped over the lower ring strand. There was no need to count, and referee Russell Mora didn't.

Canelo hadn't needed a knockout to win. But he needed a knockout to make his point. And he got it.

"The plan was patience," he said afterward. "We knew it was going to take some time for me to get him, but we stuck to our plan. It was delayed a little bit. It was a very close fight because he was defensive. He was closing up his guard. But we knew inevitably it would come. Everything came out the way we planned."

After the fight, Canelo's dressing room was filled with family and friends. Amid the celebration, the final rituals of fight night were tended to. A VADA collection officer took a post-fight urine sample from Canelo. Chepo packed up his gym bag with tape, gauze, gloves, and other tools of his trade.

One of the black leather sofas was moved to the far end of the room beneath the Mexican flag. Canelo, having showered and now wearing a stylish suit with a white shirt open at the collar, sat on the sofa with Chepo beside him. Cameras clicked. Then family and other members of Team Canelo took their turn for photographs at the fighter's side.

Great fighters have very little ambivalence about fighting. They love it. Canelo loves the challenge of competing in the ring at the highest level. When asked just prior to the final pre-fight press conference for Canelo–Kovalev where he thought he stood on the list of great Mexican fighters, Canelo answered, "The day that I retire is the day that we can judge my place in history."

So for now, let's say simply that Canelo is working his way up the ladder of Mexico's ring immortals. He enjoys the big stage. He likes the money that comes with success. But most of all, he loves practicing the craft of boxing.

"It is an honor," he says. "I am very proud of being what I am in boxing."

He should be.

For commentary on the propriety of staging the rematch between Andy Ruiz and Anthony Joshua in Saudi Arabia, see "Cash on the Dunes" in the "Issues and Answers" section of this book.

Ruiz–Joshua 2 from Afar

Humpty Dumpty is an English nursery rhyme, the origins of which are shrouded in the mist of history. It has been said at various times to have been written as an allegory for people and events as diverse as King Richard III (whose army was defeated in the last major battle of The War of the Roses in 1485) to the fall from grace of Cardinal Thomas Wolsey in 1529. In 1797, an English composer named Samuel Arnold published a work called *Juvenile Amusements* that included the following:

> Humpty Dumpty sat on a wall,
> Humpty Dumpty had a great fall.
> Four-score Men and Four-score more,
> Could not make Humpty Dumpty where he was before.

Since then, Humpty has appeared in creative works as diverse as *Through The Looking Glass* by Lewis Carroll and *Finnegan's Wake* by James Joyce. In its popularly accepted current form, the rhyme reads:

> Humpty Dumpty sat on a wall,
> Humpty Dumpty had a great fall.
> All the king's horses and all the king's men
> Couldn't put Humpty together again.

That brings us to Anthony Joshua.

At the start of 2019, Joshua was King of the World. After winning a gold medal in the super-heavyweight division at the 2012 Olympics, he'd moved to the professional ranks and compiled a 22–0 (21 KOs) record en route to annexing the WBA, IBF, and WBO crowns. His most impressive performance during that time was an April 29, 2017, knock-out of Wladimir Klitschko that saw "AJ" climb off the canvas in front of 90,000 screaming hometown fans at Wembley Stadium in London to stop Klitschko in the eleventh round.

"There has always been something regal about Joshua," Jimmy Tobin wrote. "A purple streak that went beyond his herculean dimensions, beyond the polish, beyond the grooming that long ago began preparing him to be not just a professional boxer but the heavyweight champion of the world."

Then came the fall.

On June 1, 2019, Joshua entered the ring at Madison Square Garden in what was billed as his "invasion of America." The opponent was Andy Ruiz, a substitute for Jarrell Miller who had been pulled from the fight after testing positive for banned performance-enhancing drugs.

Ruiz had a good amateur pedigree. But he'd fought his first pro fight in 2009 at 297 pounds and evinced an aversion to serious conditioning throughout his ring career.

There's a reason why very few fat people succeed in boxing. And it has nothing to do with body-shaming. Boxing requires that a fighter turn his body into a finely tuned instrument of destruction. Indeed, Top Rank (which promoted Ruiz for much of his ring career) grew so discouraged by Andy's eating habits and other lifestyle issues coupled with his financial demands that it let him buy his way out of his contract at the start of this year.

Joshua was a 20-to-1 betting favorite when the two men met in the ring on June 1. It was expected that Ruiz would be relegated to a place in boxing history alongside "Two-Ton" Tony Galento who was knocked out in the fourth round by Joe Louis eighty years ago. But once the bell rang, AJ's "invasion of America" evoked memories of England's performance against the colonies in the Revolutionary War.

After dropping Ruiz with a right-uppercut-left-hook combination in round three, Joshua was staggered by a counter left hook to the temple and pummeled around the ring. Four knockdowns later, Andy Ruiz was the WBA–IBF–WBO heavyweight champion of the world.

Within the hour, Deontay Wilder (Joshua's WBC rival) tweeted, "He [Joshua] wasn't a true champion. His whole career has consisted of lies, contradictions and gifts. Facts and now we know who was running from who!!!"

That earned a rejoinder at the post-fight press conference from Joshua's promoter, Eddie Hearn, who declared, "Deontay Wilder has zero class for kicking Joshua while he's down."

Tyson Fury, who styles himself as the lineal heavyweight king, was kinder on fight night, tweeting, "We have our back and forths but @anthonyfjoshua changed his stars through life. Heavyweight boxing, these things happen, rest up, recover, regroup and come again."

Then, two days later, Fury abandoned his gracious position and told ESPN Radio, "It was a little fat fella from California who chinned him. He'll never live it down. Can you imagine? You're built like an Adonis, you're six-foot-six, you're ripped, carved in stone. And a little fat guy who has eaten every Snickers and Mars Bar in the whole of California comes in there and bladders you all over? What a disgrace. If that was me, I'd never show my face in public again."

Meanwhile, in a video released on his YouTube channel several days after the defeat, Joshua declared, "I took my first loss. How to explain that feeling? It hasn't really changed me, my work ethic, my mindset, what I stand for, the people I'm still loyal to. I'm a soldier and I have to take my ups and my downs. On Saturday, I took a loss and I have to take it like a man. I'm the one who went in there to perform, and my performance didn't go to plan. I'm the one who has to adjust, analyze, and do my best to correct it and get the job done in the rematch."

But it's never that simple. Recalling his own loss of the heavy-weight title to Muhammad Ali in Zaire, George Foreman told boxing scribe Gareth Davies, "There is a process of grieving after a loss like this. When you are the heavyweight champion of the world, it's not like you have lost a fight. You have lost a part of yourself. You have got to find it again."

As for what might come next, Bob Arum weighed in on the subject just prior to the June 15 bout between Tyson Fury and Tom Schwartz. After saying that Fury (who he co-promotes) reminded him of Ali and Foreman, Arum declared that Team Joshua opting for an immediate rematch against Ruiz would be "the stupidest thing they can do." In response, it was noted that Arum letting Ruiz buy his way out of his Top Rank promotional contract turned out not to be so smart either.

Meanwhile, Ruiz was spending money like it would lose its value by the end of the year. A mansion, a $450,000 Rolls-Royce, lots of bling. In August, he hosted an elaborate thirtieth birthday party for himself that was notable for a bevy of buxom lingerie-clad waitresses, a naked sushi girl, a large ice sculpture with the initials "AR" carved into the ice, free-flowing champagne, a live performance by rapper Scotty Music, and more.

Soon after, trainer Manny Robles acknowledged that Ruiz had been slow to get back to the gym.

"We're working on getting back together this week," Robles told *SB Nation* on August 20. "I was hoping it would be yesterday but it wasn't, so we're definitely working on that right now. We're scheduled to start training this week. He's not in great shape. Let's hope we can get him back in the gym real soon and get him going again."

It soon became clear that a Joshua–Ruiz rematch would be the next fight for each man. The open issues were when and where. Ruiz wanted the fight in the United States. But Joshua wanted it in Cardiff and, by contract, his side of the promotion was entitled to choice of venue. Ultimately, Hearn chose December 7 in Saudi Arabia because of lucrative financial incentives extended by the Saudi Kingdom.

A purse sweetener quickly overcame Ruiz's safety and humanitarian concerns, and the fight was on.

The morality of Ruiz–Joshua 2 being contested in Saudi Arabia has been discussed at length by this writer in another article. Suffice it to say here that boxing is not known for high moral standards, a point that was emphasized at the final pre-fight press conference in Diriyah on December 4 when Hearn introduced Prince Khalid bin Salman who spoke from the dais. Prince Khalid has been named in reliable intelligence reports as having been complicit in the murder of *Washington Post* journalist Jamal Khashoggi in the Saudi Arabian consulate in Istanbul on October 2, 2018.

Glossing over that history, Hearn advised the assembled media, "I can't tell you how glad and honored we are to be here in the Kingdom of Saudi Arabia to stage this event. There was a little bit of criticism. [But] I can tell you that, sitting here today, it was a wonderful, wonderful decision that we are so happy with. This is a new dawn for the sport of boxing. And we cannot thank the Kingdom of Saudi Arabia, Skill Challenge Entertainment [the Saudi Kingdom's official event partner], and the GSA [Saudi Arabian General Sports Authority] enough for everything they have done."

Joshua had arrived in Saudi Arabia two weeks before the December 7 bout, Ruiz several days later. For the most part, the pre-fight exchanges between the boxers were pleasant.

"I respect him," Joshua said of Ruiz. "He came into the ring [in our first fight] and did what he had to do."

Ruiz responded in kind saying, "I have a lot of respect for Anthony. Outside the ring, he's a very good man."

There were the usual expressions of confidence.

"When I came to boxing," Joshua declared, "I didn't come to take part. I came to take over. I'm not here to put on a show. I'm here to win."

"I know he's gonna try to box me around," Ruiz countered. "But it's my job to prevent that. I'm ready to rock and roll."

Ruiz also shared the thought, "I'm still the same Andy Ruiz. I'm still the same chubby little fat kid with the big dream. But inside the ring, I'm the champion of the world. This journey now is what I've been dreaming about all my life. I don't want to give it away. I want a legacy, not just fifteen minutes of fame."

There were other huge upsets in heavyweight championship history before Ruiz toppled Joshua. James Braddock decisioned Max Baer. Buster Douglas knocked out Mike Tyson. Hasim Rahman beat Lennox Lewis. In each of these instances, the upset winner lost in his first title defense. By contrast, Cassius Clay "shook up the world" when he dethroned Sonny Liston and had a long glorious reign as Muhammad Ali.

Within that framework, Ruiz–Joshua 2 was seen primarily as a measuring stick for Joshua.

"Now we find out who he is," Jimmy Tobin wrote. "Is he a better version of his countryman Frank Bruno? A physical specimen good enough to pick up some hardware but too psychologically fragile to persist at the top? Or is he closer to Lennox Lewis, an Olympic gold medalist who could be chinned but who never abandoned his malice despite the risk it introduced, whose multiple title reigns were a testament to his talent but also his ability to rebuild?"

The consensus was that Joshua should take a page from Wladimir Klitschko's playbook, use his advantage in height and reach over Ruiz, and fight a cautious fight. Klitschko was mocked after he lost by knockout to Ross Puritty, Corrie Sanders, and Lamon Brewster. But things turned out well for Wladimir once he retooled his defense and embarked on a 22-fight winning streak. Lennox Lewis met with similar success after knockout defeats at the hands of Oliver McCall and Hasim Rahman. When Lewis and Rahman readied for their rematch, most onlookers who had picked Lewis to win big the first time were on the fence. They questioned whether Lennox could take Rahman's punch any better in Las Vegas than he did in South Africa. He could and he did.

Joshua was a 2-to-1 betting favorite over Ruiz in the rematch. The odds reflected his superior physical assets and the belief that he would come into their second encounter in far better physical condition than Ruiz. But there was more to it than that.

"It's not just about coming in strong and fit," Joshua said at a September 5 press conference in New York. "This training camp will be based on being quicker. I've spent the last three months sharpening the tools in my box that I didn't use before."

Joshua's jab was widely viewed the key to his winning the rematch. He had to work it effectively as both an offensive and defensive weapon.

"If he knows how to use that lead hand to stop Ruiz from coming in," Virgil Hunter (who trained Andre Ward) said, "he can control that whole situation and use his follow-up punches at the right time. And he has to set a footwork pace on Ruiz. [In the first fight] he let Ruiz take the steps that he was comfortable with. He needs to set up a footwork pace to make Ruiz step quicker, move quicker, work harder to get in range, and test his conditioning."

Joshua weighed in at 237½ pounds for Ruiz–Joshua 2, ten pounds lighter than for their first encounter. That suggested a decision on his part to trade muscle mass for speed and quickness

By contrast, Ruiz weighed in at 283½, the most he'd weighed for a fight since his second pro outing more than ten years ago. Granted, Andy was wearing undershorts, a shirt, and sombrero when he stepped on the scale. But many observers thought that the 15½ pounds he'd added since June bespoke of a lack of conditioning and commitment.

That said; when talk turned to Joshua winning the rematch with his jab, Ruiz's proponents noted that Andy had backed AJ up with his own jab in rounds one and two of their first encounter and was elusive when Joshua tried to find him with jabs of his own.

Asked what he thought would be the key to the rematch, Ruiz

answered, "Me staying small. I don't think he likes fighting against that style. I don't think he's ever fought a short guy that pressures and is pretty slick. I felt like I was boxing him around even though I was the shorter guy."

"He'll try to box me and use his jab," Ruiz continued. "But how long can he keep me away from hunting him down? That's what we've been working on most of all heading into the fight. The main thing is pressure, throw combinations and use my speed. I can't let him grow balls in there. I want to impose myself in this fight."

Having grown tired of hearing that a "lucky punch" in round three led to Joshua's downfall, Ruiz cited his own trip to the canvas in round three and told Sky Sports, "That was a lucky shot for him, too."

When Joshua looked back on the defeat and said, "The first time I had him down, I could have been smarter. I got trigger happy and he landed," Ruiz countered by noting that he'd also made a stupid mistake and got whacked just as hard as Joshua. But he had gotten back up ready to fight and survived.

And there were the intangibles.

Joshua's victory over Wladimir Klitschko had been his greatest ring triumph. But in some ways, he seemed to be a lesser fighter after beating Wladimir. Rather than emerge from the Klitschko fight with increased self-belief and the idea that he could fight through all kinds of adversity to win, Joshua had seemed more tentative and vulnerable in fights since then, as though the Klitschko experience had scared and scarred him.

Confidence is a fragile thing for a fighter.

"Joshua says all the right things," Bart Barry wrote. "Back to basics, trust his intuition, go with what got him there, a brand new fitness regimen. None of these things fixes the technical flaws Ruiz brought to light, much less the mental weakness Ruiz amplified. Andy Ruiz knows exactly what he is when he looks in the mirror. Anthony Joshua does not any longer, if he ever did. He knows his career's greatest advocates either overestimated him or lied about it."

Frank Lotierzo concurred, writing, "The thing that will make Ruiz so tough to beat is this. He's coming to fight and is confident Joshua is coming to survive and box. Ruiz is certain he has the style to beat Joshua and shake off anything he might try to do. That's a great mindset to have going into a big fight: the total belief that the opponent fears you; that he doesn't want to trade; that he can't box as well; that he isn't as fast, tough, or confident. If Joshua can overcome that, he's a remarkable fighter. Ruiz is going to ask Joshua the same questions he had no answer for the last time."

And Deontay Wilder played on that theme, opining, "Joshua always had a weak mindset—always. And you can't train for a mindset. Either you've got it or you don't. Either you believe in yourself or you don't. Either you know you've got the goods or you don't. It ain't no guessing. It ain't asking no questions. No, fuck that! You got it or you don't. And if you don't have it, you don't belong in this sport. Who knows? Maybe he's got it together. Maybe he's gonna go in there and knock Ruiz out. There's a lot of maybes. I'm just going off of what I've seen in the first fight. And just a few months is not gonna correct what happened to him that night."

Joshua's mental state was the key imponderable. And no one would be able to measure that until the fight began. If the time came to walk through fire, would AJ be able the rekindle the toughness he showed when he climbed off the canvas to knock out Wladimir Klitschko? Or would he crumble?

With that in mind, AJ's supporters were discomforted by a statement that he made as the rematch neared: "Even though I lost, it was only in my quiet times, like going to bed or something like that, that I really thought about it. In a weird way, it was kind of like a relief."

Losing was a relief? Was the pressure that came with being King of the World that crushing? What great heavyweight champion ever thought that losing was "kind of like a relief?"

It's hard to think of a fighter considered elite who fell as far and as fast as Joshua did after losing to Ruiz. Virtually no one had picked Ruiz to win the first fight. Now most boxing people were saying that it was hard to pick a winner. And most insiders who were picking were picking Ruiz.

"You roll the dice," commentator Paulie Malignaggi said of Joshua opting for an immediate rematch. "This is what boxing is, right?"

A stadium seating 15,000 fans had been built for the fight in Diriyah on the outskirts of Riyadh. The televised undercard was forgettable. Then came Ruiz–Joshua 2, the most anticipated fight of the year.

DAZN had told viewers that the fighter ring walks would begin at 3:45 p.m. eastern time and that round one would start fifteen minutes later. But a swing bout pushed the start of the walks past 4:00 p.m. and that was followed by three national anthems.

It was not an entertaining fight. Someday, if someone prepares a list of boxing oxymorons, "Ruiz–Joshua 2 highlights" will be on the list.

Ruiz looked like the last-place finisher in a wet tee shirt contest. He lumbered forward for most of the fight while Joshua circled away and jabbed. Before fighting Joshua earlier this year, Ruiz wasn't known as a puncher. Six of his previous ten fights had gone the distance. But Joshua kept his distance this time as though Andy was Mike Tyson in his prime.

Ruiz was cut above the left eye by a sharp right hand late in round one, but the cut wasn't a factor in the fight. And he landed a few solid blows, mostly in rounds eight and nine. But that was all. He evinced no understanding of how to cut off the ring to get to Joshua. When he did get inside, either AJ tied him up or referee Luis Pabon prematurely broke the fighters. On the few occasions when Andy managed to land solidly, Joshua immediately got back on his bike. By the late rounds, Ruiz had the look of a frustrated fighter who was just going through the motions.

The lack of action was reflected in the fact that, according to CompuBox, Ruiz landed only 60 punches over the course of twelve rounds while Joshua landed 107. The judges' scorecards correctly read 119–109, 118–110, 118–110 in AJ's favor.

"He won," Ruiz acknowledged afterward. "He boxed me around. I don't think I prepared as good as I should have. I gained too much weight. It kind of affected me a lot. I thought I would come in stronger and better. But you know what; next time I'm going to prepare better."

"Look, this is about boxing," Joshua said in a post-fight interview when asked about the tactical nature of the proceedings.

Or as Rocky Marciano, one of boxing's great warriors, once noted, "You're not in the ring to demonstrate your courage. You're in there to win the fight."

Give Joshua kudos for always carrying himself like a champion outside the ring. And add on credit for his winning the rematch. A second loss to Ruiz would have been a devastating blow to his career. But despite what was said throughout the promotion, Ruiz–Joshua 2 was for some belts, not THE heavyweight championship of the world. The #1 heavyweight in the world right now is Deontay Wilder with Tyson Fury in second place.

After Lennox Lewis lost to Hasim Rahman, he came into their rematch determined to seek out and brutally destroy his conqueror. And he did. Joshua, on the other hand, looked almost fragile on Saturday night. He'd be an underdog against Wilder or Fury. And it's not a stretch to say that contenders like Jarrell Miller and Luis Ortiz would give him trouble.

As for Ruiz; the good paychecks should last for a while now. He'll always be a bit of a name, the guy who beat Anthony Joshua.

Curiosities

Street fights are mixed martial arts without rules.

Street Fights:
Violence Outside the Ring

Most boys were in a schoolyard fight at one time or another. Generally, they're encounters of modest magnitude, as most childhood scuffles are. But for some, the world of violence outside the ring extends through adolescence and into adulthood. That's when things get scary.

The violence can be planned or arise on the spot. It can be on the street, in a bar, or any other place that fate might have it. It can be between people who know each other or total strangers. It can result in nothing more serious than a bruised ego or in Don King beating Sam Garrett to death on a city sidewalk over an unpaid gambling debt.

There's something primitive about a street fight. The rules of society have broken down. Survival of the fittest reigns.

"Being mean is the key to a street fight," says Don Turner, who trained Evander Holyfield and Larry Holmes. "Mean, sneaky, and willing to do anything. There's no such thing as clean play or honor. Joe Frazier, George Foreman, Larry Holmes, Mike Tyson; they were all mean. And I'll give you another name," Turner continues. "If all fights were fought in the street, Chuck Wepner might have wound up as champion. Wepner is a big mean rough tough guy who would do anything in a street fight. No, I take that back. There's one thing Chuck Wepner would never do in a street fight. He'd never give up."

Wepner, a large hulking man, six feet, five inches tall, who fought professionally for fourteen years against the likes of Muhammad Ali, George Foreman, and Sonny Liston, concurs with Turner's assessment.

"The only rule in a street fight," Wepner says, "is that there are no rules. A street fight is whatever you can get away with. Anything goes. Guys know how to break your fingers, poke out an eye. I broke a couple of guys' noses in street fights by shoving the palm of my hand into their nose. One big advantage I had in street fights was blood never bothered me. Most guys, when they get cut or blood is pouring from their nose, they quit. For me, it was no big deal."

"When you go into a boxing ring," Wepner elaborates, "it's about winning or losing. A street fight is more than that. The other guy is trying to kill you, and you have to get him before he gets you. In the ring, you're performing. On the street, you're fighting for your life. In the ring, someone is there to stop it if things get out of hand. There's no safety net in a street fight. If someone gets knocked down on the street, his head hits asphalt, not canvas."

Street fight are triggered by any number of variables. Some are about standing up for a perceived principle such as defending the turf in a neighborhood. Some start over a woman in a bar. Or there's a fender-bender and one driver takes exception to the other. Most often, they're born out of anger and people being unable to control their emotions.

ESPN commentator and boxing trainer Teddy Atlas had more than a few street fights when he was an adolescent.

"For me," Atlas explains, "I'd get to a place where, in my mind, it was about respect and self-respect. I didn't want to let someone make me feel less about myself and less than a man. That feeling would become dominant and outweigh the danger to myself. As I got older, my responsibilities to my family led me away from that and I also learned that that wasn't how I should evaluate myself as a person. But I know what it feels like because I've been there."

The thrill of fighting is like a rush for some people, even addictive. Former light-heavyweight contender Seanie Monaghan started getting into bar fights when he was fifteen.

"A fight would start," Monaghan recalls. "People would crowd around and cheer. I'd always wanted to be really good at something. And there it was. It was all about ego. I was playing a role, trying to show off for my friends. It was dumb caveman stuff, but I enjoyed the action. I wanted to be the guy who was beating someone up. There were a lot of fights, fifty or sixty over the years. I didn't want to kill anyone, but I wanted to hurt them. And then, if I did hurt someone, I'd go home in tears because I felt bad I'd hurt them."

Alcohol plays a role in a lot of street fights. Some guy in a bar gets too many drinks in him and starts swinging.

"Maybe the dumbest thing," sportswriter Jerry Izenberg notes, "is when a fight breaks out in a ballpark because some moron thinks it's incumbent upon him to defend the honor of the home team."

In a professional boxing match, a combatant knows what to expect in terms of rules and the skill level of his opponent. Street fights venture into less-charted territory. Often, a combatant doesn't know who he's dealing with and what skills his adversary brings to the table. A lot of people talk tough and act tough but aren't tough. Sometimes, the quiet guys are the best street fighters. Also, there's added danger in fighting an unknown opponent because street fighters are more likely to carry brutality to excess against someone they don't know.

Street fighting is more like MMA than boxing. But it's characterized by a very different mindset than organized combat sports and requires lesser skills. Put two street fighters in an octagon or boxing ring, and spectators would see something very crude compared to what they're accustomed to watching. There are so many subtle things that go into MMA and boxing that the vast preponderance of street fighters haven't come close to mastering.

Street fights are usually fueled by an initial outburst of emotion. They're fast and explosive with very little defensive maneuvering. The fundamental rule of street fights is to get off first. The first good punch in a street fight often ends it. By contrast, professional boxers are patient and methodical.

Teddy Atlas notes, "In the ring, the fighters have been matched ahead of time. If a fighter's team has done its homework, the fighter knows what the opponent brings to the table. They know what the opponent does well. They know what his weaknesses are. That's not true in most street fights. On the street, guys do what they do best and almost never consider their opponent's strengths and flaws."

"The biggest difference between street fighting and boxing," George Foreman says, "is endurance. Street fighters don't do roadwork for endurance. They go as hard as they can from the start and try to get it over as quickly as possible."

Chuck Wepner concurs with Foreman on the issue of endurance and adds, "People said I was a brawler and a mugger when I got in a boxing ring. Fight to the finish; have a referee that let me fight rough; don't stop the fight on cuts. I was just about unbeatable under those circumstances. Well. those are the rules in a street fight."

"I was good in street fights," Wepner elaborates. "I had maybe fifteen of them when I was a kid and a few more in school. After I retired from boxing, I had some in bars. Bar fights are easy. Guys have been drinking and they can't go more than thirty seconds without getting tired, sixty seconds at most. Guys who've been in prison can be a problem in street fights. A lot of them are violent to begin with and then they learned techniques in jail that make them even harder to fight."

Wepner knows of what he speaks. In the late 1980s, he spent twenty-two months in prison after pleading guilty to the illegal distribution of cocaine.

"I had two fights when I was in prison," Wepner recalls. "One of them was over a shower stall. The other was when a guy told me I had to give him a certain number of cigarettes each week to see that I didn't have any trouble. We threw some punches, and after that he left me alone."

Wepner's outside-the-ring fisticuffs also led to his meeting Barney Frank, who was elected to Congress in 1980 and later served as chairman of the House of Representatives Financial Services Committee which made him one of the most powerful people in government. Frank's career was also notable because, in 1987, he became only the second member of Congress to openly acknowledge being gay.

"My first day of high school [Bayonne High School]," Frank told a reporter for the *New Yorker* a decade ago, "I was sent to the vice principal for discipline because I got in trouble for talking too much. When I got to her office, Chuck Wepner was already there. He'd gotten into a fight with the toughest kid in the school."

"I remember that fight," Wepner says. "It was with a guy named Cuno Canella. But Cuno wasn't the toughest kid in the school. I was. I was never a bully, but I stood up to bullies. Cuno was giving a kid a hard time in the cafeteria for no reason. I told him to lay off. He took exception. And we went at it. It was a great fight. We were knocking over tables and I was beating the crap out of him when they broke it up. I lost sometimes in the pros, but I was undefeated in the cafeteria."

Street fights tend to be more dangerous now than they once were. People are inclined to take violence further than they did years ago. Confrontations can devolve into brutal beatings with life-changing consequences.

"When a guy in a street fight says 'I give up,'" Wepner notes, "it's supposed to be over. But then there are psychos."

Also, the dynamic of a street fight can go beyond the expected. A gun or knife is introduced. Someone from the crowd gets involved.

"You beat a guy and then you wind up having to fight the guy's friends," Teddy Atlas says. "You hope it's just you and the other guy with no weapons or someone else jumping in. But whether you like it or not, you're committing for whatever comes."

"The unknown is the scary part," Seanie Monaghan offers. "You don't know what the scene will turn into. And it can turn fast. A guy might be tougher than you thought. He can pull out a weapon. One-on-one can turn into two-on-one or twenty-on-twenty in a hurry. My nose got broken. I got cut in the head with bottles twice. One time, I got stabbed in the throat and needed thirty or forty stitches. I cleaned up my act a long time ago. I stopped drinking and reevaluated my life. I haven't had a drink in sixteen years. I look back on it all now and ask myself, 'For what?'"

Some professional boxers started training as a sanctuary from street fighting; others as a natural extension of it. But the sweet science and street fights are inextricably intertwined.

John L. Sullivan would famously walk into saloons and announce, "I can lick any man in the house."

Mickey Walker lost a fifteen-round decision to Harry Greb on July 2, 1925, at the Polo Grounds in New York. The two men then encountered one another at a nightclub in the wee small hours of the morning and had a few cordial drinks together after which things turned violent again.

No one who has walked to the center of a boxing ring can be taken lightly in a street fight. But Muhammad Ali wouldn't have been as intimidating on the street as many other heavyweights of his time. Sonny Liston, by contrast, was as feared on the street as he was in the ring. Liston engaged in innumerable street fights over the years including one in which he beat up a St. Louis police officer. On other occasions, he worked as a strike-breaker for the mob.

Shortly before Liston's 1963 rematch against Floyd Patterson, Sonny was shooting craps at the Thunderbird Hotel in Las Vegas. Cassius Clay was standing against the wall, watching. Liston was doing poorly.

"Look at that big ugly bear," Clay shouted. "He can't even shoot craps."

Liston glared at Clay, picked up the dice, and rolled again.

Another craps.

"Look at that big ugly bear. He can't do nothing right."

At that point, as recounted by several onlookers, Liston threw down the dice, walked over to Clay, and said, "Listen, you nigger faggot. If you don't get out of here in ten seconds, I'm gonna pull that big tongue out of your mouth and stick it up your ass."

Clay exited quickly.

"Cassius isn't an idiot." Angelo Dundee explained afterward. "He knows he can beat Sonny in the ring, not in a street fight."

Larry Holmes acknowledges, "I was in a couple of street fights when I was young."

How many was "a couple."

"Not that many," Holmes answers. "Three or four a year."

Three or four fights a year sounds like "many" to most people.

"It could be fighting over a girl or someone took something from me," Holmes explains. "I was big and I was good. In a street fight, you do what you can and you do what you gotta do. Pick up a rock, hit a guy in the head with a brick. You want people to say, 'Larry kicked his ass.' I never carried a gun. I carried a knife a few times when I was young, but that didn't last long and I never used it. After a while, people got smart and didn't want to mess with me no more. The word got out, 'Larry can fight.' Then I started boxing. Once you learn to really fight, you learn you don't have to fight. If someone was looking for a fight, I'd say, 'I ain't messing with this crazy motherfucker.' I figured out that I shouldn't fight unless I got paid."

In 1981, Holmes won a decision over Trevor Berbick in a successful title defense at Caesars Palace in Las Vegas. Ten years later, they had another encounter in a parking lot outside the Diplomat Hotel in Hollywood, Florida. Holmes had just scored a first-round knockout of Tim Anderson. He and Berbick, who was in attendance, had words at the post-fight press conference and their dialogue continued afterward. Berbick said some things about Holmes and women that Larry took exception to. Things came to a climax outside the hotel when Holmes climbed over two parked cars and leapt on top of Berbick, knocking him to the ground.

"That was the last street fight I had," Holmes reminisces. "Berbick was talking shit. If you're a real man, you don't talk shit about somebody else's wife or mother. So I went after him. He wasn't expecting that. He started running but I ran faster. I knocked him down and kicked his ass. I mean, like besides punching him, I kicked him in the ass. Then the cops came and broke it up."

Mike Tyson had more than his share of street fights, the most notable of which occurred in the early morning hours of August 23, 1988, when he broke a bone in his right hand in a 4:00 a.m. brawl with Mitch Green outside a clothing store in Harlem called Dapper Dan. Green who had lost a ten-round decision to Tyson two years earlier, confronted Mike regarding money that he believed he was owed by Don King. He became increasingly belligerent, and Tyson decided to strike first. After turning the rings on both hands, Mike began firing punches, closing Green's left eye and opening a cut that required five stitches to close.

Unlike Tyson, Lennox Lewis has largely avoided street fights. But he admits to having had a few.

"The last one was more than twenty-five years ago," Lewis recalls. "I wasn't champion yet, but I was a fighter on the rise. I went to meet a friend, and some guy was trying to beat him up. I said, 'Yo! Get off of him now!' And one of his friends hit me in the head, so I hit him back and knocked him down. Then another guy came at me, and I knocked him down. And that was it."

"Sometimes, because of who I am, some guy will challenge me or try to provoke me," Lennox explains. "A lot of the time, I can see right off that they want me to hit them so they can sue me and win the lottery. But I just walk away."

Ring announcer Michael Buffer might be the last person one associates with street fights. But he acknowledges having had a few before becoming the polished urbane icon that he is today,

"The last one was in the early 1970s," Buffer recalls. "It was around two in the morning. I was with a friend. We'd been to a party and got something to eat in a diner afterward. I was at the cash register paying my check when some guy who'd obviously had too much to drink started yelling at a waitress. I gave him a sideways look, and he came over to me and said in a belligerent way, 'What are you looking at?' I told him, 'Not much.' And he slapped me."

At that point, Buffer channeled his inner Hulk Hogan.

"I knew a little bit about fighting," Buffer says. "I'd been in the Army for two years. So I gave him my best shot, punched him four or five times, and rammed his face into a cigarette machine. Someone called the cops. My friend and I walked out of the diner, got in my car, and drove off just as the cops were arriving."

"I find street fights very scary," Buffer adds. "I don't want to be near one, let alone part of one."

Hall of Fame commentator Al Bernstein, one of the most genial men in boxing, had "four or five" fights outside the ring when he was young. The last was the most memorable for him.

"I went to Gage Park High School on the southwest side of Chicago," Bernstein recounts. "There were almost no Jews in the school, but I experienced very little anti-Semitism except for one guy. We were both on the football team. He played middle-linebacker and made a point of saying anti-Semitic things to me from time to time. Then, one day when we were in the locker room after practice, he urinated in my duffle bag with all of my stuff in it and gave me the finger. So I challenged him to fight."

What the bully didn't know was that Bernstein had taken up boxing and ultimately would have twenty sanctioned amateur bouts.

"I threw a jab to start things off," Al remembers. "Then I went to the body and hit him with a pretty good left hook up top. We went at it for about a minute and a half. Both of us landed some good shots. Then the coach came in and broke it up. The guy I was fighting had a bloody nose and I had a cut on my cheek."

Anyone who attends fights on a regular basis tends to become hardened to the reality of what's going on in the ring. The formality of it all tends to cosmetize the violence. Street fights are a different matter.

People are drawn to unplanned violence. If a fight breaks out among the players at a baseball or basketball game, all eyes are riveted on it. When a fight breaks out in the crowd at a professional boxing match, heads turn and those close enough to see the action roar.

Street fights are exciting and a bit scary to watch. Spectators are likely to see big showy punches. Onlookers are both attracted and repulsed by the violence. Some spectators are consumed by blood lust and celebrate the occasion.

A good prizefight is defined as one in which two boxers engage in a brutal ebb and flow and have been punched in the head and hurt multiple times. If a boxer is cut in the ring, we shrug our shoulders and expect him to continue fighting. But if that happens on the street in front of us, we're inclined to empathize with the person who's being humiliated or physically hurt and fear for his safety.

Also, on the street, violence can spread like an out-of-control fire. Unlike the crowd at a boxing match, the people who watch a street fight can become participants—willing or unwilling—at any moment.

"Street fights are bad things," Jerry Izenberg says. "Nothing good can come out of stopping to watch a street fight. One of the ways I got to be eighty-eight years old was by not standing around to watch street fights."

Should a spectator intervene if someone is lying on the ground, getting kicked in the head in a street fight? If he does, his head might be next. Only a trained law enforcement official should try to stop a street fight. The rest of us should call 911.

"I don't like unfairness," Lennox Lewis says. "I don't like seeing someone hurt on the street. If someone is getting beaten up, I want to intervene. But there are fewer limits on violence now than there used to be. Someone can pull out a knife or a gun, so I'm much more wary of playing peacemaker than I was before. If I do intervene, I'll grab the guy who's getting beaten up and pull him away. Usually, he's happy that it's over and the stronger guy doesn't feel threatened by me because I didn't put my hands on him. But to be honest with you, I stay as far away from street fights as I can."

Boxing's Satellite Promotional Tour

It's shortly before noon on Thursday, May 2, 2019. In two days, Saul "Canelo" Alvarez and Danny Jacobs will do battle at the T-Mobile Arena in Las Vegas for the middleweight championship of the world. Over the next two hours, the fighters will engage in a ritual that has become an integral part of promoting big fights—the satellite tour.

Dave Coskey, who has enjoyed a long career in media and public relations, was one of the early architects of the boxing promotional satellite tour. He was working for the Philadelphia 76ers when Julius Erving retired at the end of the 1986–87 season. There was a pregame retirement ceremony, and Coskey arranged to distribute it via satellite to stations that wanted to televise the festivities.

Later, Coskey became senior vice president for marketing at the Trump Plaza in Atlantic City. On February 3, 1990, Vinny Pazienza fought Hector Camacho at the Atlantic City Convention Center. That week, for the first time, Coskey used a satellite tour to promote boxing.

Fast-forward to April 19, 1991, when Evander Holyfield and George Foreman squared off at the Convention Center with the Trump Plaza as host hotel for the fight.

"The goal," Coskey remembers, "was to make Holyfield–Foreman bigger than a sporting event. And George was a publicist's dream. Six days before the fight, he preached in a tiny church in Atlantic City, and we set up a satellite feed for ESPN."

Mark Taffet (who served as senior vice president of sports operations and PPV for HBO) picks up the narrative.

"Bob Arum was the CEO at Top Rank, which was promoting Foreman," Taffet recalls. "Dan Duva was in charge at Main Events, which promoted Evander. They came to us with Dave Coskey, gave us the creative idea, and we implemented it. Basically, it was, get a camera, chair, and some lighting; have each fighter sit in the chair in front of the camera for an hour answering questions from a series of TV stations; and transmit it by satellite. Some of the interviews aired live. Some were taped and aired later. It was easy to do and a way to accommodate the fighters' fight-week schedules."

"We realized very quickly that this was a great marketing tool for pay-per-view," Taffet continues. "It was a win-win situation for the TV stations and the promotion. It cost next to nothing to produce. We were able to target the audience we wanted. There was very little preparation and production involved. Back then, you needed a satellite truck onsite and had to buy an hour of satellite time. Now you can do it all through the internet."

Satellite tours aren't unique to boxing. They're used to promote all kinds of commercial ventures. For example, a pharmaceutical company that's launching a new product might make a spokesperson available to media outlets for interviews.

The staging ground for satellite tours in conjunction with big fights varies. Sometimes interviews are conducted in the arena where the fight will be contested. That provides a nice camera backdrop. But often, the arena is unavailable or background noise caused by workers setting up seats or erecting scaffolding will interfere with audio transmission, and a quiet room is chosen.

For maximum impact, satellite tours are conducted as close to fight night as possible. But that can conflict with the desire of the fighters to shed media obligations and focus completely on the more difficult task of fighting. Thus, more often than not, the interviews take place on Thursday, two days before the fight. Generally, a fighter's camp gives satellite tour organizers one hour to work with.

Kelly Swanson is CEO of Swanson Communications, a public relations and marketing firm that offers satellite tours as a turnkey service.

"Obviously, you want the big national outlets like CNN and ESPN if you can get them," Swanson says. "But some regulars reach out to us for a spot and we try to accommodate them. And you look for markets that might have a special connection to one of the fighters. If Keith Thurman is fighting Manny Pacquiao, you reach out to local TV in Tampa [Thurman's hometown]."

Mike Tyson was the most sought-after fighter on satellite tours. His dance card was always full. The problem was, Tyson sometimes blew off his satellite tour obligations. And even when he showed up, there could be problems.

On January 16, 1999, Tyson fought Frans Botha after a nineteen-month layoff occasioned in part by a suspension imposed after he bit off part of Evander Holyfield's ear. During the satellite tour, Tyson was interviewed by Russ Salzberg of 9 News. The interview—reproduced here in its entirety—did not go well.

Salzberg: Mike, Francois Botha, a 6-to-1 underdog. Are there any concerns on your part?

Tyson: I don't know anything about that. I don't know nothing about numbers. I just know what I can do. How about killing this motherfucker?

Salzberg: Okay. How about the nineteen months off?

Tyson: What about it?

Salzberg: Does it pose any problem to you?

Tyson: We'll see. I doubt it seriously.

Salzberg: You take into the ring a lot of rage. Does that work for you or does it work against you at times?

Tyson: Who cares. We're in a fight anyway. What does it matter?

Salzberg: Well, for example, rage against Evander Holyfield worked against you.

Tyson: Well, fuck it. It's a fight. So whatever happens happens.

Salzberg: Mike, why do you have to talk like that?

Tyson: I'm talking to you the way I want to talk to you. If you have a problem, turn off your station.

Salzberg: You know what. I think we'll end the discussion right now.

Tyson: Then we could. Fuck you.

Salzberg: You got it. Have a nice fight, Mike.

Tyson: Fuck off.

Salzberg: Class act, buddy.

The satellite tour for Canelo–Jacobs was overseen by Ed Keenan. The first tour that Keenan worked on was for Lennox Lewis vs. Mike Tyson in Memphis in 2002. The interviews were scheduled to be conducted immediately after the weigh-in. Then Tyson refused to participate, telling those in charge to perform unnatural acts upon themselves and leaving Lewis to carry the ball. Keenan now owns Event Marketing & Communications. And he's still coordinating satellite tours.

Room 309 in the MGM Grand Conference Center has a high ceiling and is large enough to accommodate a cocktail party for a hundred people. Seventy cushioned metal-framed chairs were scattered about. One chair was set in front of a black backdrop that bore logos for Canelo–Jacobs, DAZN (which would stream the fight), Golden Boy (Canelo's promoter), Matchroom Boxing (Jacobs's promoter), Tecate (the fight's lead sponsor), Hennessy (which has an endorsement contract with Canelo), and the MGM Grand (the site hotel). There was one cameraman who would shoot one camera angle showing each fighter from the chest up.

Keenan sat at a small table, smartphone in hand with a laptop in front of him, coordinating it all.

Canelo arrived five minutes after noon, wearing a red tracksuit with white trim. Trainer Eddy Reynoso, manager Chepo Reynoso, and publicist Ramiro Gonzalez were with him.

The Spanish-language media has played a huge role in Canelo's commercial success in the United States. It's a market that DAZN needs to tap into if it's going to succeed in building a profitable subscription base. Half of the satellite interviews with Canelo would be with Spanish-speaking networks.

News is seldom made during a satellite tour interview. They're generally bland with questions and answers that tend toward the repetitive. Canelo sat through eight interviews, taking questions in English and Spanish but answering in Spanish. When called for, Roberto Diaz (whose duties with Golden Boy transcend his official role as matchmaker) translated the answers into English.

Canelo sat patiently through it all, hands folded in his lap, occasionally gesturing with his right hand to make a point. From time to time, he stretched out his legs, crossing them at the ankles.

How did he feel about the constant talk from Danny Jacobs's camp regarding whether or not Jacobs could get a fair shake from the judges in Las Vegas?

"It sounds like they're making excuses for losing already."

What was the highlight of Canelo's career to date?

"I've done a lot of good things in my career, and I'm confident that there are more to come."

How would he define himself?

"I'm a calm person."

What did he think about Jacobs having had cancer?

"It's admirable what he has overcome."

If Canelo wasn't a boxer, is there another sport he could have excelled at?

"I think I could have been a good Formula One driver."

After an hour, Canelo's interviews were done.

Jacobs arrived at 1:25 p.m. (ten minutes later than scheduled) and took his seat in front of the camera. His rich baritone voice contrasted markedly with Canelo's softer tones. There were seven interviews.

What would be the key to the fight?

"It's about me being the best version of myself that I can be . . . I'm not going to put pressure on myself to overperform and do things I'm not used to doing . . . Canelo is a great fighter, but he has weaknesses and it's up to me to exploit those weaknesses."

Most of the interviewers asked at least one question about Jacobs's battle against cancer.

"Boxing taught me to view each and every obstacle as just another opponent. Cancer was just another opponent, and I had my hand raised at the end."

What worried him most about Canelo?

"Nothing worries me about Canelo. If there's hardship for me in the fight, I'll overcome it."

At one point, there was an audio problem at one of the TV stations. The volume wasn't coming through loudly enough.

"I can't help you with that," Jacobs said. "I'm not a tech guy. I'm just a boxer."

An interviewer asked a question about The Iron Throne.

"I'm sorry," Jacobs answered. "I don't know what that means."

The question was explained.

"I'm sorry," Danny said again. "I don't watch much television. I've never seen *Game of Thrones*."

After forty-five minutes, his job was done.

Today's technology—social media, streaming video, more websites than most people can fathom—offers far more alternatives to promoting a big fight than were available when George Foreman fought Evander Holyfield in Atlantic City a quarter-century ago. But in many respects, the satellite tour is still the most cost-efficient, effective pay-per-view marketing tool available.

It's hard to imagine Rocky Marciano texting on a smartphone in his dressing room on fight night. But that was then.

Smartphones on Fight Night

Smartphones have become an integral part of business activity and social interaction for people from every walk of life. Talking, texting, accessing the internet, taking still photos, and transmitting videos are common.

In keeping with this phenomenon, smartphones are now intertwined with the boxing scene on fight night.

"It doesn't matter who you are," promoter Lou DiBella says. "You can be the promoter, the venue, the network that's televising the fights. If you're doing business in the arena, your staff is scattered all over the building. You'd be crazy to try to coordinate everything without a smartphone. It's the only way to hear about problems as soon as they happen and deal with them in a hurry."

"Social media is another reason you want a smartphone on fight night," DiBella continues. "It's a big part of how things are viewed today. I can shape how people view the fights I'm promoting by tweeting about them in real time. And I can see how the fights are being perceived by fans who are watching them."

On October 27, 2018, DiBella was at Madison Square Garden to watch Sergey Derevyanchenko (a fighter he promotes) battle Danny Jacobs for the International Boxing Federation 160-pound title. Simultaneously, Regis Prograis (another DiBella fighter) was squaring off against Terry Flanagan in the opening round of the World Boxing Super Series 140-pound tournament in New Orleans. DiBella watched Prograis–Flanagan on his smartphone from his seat at Madison Square Garden.

Like DiBella, fans onsite are often tethered to their smartphones on fight night.

"I see people sitting in the front row at ringside during an exciting fight," veteran publicist Bill Caplan says. "And they're staring at their phone. I want to go over and ask, 'What the hell did you come here for?'"

Fans also use smartphones to transmit illegal video streams that make their way onto the internet. And then there are selfies.

Spending time with Michael Buffer in a public setting makes it clear that being a celebrity can be an aggravating condition. That's particularly true for Buffer on fight night. "There are times when it seems as though everyone in the building wants a picture," he notes. "I don't want to be rude, but I can't stop for everyone."

Buffer is in an unusual position in that celebrities at ringside often do a double-take when he passes and ask to be photographed with him. "I was at a fight recently," Michael recounts, "and [Black Panther star] Chadwick Boseman asked if he could take a picture with me. I thought that was pretty cool."

Smartphones have also made their way into fighters' dressing rooms.

"I hate it," Don Turner (who trained Larry Holmes and Evander Holyfield) says. "I think it's crazy. If the fighter is on the phone, he isn't concentrating on what he's supposed to be concentrating on. It's a fighter's dressing room, not a conference center."

Pat Burns (who trained Jermain Taylor from the start of Taylor's pro career through two victories over Bernard Hopkins) is in accord and adds, "The first thing I say when we get in the dressing room is, 'Cell phones off.' You have to lock in on the task at hand. Physically, mentally. I don't want anyone calling my fighter, and I don't want my fighter calling anyone. Not his wife, not even the president of the United States."

When Taylor fought Bernard Hopkins at Mandalay Bay in 2005, Mike Huckabee (then governor of Arkansas, Taylor's home state) was escorted into the dressing room. Burns gave Huckabee a minute for a photo op with Jermain and then threw him out.

"I did it politely," Burns recalls. "But I did throw him out."

Smartphone use in the dressing room is now standard operating procedure for most fighters. Some say it helps the fighter relax. Others regard it as a negative.

"I see guys, their hands are being wrapped," promoter Don Elbaum says. "One hand is being wrapped and the fighter is on the phone with the other. No! You're supposed to be paying attention to the handwrap one hundred percent. How does it feel? Is the gauze and tape going on right? When the fight starts, your cell phone can't help you. You don't punch with your cell phone."

"It can be a problem," Lou DiBella acknowledges. "I was in the dressing room with one of my fighters—I won't tell you which one—and he got into an argument on the phone with his girlfriend right before he went to the ring. She was yelling at him about another woman. He got upset and was clearly distracted when the fight started."

Early cell phones were much bigger and clunkier than today's models and weren't nearly as smart. But there was one area where they were more useful than their 2019 counterparts. They could be wielded as weapons for purposes of assault.

On July 11, 1996, Riddick Bowe and Andrew Golota met in the ring at Madison Square Garden. Golota pummeled Bowe for most of the bout but was disqualified in round seven for repeated low blows. Immediately after the disqualification, Rock Newman (Bowe's manager) and other members of Riddick's entourage charged into the ring. One of them, Bernard Brooks Sr., punched Golota from behind. Andrew turned to confront his assailant. Several would-be peacemakers held him back. And while Golota was being restrained, Jason Harris (another member of Bowe's entourage) whacked him three times on top of the head with a cell phone, opening an ugly gash.

A riot followed. Partisans of both sides stormed the ring. Then people in the crowd away from the ring began assaulting each other as the disturbance devolved into a racially motivated series of black-white confrontations. Madison Square Garden's fifty ushers and seventy security personnel were quickly overwhelmed. The police were called with 150 police officers assigned to the operation. There were sixteen arrests.

On a more innocuous note; on March 27, 2017, Marvin Jones (then 2-and-4 with 4 KOs by) fought Ramon Luis Nicolas at the Turner Agri-Civic Center in Florida. Early in round one, a cell phone fell out of Jones's trunks. Referee Frank Santore Jr. picked it up and handed the phone to one of Jones's corner men.

Jones was knocked out in the first round. Afterward, he explained that he'd been listening to music before the fight, put the phone in his trunks, and forgot it was there. He also said that the incident caused him to lose focus during the fight and contributed to his loss because he kept thinking, "Man, my cell phone just fell out in the ring on TV."

In recent years, a ring judge was photographed using his smartphone in the middle of a round that he was supposed to be judging. Not to be outdone, a referee sought to justify his gross mishandling of a fight by taking out his smartphone and pointing to an email that praised his performance.

Trainer-commentator Teddy Atlas is vehemently opposed to the proliferation of smartphones in a boxing setting.

"I don't allow phones in the gym during training camp," Atlas says. "I don't care who it is. The fighter, his manager, anyone. It's unprofessional. And the dressing room on fight night? I don't allow it. Come on! The fighter's future and maybe his life are at stake. Be professional and treat what you're doing with respect. If you're getting ready to go into surgery, you don't want the patient and the surgeon and the anesthesiologist and the nurse talking on their cell phones."

Be that as it may; Atlas inserted cell phones into boxing lore on March 29, 1997, when Michael Moorer (who Teddy trained) defended his IBF heavyweight title against Vaughn Bean at the Las Vegas Hilton. Moorer was fighting in desultory fashion and returned to his corner after round eight to be confronted by Atlas, cell phone in hand.

"It's your son on the phone," Atlas told Moorer. "He's crying. You know why he's crying? Because his father doesn't want to be heavyweight champ. You know what he asked me? 'How come daddy don't want to be champ no more?'"

Uninspired, Moorer continued fighting as he had before and edged Bean on a majority decision.

But there's a more serious issue attached to the use of smartphones in a fighter's corner on fight night. Some trainers now use them to receive information and gain a competitive edge during the fight. The information can be that the opposing fighter was just televised telling his trainer that his ribs hurt or he broke his hand or he's tired and doesn't think he can go twelve rounds. Or it can be another trainer calling with strategic advice.

The National Football League forbids the use of electronic coaching aids such as smartphones that might give one team or the other a competitive advantage during the course of a game. The use of league-issued tablets to disseminate still photos taken by coaches is allowed.

By contrast, most state athletic commissions don't even know that a potential problem exists with regard to smartphone use in a fighter's corner during a fight. Or if they do, they haven't addressed it.

The California State Athletic Commission is staying ahead of the power curve. Mark Relyea (lead inspector for the CSAC) says that the use of electronic devices by a fighter's corner during a fight is monitored by an inspector assigned to each corner.

"We don't want a situation where using a cell phone gives one fighter a competitive advantage over another," Relyea says. "We'll allow a fighter's second to use a cell phone as a timer to keep track of how much time is left in a round but not to receive communications from outside the corner. That means no ear pieces. Right now, we're dealing with things on a case by case basis and relying on the 'best practices' provision in Rule 390 of the California Code of Regulations. We hope to have a clear written rule in the near future that deals specifically with the situation."

Similarly, Francisco Soto (chief inspector for the Nevada State Athletic Commission) says the NSAC doesn't have a formal written policy in place yet but adds, "We don't allow the use of any smart device during the contest. We simply ask the corner to put away the device until completion of the match."

By contrast, the New York State Athletic Commission is in limbo at the moment.

When Brian Viloria fought Roman Gonzalez at Madison Square Garden on October 17, 2015, Freddie Roach, who trained Viloria, was unable to make the trip to New York because of obligations to Miguel Cotto (who was in training to fight Canelo Alvarez). In Roach's place, assistant trainer Marvin Somodio worked Viloria's corner. Team Viloria requested that the New York State Athletic Commission permit Somodio to strategize by cell phone with Roach during the fight, but the NYSAC refused.

"We didn't have time to properly consider all of the ramifications." David Berlin (then executive director of the NYSAC) remembers. "The cameras and microphones sometimes reveal what the opponent's corner is saying, so a trainer with that information might coach a fighter on how to counter what is about to come his way. We didn't want to set a precedent for cell phone use during a fight until we were comfortable that it wouldn't give the user an unfair competitive advantage."

Berlin was fired as executive director in May 2016 for putting the proper conduct of his job ahead of political imperatives. In his absence, the NYSAC has become increasingly ill-informed as an institution and divorced from issues that are important to the conduct of fights.

"I know for a fact that communications devices are being used in the corner in New York," Lou DiBella says. "The trainer is there with a cell phone in his pocket and an earbud or Bluetooth in his ear. He gets information while the fight is going on, and sometimes it can give his fighter a competitive advantage."

Recently, Lee Park (a spokesperson who handles media inquiries on behalf of the NYSAC) was asked, "What is the policy of the New York State Athletic Commission regarding the use of smartphones and other communication devices by a fighter's seconds to receive information during a fight?"

Park responded that the NYSAC has "no specific policy" with regard to the issue but that it has "complete authority to prohibit or curtail specific activity that may be disruptive or call into question the integrity or safety of a fight."

Pressed for more, Park seemed unaware of the Brian Viloria precedent and cited a series of NYSAC rules and regulations that deal with disruptive or disorderly conduct by a fighter's seconds. Don't look for leadership from the New York State Athletic Commission on this issue.

Fistic Nuggets

Muhammad Ali was real. Tony Soprano wasn't. But they shared a bond as cultural icons and met, so to speak, under memorable circumstances.

The catalyst was Jules Feiler, who now owns the Pitching Staff, a New York–based public relations firm. In early 2006, Feiler was working on a project with Rasheda Ali (one of Muhammad's daughters) when Rasheda telephoned him and said, "I'm in New York with my dad, and he's bored. Can you think of something that would be fun for him to do?"

One of Feiler's clients at the time was Michael Imperioli, who played Christopher Moltisanti on *The Sopranos*. Jules telephoned Imperioli and asked, "How would you like to have dinner with Muhammad Ali tonight?"

"And he couldn't do it," Feiler recalls, "because they were in the middle of shooting an episode. But Michael said, if we wanted, he'd send an HBO van over to the hotel where we were staying to bring us to the set at Silvercup Studios."

"I was a huge fan of the show," Rasheda adds. "And Daddy had watched it a few times. I asked him if wanted to go, and he was all for it."

The average person couldn't just walk onto the set of *The Sopranos*. But Muhammad Ali wasn't an average person.

"They were on a break when we got there," Feiler remembers. "Some actors and crew people were sitting outside, smoking cigarettes. Michael and Steven Van Zandt [who played Silvio] came out to greet us. They were shooting an episode where Tony was in the hospital after he'd been shot by Uncle Junior. They brought us inside. James Gandolfini was sitting in a hospital bed. Remember, Tony was in a coma for several episodes that season. Anyway, James is sitting there dressed in a hospital gown splattered with blood, reading a newspaper and didn't look up. Ali walked over and smacked the newspaper. James ignored him. He didn't even look up to see who it was. So Ali smacked the paper again. James looked up, blurted out 'HOLY FUCK!' and jumped out of bed to hug Ali."

"It was fun," Rasheda says. "Obviously, everyone wanted to meet Daddy, and he wanted to meet them. He was always intrigued by actors who played gangsters and he had all sorts of questions. He asked James Gandolfini if he was a gangster in real life, and James said no, he was just acting."

A photographer named Shahar Azran was there and took some photos of Ali and Gandolfini together. Then Gandolfini realized that he couldn't be photographed wearing a hospital gown because the script was top secret and no one outside of the inner circle was supposed to know that Tony Soprano was in the hospital. So he changed into gym pants and a white tee shirt, and Azran took some more photos.

What does the photographer remember about that day?

At one point, Gandolfini nodded toward Ali and told Azran, "That's the difference between a celebrity and a legend."

★ ★ ★

The sad news that New York Mets pitching great Tom Seaver is suffering from dementia and will retire from public life is a reminder that all people from all walks of life are susceptible to the condition, not just fighters.

Seaver was on the list of A+ athletes who rose to prominence in the 1960s when advances in television were redefining the sports experience. Muhammad Ali was at the top of that list. Years ago, sportswriter Dick Schaap told me about an evening he spent with Ali and Seaver.

"In 1969, the year the Mets won their first World Series," Schaap reminisced, "I spent the last few days of the regular season with the team in Chicago. Ali was living there at the time. I was writing a book with Tom Seaver, and the three of us went out to dinner together. We met at a restaurant called the Red Carpet. I made the introductions. And of course, this was the year that Tom Seaver was Mr. Baseball, maybe even Mr. America. Ali and Tom got along fine. They really hit it off together. And after about half an hour, Ali in all seriousness turned to Seaver and said, 'You know, you're a nice fellow. Which paper do you write for?'"

★ ★ ★

Most of us remember our first watch with fondness. For Michael Buffer, the iconic ring announcer who has made "Let's get ready to rumbl-l-l-l-e" an international battle cry, the memory of his first watch is tinged with sadness.

"It was a Timex and I loved it," Buffer recalls. "My parents gave it to me when I was ten years old. It had a white face with some kind of silver-colored case and a black strap. One day, not long after I got it, I went swimming in a public park in Green Lake, Pennsylvania, and forgot to take it off. When I got out of the water, I realized what I'd done."

What happened next was inevitable.

"The face fogged up," Buffer continues. "The hands stopped moving. I was heartbroken. The watch didn't work anymore and I still wore it for a few weeks before I got rid of it. I was absolutely devastated. For thirty-five or forty years after that, every time I went swimming or took a shower or bath, I checked my wrist instinctively to make sure I wasn't wearing my watch."

Buffer now has an extensive collection of luxury timepieces.

"I like to dress well, and accessories are part of that," he says. "It has nothing to do with showing off. I just love good timepieces. The first good watch I had was a Baume Mercier that I got when I was in my thirties. That was a step up for me at that time in my life. As my career as a ring announcer flourished, I moved on from there."

Buffer keeps current on what's trendy but his preference in timepieces is classic elegance. There's no chance that he will look at a watch and tell the seller to "ice it."

"I don't want a watch that's trendy one year and a year later you look at it and ask, 'What is that?'" Michael notes. "I don't like the big sport watches. If a watch is too bulky, the cuff of my shirt doesn't flow down over it." And he's quick to add, "I don't need a watch that tells me how many miles I've walked or what my blood pressure is. I want a timepiece that looks good and tells me what time it is."

Buffer declines to say how many watches are in his collection other than to acknowledge that there are quite a few. "My most unique watch," he volunteers, "is probably a power reserve Panerai. They're no longer in production. And Rolexes are still my favorite. I have five of them. One of the many good things about a Rolex is that it's timeless."

So . . . Has Buffer ever thought about going to eBay and replacing his first Timex watch?

"No," he says with a shake of his head. "That's in the past now."

★ ★ ★

Every now and then, I watch an old boxing movie on television.

Gentleman Jim is a 1942 film starring Errol Flynn as James J. Corbett, the "scientific" fighter who dethroned an aging John L. Sullivan at the Olympic Club in New Orleans in 1892.

Flynn was a huge star in the 1930s and '40s. *The Adventures of Robin Hood* and *Captain Blood* were his most famous swashbuckling roles. *Gentleman Jim* was basely loosely on Corbett's autobiography. *Variety*, whose movie reviews carried considerable weight in those days, called it "a good film" before adding that it was "so far removed from fact that it's ludicrous" and concluding that the film's many fictions "take this picture out of the biographical class and into fantasy."

That's a fair appraisal. The movie is silly and unrealistic. But it's fun.

Ward Bond is engaging as John L. Sullivan, who Corbett dethrones in the film's climactic battle. Alexis Smith, a Canadian beauty who later enjoyed a successful career on Broadway (she was on the cover of *Time Magazine* during her 1971 Tony Award–winning run in *Follies*) plays Corbett's love interest, Victoria Ware.

The dialogue is vintage Hollywood.

When Corbett meets Sullivan for the first time, he tells The Great John L, "I've seen you around San Francisco a few times, but from a long distance, of course."

"Well," Sullivan responds, "seein' me from a long distance is a smart idea, young fella."

But it's Smith, as Ware, who has the film's best lines. As her romance with Corbett unfolds, she tells him, "A woman doesn't figure things out. She just knows all at once." Later, that evolves to, "I think you like me more than I like you. But it wouldn't surprise me if I loved you more than you love me."

Then, at last, Corbett and Ware kiss.

"I'm no gentleman," Corbett confesses.

"In that case," Ware counters, "I'm no lady."

★ ★ ★

Golden Boy fights in Las Vegas don't feel the same without Don Chargin there.

Chargin, who died last year at age ninety, promoted fights for more than six decades, most notably in California with Aileen Eaton and later with his wife, Lorraine. He helped build Golden Boy into a promotional power and was inducted into the International Boxing Hall of Fame in 2001.

Chargin was generous in sharing his knowledge with writers, fighters, managers, even rival promoters. And he always had a good tale to tell.

One of my favorite Don Chargin stories involves an incident that occurred at Pittsburgh International Airport. Don was walking down a corridor when his suitcase opened and the contents spilled out onto the floor. Moments like that are embarrassing. Personal belongings roll away. Fellow travelers in a hurry to get to where they're going walk by, chuckling at your plight.

Don was on his knees, gathering his belongings when a pleasant-looking man came up from behind, stopped, and said, "Let me help you with that." They finished the chore together. Don thanked him and then realized that the good Samaritan was Arnold Palmer.

★ ★ ★

Few people in boxing make a point more dramatically in or out of the ring than Bernard Hopkins. For three decades, he has confounded critics and defied expectations, inventing and reinventing himself time and again.

Unknown club fighter with an 0–1 ring record . . . Prospect . . . Contender . . . Beltholder . . . Legitimate champion . . . Ageless wonder with Hall of Fame Credentials . . . The Executioner . . . The Alien . . . BHop . . . Bernard has played all of these roles.

Hopkins agreed to pose for photographer Wojtek Urbanek at the annual Boxing Writers Association of America dinner. But before facing the camera, Bernard wanted to share some thoughts with me. Quite a few thoughts, actually. Words of wisdom like, "Anybody I fucked deserved it," and "I don't want to be a businessman; I want to be a business."

Bernard lectured nonstop for a good twenty minutes, often gesturing forcefully with his hands. At one juncture, to emphasize a point, he suggested that we simulate a pre-fight staredown.

"I'm watching this," Urbanek recalls. "And I said to myself, 'I have to capture this. Something important is going on here.'"

"Bernard is an amazing person," Wojtek adds. "He sees the big picture of things, although, very often, he is in the center of the picture."

★ ★ ★

What's it like for a promoter who feels as though he has finally made it to the big time?

Robert Waterman, who promoted fight cards in the United Kingdom and a half-dozen other countries from 1997 to 2012, recalls, "My breakthrough fight was a cruiserweight championship bout on EuroSport. I was standing in the ring before the fight, feeling quite pleased with myself, when my cell phone rang. The fighters weren't in the ring yet so I answered it. And the first thing I heard was my mother's voice saying, 'Tuck your shirt in. You look like a slob.'"

★ ★ ★

Longtime boxing writer Norm Frauenheim was chatting with Roberto Duran over dinner in Las Vegas earlier this year when "Manos de Piedra" began reminiscing about a 2001 automobile accident in Argentina that almost cost him his life.

"I was in a coma for two months," Duran recounted, underlining the gravity of his condition.

"Two months?" Frauenheim said incredulously.

Duran shrugged and responded, "Two months, two weeks, two days, two hours. It was a coma, okay?"

For the record; in Duran's 2016 autobiography—*I Am Duran*—Roberto recounts that he was "dead on the operating table for thirty seconds" and went into cardiac arrest "for two or three minutes."

★ ★ ★

"Don Elbaum," Jerry Izenberg once wrote, "lives on nerve and hustle and dreams he will never realize."

Elbaum, a 2019 inductee into the International Boxing Hall of Fame, has spent his life in boxing as a promoter, matchmaker, manager, and jack-of-all-trades. He has been referred to as "a low-grade hustler who's too low to grade" and "a charming rogue without the charm." That's by people who like him.

Elbaum gave Don King his start in the sweet science. He has connived with referees and judges and once planned to promote fights in Nevada at an upscale brothel called Sherry's Ranch. "Bordello Boxing" (as the venture was known) failed to get off the ground when the Nevada state legislature put its foot down.

The most famous tale involving Elbaum dates to 1965. Sugar Ray Robinson was nearing the end of his glorious ring career and readying to fight Peter Schmidt in Johnstown, Pennsylvania. The media was invited to a publicity dinner.

"I looked around for the two most battered boxing gloves I could find," Elbaum (who promoted the bout) later recalled. "The highlight of the evening was when I got up and said, 'Ray, don't ask me how I got these. But twenty-five years ago, you made your professional debut at Madison Square Garden, and these are the gloves you wore in that fight.' Ray's eyes actually teared up. He was genuinely moved by the moment. He took the gloves and cradled them in his arms like he was holding a newborn babe."

Then someone suggested that Robinson put the gloves on for a photo op. That was when the world discovered that Don Elbaum had given Sugar Ray Robinson two left gloves.

"I love boxing," Elbaum. told me years ago. "I've given my life to boxing. It's the reason I've been broke, in jail, lived out of crummy motel rooms. You name it, and boxing has done it to me. But if I had my life to live over again, I'd do it all the same way. Boxing is in my blood. It's a beautiful sickness."

So . . . With that as background, it's worth recounting a telephone call I received recently from Elbaum.

"I gotta tell you this," Don proclaimed. "It's a classic. I was on a train yesterday going from Philadelphia to Providence. I was reading the *New York Times* magazine section. It had a big article about Glenda Jackson playing in *King Lear. King Lear* is a great play. I think Shakespeare wrote it. And Glenda Jackson was on the magazine cover."

"Anyway," Elbaum continued, "there was this woman sitting across the aisle from me. I'm guessing she was in her sixties. I glanced over at her. We made eye contact. And then she said to me, 'It's so nice to be sitting across the aisle from an intellectual.'"

★ ★ ★

Ricky Jay, the masterful magician who captivated the world with sleight-of-hand artistry and was also an accomplished film actor, died in November 2018 at his home in Los Angeles.

Jay was a boxing fan and ardent admirer of Muhammad Ali. Ali, in turn, loved magic and delighted in performing simple magic tricks for enthralled onlookers.

Jay witnessed one of Ali's performances and was amused but not enthralled.

"Muhammad performed several crude tricks," Jay told me years later. "And when he was done, he broke the cardinal rule of magicians by explaining how each trick was performed. But his performance was so clumsy that, really, no further elucidation was necessary."

★ ★ ★

Another fistic nugget involving Don Elbaum . . . He's the promoter who put Michael Buffer in a boxing ring for the first time.

"It was in Atlantic City in the summer of 1982," Buffer recalls. "I was working as a model and pitching myself to casinos, trying to get in the door as a ring announcer. I'd met Elbaum before and been to a few of his shows at the Tropicana. I asked him if I could work one of his fight cards. And he told me no, he already had a ring announcer, but there was another life-changing opportunity he could make available to me."

And the life-changing opportunity was?

"A publicity event for his next show at the Tropicana," Buffer recounts. "He didn't pay me. But Don said it would be an incredible opportunity because hundreds, maybe thousands, of people would see me."

"And that," Buffer explains, "is how I wound up in a boxing ring in a parking lot outside a mall in Pleasantville, New Jersey, on a hot, sticky, muggy summer afternoon. At most, there were fifteen people watching.

I introduced the fighters. There were a few rounds of sparring. And that was it."

And now a word from Don Elbaum . . .

"Let me tell you my version," Elbaum says. "I was using Ed Derian as a ring announcer back then. Michael was sitting next to me at one of my shows and said, 'I could do that.' So I gave him his first break. Michael is where he is today because of the exposure he got that afternoon in the parking lot in Pleasantville, New Jersey. And because I'm such a nice guy, when Michael went on to bigger and better things, I never stood in his way."

★ ★ ★

And another memory tied to Muhammad Ali . . .

Recently, I was listening to the tape of an interview I conducted with Mickey Mantle in 1989 when I was researching *Muhammad Ali: His Life and Times*. Most of what Mantle had to say that afternoon is incorporated in that Ali biography and a collection of articles published under the title *Thomas Hauser on Sports*. But there was one exchange I'd forgotten that bears repeating now.

Toward the end of the interview, I asked Mantle if he'd ever been in a fight—not an organized amateur fight but a playground or street encounter—and whether he thought he'd had the tools to be a boxer.

"Through the years, I've had maybe three or four fights," Mantle answered. "What do you call it if you can't take a punch, a glass jaw? I might have had a glass jaw for all I know. Fortunately, nobody ever hit me in the head."

I don't remember anyone coming home from a night at the fights and saying,
"Wow! The music was great."

Fight Night Music

Music has been part of sports for well over a century. The Notre Dame band played at the first football game between the Fighting Irish and Michigan in 1887 and hasn't missed a home game in 132 years.

Gladys Goodding played the organ for the Brooklyn Dodgers from 1942 until the Dodgers moved west after the 1957 season and was an integral part of the Ebbets Field experience. She was also a fixture at Madison Square Garden, playing the National Anthem before boxing matches and entertaining crowds during Knicks and Rangers home games until her death in 1963.

In recent years, music has been increasingly prominent in sports settings. Don't expect to see Tiger Woods readying for a birdie putt at the Masters while "We Will Rock You" blasts in the background. But onsite music keeps expanding.

"Na Na Hey Hey Kiss Him Goodbye" has been heard at sports events dating back to 1977 when Chicago White Sox organist Nancy Faust began playing it to serenade opposing pitchers who walked from the mound after being knocked out of the game: "Na na, na na na na, hey hey-ey, goodbye."

The New York Yankees have played "YMCA" by the Village People during the seventh-inning stretch since 1996 with the grounds crew acting out the letters.

NFL cheerleaders and NBA dancers have danced to music during timeouts for decades.

And let's not forget the familiar guitar riffs from Gary Glitter's "Rock and Roll" and the White Stripes's "Seven Nation Army" that rev up the crowd.

Cedric Kushner, who died in 2015, was the first promoter to use music as a significant component of fight night shows. Jim DiLorenzo, who worked with Kushner and was the driving force behind the effort to blend boxing and music, recalls, "We started experimenting with music at the Hammerstein Ballroom in New York in early 2000. It was an effort to create a club-party vibe. We had a DJ and invited the right people. We felt we were onto something. Then we launched *Thunderbox*, which joined live hip-hop music and boxing."

Kushner's *Thunderbox* fight cards were syndicated nationally with most of the events originating in New York or Las Vegas. Cedric had been a concert promoter before turning to boxing, so he was comfortable in that world.

"We brought in some great talent to go with the fights," DiLorenzo reminisces. "Wyclef Jean opened the debut show. Later, we had Fat Joe, Ultra V, Doug E. Fresh, Eve, a lot of great performers. But the productions were too expensive. Not the talent, the productions. We could never get the advertising to support what we were doing. The numbers just didn't add up."

Meanwhile, in mid-2000, HBO launched *KO Nation*, a Saturday afternoon series that mixed hip-hop artists and dancers with boxing. Dave Harmon, who was the coordinating producer, remembers, "We wanted to do something different and expand the appeal of boxing on HBO to a younger demographic. We put a DJ in the arena. We had music between fights, music between rounds, and the KO Nation Dancers. No one would think twice about any of that now. Every big show has a DJ in the arena. But there was a lot of debate about it at the time."

More significantly, ratings were consistently low and *KO Nation* was cancelled the following year.

Fast-forward to 2007 when Top Rank took the lead in bringing onsite music back to boxing. Top Rank president Todd duBoef recounts the impetus for the move.

"We began adding music to our in-arena production when Miguel Cotto fought Zab Judah at Madison Square Garden," duBoef says. "There's so much unpredictability on fight night. There are times when fights run short and, because of the demands of television, a forty-five-minute delay is unavoidable. You need something to fill the downtime. The question is what. At first, the music was considered disruptive because people were used to being in an environment where they could hear a pin drop. And the HBO producers were screaming at us, 'What are you doing? You're killing our production.' Can you imagine a Notre Dame football game and telling the Irish marching band to be quiet because the announcers are talking? But eventually, they got used to it."

Rick Bernstein (executive producer for HBO Sports since 2000) has his own memories of the music and notes, "You have to balance the experience for the thousands of fans who are watching a show in the arena against the experience for the millions of fans who are watching on television. During a round, the announcers can wear headsets. But you don't want them wearing headsets when they're on camera between fights. You want them to use stick mics then. And there were times when the music was so loud that, without headsets, the announcers literally couldn't hear what the announcer standing next to them was saying."

"Also," Bernstein continues, "as producers, we wanted to hear what was being said in the corner between rounds. You do that by holding a fishpole mic over the fighter and the trainer wearing a clip-on. But there were times when the music made that impossible. We were literally begging the promoter to turn the volume down."

Eventually, HBO solved the between-fights problem by outfitting its announcers with the kind of noise-cancelling earpieces that musicians use in live concerts so they can hear themselves play. And the use of directional microphones in given situations enabled viewers at home to hear most of what the production truck wanted them to hear.

Music is now part of the in-arena experience for virtually all big fights and many small fight cards. In addition to fighter ringwalks, it has made its way into the break between fights and even the one minute rest period between rounds. In essence, it's mood music designed to give onsite fans the feeling that they're at a happening.

"Some people love it; some don't," duBoef acknowledges. "I understand that. But when it's done right, audio entertainment helps keep the crowd engaged. It's another element, along with lighting and video, that creates an entertaining environment and enhances the in-arena experience. Let's be realistic. If the arena is quiet, it feels less exciting."

Most discussions about fight-night music focus on two variables: what's played and at what volume.

Almost always, the promoter hires the DJ and the DJ chooses the music subject to the promoter's instructions. For most big arenas and many small sites, the license fee for the music is covered by the venue's

ASCAP, BMI, and SESAC performance rights licenses so the promoter and DJ have free reign regarding what to play.

Hip-hop and heavy beat are the sounds most often heard. Often, that's at odds with audience demographic. And in truth, there are times when no one in the crowd (including young people) seems engaged. That said; the theory behind the choice of hip-hop and heavy beat is that they create the feeling among those in attendance that they've stepped into the fighters' world.

Counterintuitively, "Sweet Caroline" has become enormously popular among boxing fans in the United Kingdom. The song was written and recorded by Neil Diamond in 1969. The Boston Red Sox have played it during games at Fenway Park since 1997, and the tradition has spread to other venues. In England, it's played just before the ring walk for big fights promoted by Matchroom. And the crowd loves it. It energizes the fans. They sing along.

One might ask, "Would anyone object if a fight card also featured Mick Jagger singing 'Satisfaction'?"

And of course, national anthems are often sung. Some fight cards have live performances of as many as three anthems (the host country and the respective homeland for each main event fighter). Singers range in ability from accomplished musicians to unskilled local talent.

Most anthem performances are eminently forgettable. But Joe Frazier is remembered musically for having sung the national anthem before the September 15, 1978, rematch in New Orleans between Muhammad Ali and Leon Spinks. And R. Kelly raised eyebrows with his rendition of "The Star Spangled Banner" prior to the 2005 rematch between Jermain Taylor and Bernard Hopkins when he exhorted the crowd to "clap your hands" while two dancers simulated ballroom dancing in the ring.

Then there's the question of volume. Music is played at other sports events. But it isn't as omnipresent or loud as is often the case at fights.

At its worst, fight night music is intrusive and diminishes the onsite experience.

Here, Todd duBoef agrees, saying, "The music can't be so loud that it assaults the senses. Different arenas have different sound systems. The Theater at Madison Square Garden has a low ceiling and the speakers turn inward so it can get very loud in there, particularly for fans who are sitting in the direct path of a speaker. There have been times at The

Theater when the music was too loud and I asked the DJ to turn it down. The idea is to give people in the arena a pleasurable experience and add to the excitement, not blow them out."

Some criticism of fight night music is generational.

Hall of Fame promoter Russell Peltz opines, "One of the great things about going to the fights used to be talking to the person sitting next to you about the fight you just saw or the round that was just fought. And you can't do that as much anymore because the music is so loud. You have to shout to talk to the person sitting next to you. It's another example of boxing today being too much sizzle and not enough steak. Forget the music and have better fights."

Don Elbaum, who will join Peltz in Canastota this June, is in accord and adds, "Most of the time, the music is a poor attempt to cover up the lack of action. Part of boxing's appeal is that it's the most basic of all sports, and the music detracts from that. The fans are coming to fights, not a hip-hop concert."

Then there's veteran publicist Bill Caplan, who recalls, "There used to be a wonderful stadium called the Hollywood Legion Stadium that had boxing through the 1950s. There was a band there called the Hollywood Legion Band that played march music—John Philip Sousa, stuff like that—between fights. That was good. People loved the music. It wasn't intrusive. It lit the place up. And now—"

Caplan shakes his head.

"I don't mind it that they play music," he says. "The truth is, I mind the music they play. I love almost everything about going to the fights, but I loathe the music. And if you look around the arena when it's playing, no one seems to be enjoying it. No one is dancing. No one is singing."

Then Caplan tells one of his favorite stories.

On August 25, 2012, Don Chargin promoted a fight card in Fairfield, California. Earlier in the day, Bill had given him a gift: a CD of Frank Sinatra's greatest hits. That night, Chargin handed the CD to the arena DJ and told him, "This is what you play tonight."

"What about the fighters' ringwalk music?" the DJ asked.

"They can walk out to Sinatra," Chargin instructed. "If you play anything else, you're fired."

"None of the fighters or fans complained," Caplan notes in closing.

This was one of several articles about other sports that I wrote for Sporting News in 2019. If I was prescient, I would have kept my old baseball cards. Instead, I kept a board game called All-Star Baseball.

Before Video Games,
There Was All-Star Baseball

You've probably never heard of Ethan Allen. He was born in 1904, died in 1993, and played for the Cincinnati Reds, New York Giants, St. Louis Cardinals, Philadelphia Phillies, and St. Louis Browns from 1926 to 1938. He had a career batting average of .300 and amassed 1,325 base hits. From 1948 through 1968, he was the head baseball coach at Yale, where his players included future United States president George Herbert Walker Bush.

And Allen's real claim to fame?

He invented a game called All-Star Baseball that was manufactured by Cadaco-Ellis and became the best-selling baseball board game of all time.

Before the *Ping-BOOM-Splat!-Bonk* of the video age, sports games for children involved throwing dice, spinning a wheel, or pointing a piece in the right direction. No quick hands or hand-eye coordination were necessary. The games were durable. More than a few baby boomers still have their old Monopoly and Scrabble sets in a closet, not to mention chess and checkers. They're half a century old and remain in vintage working order. Kids never had to buy new software or a new operating system.

In a 1983 interview with Bill Madden of *Sporting News*, Allen recalled, "I had this idea, even when I was playing, that you could put a man's playing record on a disc. While I was with the Cubs, I went to various manufacturers with the hope of selling the idea to them as a game, only to have most of them practically kick me out of their offices."

In 1941, five years after his quest began, Allen brought his concept to Charles Mazer (head of Cadaco-Ellis, a Chicago-based game manufacturer). Ellis liked the idea, and All-Star Baseball was born.

The first edition, manufactured in 1941, sold for $1.25. It had a cardboard playing field that fit snugly into the game box, a scoreboard, two cardboard blocks with spinners attached (one for each team), and forty round cardboard discs with die-cut centers.

Each disc represented a different all-star player from the 1941 season. They were designed like pie charts and were the key to the game. Sections numbered one through fourteen were irregularly arranged around the circumference of each disc. One represented a home run. Ten was a strike out. The design of each disc reflected probabilities based on the player's real-life batting statistics. For example, Babe Ruth had the largest home run zone of any player. He also walked and struck out a lot.

In choosing teams, the two players (managers, if you will) usually divided the discs into American League vs. National League. But if they preferred, they could hold their own draft. There was a designated field position for each player. Under the rules of the game, each position had to be included in the lineup.

In terms of strategy, managers wanted their best hitters in the lineup. Babe Ruth (who hit for average and power) was an obvious choice. So was Ted Williams. Ty Cobb was a good bet too. If the opposing manager allowed it, playing Ruth as a pitcher (even though his disc designated him as a right fielder) was a smart move since it removed a weak hitting pitcher from the lineup in favor of another good-hitting outfielder.

Once the managers had chosen their lineups and put their hitters in order, they placed their player discs on the spinner block batter-by-batter to determine each batter's fate. The manager flicked the spinner with a forefinger. Whatever number the point of the spinner came to rest on dictated the result of a given at bat. If the spinner landed directly on the line between two numbers, the resolution went in favor of the batter just as, in baseball, a tie goes to the runner.

The manager of the team at bat could also choose to insert one of two strategy discs for steals, hit-and-run plays, squeeze plays, and sacrifice bunts. If a weak hitter was at bat, advanced strategy made sense. But not if Babe Ruth was at the plate.

Later editions of the game incorporated a third specialty disk to determine the result of fly balls, ground balls, and singles (for example, the possibility of an error or the batter being thrown out trying to stretch a single into a double).

Baseball is unique among team games in that the defense has the ball at the start of each play and initiates the play when the pitcher chooses to do so. But All-Star Baseball was all about the batter. The skill of the opposing pitcher was irrelevant. So was speed. When stealing a base, the fleet-of-foot Ty Cobb had no more of an edge than the legendarily slow Ernie Lombardi.

The initial target audience for the game was boys ages nine through twelve. It allowed them to manage their own big league baseball team. And just as important, All-Star Baseball was a level playing field where a boy could compete with his older brother on even terms and the class klutz was the equal of his most athletically gifted schoolmates.

Each year, Cadaco-Ellis manufactured new player discs, adding some players and replacing others. The latest set of player discs could be purchased annually by mail directly from Cadaco.

Nineteen of the forty players from the 1941 edition also appeared in the forty-player 1942 edition. Succeeding years brought further personnel changes and slightly altered pie charts based on updated career statistics. A 1946 edition added Hall of Fame immortals to the player lineup.

All-Star Baseball fired the imagination. In the first decades of its existence, there were few if any sports events on television and, except for films, no other available video images. Thus, for generations of children, a small round cardboard disc three-and-a-half inches in diameter was the physical embodiment of Babe Ruth. The wide number one sector on his disc stood out as boldly as the record 714 career home runs that The Babe had walloped.

The game was also an entry point into baseball history for boys who were unfamiliar with Hall of Fame greats like Rogers Hornsby and Honus Wagner.

Ultimately, tens of millions of sets were sold As sales mounted, Mazur was acclaimed as a "genius" for having had the foresight to purchase rights to All-Star Baseball. But he eschewed the label, ruefully acknowledging that, a decade earlier, he'd passed on the opportunity to buy and manufacture a board game called Monopoly.

Eventually, All-Star Baseball player discs were manufactured annually for every team in the major leagues. In 1968, the cutout was eliminated from each disc and the spinner blocks were replaced by plastic sleeves. But by then, the game's long run of success was nearing an end.

Strat-O-Matic—a new dice game—had begun production in 1961 and was eating away at sales of All-Star Baseball. Then the video game revolution began. In 1989, All-Star Baseball added photographs to the player discs in an effort to make them attractive to collectors. But the new "collectibles" never caught on.

Meanwhile, another problem loomed. For a half century, Ethan Allen had contacted each player represented on an All-Star Baseball disc to get permission to use his name and statistics. As noted by Bernard Crowley of the Society for American Baseball Research, "The players, many of whom felt honored to be included in the game, were not paid."

In 1993, the Major League Baseball Players Association demanded licensing fees for the use of players' names, statistics, and images. At that point, economic reality dictated an end to new editions of All-Star Baseball. A 2003 agreement with the MLBPA led to one more year of manufacture but that was all. The arrival of Fantasy Baseball shoveled dirt on the grave.

Vintage editions of All-Star Baseball are now sold on eBay. Some independent entrepreneurs (in apparent violation of licensing and trademark laws) design and print player discs from all eras, including the present, which they sell online today.

That brings us to contemporary times. My 1950s edition of All-Star Baseball has been in a hall closet for decades. Recently, I decided to revisit my youth by playing a game.

Steve Albert is the youngest of three Albert brothers, who comprise the first generation of one of sportscasting's royal families. Steve's stint as a Major League Baseball commentator began in 1979 when he replaced Lindsey Nelson as a TV and radio play-by-play announcer for the New York Mets. The job lasted for three years, during which he shared a microphone with Bob Murphy and Ralph Kiner. Steve has also called NFL, NBA, and NHL games, and spent two decades as a blow-by-blow commentator for Showtime Championship Boxing. I can't think of another announcer with all five of these credits on his résumé.

"All-Star Baseball was my favorite game when I was a boy," Steve told me when I raised the possibility of our playing against each other. "I didn't play it much with Marv because of the age difference between us. But I played it with Al all the time."

Several days later, I brought my All-Star Baseball game to Steve's apartment. That meant he was the home team. Clearly, Steve was into the spirit of things. When I arrived, he was wearing an old Brooklyn Dodgers game jersey with what looked like a tobacco stain on the front.

"Not tobacco, guacamole," he explained.

Steve had also rummaged through a closet and taken out an old Louisville Slugger baseball bat and two gloves, one of which looked like it had been used as a teething ring by a family of pit bulls.

"That's the first glove I ever had," he told me.

Rather than play American League vs. National League, we divided the discs into two teams based on the era in which the players played. Steve had choice of team and chose the modern all-stars ("modern" being a relative term). I had the old-timers.

As kids, we'd played All-Star baseball sitting on the floor. Now, as a concession to aging muscles, tendons, and ligaments, we sat on a sofa and set the playing field and discs out on the coffee table in front of us.

Our game was scheduled for five innings since a nine-inning game seemed a bit long for our attention span.

The starting lineup for my Old Timers team was:

LF   Ty Cobb
2B   Rogers Hornsby
RF   Babe Ruth
1B   Lou Gehrig
CF   Joe DiMaggio
SS   Honus Wagner
C   Bill Dickey
3B   Pie Traynor
P   Walter Johnson

Steve's Modern All-Stars were:

2B   Jackie Robinson
SS   Ernie Banks
1B   Stan Musial
CF   Mickey Mantle
LF   Ted Williams
C   Yogi Berra

3B   Eddie Matthews

RF   Al Kaline

P   Bob Feller

"It pains me to leave Hank Aaron out of my starting lineup," Steve said. "But I have to go with Ted Williams."

Before the first spin, we stood for the national anthem which was sung via laptop by James Taylor.

I placed my Ty Cobb disc on the spinning block.

Steve segued to play-by-play mode: "Top of the first inning. Leading off for the Old Timers, Ty Cobb."

Cobb flied out.

Rogers Hornsby drew a walk.

Babe Ruth advanced to the spinning block.

I spun . . . Round and round the spinner went. . . .

YES !!!

The point of the spinner came to rest in the middle of the sector labeled "#1" . . . HOME RUN !!! The Old-Timers led 2–0.

Lou Gehrig singled and advanced to second on a groundout by Joe DiMaggio. Honus Wagner doubled Gehrig home, and I was up 3–0.

When the top of the first inning ended, Steve and I sang a beer commercial from our younger days: "Schaefer is the one beer to have when you're having more than one."

Then it was Steve's turn at bat. Or to be more precise, Jackie Robinson at the plate.

"This is my first All-Star Baseball spin in more than fifty years," Steve noted.

Robinson singled. Ernie Banks was up next and also singled. But Robinson was thrown out when he went too far while rounding second base.

"Jackie Robinson making a base-running mistake? Never!" Steve groused.

Stan Musial singled Banks to third. But Mickey Mantle and Ted Williams flied out to end the inning.

"The Mick had a rough night last night," Steve hypothesized. "He was out late drinking."

I scored two more runs in the top of the second inning on RBI singles by Ruth and Gehrig. Steve picked up a run on a solo homer by Eddie Mathews in the bottom of the frame . . . The score stood 5–1 in my favor.

Top of the third inning. Bill Dickey, my catcher, came to the plate. Dickey was playing injured. At least, that's what we presumed since his disc was held together by yellowing scotch tape. Dickey tripled and was singled home by Pie Traynor, who then scored on a triple by Nap Lajoie . . . 7–1.

"The crowd is not in a great mood right now," Steve informed me. "I'm getting annihilated."

There was a break in the action while we sang "Take Me Out to the Ballgame."

Then the roof caved in on my head. Steve sent eleven batters to the plate in the bottom of the third inning and scored six runs to knot the game at seven runs apiece.

Now, suddenly, the Old-Timers' bats were cold. And the Modern All-Stars stayed hot, scoring two more runs in the bottom of the fourth to take a 9–7 lead.

"This could be a comeback of historic proportions," Steve proclaimed.

Top of the fifth inning. My final at bat. I was trailing by two runs.

Strike out . . . Fly out . . . Down to my last out. . . .

Steve began to applaud rhythmically and stomp his feet.

George Sisler, who was pinch hitting, grounded out . . . Game over.

"Don't feel bad," Steve told me over dinner that night. "I'll give you a rematch in fifty years."

It wasn't Peggy Sue Got Married *or* The Best of Times. *But it was fun.*

Going Home for a High School Football Game

I've spent a lot of time over the years watching football.

I got interested in the sport at age ten.

Football is omnipresent on television now from the preseason in August through the Super Bowl in February. But when I was young, only a handful of games, college and pro, were televised each week. There was no cable TV, no *Monday Night Football*.

In the early 1960s, I was a student at Mamaroneck High School—a public school in the suburbs of New York. I went to almost every MHS home game, but the NFL mattered more to me at that time in my life. Then I enrolled at Columbia and the hapless Lions captured my heart. I still go to a Columbia football game each year. I've been to a few big-time college encounters and a handful of NFL contests. Mostly, I watch football on television. I don't sit through many games in their entirety but enjoy watching bits and pieces of them.

At a guess, I'd say that, over the years, I've watched an average of three hours of football a week on television when the game is in season.

"That's not a lot," you say?

Do the math.

I'm seventy-three years old, so I've been watching football for sixty-three years times twenty-two weeks a year times three hours a week. That comes to four thousand hours of my life spent watching football on television. One hundred work weeks. Two years of a fulltime job.

Sometimes I say to myself, "Football is a very stupid game." Young men push each other around and knock each other down while someone runs around with a funny-shaped ball. They inflict physical damage on each other that, at its worst, ranges from broken bones and torn muscles that will cause chronic pain and hobble movement later in life to long-term brain damage.

So why do we celebrate high school football?

For starters, it's a unifying force. Rooting for the team makes students part of a group and brings disparate elements of a community together.

For the players, there's pleasure in playing and lessons to be learned. Lessons about hard work, lines of authority, trusting co-workers, and being part of a team. Football is a great team sport. The plays work because eleven young men coordinate their efforts on each play to make them work. Players are dependent on their teammates to make things happen.

Also, it's pretty cool to be a high school football hero.

Jerry Izenberg knows football. He's the dean of American sportswriters and one of two journalists who has been credentialed to cover every Super Bowl ever. He's also the author of *Rozelle* (the definitive biography of the commissioner who remade pro football) and *No Medals for Trying* (an inside look at the 1989 Giants under coach Bill Parcells).

"I love high school football," Izenberg says. "I love watching the players play." He pauses. "I said 'play.' They're working hard. They're busting their butts. But they understand that it's a game, and they have the game in perspective."

Earlier this month, I decided to go home for a Mamaroneck High School football game for the first time in more than fifty years.

We're not talking Pennsylvania coal country or *Friday Night Lights*. Some of the teams that Mamaroneck plays each year have an impressive roster of NFL alumni. Eleven White Plains High School graduates suited up in the pros, most notably Hall of Fame receiver Art Monk. Nine New Rochelle High School graduates played in the NFL including George Starke ("head hog" for the 1983 Super Bowl champion Washington Redskins) and the infamous Ray Rice.

One Mamaroneck Tiger made it to the bigtime.

Billy Van Heusen graduated from MHS in 1964 (one year after I did). Between 1968 and 1976, he played 109 games with the Denver Broncos. He was a punter in the pros, averaging 41.7 yards per kick on 574 punts during his career. He also saw time as a wide receiver (82 receptions for 1,684 yards and 11 touchdowns), rushed for 171 yards and a touchdown on 13 carries, and completed two of five passes for 71 yards. In 1974, he was chosen as a second-team All-Pro by the Pro Football Writers Association.

Van Heusen turned seventy-four this summer. I tracked him down in Denver, where he oversees a residential real estate brokerage company called the Billy Van Heusen Team. We didn't know each other well when we were young, but we grew up with the same teachers and peers in the same surroundings.

"I learned to punt in elementary school," Van Heusen told me. "Jim Smith [the gym teacher] taught me. I never thought punting would take me anywhere in life, but that was what got me to the pros. It's been a long time since I went to a Mamaroneck game, but my memories of Mamaroneck are all good."

A growth spurt and summer of working out with weights pushed Van Heusen to six feet tall and close to 200 pounds before his senior year of high school.

"I got big enough that year to be good," Billy reminisced. "We had good players who were great guys. Coach [Roy] O'Neill put discipline in the program but he made it fun. I had pretty good stats and learned what it meant to be part of a team. Football was an important part of that growing up time in my life when I became more serious and more responsible."

Those "pretty good stats" included a season average of 15.2 yards per carry and a game against Scarsdale when Van Heusen scored three touchdowns on runs of 60 yards or more.

Then came The Game.

Mamaroneck had won its first six outings in 1963 by a combined score of 180 to 14. The season finale was against Port Chester, a rivalry that dated back to 1920 and continues to this day.

"Port Chester was our biggest rival," Billy recalls. "We were up 21–0 at the half. Then we got complacent. We knew what we had to do. Port Chester just executed better."

A missed extra point left Mamaroneck clinging to a precarious 21–20 edge as the clock ticked down. But it didn't click fast enough. Port Chester scored with 33 seconds left in the game for a 27–21 triumph.

"It was the worst thing that ever happened to me in football," Van Heusen says. "The hardest loss on the football field I ever had."

That brings us to Mamaroneck High School football today.

High school football has changed radically over the years. Some high school programs are geared toward producing Division I college football players. Signing days are huge. Students host their own press conferences to announce where they'll be playing ball in the fall.

Mamaroneck football is a throwback to an earlier era when amateur sports were more innocent than they are now and high school football certainly was. At MHS, the gridiron values are pretty much the same today as they were fifty years ago. Four players from last year's 7-and-2 squad are now in college football programs—at Amherst, Hamilton, St. Lawrence, and Macalester. It's rare that an MHS graduate plays bigtime college football. Going back five years, Alex Parkinson (MHS '14), who went on to play wide receiver at Princeton, comes the closest.

But there have been changes.

When I was in high school, sports was a male-dominated world. Mamaroneck had a full complement of boys' varsity teams but no girls' varsity sports. That's different now. And Bari Suman (a graduate of SUNY Courtland) is in her sixteenth year as the school's athletic director.

Fifty years ago, the MHS student body was almost uniformly white with a few students of color sprinkled in. The poor Italian American kids—many of whom lived near the railroad tracks—were the "minority" students. The student body today is classified as 70 percent white, 20 percent Hispanic, 5 percent Asian, 4 percent black, and 1 percent other.

Anthony Vitti is Mamaroneck's current football coach. Both of his parents graduated from MHS. He grew up in Mamaroneck, played football for the Tigers, and earned an undergraduate degree at the University of Albany followed by a master's degree from Iona. He joined the MHS coaching staff in 2000 and was named head coach before the start of the 2010 season. He also teaches biology.

Vitti is in his early forties, outgoing, articulate, and a good coach.

"We want our kids to understand that they're part of something that's larger than themselves," he says. "They're part of a team. And the team is part of a larger community. Our program is motivated by five core values. Be honest; be accountable; be tough, mentally and physically; compete; and finish. I tell our kids that we have a twenty-year plan. Learn your lessons on the field and apply them later in life. Wins and losses come and go. Your character and values will stay with you forever."

A recent study by the National Federation of State High School Associations revealed that, although the population has grown by 7.5 percent over the past decade, participation in high school football has dropped by 9.5 percent, largely because of parental concern regarding head injuries.

"An awareness of head injuries is at the forefront of everything we do," Vitti says when the issue is raised. "Everything from how we block and tackle to how we practice."

A half-century ago, Mamaroneck football games were played on Saturday afternoon. Now most games are scheduled for seven o'clock on Friday evening, a better fit with student and administrator schedules.

On September 6, I boarded a 4:51 p.m. train from Grand Central Station in New York and arrived in Larchmont (adjacent to Mamaroneck) at 5:27 p.m. I'd planned to walk the mile to the high school and hoped to write about a warm September evening with a gentle breeze. But there had been gray skies with intermittent showers during the day and it was raining when the train pulled in so I took a taxi.

Most of the places that anchored my high school years are now off limits or long gone. My father died in 1994 and the house that I grew up in was sold. The local pizza hangout and once familiar stores exist only in memory.

Memorial Field, where MHS plays its home games, now has lights and artificial turf. But sitting on the Mamaroneck side, the view is pretty much the same as it was a half-century ago. Seven rows of aluminum bleachers stretch between the twenty yard lines. There's seating for about sixty people on the opposite side of the field and a small electronic scoreboard behind the east end zone.

There was no *Twilight Zone* time warp when I walked to the edge of the field. I wasn't transported back decades in time.

About forty minutes before kickoff, a hard rain began to fall and I sought sanctuary in a corridor outside the gym.

Eight minutes before the seven o'clock kickoff, Coach Vitti addressed the team. He told them the game was "our little slice of heaven," that their classmates and people who live in the community want to be "part of the pomp and glitz of football. But you guys," he reminded them, "get to live it." He closed with the thought, "You are all one."

Mercifully, the rain stopped shortly before kickoff. But there was a sharp damp wind for most of the game and it was unseasonably cold for early September. I had come up from the city with a very light jacket. Most of the locals were wearing parkas.

No ticket was necessary for admission. There were only a few hundred spectators on hand when the game began, but the stands filled up nicely as the first quarter progressed. A lot of the fans appeared to be between the ages of twenty-five and forty. There were fewer students than I'd expected. Those who were there looked very young to me. And I'm sure I looked old to them.

It was the opening game of the season for both teams. Four twelve-minute quarters.

Mamaroneck, as befitting Tigers, wore black uniforms with orange trim. The North Rockland Red Raiders wore red and white.

North Rockland had eight players who weighed 240 pounds or more. That would be decisive as the game wore on.

Mamaroneck went three-and-out on its first possession and a fumbled snap led to a 7-yard punt which gave North Rockland the ball on the Mamaroneck 44 yard line. The Red Raiders immediately marched in for a score with less resistance from the defense than Tiger fans would have liked. The extra point attempt was low and to the left leaving the score 6–0 North Rockland.

Mamaroneck went three-and-out again on its next possession and was forced to punt. This time, the Tiger defense held. And a snap over the North Rockland punter's head gave MHS the ball on the Red Raider 5 yard line. Three plays from scrimmage resulted in a loss of four yards. Mamaroneck settled for a 26-yard field goal to pull within 6–3.

On the next series, the Tiger defense held yet again. And the crowd came to its feet when Jack Betton, an MHS junior, returned a punt 60 yards for an apparent touchdown. But the return was nullified by an illegal block.

A punt left North Rockland with the ball on its own two-yard line, pinned against its own end zone. Again, the Tiger defense held. After a poor punt, the Tigers had the ball on the North Rockland 32 but the drive ended with an interception.

Near the end of the half, the North Rockland kicking game (which was abysmal) came up short once more when a Mamaroneck punt was fumbled and recovered by the Tigers on the Red Raider five-yard line. But again, Mamaroneck was forced to settle for a field goal making the score 6–6 at the half.

Coach Vitti addressed the defense at halftime outside the gym.

"Defense! Great job! We're okay with what we're doing."

Speaking to the offense, an assistant coach was less complimentary to his charges.

"Can we stop messing around? Can we go out and run the offense?"

The third quarter was scoreless. Again, Mamaroneck's defense was heroic. But in the fourth quarter, North Rockland's huge advantage in size began to tell.

Izaiah Battle, a 210-pound senior running back, began ripping off large chunks of yardage and scored on a 9-yard run with 9:39 left in the game. The Red Raiders missed the extra point. But two minutes later, North Rockland closed the show with another rushing touchdown. This time, the extra point was good, making the final score 19–6.

The kicking game (punts, field goals, extra points) had favored Mamaroneck. And North Rockland had zero yards passing. But the rest of the game belonged to the Red Raiders. They rushed for 290 yards while Mamaroneck gained only 23 yards on the ground and 117 yards through the air.

That said; Mamaroneck is a young team that will get better with the passage of time.

As for my own personal adventure; people sometimes use sports as a vehicle to journey back to an earlier time in their life. But I experienced no great epiphany or memorable flashback.

Although I was rooting for Mamaroneck, the loss didn't hurt as much as it would have when I was seventeen. In fact, despite the wind and cold and final score, I rather enjoyed myself. It was nice to watch young men with no thought of a professional career playing football on a damp cold night for each other and themselves.

Issues and Answers

Behind the Facade at the New York State Athletic Commission

Part One

In July 2017, soon after Kim Sumbler was named acting executive director of the New York State Athletic Commission, I wrote, "Sumbler is entitled to a grace period to show what she can do in the job."

Twenty months have passed since then. In June 2018, the New York State Senate confirmed the appointment of three new commissioners designated by New York governor Andrew Cuomo, bringing the total number of NYSAC commissioners to five. And Sumbler has begun to put her imprint on the commission. It's now time to evaluate what's happening.

The first thing to be said about the New York State Athletic Commission is that it's better than most state athletic commissions in the United States.

It should be. New York and boxing have been intertwined for a century. In 2016, mixed martial arts was added to the mix. And the NYSAC costs taxpayers a lot of money. There are some dedicated hardworking public servants who work for the commission. But there are also problems.

Many of the problems start with the fact that the NYSAC might be the most politicized state athletic commission in the country. Politics is essential to proper governance. But at a time when Andrew Cuomo's supporters hope that he'll be in the vanguard of public officials demonstrating how government and politics can work to better the lives of citizens, the NYSAC is often hamstrung by a politics-first environment that negatively influences decisions.

Larry Merchant once said, "Boxing and politics are the two best places in the world to study human behavior." At the New York State Athletic Commission, they coincide.

The NYSAC is part of the New York State Department of State. That places it directly within Governor Cuomo's political domain. The Department of State hires and fires key commission personnel. In an environment like that, political connections can take priority over performance. This applies to some—not all—fulltime jobs at the commission. And it filters down to the selection of fight-night officials such as inspectors, referees, and judges. An all-too-familiar refrain heard at the NYSAC is, "We can't touch him; his father is friendly with a state senator," or "This one is off limits; one of Andrew's political backers is in his corner."

Speaking on condition of anonymity, one commission employee says, "Every major decision gets bounced up to the Department of State. We're told that the lines of communication with the governor's political people are always open. You can look at that and say that they're available to help. Or you can look at it and say they're interfering."

"Which do you say?"

"The latter."

Success at the New York State Athletic Commission should be measured in terms of how well employees are doing their respective jobs. Instead, undue attention is paid to the optics of a situation—the way in which an event or course of action is perceived by the public.

Two years ago, an article by Carl Campanile in the *New York Post* noted, "Governor Cuomo's office has warned public-relations officers at fifty-five state agencies to start churning out a lot more good news about the administration—or else. Cuomo's communications director, James Allen, delivered the stern message in a conference call last week, leaving some of the agency officials rattled. 'If you don't generate more press releases, changes will be made!' Allen declared, according to one source."

Nine months later, Luana Ferreira (then the licensing access and language access coordinator for the New York State Athletic Commission) sent out a memorandum to all commission staff that began, "Greetings to all! The holiday season is upon us and there has been much conversation about bringing together our wonderful NYSAC community to join in the festivities. There is much to celebrate, such as the good press we have been getting (including the article in the *NY Post*, YES! the *NY Post*)."

As former NYSAC commissioner John Signorile declared, "Our job is to protect the fighters, help the promoters make some money, and make the governor look good."

Optics has been a point of instruction at training symposia for NYSAC personnel. NYSAC commissioner Ndidi Massay has denounced critics of the commission as "haters" and stated at a commission meeting, "I'm a little concerned about creating policy like this. Are we gonna be, you know, what's the public gonna think? Let's take the haters out there. How are we gonna get criticized on this? What are they gonna say? I wanna be prepared for any negative backlash."

That's not politics. It's bad politics. When a government entity is operating properly, the optics take care of themselves.

One of the most frustrating things for journalists who deal with the New York State Athletic Commission is its circle-the-wagons approach.

If a writer calls Bob Bennett (executive director of the Nevada State Athletic Commission), Bennett picks up the telephone and answers questions. The same is true of Andy Foster in California, Larry Hazzard in New Jersey, Greg Sirb in Pennsylvania, Mike Mazzulli at Mohegan Sun, and most other point people at athletic commissions in the United States.

By contrast, in New York, all formal inquiries to NYSAC personnel are channeled through Department of State media specialists who ask that questions be submitted in writing. Then, more often than not, they send back bland, politically attuned responses or don't respond at all.

On February 11, 2019, Lee Park (director of communications for the New York State Department of State) refused a request by this writer to make Kim Sumbler, Theresa D'Andrea (counsel for the NYSAC), and James Vosswinkel (the most engaged of the five NYSAC commissioners) available for interviews. A number of NYSAC employees were willing to provide information for this series of articles on condition of anonymity.

It's difficult to present the position of NYSAC officials with regard to criticism regarding their performance when they refuse to answer questions. Then again, maybe their refusal is an indication that they don't have answers.

Meanwhile, secrecy begets mistakes. In a secretive environment, fewer people are aware of the existence of problems. That makes it less likely that the problems will be brought to the attention of people who should know about them and less likely that solutions will be found.

The most important function a state athletic commission performs is overseeing the health and safety of fighters. This goes beyond what happens on fight night. A host of related issues are involved.

Fight night medical care in New York is much better now than it was before. Part of this is due to the revision of NYSAC medical protocols after Magomed Abdusalamov suffered life-altering brain damage in a fight against Mike Perez at Madison Square Garden five years ago. It's also attributable to Nitin Sethi, a neurologist affiliated with Weill Cornell Medicine in New York. Dr. Sethi became chief medical officer for the NYSAC in the aftermath of the Abdusalamov tragedy. He has been instrumental in the revision of medical protocols and oversees the NYSAC medical team on fight night.

But there's need for improvement.

The most glaring medical deficiency at the New York State Athletic Commission is the lack of understanding and resolve with regard to the use of illegal performance-enhancing drugs. Illegal PED use is not a victimless crime. It results in fighters being hit in the head harder than would otherwise be the case and thus sustaining more short-term and long-term brain damage. It is one of the reasons that fighters die.

Last year, the Nevada State Athletic Commission pulled down what was expected to be the biggest fight of the year—a scheduled "Cinco de Mayo" rematch between Canelo Alvarez and Gennady Golovkin—when it suspended Alvarez for six months after he tested positive for Clenbuterol. On a smaller scale, the Massachusetts State Athletic Commission denied a request for a license by Billy Joe Saunders to defend his WBO 160-pound title against Demetrius Andrade after it learned that Saunders had tested positive for oxilofrine.

Contrast that with New York's handling of situations involving Luis Ortiz, Jermall Charlo, and Jermell Charlo.

Ortiz, who had tested positive for illegal performance-enhancing drugs on multiple occasions, was scheduled to fight Deontay Wilder at Barclays Center in Brooklyn on March 3, 2018. How did the NYSAC handle the PED issue? On January 10, 2018, the commission sent a letter to DiBella Entertainment (which was promoting the fight) advising it that Ortiz would be required to undergo testing for anabolic steroids, diuretics, masking agents, and a ten-panel drug urine test no later than January 19 and again fifteen days before the fight, as a condition of licensure.

This is the equivalent of law enforcement authorities giving a suspect nine days' notice before executing a search warrant to raid his apartment for drugs.

Similarly, Jermall and Jermell Charlo were scheduled to fight in co-featured bouts at Barclays Center on December 22, 2018. But a problem arose when both brothers were unavailable for required PED tests that were to be administered on November 1 by the Voluntary Anti-Doping Association and failed to answer their telephones or otherwise provide VADA with information regarding their whereabouts for the entire day.

Jermall Charlo later maintained that the brothers were "out of town doing promotional stuff." A diligent inquiry by the NYSAC would have followed up with questions like, "Where were the Charlos doing their out-of-town promotional work?" Presumably, there would have been a record of their travel. "What, specifically, was the promotional work? Who did they meet with? Where did the promotional work appear? And why didn't the Charlos answer their telephones when VADA's collection agents attempted to reach them?" VADA could have tested them in whatever city they were in.

The New York State Athletic Commission did, in fact, request some information from the Charlos regarding their missed tests. But according to a well-placed source within the commission, the Charlos refused to provide it.

Rather than press the issue, the NYSAC then asked the Charlos to provide test samples to Quest Diagnostics and Labcorp (each company tested a different brother).

In today's world of microdosing, twenty-four hours is often more than enough time for a dirty fighter to get clean.

There's no evidence on the public record that the Charlos were using illegal performance-enhancing drugs. That said; the unfortunate message sent by the New York State Athletic Commission in this instance was, if fighter were to take an illegal performance-enhancing drug and, by chance, VADA showed up to test him while the drug was still in his system, he could simply miss the test.

Do the people who run the NYSAC really think that's how to protect the health and safety of fighters? Or were they more interested in not making waves and not interfering with a fight that powerful economic interests supported?

Also, laying these individual cases aside, the New York State Athletic Commission's drug-testing program is fundamentally flawed. The commission takes a pre-fight urine sample from each fighter on fight night. For championship bouts, a post-fight urine sample is also taken.

Having fighters urinate into a cup on fight night does not constitute a comprehensive PED-testing program. And more significantly, neither Quest Diagnostics nor Labcorp (where samples are sent by the NYSAC) is accredited by the World Anti-Doping Agency. Here, the thoughts of VADA president Dr. Margaret Goodman are instructive.

"There's a reason that VADA and USADA use WADA-accredited labs," Dr. Goodman says. "WADA enforces standards that a WADA-accredited lab must meet. Quest and Labcorp are good labs, but they don't have the ability or the equipment to perform certain tests. They aren't as sophisticated as a WADA-accredited lab. They don't test for everything that a WADA-accredited lab tests for. They don't have the same equipment and the same sensitivity levels in terms of their ability to pick up certain illegal substances. If you're serious about PED testing, you use a WADA-accredited lab."

In some respects, the NYSAC is more conscientious in its treatment of medical issues than other commissions. For example, fighters who aren't allowed to fight in New York are often licensed to fight elsewhere in the country. The NYSAC refused to license Abner Mares to fight Jesus Cuellar on a June 25, 2016, card at Barclays Center because eye issues (including surgery for a detached retina) had left Mares with what one source says was 20/400 vision in his left eye. Thereafter, Mares fought three times in California before suffering a detached retina in his right eye that forced him out of a scheduled February 9, 2019, bout against Gervonta Davis (also in California).

But while the NYSAC has a good record of denying impaired fighters a license to fight, it doesn't take the next step of red-flagging fighters who have been denied a license and advising other states to contact the NYSAC medical staff if that fighter applies for a license to compete in another jurisdiction.

The NYSAC does have what it calls a "red flag" policy of its own that was instituted because of internal concern that its medical staff wasn't observing certain fighters for a long enough period of time after a bout. Fighters who had minor headaches, balance issues, or blood in their urine were allowed to leave the arena without further observation. Now

NYSAC doctors can require a fighter to remain on site for further observation and determine if the symptoms in question clear up or worsen.

That's a step in the right direction, but it's not enough. Suppose Magomed Abdusalamov had been red-flagged? By the time he started showing neurological symptoms and was taken to the hospital, much of the "golden hour" necessary for effective surgical intervention would have been lost.

If a fighter's condition warrants his being red-flagged, he should be sent to the hospital for observation. This is a man or woman who has been punched in the head, often more than a hundred times, by a professional fighter trained in the art of hurting.

But no medical protocols will be effective if they aren't properly administered. This requires standing up to powerful economic interests—such as UFC—when warranted.

On November 4, 2017, Michael Bisping tapped out while being choked by Georges St-Pierre at UFC 217 at Madison Square Garden. A left hook and series of forearms smashes had immobilized Bisping. Then St-Pierre applied a naked chokehold that ended the bout.

Bisping appeared to temporarily lose consciousness. That night, he was placed on a thirty-day medical suspension by the NYSAC medical staff. Then, in mid-November, UFC contacted Kim Sumbler, told her that Bisping had been judged fit to fight by a neurologist in California, submitted supporting medical documentation, and asked that the suspension be lifted. Sumbler passed the request on to the appropriate NYSAC medical personnel, and the suspension was lifted. On November 25, three weeks after enduring a beating in New York, Bisping was knocked out by Kelvin Gastelum on a UFC fight card in Shanghai. He has not fought since. In May 2018, Bisping announced his retirement from MMA competition. Later, he said that he retired as a consequence of an injury suffered in the Gastelum fight.

The Michael Bisping situation left many in the MMA community aghast.

Dr. Tad Seifert, a neurologist and member of the Association of Boxing Commissions medical advisory committee, told Mark Raimondi of MMA Fighting that he believed allowing Bisping to fight in Shanghai was "grossly negligent."

"I think it's incumbent upon us that are involved with commissions to be vigilant in fighter health and safety," Seifert explained. "That's got to be our utmost priority. And a guy that's thirty-eight years old and historically been downed more than any other fighter in the history of the UFC, that was at least visibly—through the eyes of what the videos tell us—concussed twenty-one days prior; to lift that suspension, I think, was a bit reckless. I try not to be critical of scenarios like this, but this is one of those that I couldn't keep my mouth shut."

MMA writer Ben Fowlkes observed, "The second [stoppage] was a lot harder to watch than the first. That's at least in part because the memory of the first one was still so fresh. While doctors know it's probably not great to group your brain traumas too close together, there's no way to determine in advance when it's bound to be especially bad."

UFC commentator Joe Rogan declared, "You really can't be letting a guy fight three weeks after an absolutely brutal fight like that. It just does not make sense. It does not make sense."

Former UFC commentator Brian Stann added, "This was an awful decision to allow him to fight. He was rocked badly against Georges St-Pierre. He wasn't just choked out. The human brain does not recover that fast."

Dr. Michael Schwartz (founder and first president of the Association of Ringside Physicians) says that he's not in a position to comment specifically on Michael Bisping since he didn't examine the fighter or the fighter's medical records. But Schwartz does say, "In general, suspensions are based on medical evidence that suggests a minimum amount of time and should be upheld unless there's overwhelming compelling evidence that the initial suspension was inappropriate. Also, it's important to consider whether a medical examination cited in support of lifting a suspension was conducted by a truly neutral party or a doctor sought out on behalf of the suspended fighter."

It's safe to say that the NYSAC would not have allowed Michael Bisping to fight in New York twenty-one days after he'd been beaten badly and choked unconscious. It should not have paved the way for him to fight in another jurisdiction either. It's unlikely that the NYSAC would have done this for a promoter other than UFC.

"I think Nitin has done a great job," a doctor who has worked closely with Dr. Sethi at the NYSAC says. "Overall, his presence at the

commission has been a huge plus. He cares. He has tried very hard to educate the medical staff and other commission personnel regarding issues
of fighter safety. He's hands-on on fight night. But the Michael Bisping
situation troubles me. He should have put his foot down on that one."

The men and women who run the New York State Athletic Commission are regulators. They shouldn't be enablers.

Meanwhile, one way to advance the health and safety of fighters is to
have an active knowledgeable medical advisory board.

The NYSAC has a medical advisory board. But according to the
New York State Athletic Commission website, this board has met only
once since June 2017. That was on September 19, 2018. Four of the
nine board members were physically present. Two more participated via
an electronic hookup. The meeting lasted twenty-four minutes. Business
consisted of approving the minutes of the board's previous meeting
(which had occurred fifteen months earlier) and approving the appointment and reappointment of NYSAC physicians. Dr. Sethi also answered
one question put to him by a committee member.

"They're playing Russian roulette with fighter safety," a commission
doctor says of the board. "And some of them don't even know it."

Part Two

On December 29, 2017, a *New York Times* investigative report explored
New York governor Andrew Cuomo's oversight of the Metropolitan
Transportation Authority. In one instance, 900 workers were paid to perform 700 jobs as part of a 3.5-mile subway tunnel construction project.
"Officials," the report read, "could not find any reason for the other 200
people to be there." The resulting project cost nearly $3.5 billion for each
new mile of track, multiples more than similar projects in other cities
throughout the United States.

There was a trade-off, of course. As reported by the *Times*, "Trade
unions, which have closely aligned themselves with Cuomo and other
politicians, have secured deals requiring underground construction work
to be staffed by as many as four times more laborers than elsewhere in the
world. Construction companies, which have given millions of dollars in
campaign donations in recent years, have increased their projected costs
by up to 50 percent when bidding for work from the M.T.A."

A subsequent *New York Times* editorial entitled "A Gold-Plated

Ramshackle Subway" declared, "Billions of dollars that could have gone to maintaining and improving the subways have been wasted."

It's difficult to fully comprehend the corruption and waste in massive government undertakings like public transportation because of the size of the bureaucracy involved. The New York State Athletic Commission is more easily studied. But even here, details are hard to come by.

The NYSAC doesn't have a budget like its counterparts in states like California and Nevada. Its economic mysteries are folded into the New York State Department of State budget. Thus, much of its cost to taxpayers is hidden from public scrutiny.

To date, both the NYSAC and Department of State have refused requests to provide information stating the total annual cost of operating the commission and a breakdown of these costs (e.g. salaries, travel expenses, office space, etc).

Meanwhile, Governor Cuomo has touted combat sports as a moneymaker for the State of New York. On December 20, 2018, the governor's press office issued a media release praising "the success of New York State's mixed martial arts, boxing, and wrestling industries," and declaring that, since September 2016 when MMA became legal in New York, "overall revenue from combat sports" has jumped from $15,950,000 to $48,500,000 annually.

But let's look more closely at the numbers. The bulk of this revenue goes to out-of-state corporations and fighters who live out of state. There has been a modest increase in economic activity surrounding big fights (e.g. at hotels and restaurants). But this increase has been offset in part by the near-extinction of small boxing cards due to an insurance requirement that has killed boxing upstate and decimated small club shows in New York City.

Moreover, using the Governor's own data, only $3,788,082 per year in state taxes has been paid on the revenue that he cites. That's because the state has agreed to cap the TV revenue taxes and ticket revenue taxes that promoters pay at $50,000 for each item per event.

Are combat sports a moneymaker for the State of New York? In 2017, the state agreed to pay $22 million to Magomed Abdusalamov and his family to settle claims alleging substandard medical protocols and improper conduct by New York State Athletic Commission employees after Abdusalamov suffered permanent brain damage in a 2013 boxing match at Madison Square Garden.

Want more? The Cuomo press release states, "An April 2017 UFC event in Buffalo generated $3 million in salaries and wages for 72 jobs."

Think about that for a minute. Do the math. It comes to $41,667 per job for one night's work. These numbers might average out if the main event fighters' purses are included, but that's hardly an economic boom for the State of New York.

Also, one has to consider the cost of operating the New York State Athletic Commission. Government agencies don't have to be money-makers. They're providing a service. But let's be honest about what the numbers are.

It's an open secret that fighter's purses are sometimes underreported to the NYSAC, which enables these fighters and others to escape the full state and city tax payments that should be made.

Similarly, it's well known that at least one boxing impresario arranges to sell tickets for cash on the street outside the arena on fight night and then facilitates the filing of false reports listing the tickets as comps to avoid taxes.

The New York State Athletic Commission burns taxpayer dollars by overstaffing fights at taxpayer expense. The Pennsylvania State Athletic Commission has twenty-five to thirty people on site for its biggest events. For the biggest fight cards in Nevada, the NSAC has up to forty-five people on site. By contrast, the New York State Athletic Commission regularly assigns more than sixty people to fights at Madison Square Garden and Barclays Center.

Are all of these employees (most of whom are paid on a per diem basis) necessary? Let's look at the numbers.

Approximately forty NYSAC personnel were assigned to the UFC event in Buffalo that Governor Cuomo referenced in his December 20, 2018, press release. If more than sixty NYSAC employees are necessary to properly regulate a ten-fight card in New York City, shouldn't the same number be necessary to properly regulate a thirteen-fight card upstate? Or are assignments made (and taxpayer dollars unnecessarily spent on transportation, hotel, meals, and salary) so NYSAC personnel can travel from upstate New York to New York City and have a good time?

Another example of waste is the amount of money that the New York State Athletic Commission spends to regulate professional wrestling in New York. Section 213 of the rules promulgated by the NYSAC in 2016 requires that promoters of professional wrestling matches be licensed by the state. The NYSAC assigns at least one official (an inspector or deputy commissioner) to each show. Their job is to ensure that a licensed physician and ambulance are on site. The cost to the state is the per diem salary of the inspector or deputy commissioner and, sometimes, travel expenses.

Isn't it time that the New York State Athletic Commission stopped wasting taxpayer dollars by "regulating" professional wrestling? If *The Great White Hope* returned to Broadway, would the NYSAC regulate it?

Presumably not. Why not? Because like professional wrestling, a Broadway theatrical production is not a real athletic competition. It's scripted entertainment.

Why did New York State taxpayers pay to regulate 272 wrestling events in New York last year?

Governor Cuomo might say, "WWE combatants can get hurt."

That's right. They can. And a Cirque du Soleil performer was killed several years ago when her harness separated from a safety wire and she plunged ninety-four feet to the stage below. An actor in the Broadway production of *Spiderman* suffered serious injuries when a line holding him snapped and he fell into the orchestra pit. There are federal, state, and city agencies that deal with these issues. The NYSAC shouldn't be one of them.

Too many people at the New York State Department of State and New York State Athletic Commission don't understand that specialized knowledge is required to regulate combat sports. They have no background in combat sports, don't understand combat sports, and have little or no respect for what fighters go through. As one deputy commission said recently, "What they know about boxing and MMA would fit in a thimble with room to spare for a finger. All they know about combat sports is that people hit each other."

The NYSAC is out of touch with the combat sports community. Many people at the commission don't have a clue as to how much there is that they don't know. No one is on the ground, following the day-to-day minutiae. Matt Delaglio (the NYSAC director of boxing) comes the closest.

No one from the commission attends pre-fight press conferences or other fight-related events other than weigh-ins and the fights themselves. Often, the commission fails to address a specific issue or problem because its employees don't even know that the issue or problem exists.

In theory, the New York State Athletic Commission is overseen by five commissioners. But that's more fiction than fact.

Traditionally, the NYSAC had three commissioners. In 2016, the New York State legislature increased that number from three to five. The commissioners then were Edwin Torres, John Signorile, and Ndidi Massay. Two years passed before the new seats were filled.

On June 30, 2017, Michelle Nicoli-Rosales (Andrew Cuomo's deputy director of communications for economic development) confirmed that the governor had nominated Dr. James Vosswinkel, Dr. Philip Stieg, and Donald Patterson as new NYSAC commissioners subject to approval by the New York State Senate. Massay's term was scheduled to run until January 2019. It was unclear whether Torres or Signorile (both of whom were serving on holdover terms) would be replaced. One year later, on June 19, 2018, the state senate voted to approve the appointments of Vosswinkel, Stieg, and Patterson. Signorile was axed.

If Andrew Cuomo truly cared about the mission of the New York State Athletic Commission, he would have used his influence and the power of his office to ensure that five able commissioners with an understanding of combat sports were put in place in a timely manner. Two years is not timely. Moreover, except for Patterson (who has been involved with amateur boxing in Buffalo), it appears as though none of the five current commissioners has had any experience with combat sports.

Torres served as a New York State Supreme Court judge in the Bronx for many years. A biographical sketch on the NYSAC website states, "He is a lifelong boxing enthusiast and was chosen for his legal acumen and his ability to apply his judicial skills in disputed matters that come before the Commission." But Torres is now eighty-eight years old and no longer has this ability.

Massay is an attorney. The NYSAC website states that she is Executive Director of RISE (Ross Initiative in Sports for Equality). But a review of the RISE website indicates that she no longer has that role.

Steig is a neurosurgeon who currently serves as chairman of the Weill Cornell Brain and Spine Center.

Vosswinkel is medical director of the Stony Brook University Trauma Center and Surgical Intensive Care Unit. Of the five commissioners, he has been the most engaged in the work of the commission and is the commissioner who has made the most significant commitment in terms of time and effort to the job.

Because of a quirk in state law, Stieg, Massay, and Torres are now serving on a holdover basis and can be dismissed from their positions at any time. Indeed, Torres has been serving on a holdover basis since January 1, 2014. Vosswinkel and Patterson are serving terms that expire on January 1, 2021.

Except for Vosswinkel, the commissioners don't regularly attend fight cards in New York. When they do, they tend to arrive well after the fights have started. There are occasions when no NYSAC commissioner is on site. They're more often seen at high-profile events such as Canelo Alvarez vs. Rocky Fielding at Madison Square Garden on December 15, 2018 (when four of the five commissioners were present).

The commissioners have been inclined to forgo attendance at staff training seminars. On June 30, 2018, the NYSAC held a mandatory staff symposium for doctors, deputy commissioners, and inspectors that was devoted largely to medical issues. None of the five commissioners attended.

In the aftermath of the Magomed Abdusalamov tragedy, the Office of the New York State Inspector General conducted an extensive investigation of the New York State Athletic Commission. In July 2016, it issued a blistering report that, among other things, declared that investigators had "found a lack of appropriate engagement and oversight by Athletic Commission commissioners."

With the exception of Dr. Vosswinkel, this lack of appropriate engagement and oversight appears to be continuing, as evidenced by a review of recent NYSAC meetings.

Article 7 of the New York State Public Officers Law, otherwise known as the "Open Meetings Law," requires that meetings of public bodies be open to the general public. Section 100 of this law states, "It is essential to the maintenance of a democratic society that the public business be performed in an open and public manner and that the citizens of this state be fully aware of and able to observe the performance of public officials and attend and listen to the deliberations and decisions that go into the making of public policy." Certain issues, such as "matters which will imperil the public safety if disclosed," may be discussed in a closed "executive session."

On September 26, 2018, the New York State Athletic Commission met for the first time in 357 days. The five commissioners—Edwin Torres, Ndidi Massay, Donald Patterson, Philip Stieg, and James Vosswinkel—were all present. So were executive director Kim Sumbler, director of boxing Matt Delaglio, chief medical officer Nitin Sethi, and commission counsel Theresa D'Andrea. Sumbler began the session with a series of laudatory remarks about those present. The only substantive action the commissioners took was to approve nine new models of boxing gloves based on Delaglio's recommendation. The entire proceeding lasted thirty minutes.

The next commission meeting took place on December 10, 2018. This time, three of the five commissioners—Vosswinkel, Torres, and Patterson (by telephone)—were present. Sumbler, Delaglio, and D'Andrea were also there. The meeting lasted for seven minutes. The only substantive business conducted was the approval of a new brand of boxing gloves for use in New York.

The following, and most recent, NYSAC meeting occurred on February 28, 2019. Four commissioners—Vosswinkel, Stieg, Massay, and Patterson (via Facetime)—were present, as were Sumbler, Delaglio, Sethi, and D'Andrea. Sumbler reported that the NYSAC had overseen 28 boxing events in 2018, 9 major MMA events, 72 smaller MMA competitions, and 272 wrestling events. The commissioners then approved two new boxing gloves and one new MMA glove for use in New York. The meeting lasted eight minutes.

There was no discussion or acknowledgement at any of these meetings of the many important issues facing the New York State Athletic Commission.

Leadership starts at the top. This isn't a good start.

Part Three

At present, the point person for the New York State Athletic Commission is executive director Kim Sumbler. Prior to joining the NYSAC, Sumbler oversaw combat sports for the Seneca Nation of Indians Athletic Commission in western New York.

Sumbler is adept at forming alliances. Early in her tenure, she prevailed over then-commissioner John Signorile in a messy power struggle.

There are good people at the NYSAC who support Sumbler. Among other things, they say, "I like Kim . . . I trust Kim . . . We're moving in the right direction . . . So far, I think Kim is doing a good job."

Others believe that Sumbler is "sloppy on details." They complain that, too often, she instructs the commission staff to be at the venue on fight night at a specific hour but doesn't arrive herself until later. They also say that she doesn't spend enough time at the NYSAC office at 123 William Street in New York City (the only commission office) and doesn't understand the nuances of the sport and business of boxing.

Sumbler labors under two handicaps. First, at the Seneca Nation of Indians Athletic Commission, she had free reign to do her job. But at the NYSAC, her hands are sometimes tied by political imperatives. And second, overseeing the NYSAC workforce is a challenge.

"It's a difficult agency to run," one insider says. "For most people who work at the commission, it's not their primary job. It's something they fit in around other commitments. That's for starters. Some of the commission personnel are dedicated and talented. Others are well intentioned but simply don't have the tools to do the job right. Things that are common sense to you and me aren't common sense to them. You have team players and you have prima donnas. It's not easy."

Matt Delaglio (who once worked for Main Events) is the commission's director of boxing. Most matters that require expertise in the sweet science are steered to him.

At present, Sumbler is deeply involved in day-to-day decision-making with regard to mixed martial arts. But on February 19, the Department of State posted a job listing for an "athletic activities assistant" who will assume the position of director of mixed martial arts.

Theresa D'Andrea is assigned by the Department of State to work full-time as counsel for the NYSAC, a position she has held since September 2018. D'Andrea replaced Ryan Sakacs, a former assistant district attorney in the Manhattan District Attorney's Office, who was employed by the commission on an hourly basis.

D'Andrea's profile on LinkedIn states that she spent two years in private practice at a law firm where she specialized in consumer finance litigation. Prior to that, she was in the New York City Law Department for twenty-seven months, the last ten of which were spent in its Division of Labor & Employment Law. She has no apparent legal expertise relating to combat sports. This means she has to feel her way through the nuts-and-bolts issues inherent in her job on a day-to-day basis.

As previously mentioned, the Department of State refused to make D'Andrea available for an interview in conjunction with this series. Thus, it's impossible to gauge her understanding of the larger issues that affect the sport and business of boxing in New York and her ability to handle them.

D'Andrea's precise duties at the NYSAC are unclear. Several commission employees report that she was responsible for recording RSVPs for a January 4, 2019, office holiday party that were sent to almost one hundred commission personnel. At an annual salary of $123,000 a year (as reported by seethroughny.net/payrolls/state-government) this seems like an inefficient use of state resources. However, given D'Andrea's background in labor and employment law, there's one issue that she might want to address.

At present, the minimum wage in New York City is $13.30 per hour. For businesses in New York City with eleven or more employees, it's fifteen dollars per hour. The New York State Department of Labor website states, "The Minimum Wage Act requires that all employees in New York State receive at least the applicable hourly minimum wage rate."

NYSAC inspectors are paid one hundred dollars per show. They're frequently ordered to report to fights at Madison Square Garden and Barclays Center at 2:30 p.m. Many of them are on the job until 12:30 a.m. or later. This comes to ten dollars an hour, five dollars per hour below New York's legal minimum wage. Multiple sources say that, as a matter of course, administrators fill out false time sheets for the inspectors to cover up the infraction. Moreover, there are no scheduled breaks for NYSAC employees on fight night as required by state law.

If a factory had sixty employees, paid them below minimum wage, and filed false paperwork with the state to cover up the shortfall, there would be a criminal investigation.

At present, the New York State Athletic Commission has eleven deputy commissioners, as many as nine of whom have been assigned to work on a per diem basis on a given night.

Deputy commissioners are responsible for coordinating what

transpires in the technical area at ringside and in the back of the house on fight night. Some NYSAC deputy commissioners are conscientious, capable, hardworking public servants. Others leave fighter urine samples unattended (a violation of medical protocols) and refuse simple requests such as helping to move a table on fight night ("It's not my job"). One deputy commissioner needs training with regard to sexual harassment (although removal from his position would be more appropriate).

There's also an area where some NYSAC deputy commissioners—including some of the best—should rethink their modus operandi. The job does not require a deputy to get up on the ring apron or into the ring and stand directly beside or behind a fighter during the pre-fight introductions and reading of the judges' scorecards before and after a featured television fight. This jockeying for camera time is unnecessary. The same deputy commissioners don't consider it part of their job description to climb onto the ring apron or into the ring and stand beside or directly behind a fighter in undercard fights.

Sometimes, there are so many deputy commissioners positioning themselves to be close to the action and sit in or near the corner during a fight that it's difficult for the ring doctors and inspectors to do their job. And this fondness for the camera extends to fighters' dressing rooms, where some inspectors make a point of standing directly behind a fighter when a television camera cuts to a shot of the fighter warming up.

There are times when it's inevitable that a commission employee will be seen on camera. But the groping for the spotlight that some deputy commissioners and inspectors engage in (which at times results in members of a fighter's team being pushed aside) pisses some fighters' camps off. People who work at the NYSAC should find their jobs gratifying, but they're not there for self-gratification.

Inspectors are the eyes and ears of the commission in a fighter's corner and dressing room on fight night. Some inspectors perform their work in exemplary fashion. Others arrive at the arena on fight night with alcohol on their breath, leave fighters alone without proper supervision after a pre-fight urine sample has been taken, and check their smartphones or scratch off lottery tickets while a fighter's hands are being taped.

This leads to another issue. Most NYSAC inspectors don't have a clue as to what constitutes a legal or illegal handwrap. At one point in their training, they were told that, pursuant to commission regulations, a trainer is allowed to use "soft surgical bandage not over two inches wide, held in place by not more than ten feet of surgeon's adhesive tape for each hand" and that "up to one 20-yard roll of bandage may be used to complete the wrappings for each hand." But the majority of inspectors have forgotten this information. And they don't know what constitutes "stacking" or other illegal handwrap practices.

For big fights, NYSAC inspectors rely on a representative of the opposing fighter's camp to call attention to irregularities in taping. For small fights, in some instances, anything goes.

Medical protocols put in place after the Magomed Abdusalamov tragedy provide that, if a fighter has to go the hospital after a fight, the inspector assigned to him (or her) is supposed to escort the fighter to the ambulance with an EMT and give the fighter his paycheck in the ambulance. The logic behind this is that (1) the fighter should be carefully monitored at all times and (2) if he receives his paycheck in advance, there's an increased chance that he might not get in the ambulance and go to the hospital.

On September 8, 2018, Ve Shawn Owens lost to Chordale Booker in a swing bout at Barclays Center that wasn't contested until well after midnight when the main event was over. The NYSAC medical staff said that Owens should go to the hospital for a more thorough checkup. But it was late and a source says that the inspector assigned to Booker gave him his paycheck and didn't walk him to the ambulance.

As for in-the-ring and ringside officials, the New York State Athletic Commission has some excellent referees and it has some awful referees.

Refereeing a prizefight is a demanding job. It requires the ability to make sound split-second judgments and then implement them immediately. Among other things, a referee has to be in good enough physical condition to move deftly around the ring and be properly positioned at all times.

Harvey Dock (who plies his trade primarily in New York and New Jersey) is widely recognized as one of the best referees in the country. But at the other end of the spectrum, the NYSAC has referees who consistently make mistakes such as ignoring fouls, miscalling knockdowns, and stopping fights too late.

The NYSAC Combative Sports Officials Fee Schedule mandates that the referee for a championship fight receive .13 percent of the fighters' combined purses or $3,000 (whichever is greater). This means, for Anthony Joshua vs. Jarrell Miller (which is scheduled to be contested at Madison Square Garden on June 1 with estimated purses in excess of $30 million), the referee will be paid in the neighborhood of $40,000. That's a lot of money and, for some referees, a powerful incentive to please a promoter who might influence their appointment.

As with its referees, the NYSAC has some excellent judges and some awful judges. On the positive side, Steve Weisfeld has evolved into one of boxing's most reliable arbiters. But some NYSAC judges are notorious A-siders while others seem to score fights without any comprehensible criteria.

A ring judge can have a bad night. But looking at recent bad decisions in New York, one sees the same judges' names popping up again and again. It's not hard to connect the dots.

Judges sit on the ring apron. They have the best seats in the house. The men and women who sit in these seats have a responsibility to turn in accurate scorecards. Fighters' careers are at stake. Their economic future is on the line.

Hint: When the crowd boos a decision in favor of the hometown favorite, one can assume that the judging was poor.

New York doesn't have a monopoly on bad decisions. They're endemic throughout boxing. No sport does less to ensure quality officiating. But the fact that there are poor decisions in other jurisdictions doesn't justify a cavalier attitude with regard to the problem. If judges render an unjust decision that devastates a young man's career, the prevailing ethic at the NYSAC seems to be to ignore it and move on. That's unacceptable.

Part Four

To function properly, an organization needs standards and accountability. A lack of standards and accountability in one area seeps into another.

Too often, the New York State Athletic Commission doesn't train or evaluate its personnel as well as it should. In some instances, mediocrity has been institutionalized. Good NYSAC employees learn something new every day. There are other people at the commission who think that they already know it all.

Well-run sports organizations acknowledge when their officials make a mistake. The New York State Athletic Commission doesn't.

Boxing insiders know who the competent and incompetent referees and judges at the NYSAC are. But below-par officials are allowed to keep working, often in high-profile situations. There's no comprehensive plan in place at the commission to evaluate referees and judges. No one at the NYSAC sits down with them after a flawed performance to watch videos of a fight and ask what their thought processes were?

The practice of assigning officials of questionable competence to preliminary fights is sometimes utilized to shield them from public scrutiny. But that doesn't solve the problem. Fighters' careers—and lives— are still in their hands.

One way to improve the quality of judging in New York would be to train former fighters as ring judges.

In recent months, the commission has hired a group of new inspectors. But they aren't being properly trained. Kim Sumbler has sought to institute standardized protocols for the performance of inspectors on fight night. In theory, inspectors are evaluated by deputy commissioners at the close of each fight card. But it's a haphazard process.

At times, the interaction among commission personnel resembles a food fight in a junior high school cafeteria.

Multiple sources say that, on several occasions, a deputy commissioner assigned to watch urine samples in the dressing room area left his post because he wanted to be at ringside to watch the fights. In one instance, the person he recruited to oversee the samples in his absence didn't understand the sensitivity of the situation and left the samples unattended to go to the ladies' room. Later, she complained that the deputy commissioner was verbally abusive to her, telling her to shut up and embarrassing her in front of other commission personnel.

On April 21, 2018, according to one source, the NYSAC licensing access coordinator approved a request that a fighter's ten-year-old son be in his father's corner to translate during a fight at Barclays Center. This is not good judgment. A deputy commissioner heard about the plan and put an end to it.

At another fight card at Barclays Center, a New York State Department of State media relations specialist was seated by the ring apron, leaning into the ring to take smartphone photographs of the fights to tweet out over social media on behalf of the DOS. Earlier in the day, NYSAC executive director Kim Sumbler had told commission personnel to strictly enforce rules against photographers leaning into the ring. Two months later, the same DOS employee was moving around the technical area at Madison Square Garden, standing up and taking photos while blocking the view of paying spectators.

There's a depressingly familiar routine at the New York State Athletic Commission. A referee, judge, inspector, or deputy commissioner makes a mistake. If the mistake is serious enough (for example, forgetting to take a fighter for his pre-fight physical and then lying about the oversight when asked), the employee is dismissed. But often, when there's an attempt to correct inadequate performance, the employee in question complains to his or her political backer or threatens to institute legal proceedings for discrimination and the commission backs off.

Often, the political process prevents things that need to be done from being done or precludes them from being done quickly enough. When a problem employee is identified, the guiding philosophy is to "give the employee enough rope to hang himself." Meanwhile, the lives of fighters are at risk.

For years, it was known that an NYSAC inspector was suffering from cognitive issues. On one occasion when a fight called for the combatants to wear 8-ounce gloves, one pair of 8-ounce gloves was lost. However, a pair of 10-ounce gloves was readily available. The inspector suggested that each fighter wear one 8-ounce glove and one 10-ounce glove. Fortunately, he was overruled. Last year, the same inspector was assigned to a fighter's dressing room at Barclays Center. He lost the fighter's gloves ("I put them down someplace and forgot where") and had to go back to the onsite commission office for a second pair. Then he fell asleep in the dressing room. Soon after, his employment was terminated by the commission.

Why wait that long? By definition, this inspector's continued employment was jeopardizing the integrity of the fights that he was assigned to and, by extension, the lives of fighters. It wasn't his fault that he couldn't do the job anymore. He was suffering from a debilitating medical condition. Standards are empty vessels if there's an absence of accountability for the failure to meet them.

One former commission inspector, Dorothea Perry, has been a lightning rod for controversy for years. There have been complaints that she left fighters unattended in dressing rooms and used her badge to gain entry to the dressing rooms of high-profile fighters whom she hadn't been assigned to monitor. David Berlin (who served as NYSAC executive director for two years beginning in May 2014) wanted to dismiss Perry from her position with the commission because he believed she had failed to properly carry out her duties on multiple occasions. But he was overruled by his superiors.

Perry's employment with the commission was finally terminated on April 25, 2018. In an email written that day to NYSAC director of boxing Matt Delaglio, she noted that her termination had come "only two weeks after my submitting a complaint to another State Office regarding being passed over for the Deputy Commissioner's position." Perry then declared, "This termination appears to be an illegal act of retaliation."

Multiple sources say that Perry's termination was related to events that occurred during a fight card at Barclays Center on April 21, 2018. There had been security concerns leading up to that night, in part because of a social media feud between Adrien Broner (who was fighting in the main event) and a rapper who goes by the moniker "Tekashi69." An April 18 open media workout had been canceled as a security precaution and the final pre-fight press conference (previously scheduled for the Highline Ballroom in Manhattan) was moved to Barclays Center, where there was heightened security. In addition, the Friday weigh-in was closed to the public. When fight night came, there was a heavy police presence at Barclays Center including gang units. Even then, a temporary lockdown was necessary when a gun was fired in the building. Perry was the senior inspector in the dressing room for one of the undercard fighters and allegedly violated commission protocols with regard to the lockdown.

Over the years, Perry has filed discrimination complaints against Ron Scott Stevens (a former NYSAC chairman), Felix Figueroa (a former NYSAC chief inspector), and David Berlin. In each instance, there was no finding that they had discriminated against her. In a November 30, 2017, email to Matt Delaglio, she complained, "Senior staff members and superiors are making derogatory comments about me and making false claims." She also wrote, "I accuse the New York State Athletic Commission's senior staff of creating a hostile work environment and other Title VII violations. Furthermore, I accuse [affirmative action

officer] Maria Herman of being complicit and conspiring with others at
the athletic commission to cover up the wrongdoings by submitting false
reports to indemnify and hold harmless the commission staff."

In addition, Perry filed a complaint with the New York City Police
Department alleging criminal conduct and a second complaint with the
New York State Department of State alleging workplace violence that
she said was committed against her by an employee of a media relations
company that was onsite for the April 21, 2018, fight card at Barclays
Center. More specifically, she alleged that the employee had threatened,
"I'm going to kill you." Neither of these complaints resulted in a finding
of wrongdoing by the alleged perpetrator.

A Google search further reveals that Perry has filed at least two law-
suits alleging racial discrimination against private-sector employers.

On June 4, 2014, Robert Werner (chief investigator for the New
York State Inspector General's Office) interviewed Mike Paz (a former
NYSAC inspector) in conjunction with the Inspector General's investigation into the injuries suffered by Magomed Abdusalamov in his fight
against Mike Perez at Madison Square Garden. At one point, Werner
told Paz, "Although this most recent investigation started as a result of
the November 2nd fight, you start looking at policies, procedures. We
start looking at the old IG reports. It's a very small agency, the athletic
commission. You guys have been investigated five times. When you start
looking at that type of stat, what's wrong with this picture?"

What's wrong the picture is that too many decisions at the NYSAC
are made on the basis of political expediency rather than what's right.
And too often, standards and accountability are lacking. This culture has
to change.

A driver can run a red light ten times without adverse consequences.
Then, one day, there's a truck. The New York State Athletic Commission
is running red lights. NYSAC personnel who don't do their jobs properly are damaging fighters' careers and, in some instances, endangering
fighters' lives.

Concussions are like snowflakes. No two are exactly alike.

Fighting with a Concussion

Trainer Rob McCracken was widely criticized for remarks he made to the BBC during the early stages of promoting the December 7, 2019, rematch between Anthony Joshua and Andy Ruiz. Referencing the aftermath of round three of their first fight, McCracken said, "I know [Joshua] better than all these experts who virtually don't know him or have met him once or twice. So I knew he was concussed and I'm trying to get him through a few more rounds, one round at a time, and see where he's at. Can he recover? Can he get back into this? But he was glassy-eyed from when he got caught with that initial shot in round three and he carried that with him up until the end. It's a nightmare situation. Pro boxing is deadly, and you're in the corner with a heavyweight not responding as he should."

"How could McCracken let AJ fight with a concussion?" the critics responded. "That's horrible."

But boxers often continue fighting after being concussed during a fight. That's not a secret to those in the know or anyone with enough sense to understand what's going on.

A concussion is a temporary loss of normal brain function caused by a blow to the head. Depending on its severity, a concussion can affect memory, judgment, reflexes, speech, balance, and muscle coordination. Additional physical symptoms can include a prolonged headache, vision disturbances, dizziness, nausea, vomiting, ringing ears, sensitivity to light, and a loss of smell or taste.

A person who suffers a concussion does not necessarily lose consciousness. A "mild" concussion might result in someone being dazed or buzzed. A person who experiences a "moderate" concussion might lose consciousness for a second. A "severe" concussion can involve a longer period of unconsciousness. The severity and duration of other symptoms are also factored into evaluating the seriousness of a concussion.

No two concussions are exactly alike. And there are no scientifically validated treatments for concussions other than a few medications that are used to treat the symptoms of a concussion, not the concussion injury itself.

Let's look at what the long-term after effects of a severe concussion can be.

The injured person might look healthy. But dizziness and blurred or double vision can last for a year or longer. He, or she, might have trouble sequencing (for example, remembering the order in which to perform three simple chores). Constant fatigue, anxiety, and depression are common.

Boxing writer Clay Moyle (who has authored biographies of Sam Langford, Billy Miske, and Tony Zale) experienced the after effects of a severe concussion when he fell ten feet from a ladder, hit his head on the root system of a tree, and was unconscious for approximately nine minutes. Moyle's condition has improved steadily since then. But more than three years later, he still suffers from motor-skill issues and other symptoms.

Recently, Moyle told me, "There was absolutely nothing more frustrating to me than the fact that almost everyone thought I not only looked perfectly fine, but was, and that it was all in my head so to speak. My sister essentially convinced my mother and siblings that my only problem was that I was suffering from anxiety. Hell, yes, I was suffering from anxiety. But it was because my brain didn't feel remotely the same and simply trying to function on a daily basis had become such a struggle for me."

If a player in the National Football League is knocked down and struggles to get to his feet because "his bell has been rung," he's removed from the game and evaluated in a concussion protocol tent before being allowed to return to the playing field. The examination explores physical and cognitive symptoms.

By contrast, if a fighter is knocked down and struggles to get to his feet, there's no concussion protocol tent to put him in where he can be examined for ten minutes before a determination is made as to whether or not he's fit to continue fighting.

The referee has the authority to stop a fight. But insofar as neurological symptoms are concerned, it's primarily a call for the ring doctor.

We've all seen ring doctors shine a penlight into a fighter's eyes between rounds. But that's not about concussions. The doctor is looking to see if the fighter's pupils are the same size and if they're reacting differently from one another. If the pupils are not the same size or are reacting differently, that's often indicative of bleeding in the brain. The fighter should be taken to a hospital as soon as possible.

How does a doctor determine in the middle of a fight whether a fighter is suffering from concussive symptoms sufficient to warrant the fight being stopped?

It's an art as much a science, a gray area with no simple answers. There are no clear guidelines for ring doctors to follow. Standards are still evolving. The steps taken vary from doctor to doctor and state to state.

Boxing is legalized assault. Conduct that would otherwise be unlawful is allowed in a boxing ring. The rules for medical care during a fight are also different from the norm. Continued participation that wouldn't be permitted elsewhere is allowed during a fight. A fighter who is "buzzed" is more likely than would otherwise be the case to suffer a second, more serious, loss of normal brain function during the fight. But often, he's allowed to fight on.

Reality dictates that the magnitude of a fight and what has happened in the earlier stages of the fight are also weighed in the process.

Deontay Wilder was involved in two high-profile concussion incidents. In round seven of Wilder's March 3, 2018, fight against Luis Ortiz, Ortiz stunned Wilder and followed with a barrage of punches that pummeled Deontay around the ring. Wilder appeared to be out on his feet. But he stayed on them. From all appearances, he suffered a mild concussion from which he quickly recovered. In the tenth round, he knocked Ortiz out.

Nine months later, Wilder decked Tyson Fury in the final round of their championship fight. Fury lay on his back, seemingly only barely conscious. Then he rose to his feet just before the count of ten, a heroic effort that evoked images of a barely conscious Larry Holmes climbing off the canvas against Earnie Shavers and Renaldo Snipes. That, most likely, was a moderate concussion. At the end of twelve rounds, the judges ruled the fight a draw.

Neither Wilder fight would have been allowed to continue had it been a four-round preliminary bout. But given the attendant circumstances, each fight went on. Maybe things shouldn't be that way, but that's the way they are.

Let's be honest. If fights were stopped every time a boxer was dazed or buzzed, there would be no boxing.

There are lots of lessons that Donald Trump never learned. One of them could have been taught to him by Gerald Ford.

When Muhammad Ali and Gerald Ford Met

On June 25, 2019—one day after the United States Women's National Team advanced to the quarter-finals of the World Cup—*Eight by Eight* magazine posted a video clip from an interview conducted in May in which Megan Rapinoe was asked, "Are you excited about going to the White House?"

Rapinoe is white and openly gay. She's also the heart and soul of the United States Women's National Team. On multiple occasions, she has followed Colin Kaepernick's lead and declined to stand for the playing of the National Anthem.

"I'm not going to the fucking White House," Rapinoe responded. "No, I'm not going to the White House." Then, taking note of Donald Trump's proclivities, she added, "We're not going to be invited."

The following day, Trump responded with a three-part tweet that read, "Women's soccer player, @mPinoe, just stated that she is 'not going to the F...ing White House if we win.' Other than the NBA, which now refuses to call owners, owners (please explain that I just got Criminal Justice Reform passed, Black unemployment is at the lowest level in our Country's history, and the poverty index is also best number EVER), leagues and teams love coming to the White House. I am a big fan of the American Team, and Women's Soccer, but Megan should WIN first before she TALKS! Finish the job! We haven't yet invited Megan or the team, but I am now inviting the TEAM, win or lose. Megan should never disrespect our Country, the White House, or our Flag, especially since so much has been done for her & the team. Be proud of the Flag that you wear. The USA is doing GREAT!"

Despite Trump's tweet, no invitation to visit the White House was extended to the team after it won the World Cup.

Trump's conflict with Megan Rapinoe brings back memories of a conversation I had with Gerald Ford in 1989 when I was conducting research for a biography entitled *Muhammad Ali: His Life and Times.*

Ali was once one of the most reviled men in the America. He had accepted the teachings of a black separatist religion known as the Nation of Islam. Then, at the height of the war in Vietnam, he refused induction into the United States Army after uttering the immortal words, "I ain't got no quarrel with them Vietcong." He was stripped of his championship, precluded from boxing for more than three years, and faced five years in prison before his criminal conviction was overturned by the United States Supreme Court. Through it all, Ali persevered. On October 30, 1974, he dethroned George Foreman to reclaim the heavyweight championship of the world.

Then came an occasion that would have been unthinkable if today's race-baiting president had been in office. On December 10, 1974, at the invitation of Gerald Ford, Muhammad Ali visited the White House.

"When I took office," Ford told me thirty years ago, "we as a nation were pretty much torn apart. There were conflicts between families, in colleges, and on the streets. We'd gone through some serious race problems. The Vietnam War had heightened differences. And of course, there was the heritage of Watergate. One of the major challenges my administration faced was how we could heal the country. Not that everybody had to agree, but at least we should lower our voices and listen to one another. I think that, during the two-and-a-half years I was president, we did that. And having Muhammad Ali come to the Oval Office was part of our overall effort. I felt it was important to reach out and indicate individually as well as collectively that we could have honest differences without bitterness. So I wanted to meet Muhammad, not only because of my interest in sports, but because it was part of my overall effort to heal the wounds of racial division, Vietnam, and Watergate."

How did the meeting go?

"I recall it quite well," Ford reminisced. "I've always been interested in boxing. It goes back to my youth, when I can recall very vaguely Jack Dempsey and Gene Tunney and then, later, Joe Louis. And I've always been a sports enthusiast. I always liked to meet the best in any part of the sporting world, and certainly Muhammad Ali was representative of that group. His visit was an enjoyable time for me. Muhammad never lacked for words, and it was a real pleasure to chat with him. We talked about some of his successes and my interest in sports. I've always respected what he accomplished in boxing. And he was a man of principle. I know there were some who thought he evaded his military responsibility, but I've never questioned anybody's dedication to whatever religion they believe in. I give people the maximum benefit of the doubt when they take a stand predicated on conscience. That's always been my philosophy, so I never joined the critics who complained about what he did and didn't do during the Vietnam War. I accepted his decision."

It's sad how times have changed.

Jarrell Miller, PEDs, and Boxing

Jarrell Miller is the poster boy this week for the use of banned performance-enhancing drugs in boxing. But there's plenty of blame to go around and people who are more culpable than Miller.

Let's start with some facts.

Miller was suspended by the California State Athletic Commission in 2014 after testing positive for methylhexaneamine following a Glory 17 kickboxing event. More recently, he was dropped from the World Boxing Council rankings because he refused to join the WBC Clean Boxing Program. When it was time to sign up for PED testing by the Voluntary Anti-Doping Association (VADA) as required by his contract to fight Anthony Joshua at Madison Square Garden on June 1, 2019, Jarrell dragged his heels before submitting the necessary paperwork. Meanwhile, at press conferences in New York and London to promote the bout, he accused Joshua of using illegal performance-enhancing drugs.

On April 16, it was revealed that a urine sample taken from Miller by a VADA collection officer on March 20 had tested positive for GW1516 (a banned substance also known as Cardarine and Endurobol). GW1516 was developed in the 1990s to treat diabetes, obesity, and cardiovascular disease. Its use was largely discontinued in 2007 after it was linked to the development of cancer during trials on mice. It's not classified as an anabolic steroid but is considered an anabolic compound and has anabolic properties because it helps build muscle mass. Essentially, it forces skeletal muscle to use fat rather than carbohydrates as an energy source and is also an endurance aid.

On April 17, the New York State Athletic Commission denied Miller's request for a license that would have allowed him to fight Joshua. In so doing, the commission indicated that if the B-sample taken from Jarrell on March 20 were tested and came back negative, he could reapply for the license.

That same day, Team Miller formally requested that Jarrell's B-sample be tested, and Miller posted a statement on social media that read, "I am absolutely devastated upon hearing the news my boxing license has been revoked in NY State and I will be vigorously appealing this decision. I have NEVER knowingly taken any banned substance and, when I found out the news, I was totally shocked. My team and I stand for integrity, decency & honesty and together we will stand to fight this with everything we have! This was a voluntarily test that I was very happy to do and these results came just one week after another voluntarily test that I had taken which was completely clean. I refuse to just lie down and let my dream be taken away from me when I know in my heart that I've done nothing wrong. 15 years of hard work. I'm WARRIOR. I don't need a banned substance."

One day later, on April 18, VADA notified the New York State Athletic Commission, promoter Eddie Hearn, and both the Joshua and Miller camps that a blood sample taken from Jarrell on March 31 had tested positive for human growth hormone, another banned substance.

On April 19, Miller hit the trifecta when it was announced that a urine sample taken from him by VADA on March 31 had come back positive for EPO (erythropoietin), a banned performance-enhancing drug that stimulates the production of red blood cells.

That evening, Miller posted a video on social media in which he acknowledged, "This is your boy, 'Big Baby' Miller here, A lot can be said right now. I'ma get straight to the point, I messed up. I messed up. I made a bad call. A lot of ways to handle a situation. I handled it wrongly. And I'm paying the price for it. Missed out on a big opportunity and I'm hurtin' on the inside. My heart is bleeding right now. I hurt my family, my friends, my team, my supporters. But I'm gonna own up to it. I'm gonna deal with it, I'ma correct it and I'm gonna come back better. I'm humbled by the experience. I understand how to handle certain things. I'm gonna leave it at that. I love you guys and I appreciate you guys out there, and as fighters we go through a lot, I don't wanna make it a bad name for ourselves. It's time to do right and get right. So I thank you guys."

Miller got caught, but he wasn't alone in his wrongdoing. Forty years ago, Ken Norton was known for his chiseled physique. In boxing's current PED era, most elite fighters are more chiseled than Norton ever was. They aren't all clean.

It's a matter of record that numerous fighters have had adverse findings with regard to the use of performance-enhancing drugs. The list includes—but is not limited to—Luis Ortiz, Alexander Povetkin, Antonio Tarver, Lamont Peterson, Andre Berto, James Toney, Shannon Briggs, Tyson Fury, Ricardo Mayorga, Lucas Browne, Fernando Vargas, Frans Botha, J'Leon Love, Orlando Salido, Brandon Rios, and Canelo Alvarez. In addition, suspicions have been raised with regard to stars like Floyd Mayweather, Manny Pacquiao, Shane Mosley, and Evander Holyfield.

The United States Anti-Doping Agency began testing professional boxers for performance-enhancing drugs in 2010. USADA could have been instrumental in cracking down on the use of PEDs in boxing. Instead, it became an instrument of accommodation. USADA's website states that it administered 1,501 tests on 128 professional boxers. Yet it reported only one adverse finding regarding a professional boxer to a governing state athletic commission.

By way of comparison, Dr Margaret Goodman (president of the Voluntary Anti-Doping Association) says that close to four percent of the tests for illegal performance-enhancing drugs conducted by VADA come back positive. Using the four-percent benchmark, one would expect that 60 of the 1,501 tests conducted by USADA would have yielded a positive result.

In recent months, USADA has conceded to multiple third parties that there was more than one positive test result with regard to a professional boxer but that it chose to "adjudicate these matters internally" without reporting the positive result to the opposing fighter's camp or state athletic commission that had oversight responsibility with regard to a given fight.

Moreover, it appears as though USADA—with public scrutiny focusing on its test results—has stopped testing professional boxers for PEDs. According to the USADA website (updated through April 20, 2019), the most recent tests conducted on professional boxers by USADA were administered to Danny Garcia and Shawn Porter, who fought each other at Barclays Center on September 8, 2018.

In other words, a company that conducted more than fifteen hundred tests on professional boxers over the course of eight years (and reaped hundreds of thousands, if not millions, of dollars from the procedure) suddenly stopped testing professional boxers.

Good riddance.

The various state athletic commissions have also been delinquent in their oversight responsibilities as they relate to illegal performance-enhancing drugs. Not one commission has developed the expertise, committed the financial resources, and otherwise demonstrated the resolve to eliminate the use of illegal PEDs.

Four of Miller's most recent six fights have been under the jurisdiction of the New York State Athletic Commission. One can speculate that Jarrell didn't suddenly decide to load up on a cornucopia of banned performance-enhancing drugs for his fight against Anthony Joshua without having tried any of them before. Hypothetically speaking, he could have been using the same banned substances prior to all of his recent fights.

VADA president Dr. Margaret Goodman says that, had Miller's samples been collected by the New York State Athletic Commission and tested pursuant to current NYSAC protocols, none of the three banned substances would have been detected. It's unlikely that the three drugs would have been detected pursuant to the PED testing protocols of any other state athletic commission either unless the tests were administered by VADA.

Does the attention focused recently on Jarrell Miller represent an opportunity to change the culture of PED use in boxing? And if so, how can the culture be changed?

No one entity can rid boxing of performance-enhancing drugs. But a coordinated effort by the powers that be can take significant steps in the right direction.

First, a shout out to Margaret Goodman and VADA. Dr. Goodman has waged a courageous, often lonely struggle against the spread of performance-enhancing drugs in boxing. She has put an enormous amount of time and quite a bit of her own money into the cause.

Each state athletic commission should demand that a fighter submit to VADA testing as a prerequisite to that fighter being licensed within its jurisdiction. The Association of Boxing Commissions should encourage its members to adopt this policy. If the various state athletic commissions act in concert, it will preclude forum shopping by PED users.

State athletic commissions should also, where appropriate, enlist the aid of law enforcement authorities.

Government entities don't effectively combat heroin use by

prosecuting addicts. In addition to providing treatment for addiction, they combat heroin use by prosecuting the drug traffickers.

There are gyms in the United States that are known as distribution centers for illegal performance-enhancing drugs. There are physical conditioners who have a known affinity for these substances. Fighters who have tested positive for illegal PEDs should be asked under oath, "Where did the drugs come from? Who, what, how, when, and where?" We already know why.

The New York State Athletic Commission might try to wash its hands of Miller. The commission might say, "We denied Jarrell a license. He's not a licensee. Therefore, we have no further jurisdiction over him."

That would be consistent with the NYSAC looking the other way when Jermall and Jermell Charlo missed drug tests prior to fighting at Barclays Center last December.

The NYSAC might also feel that it doesn't have counsel capable of properly handling the matter. Ryan Sakacs (who previously served as counsel to the commission) once served as a criminal prosecutor and has expertise in drug cases. The current commission counsel seems less suited to the task. But the NYSAC could reach beyond its immediate staff to find more experienced counsel in the New York State Department of State or Attorney General's Office. The NYSAC could also reach out to Sakacs and retain his services on an hourly basis (which was his arrangement with the commission prior to his departure).

Promoters should encourage VADA testing to protect their clean fighters. In that regard, a special message is in order for Premier Boxing Champions and Al Haymon. They haven't done the majority of their fighters any favors by steering them clear of meaningful VADA testing. What they have done is ensure that many PBC fighters are getting hit in the head harder than would otherwise be the case.

The television networks and streaming video channels that now provide the bulk of the money for boxing should require VADA testing for every fighter who appears in a main event or co-featured bout on their network.

The world sanctioning organizations should follow the lead of the World Boxing Council and institute drug-testing programs similar to the WBC Clean Boxing Program.

The media has to be more vigilant and more involved in exposing the use of illegal performance-enhancing drugs in boxing.

And most important, fighters should demand VADA testing. They're the ones who are most at risk.

Right now, many elite fighters feel that they have to use performance-enhancing drugs to be competitive against other fighters who are juicing. But as years pass, this escalation of weaponry will take a hideous toll on them.

Credible PED testing is expensive. It's impractical to think that it can be put in place for every fighter and every fight. But spot testing is a partial deterrent. Some of the hundreds of millions of dollars being poured into boxing now by DAZN, ESPN, and Fox should be used to fund VADA PED-testing programs.

Talking about performance-enhancing drugs several months ago, Jarrell Miller said, "Your life is on the line. Your career is at stake. Guys are gonna do what they gotta do."

So a thought in closing:

The Bible tells us that Jesus told those who would stone an adulteress, "He that is without sin among you, let him first cast a stone" (John, Chapter 8, Verse 7).

Let's adapt that thought for today's fighters: "He that is without sin among you, let him sign up for VADA testing."

When Jarrell Miller tested positive for illegal performance-enhancing drugs prior to his scheduled June 1, 2019, fight against Anthony Joshua, Matchroom Sport managing director Eddie Hearn expressed outrage. But Hearn appeared to thumb his nose at procedures and protocols intended to rid boxing of illegal performance-enhancing drugs when Danny Jacobs was scheduled to fight Julio Cesar Chavez Jr.

Matchroom, Chavez Jr., PED Tests, and Forum Shopping

Matchroom Boxing USA plans to promote—and DAZN plans to stream—a super-middleweight fight between Danny Jacobs and Julio Cesar Chavez Jr. on December 20, 2019. Few boxing insiders think the bout will be competitive. Jacobs is a prohibitive favorite. But DAZN wants Chavez on the network because it believes his presence will drive subscription buys in the Hispanic American community. Matchroom Sports managing director Eddie Hearn wants the dollars that will come with promoting the fight. Chavez wants the payday. And Jacobs wants to get back in the win column while making as much money as possible after losing to Canelo Alvarez this past May.

Initially, Jacobs–Chavez was slated for the MGM Grand Garden Arena in Las Vegas. Then, on October 24, pursuant to a request by the Nevada State Athletic Commission, a Voluntary Anti-Doping Association (VADA) collection officer went to the Wild Card Gym in Hollywood where Chavez was training to collect a urine sample from the fighter to be tested for illegal performance-enhancing drugs.

According to information transmitted by VADA to the NSAC, Chavez arrived at the gym shortly before 2:00 p.m. At that time, the VADA collection officer introduced himself and Chavez refused to provide the sample. He repeated his refusal several times as the afternoon progressed. VADA president Dr. Margaret Goodman was contacted by Matchroom Boxing CEO Frank Smith and Shaun Palmer (counsel for Matchroom), who asked that the VADA collection officer remain on site while they sought to convince Chavez to provide the sample. At 4:35

p.m., after Chavez had left the gym and it was clear that he would not return to provide the sample, the VADA collection officer left.

On October 30, at the behest of executive director Bob Bennett, the Nevada State Athletic Commission placed Chavez on temporary suspension pending the result of a November 20 commission meeting. An attorney representing Chavez reached out informally to the Nevada Attorney General's office (which has jurisdiction over the NSAC) for relief. But the AG's office stood by Bennett.

Thereafter, Eddie Hearn found what he was looking for in the form of a more compliant state athletic commission. Francisco Meneses (executive director of the Arizona Boxing and MMA Commission) said that the fight could proceed in Arizona and that drug testing would be conducted by Drug Free Sport US (an organization that lacks the credibility of VADA).

After Arizona was announced as the site for the fight, Hearn told FightHype.com, "Chavez hadn't signed for the fight, hadn't signed up for VADA, and Nevada through VADA turned up to test him. And he said, 'Well, I haven't signed for the fight yet.' So he didn't test and they chose to not license him. So I went to the ABC, went to the other boxing commissions, who said, 'We'll license him, no problem. He just has to sign up for testing, which he's done in full. And on we go."

But Hearn's explanation is flawed.

First, under Nevada law, the Nevada State Athletic Commission has jurisdiction to test a fighter for performance-enhancing drugs once a promoter requests a date for a fight from the commission. And Matchroom had previously requested December 20 as the date for Jacobs–Chavez.

Moreover, the Muhammad Ali Boxing Reform Act provides that each boxing commission shall establish procedures to ensure that no boxer is permitted to box within its jurisdiction while under suspension from any other boxing commission as a consequence of a failed drug test. And the World Anti-Doping Agency (WADA) code expressly treats evading, refusing, or failing to submit to a drug test as a violation with penalties that are the same as the penalties for a failed drug test.

The Ali Act was designed to prevent forum shopping of the kind that is happening now in conjunction with Jacobs–Chavez.

Before Matchroom settled on Arizona as the site for Jacobs–Chavez, it reached out informally to the California State Athletic Commission to determine whether Chavez might be licensed in California. But Chavez has had a troubled relationship with the CSAC. He was supposed to fight on the Deontay Wilder vs. Tyson Fury undercard in Los Angeles last December but missed multiple appointments with CSAC medical personnel (at least one of which would have included testing for PEDs). Thereafter, he was pulled from the Wilder–Fury undercard.

The response of CSAC executive director Andy Foster to Matchroom's inquiry regarding Jacobs–Chavez was such that Hearn decided to look elsewhere for a site.

Hearn's claim that he "went to the ABC [Association of Boxing Commissions], went to the other boxing commissions, who said, 'We'll license him, no problem. He just has to sign up for testing," is particularly problematic.

Hearn may, or may not, have spoken with Mike Mazzulli (a former ABC president who is still a member of the ABC executive board). But Mazzulli no longer speaks with the authority of the ABC. And even if he did, he wouldn't have the authority to waive a violation of the Ali Act.

In that regard, the thoughts of Brian Dunn (the current ABC president) are instructive. On November 12, Dunn told Boxing Scene, "I did not speak to Eddie Hearn. I did speak with Bob Bennett and Francisco Meneses [executive director of the Boxing & MMA Commission at the Arizona Department of Gaming]. And I'm not happy about this. I don't like the commission shopping aspect of it. I don't think it's legal under the Ali Act for the fight to go forward in Arizona if Chavez is on suspension in Nevada for refusing to take a test. I just don't think it's a good idea for Arizona to proceed with this fight under these circumstances."

There is one sliver of hope for Matchroom and Chavez. As earlier noted, the NSAC placed Chavez on temporary suspension pending the result of a November 20 commission meeting. At that meeting, the five commissioners are expected to review the temporary suspension and set it down for a hearing on December 18.

The key question is whether, in the interim, the NSAC commissioners will classify Chavez's suspension as an administrative suspension or a suspension for refusing to submit to a sample collection. In the first instance, Jacobs–Chavez might be viable. If the NSAC chooses the latter option, the Arizona commission would be in violation of federal law if it allowed Jacobs–Chavez to be contested.

Here, one might note that, in the past, Chavez has had an adversarial relationship with the NSAC. In 2009, he tested positive for Furosemide (a banned diuretic) following a decision victory over Troy Roland and the result of the fight was changed to no decision. He also tested positive for marijuana following a decision loss to Sergio Martinez in Nevada in 2012 after which he was fined and suspended.

As for Arizona, one source who has spoken with Francisco Meneses says that Meneses assured him he would not let Jacobs–Chavez proceed in Arizona if the Nevada State Athletic Commission classifies and upholds Chavez's suspension as being for refusing to take a drug test. "But from Francisco's point of view," the source explains, "that's okay. At that point, Arizona will still have a Danny Jacobs fight. It's just that it will be against Gabriel Rosado instead of Chavez Jr."

Rosado is Jacobs's backup opponent in the event that Chavez doesn't make it to ring center for the opening bell on December 20. Gabriel has had twelve fights over the past seven years and won three of them. He has never fought at a weight above 160 pounds. If Jacobs–Chavez turns into Jacobs–Rosado, it will be a classic case of bait-and-switch.

In an era when "crazy money" is being thrown around in boxing, at least one company has stayed grounded in reality.

The Future and FITE

Streaming video is playing an increasingly important role in sports. Boxing fans are already familiar with DAZN and ESPN+. Now meet FITE.

FITE is a subsidiary of Flipps Media, a small technology company that patented a technology that allows users to download programming from the cloud and cast it to a smart TV by means of an application on the user's smartphone. In other words, users no longer need a computer to watch internet programming on their television set.

Flipps founded FITE in 2016 to exploit this technology in conjunction with combat sports. FITE also allows viewers to watch programming on a computer or tablet without downloading its app by going directly to the FITE website.

FITE's only permanent office is in Bulgaria. That's where company CEO and founder Kosta Jordanov lives and a 20-person technology team is located. It has six employees in the United States.

"That's modern business," executive advisor Roy Langbord (FITE's point person on boxing) notes. "FITE has servers around the world. It doesn't need offices around the world."

FITE began acquiring content in 2016 and streamed several small events that year. Since then, its footprint has grown.

There's an enormous amount of boxing available now on television and streaming video. This means that fans are becoming more discriminating about what they watch, which is a problem for some networks and promoters. But not for FITE.

FITE is a distributor. It's a vehicle (often one of many) by which viewers can buy a given pay-per-view combat sports event. It has the ability to stream dozens of live events and accommodate an unlimited number of viewers simultaneously with HDTV transmission and no buffering. It can throw as many events as it wants against the wall and see what sticks.

"We don't reach into our pocket for millions of dollars to buy programming," Langbord explains. "We don't produce shows or control content. You provide us with a signal and, at no further cost to you, we'll distribute it on a revenue share basis. We're not looking for exclusives. We're happy to be one piece of your puzzle. It's as simple as that."

But not simple from a technological point of view. By way of example; FITE was rebuffed in its attempt to participate in distributing streaming video of last November's match between Tiger Woods and Phil Mickelson. The promotion opted for an exclusive digital distributor instead. Then the online pay-per-view ordering system crashed under the weight of last-minute orders; the promotion opened up a free internet stream; and cable companies refunded the cable purchase price to buyers who had paid for the promotion.

"We've handled much bigger events than that and much heavier traffic without a problem," Langbord says.

For each pay-per-view event that FITE distributes, there's a negotiated split of revenue between FITE and the content provider. The split (which industry sources say ranges from fifty-fifty to seventy-thirty in favor of the provider) is always more favorable that the split offered to the provider by basic cable or satellite distributors.

The price to the public to watch an event on FITE matches the "suggested retail price" in whatever market an event is streamed. Content can be geo-priced and geo-blocked.

If FITE distributes an event in a foreign country, it's distributed in the language (or languages) supplied by the content provider. The exception to this is an agreement by FITE to provide Spanish-language audio for some of Canelo Alvarez's fights.

In marketing events, FITE can turn to a list of 1.5 million registered users, many of whom have downloaded the FITE app and each of whom has provided the company with an email address. There's some free programming, most of which is promotional material for pay-per-view events that FITE intends to distribute.

"Our pitch to content providers is simple," Langbord says. "We tell them, 'We're willing to come in at the last minute and fill in the gaps on your map around the world. Come to us and you can get worldwide distribution with one contract. If you haven't sold rights to distribute your event in Serbia, we'll make it available in Serbia for whatever price you want. No matter how many buys we get, it's found money for you at no cost to the promotion.'"

"And there's a nice side benefit to working with FITE," Langbord adds. "We can track numbers as they're coming in. How many households are buying an event? Where are they located? How many are watching at any given time? It takes days, sometimes weeks, to get these numbers from traditional cable-TV distribution. With FITE, you get them in real time."

FITE now streams roughly two dozen events each week, most of them on Friday and Saturday nights. It's the sole distributor for many small independent shows and participates in the distribution of larger ones. It has reached a point where it turns down content if the proposed programming falls short of its production standards or will appeal to too small an audience. It has been unable to close a deal with WWE, and an old deal with UFC expired. But FITE currently distributes programming for Top Rank, Premier Boxing Champions, and Golden Boy among other content providers.

It also distributes Canelo Alvarez's fights in markets where DAZN doesn't have a channel and hasn't otherwise disposed of rights to a given Canelo bout. FITE doesn't reveal buy numbers to the public. But industry sources say that its most successful distribution effort to date was Canelo–Golovkin II where FITE generated almost 50,000 additional PPV buys for the promotion.

That brings us to the July 20, 2019, fight between Manny Pacquiao and Keith Thurman.

Initially, PBC granted nonexclusive rights to FITE to distribute Pacquiao–Thurman in the United States, Canada, and (jointly with ITV) the United Kingdom and Ireland. Other markets were off limits while PBC tried to sell rights on its own, often on an exclusive basis.

Then, during fight week, PBC contracted for FITE to distribute Pacquiao–Thurman in Austria, the Czech Republic, Denmark, East Timor, Estonia, Finland, Germany, Hong Kong, Hungary, Iceland, India, Italy, Kazakhstan, Latvia, Lithuania, Macau, Malaysia, Mongolia, Myanmar, Norway, Romania, Slovakia, South Korea, Sweden, Switzerland, Taiwan, and the Caribbean Islands.

"We make it easy to do business with us," Langbord says. "Our feelings aren't hurt if you come to us after you couldn't sell something somewhere else."

Most of the orders for Pacquiao–Thurman were placed on fight night.

"Wrestling fans buy shows in advance," FITE COO Michael Weber notes. "Boxing fans buy late. At least one-third of our buys for boxing come in after the pay-per-view event has started; some as late as the first round or two of the main event."

So far, FITE has spent small and smart. It was built with a modest capital investment of roughly $9 million. Startup costs have not been recouped yet, but the company began operating in the black this year. Its technology is constantly being upgraded to accommodate new equipment and new platforms. Growth has been constant.

At some point in the future, FITE might expand its one-event-at-a-time formula to offer subscriptions to sites like DAZN and Box Nation. It's also considering expanding into the distribution of music events and other sports like motor racing.

"Streaming video is only going to get bigger," Mike Weber says. "Cord-cutting is the wave of the future. When FITE launched in 2016, twenty percent of households in the United States didn't have cable or satellite TV. Now that number is thirty-five percent."

And there's another significant change that Weber sees unfolding: "Promoters are now starting to call us rather than our having to call them to pitch our product."

In boxing, the bullies reign.

When Red Corner vs. Blue Corner is Unfair

In the early years of boxing in the United States, fighters flipped a coin to determine which fighter sat in which corner. Or alternatively, the fighter who entered the ring first had choice of corner. That was important for outdoor fights since it was often the difference between a fighter facing the sun between rounds or sitting with his back to it.

Over time, traditions evolved.

Aileen Eaton promoted fights at The Olympic Auditorium in Los Angeles for four decades during the mid-twentieth century, first with her husband and later with Don Chargin. There was an informal "gamblers section" at The Olympic where bets were placed on one corner or the other before the fighters entered the ring. Ring announcer Jimmy Lennon Sr., holding a wooden disk in his hand, would meet the fighters as they climbed through the ropes. One side of the disk was black, the other white. Lennon instructed the fighter who entered the ring first to "call it." The fighter would call "black" or "white." Lennon would flip the disk. And whichever fighter won the toss had choice of corner.

Octogenarian boxing publicist Bill Caplan recalls, "A lot of gamblers held their breath on that one."

Then television dictated a change. ESPN, USA Network, and HBO began demanding that favored fighters sit in certain corners to be more easily seen on camera between rounds. And things went from there.

Now most fight cards have a "winners" corner and a "losers" corner. For major bouts, the televising network often tells the promoter which fighter it wants in which corner. For undercard bouts, it's the promoter's call. But almost always, fighters who are expected to win are assigned to the same corner throughout the night.

"And it's not just the pros," trainer Pat Burns says. "You see the same winners-corner, losers-corner setup at big amateur tournaments too."

Moreover, this delineation often extends to dressing rooms with all of the favored undercard fighters in one big room and the designated losers in another.

Fighters in the underdog corner know why they're there. They understand their role going in. Some of them are motivated by their B-side status. Others fight down to expectations. On occasion, a B-side fighter returns to the losers dressing room with a victory and his brethren erupt in cheers.

If he did it, I can too.

But these moments are few and far between. Most of the time, underdog dressing rooms are dreary places.

Trainer Don Turner objects to the winners-corner, losers-corner dichotomy.

"Most fights today aren't competitive," Turner says. "But why would you announce that to everyone in the arena by putting all the guys you know are going to win in one corner and all the guys you know are going to lose in the other?"

The answer is simple. The playing field has always been tilted more toward the house favorite in boxing than in other sports. Promoters do it to give the fighter they expect and want to win an additional advantage.

"As long as the present system is in use," promoter Lou DiBella says, "I'll do what I can within the rules to benefit my fighter. But let's be honest about it. The present system isn't fair. It makes the point to the judges who the favored fighter is and who's supposed to win. And in a close round that a judge has trouble deciding, that can be a factor."

"I'd love to say that, once the bell rings, the corners don't matter," trainer-commentator Teddy Atlas adds. "But that's not true. Consciously or subconsciously, some judges are influenced by which corners the fighters are in. The whole situation makes it easier for some judges to do the wrong thing. It greases the skids a little bit more than they're already greased and gives another advantage to the fighter who's already protected by the house money."

And there's more.

"You talk about the judges being influenced," longtime promoter Don Elbaum observes. "And they are. But the ring doctors are influenced too. They're much more likely to stop a fight in the corner when they know a certain guy is expected to lose. And it can affect the referee's rulings too."

What should be done to remedy situation?

David Berlin, who served as executive director of the New York State Athletic Commission several years ago, says, "I don't like the practice. I think it sends the wrong message. But I don't think it's a proper subject for regulation. It's the commission's job to appoint competent officials who aren't influenced by which corner a fighter is in. Beyond that, it's the promoter's show, and the promoter should be able to present it the way he or she wants to."

Pennsylvania State Athletic Commission executive director Greg Sirb is in accord and notes, "We talked about it with some of the promoters last year. I'd like to see them mix the corners up a bit, but it's not enough of an issue for us to mandate it."

That said; fights would be a bit more equitable if corners were assigned at random by a coin toss.

"I don't have a problem with which fighter walks to the ring first and which fighter is introduced first," Don Turner says. "But once the bell rings, the fighting should speak for itself."

So let's give the final word to Teddy Atlas, who declares, "For most of the fights I've been involved with as a trainer, my guys have been in the favorite corner. But that doesn't keep me from seeing how unfair the situation can be. You're putting up a sign that tells the judges that the person who's paying them to judge wants a certain fighter to win. And you're announcing to the world, 'This guy is just an opponent. We brought him here so our guy can get another win.' It doesn't seem right to me. Most B-side guys are trying to win whether they have a realistic chance of winning or not and whether the people running the show want them to have a chance or not. They're telling themselves, 'This could be my big moment. This could be the night I turn my life around.' They're putting their future, they're putting their life on the line. Don't tilt the playing field more than it's already tilted."

2019 marked the end of another decade for the sweet science.

Fighter of the Decade

Ever since John L. Sullivan became America's first sports superstar in the 1880s, each ten-year period has seen one or more fighters who were worthy of being designated "Fighter of the Decade."

History judges elite fighters in large measure by their record against other elite fighters and how they performed in their most difficult challenges. History also awards points for longevity because, as A. J. Liebling wrote, "Only the great ones win the title young and hold onto it." And consideration is given to whether a fighter's reign was special in a way that went beyond boxing.

Looking at past eras, my choices for Fighter of the Decade are:

1880–1889: John L. Sullivan

1890–1899: Bob Fitzsimmons with honorable mention to
James J. Corbett

1900–1909: Joe Gans with honorable mention to James
Jeffries and Stanley Ketchel

1910–1919: Jack Johnson

1920–1929: Jack Dempsey and Gene Tunney with honorable mention to Benny Leonard

1930–1939: Joe Louis with honorable mention to Henry
Armstrong

1940–1949: Sugar Ray Robinson

1950–1959: Rocky Marciano with honorable mention to
Archie Moore

1960–1969: Muhammad Ali

1970–1979: Roberto Duran with honorable mention to
Carlos Monzon

1980–1989: Sugar Ray Leonard with honorable mention
to Larry Holmes, Mike Tyson, Marvin Hagler, and Julio
Cesar Chavez.

1990–1999: Roy Jones with honorable mention to Evander
Holyfield, Lennox Lewis, and Pernell Whitaker

2000–2009: Manny Pacquiao with honorable mention to
Floyd Mayweather and Bernard Hopkins

These men were dominant in their time. Many brought never-before-seen skills to their craft, captured the public imagination, and engaged in legendary fights. They were champions—often in multiple weight classes and in eras when the term "champion" was synonymous with greatness. A few changed the social fabric of America. Their ring exploits were the stuff of legend.

Significantly, only one of the men designated above as "Fighter of the Decade"—Rocky Marciano—was undefeated over the course of his career. All but three—Sullivan, Marciano, and Ali—lost fights during the decade in which they reigned supreme. When a fighter fights the best again and again, sometimes he loses. When Sugar Ray Robinson was young and great, he lost to Jake LaMotta.

At the end of 2019, writers and fans will decide who deserves to be called boxing's latest "Fighter of the Decade." In prior eras, there were more than enough worthy candidates for the honor because fighters went in tough and fought other great fighters in their prime.

But that doesn't happen much anymore. Most elite fighters today lack the inquisitors to be considered great. Instead, they're "all-time goods." The days when Ray Leonard, Thomas Hearns, Roberto Duran, and Marvin Hagler engaged in their extraordinary round-robin warfare are long gone. Too often now, hype and glitz take priority over the best fighting the best.

Still, someone will be named "Fighter of the Decade." Who deserves the honor?

Manny Pacquiao entered the decade as the hottest property in boxing with devastating knockouts of Oscar De La Hoya, Ricky Hatton, and Miguel Cotto in his previous three fights. But Pacquiao's record in the current decade (12–4, 1 KO) falls short of the mark. Two of the four blemishes on his record during the past ten years came on questionable decisions. But Manny was outclassed by Floyd Mayweather and starched by Juan Manuel Marquez. And none of his victories since January 1, 2010, were notable with the exception of his triumph over Keith Thurman. He doesn't make the final ballot.

Other fighters are victims of the calendar. Terence Crawford, Vasyl

Lomachenko, and Deontay Wilder have begun to construct impressive bodies of work. But none of them has accomplished nearly enough to warrant consideration for decade-end honors.

The conversation is likely to focus on five fighters:

* Andre Ward (11–0, 3 KOs): Ward entered the decade as a participant in Showtime's "Super Six" tournament and scored victories over Arthur Abraham, Carl Froch, Chad Dawson, and Sergey Kovalev (twice). He's a craftsman who stayed in his lane and got the job done.

* Floyd Mayweather (10–0, 2 KOs): Mayweather is a worthy candidate. But as in the previous decade, he avoided top fighters in their prime. Shane Mosley, Miguel Cotto, and Manny Pacquiao were past their peak when Floyd fought them, and Canelo Alvarez had yet to mature. Victor Ortiz, Robert Guerrero, Marcos Maidana (twice), Andre Berto, and Conor McGregor round out Floyd's résumé for the decade.

* Wladimir Klitschko (11–2, 7 KOs): Klitschko entered the decade with the IBF and WBO belts around his waist and added the WBA bauble. But his victories came against a "who's who" of mediocrity, and he ended the decade with losses to Tyson Fury and Anthony Joshua. Wladimir was an imposing presence on the boxing scene and he wore his crown with grace. But to be "Fighter of the Decade," a boxer needs to have beaten worthy inquisitors. Klitschko didn't.

* Gennady Golovkin (22–1–1, 20 KOs): Golovkin has to answer the same question put to other "Fighter of the Decade" candidates —"Who did you beat?" He amassed a string of impressive victories against workmanlike competition. But when the time came for Gennady to step up the level of opposition, he was less than great. Golovkin's supporters say that he was "robbed" against Canelo Alvarez. But Danny Jacobs partisans say that Jacobs was robbed against Golovkin.

* Canelo Alvarez (24–1–1, 14 KOs): Canelo scored victories over an aging Miguel Cotto and an old Shane Mosley. But he has been willing to go in tough. His competitive spirit led him to challenge Floyd Mayweather too soon. He fought and beat Austin Trout and

Erislandy Lara when most name fighters were avoiding them. He battled Gennady Golovkin twice, adding a win and a draw to his résumé. And he closed out the decade with a clear-cut decision over Danny Jacobs and an impressive knockout of Sergey Kovalev.

This is my book. And in my book, Canelo Alvarez is "Fighter of the Decade."

In 2019, one of Muhammad Ali's daughters—Hana—added a new leaf to the tree of remembrance for Ali.

At Home with Muhammad Ali

Muhammad Ali had four wives. Each was important to him in a different way.

Sonji Roy was his first love. They met on July 3, 1964, four months after Ali dethroned Sonny Liston. Muhammad was twenty-two years old, one year younger than she was. Sonji was a strikingly sensuous woman who supported herself by working in nightclubs, entering beauty contests, and modeling. Ali married her forty-one days after they met.

Ali adored Sonji. They were young and full of hope at a time when the most electrifying years of his life had just begun. He was faithful to her throughout their marriage. But Sonji found herself at odds with the Nation of Islam hierarchy, and that brought their marriage down. They divorced on January 10, 1966.

Once, on a sunny afternoon three decades ago when Ali and I were walking near his home in Berrien Springs, Muhammad told me, "If I go to heaven, I want to be there with Sonji."

On August 17, 1967, Ali, then twenty-five years old, married seventeen-year-old Belinda Boyd. Belinda had been raised in the Nation of Islam. She and Ali had four children together: three daughters (Maryum, Rasheda, and Jamillah) and a son (Muhammad Jr.). They divorced in 1977 after years of womanizing on Ali's part. During their marriage, Ali had three daughters out of wedlock. One of these daughters, Hana (born on August 6, 1976), was the love child of Ali and Veronica Porché who would become his third wife.

Veronica was uncommonly beautiful with an elegance about her. She and Ali met in 1974 when she was an eighteen-year-old student at USC and entered a beauty contest to choose poster girls for Ali's upcoming fight against George Foreman in Zaire. Out of seventy entrants, four were chosen to travel around the United States promoting the bout and ultimately to go to Zaire. Veronica was one of them. She and Ali married on June 19, 1977, had a second daughter (Laila, born on December 30, 1977) and divorced nine years later.

On November 19, 1986, Ali married Lonnie Williams, who was his primary companion, caretaker, and rock for the final thirty years of his life.

Now Hana Ali has written a memoir. *At Home with Muhammad Ali* was published by Bantam Press in the United Kingdom and will be published by Amistad this spring in North America. It tells the story of Ali and Veronica from their older daughter's perspective.

Veronica Porché was born on December 16, 1955. Hana recounts that, in high school, her mother was prom queen, senior class president, a straight-A student, and received scholarship offers from USC, UCLA, Princeton, and Yale.

Ali's "courtship" of Veronica is recounted in detail in *At Home With Muhammad Ali.*

"I met him when I was eighteen years old," Veronica recalled years later. "He was tall, handsome, incredibly charismatic, charming, and—to my surprise—shy. He told me that his marriage was really over. I was convinced that his marriage was over emotionally and they were going to get a divorce."

Thereafter, Veronica became a regular presence in Ali's life. At age eighteen, she was being pursued by the most charismatic, exciting, handsome man on the planet.

"Mom never stood a chance," Hana writes.

And of course, Ali would never be unfaithful to her. Or so Veronica thought. After all, Muhammad truly loved her.

Ali bought a condo for Veronica near his home in Chicago. Their relationship became tabloid fodder when he brought her to the Presidential Palace in Manila prior to his October 1, 1975, fight against Joe Frazier. Ten months later, Hana was born. After Ali's divorce from Belinda became final, he and Veronica were married.

Hana's early years were spent in a thirty-room mansion in Fremont Place, a gated community in Los Angeles. Not many kids come home from school and find Michael Jackson sitting in their living room. Then again, not many kids come home from school and find Muhammad Ali in the house.

"I grew up inside a fairy tale," Hana writes. "A family of four living in a beautiful mansion with a trellis and floral vine balcony. My father was the most famous man in the world and my mother one of the most beautiful women in the world. Then, one day when I was ten years old, the fairy tale ended. We were moving to a new house and Daddy wasn't coming."

Long before that, Muhammad and Veronica had begun sleeping in separate bedrooms.

"One morning," Hana recounts, "I had woken up to find my father in the guest bedroom."

"Daddy, why aren't you in bed with Mommy?"

"I snore too loud. I don't want to disturb her."

"But as time passed," Hana recalls, "my mother kept locking her bedroom door, distancing herself from my father."

There was marriage counseling to no avail.

"Those final two years of my parents' marriage," Hana writes, "they traveled the world together making appearances, always friendly and cordial with each other. Everything appeared normal to the press."

But on June 26, 1985, Veronica's lawyers issued a statement saying that she and Muhammad had filed for divorce. And Hana was left to think about Maryum, Rasheda, Jamillah, and Muhammad Jr.—her siblings from Ali's marriage to Belinda: "I wondered what it must have been like for them when he moved away. Did they also cry themselves to sleep night after night when they realized Daddy was never coming home?"

Hana blamed her mother for the breakup of the marriage. Laila was neutral in assigning blame. But given the omnipresent governesses and nannies in their home, both sisters questioned whether their mother loved them.

"For a long time, we didn't believe she did," Hana acknowledges. "She often ate alone, was off riding horses, practicing opera in her room, or running errands. She didn't play on the floor with us very long or sit on the sofa and watch television with us. She often seemed preoccupied and busy. I never really felt her love as strongly as I felt my father's."

But as Hana matured, she came to see her mother's strengths and her father's flaws more clearly.

Marriage to Ali wasn't what Veronica had signed up for. There was an endless stream of visitors in the home with virtually no privacy. And more troubling, as Ali's old ring adversary Earnie Shavers observed, "When a man marries his mistress, he creates a vacancy."

"It's no secret my father fooled around," Hana notes.

Veronica, of course, had been an active participant in Muhammad's earlier infidelity. Now she was on the receiving end of unwanted blows. In a 1979 interview, she had told Marilyn Funt, "When I first met him, I had to get used to his hugging everyone. Now I'm used to it. I can't say I like it, but I try not to pay attention to it. If I had a choice, I would rather that he didn't do it. But it's his personality. Sometimes I just get disgusted with the boldness of the women. Even in front of me, they sort of push you aside and don't acknowledge you. They are really bad sometimes."

But the problems went far deeper than that.

In the late 1970s, Ali made a series of audiotapes that he later gave to Hana as a legacy gift when she was old enough to understand them. Some of the tapes are soliloquies. Others are recordings of telephone calls or in-person conversations. One of the tapes that Hana excerpts in her book reads as follows:

> Veronica: "You shouldn't be out with a woman. That's all. You should just keep away from them. And don't give me any excuse because, too many times before, I trusted you with people like that and something happened. I don't know what you might do. I would never have thought you would have messed with Tammy [one of the family's babysitters]. I would never have thought that."
>
> Muhammad: "Allah is my witness. I never—"
>
> Veronica: "Muhammad; don't you say Allah because you already told me you did."
>
> Muhammad: "But I didn't."
>
> Veronica: "You did too, at the farm. You finally admitted it to me. Tammy was blaming the baby on you and she was going everywhere with us and telling people that she was pregnant. And another time, I came home and you had a lady sitting on your lap. And then, another time, you were in the bus with that woman in the bathroom."

Eventually, Hana stopped blaming her mother for her parents' divorce and confronted her father about his infidelities. After initial denials, he acknowledged his philandering.

Now, recounting her own voyage of self-discovery, Hana writes, "My father was my world. In my eyes, he was responsible for making the sun rise, and I had unfairly cast my mother in the role of the villain, blaming and punishing her ever since I was ten for leaving my beloved father. But really, if anyone is to blame, it is the partner who is being unfaithful. Now, for the first time in my life, I was forced to consider her feelings, what she went through. I knew it was time to face it, to finally admit to myself and the world after all these years that it was not entirely her fault. Dad may have suffered acutely at the end. But my mother's pain was drawn out over many years with each act of betrayal."

And Hana quotes Veronica as saying of Muhammad, "He was a decent, loving human being. His biggest fault was fooling around. I didn't always know when he was fooling around. Sometimes I wouldn't find out until years later. They were mostly one-night stands. But there were too many broken promises. After being hurt so many times, my feelings gradually numbed. Divorce is hard on the person leaving too. I always cared about him, but I had to distance myself."

After the divorce, Veronica went back to school and earned a graduate degree in clinical psychology. In 1992, she married actor Carl Anderson, who died of leukemia in 2004. She currently has a private practice affiliated with the Cedars-Sinai Medical Center in Los Angeles.

The tale of infidelity in marriage is a story that has been told millions of times. But when the main protagonist is Muhammad Ali, it has special meaning. The recounting of Ali's philandering isn't pretty. But Hana has chosen to write it.

At Home with Muhammad Ali has several strengths. For more than three decades, Veronica has maintained a discreet silence regarding her years with Ali and the breakup of their marriage. The books gives us more information in that regard than we had before.

There's occasional humor. One fear Ali had was that someone would kidnap one of his children when they were young. But Hana was such a difficult child that one governess assured him, "Don't worry, Muhammad. If anyone took this child, they'd bring her right back."

And it's entertaining to read about the complexities of the most famous Muslim in the world agreeing to have a Christmas tree for his children in their home.

But there are also flaws.

The audiotapes that Ali recorded in the late 1970s are both a strength and weakness of the book. A strength because on occasion the material is fascinating. A weakness because, too often, Hana quotes from them excessively.

Also, in 2012, Hana discovered a cache of what she describes as love letters that Ali wrote for Veronica as their marriage was disintegrating but never sent to her. These letters are written in Muhammad's hand but phrased in a way that strongly suggests they were written with help from a third party. Indeed, one of the letters states, "I had someone help me with the big words." The letters total twenty-eight handwritten pages and were written over the course of three years. There are places where it feels as though they were forced into the narrative.

And Ali had a tendency to tell stories that weren't true because they were good stories. For example, he once claimed that he put on a white hood and robe and went to a KKK rally. In that vein, the book recounts a purported incident when Muhammad and Elvis Presley went to a "redneck" bar in Pennsylvania and Elvis sang *Hound Dog* for the startled patrons. Hana presents "both sides" of the issue as to whether or not this actually happened. But there's really only one side. It didn't happen. And she hurts her credibility by saying that the truth "will always be a mystery."

The book repeats as true the allegorical tale fashioned for Ali's 1976 autobiography written with Richard Durham that young Cassius Clay threw his Olympic gold medal in the Ohio River. That never happened. And at one point, Hana says that Ali estimated he boxed 150,000 rounds and took 1.5 million blows to the head. Those are ridiculously inaccurate numbers. Ali started fighting at age twelve and retired at age thirty-nine. During his years in exile and the downtime between fights, he was out of the ring altogether. But let's give him credit for fighting four days a week, forty weeks a year, for all twenty-seven years. That would come to 4,300 sessions with—by Ali's reckoning—an average of 35 rounds and 349 blows to the head per session. To repeat; those are ridiculously inaccurate numbers.

Also, there are places in the book where the narrative meanders. And there's too much repetition. For example, readers are told and then retold the same anecdote about Ali leaving home to train for the Larry Holmes fight and Hana crying out in frustration, "You're not my Daddy. You're Muhammad Ali." It's a good story, but it doesn't have to be told twice.

That said; *At Home with Muhammad Ali* adds new insights regarding Ali as a husband and father to the historical record. And it gives Veronica her due.

"My parents shared a great romance," Hana concludes. "Laila and I were born out of their love, and a lot of beautiful memories, adventures, and sometimes pain and sorrow were experienced in the twelve years they were together. They were two remarkable people trying to find their way in the world."

Fistic Notes

George Foreman is in the history books as the oldest man to claim the heavyweight throne, a distinction he earned at age forty-five when he knocked out Michael Moorer on November 5, 1994. But as of this writing, Foreman holds another distinction related to his age. He's boxing's oldest living former heavyweight champion.

Foreman was born on January 10, 1949. That makes him almost ten months older than Larry Holmes, who was born on November 3, 1949. George also has the distinction at present of being the earliest reigning heavyweight king who's still alive.

Asked how he has dealt physically and emotionally with the passage of time, Foreman notes, "Physical things are done now purely as entertainment and for well-being. Such a joy that it's never done for pride and bill paying."

As for his thoughts on being boxing's oldest living former heavyweight champion and the earliest reigning heavyweight champion who's still alive, George responds, "I remember how much I miss the old champs. How I tried to get the attention of Jack Dempsey; my friendship with Sonny Liston; how Joe Frazier was such a frightful boxer and gentle man; the funny and exciting days of Muhammad Ali. The years have now made me the spokesman for every heavyweight champ that I met. So I have many years and also a great responsibility."

Meanwhile, any thoughts that Foreman might have of becoming the oldest living former heavyweight champion ever should be put on hold. Max Schmeling, who claimed the vacant heavyweight throne with a victory over Jack Sharkey in 1930, lived to be ninety-nine years old.

★ ★ ★

Teddy Brenner, who made fights for Madison Square Garden during the glory years when every fighter wanted to ply his trade at MSG, often said that each undercard fight is a brick in constructing a card that sells tickets and entertains the crowd.

Brenner took it for granted—as boxing fans do today—that undercard fights are part of the show. But it wasn't always so.

Boxing was illegal for much of its early history in the United States. Promoters were happy to get in one fight—forget about an undercard—before the police arrived and shut down the show.

Historian Craig Hamilton says that, when John L. Sullivan fought Dominick McCaffrey on the outskirts of Cincinnati on August 29, 1885, there was an undercard bout between Tommy Warren (who eventually fought 35 recorded fights) and Tom (or John) King (who never fought again).

That's the only time Sullivan is known to have fought with an undercard bout preceding his own. The historic September 7, 1892, contest between Sullivan and James Corbett at the Olympic Club in New Orleans was preceded by two championship fights, but they were contested on different days. On September 5, Jack McAuliffe knocked out Billy Myer to successfully defend his world lightweight title. Then, on September 6, George Dixon stopped Jack Skelly in a featherweight championship bout.

State prohibitions against the sweet science began to ease in the first decade of the twentieth century. By 1910, multibout cards were common but considered unnecessary to draw fans to big fights. There was no undercard in Reno prior to Jack Johnson vs. James Jeffries on July 4, 1910. Only one fight preceded Johnson vs. Jess Willard in Havana on April 5, 1915.

Then Tex Rickard (who had promoted Johnson–Jeffries) saw the future. Rickard arranged for six undercard fights when Jack Dempsey challenged Jess Willard for the heavyweight throne on July 4, 1919, in Toledo, Ohio. History tells us that Serafino Sinatra (a Toledo resident who fought under the sobriquet "Wop English") brought a string of newspaper decisions into the ring and scored a first-round knockout over Walter "Whirlwind" Wendt (who was entering the squared circle for the first time as a pro). Then Johnny Lewis (4–2–1) stopped Tommy Long (0–3) in three rounds. Four other undercard bouts went the distance.

A new tradition had been born. Fourteen months later, when Dempsey fought Billy Miske in Benton Harbor, Michigan, Sam Langford and Harry Greb were in separate fights on the undercard.

★ ★ ★

Marvin Miller is a towering figure in sports history. In 1966 when he was elected executive director of the Major League Baseball Players Association, players were bound to their club by a "reserve clause" that precluded free negotiation. Pensions were negligible. Most labor issues were resolved by club owners in a dictatorial manner.

In 1968, Miller negotiated the first collective bargaining agreement in the history of professional sports. That began the process of laying a foundation for an effective labor movement. In 1970, the average salary for a major league baseball player was $29,303. In 2018, it was $4,095,686.

But there was one area where Miller failed the players he represented. He steadfastly opposed meaningful testing for performance-enhancing drugs. In part, his position was born of the fear that players who used recreational drugs might be snared in the dragnet. But as a consequence of his intransigence on the issue, a wave of steroid abuse washed over baseball. Records were tainted. "Clean" players were put at a competitive disadvantage. And the health of users was jeopardized.

It's no secret that the use of illegal performance-enhancing drugs plagues boxing today. But we're not talking about hitting a baseball further. We're talking about fighters getting hit in the head harder.

Al Haymon could take a big step toward changing that.

Like Miller, Haymon has delivered increased purses to the athletes he represents. But over the years, he has shown no inclination to eliminate illegal PED use from boxing. To the contrary, from a questionable alliance with USADA to providing a protective umbrella for fighters who have "missed" tests, he has contributed to exacerbating the PED problem.

Premier Boxing Champions, more than any other promoter, controls its own universe. PBC and its TV partners—Fox and Showtime—could make a difference now if they wanted to. All they would have to do is say that, to be eligible to fight under the PBC banner and appear on Showtime or Fox, a fighter would have to submit to year-round VADA testing. A small percentage of each TV license fee would be sufficient to fund the entire program.

Will Haymon press the issue? I doubt it. And that's a shame. Because if he did, it would be his most important contribution to boxing. As long as the status quo with regard to PEDs is maintained in boxing, more fighters than would otherwise be the case—including PBC fighters—will suffer brain damage.

★ ★ ★

Hundreds of notable fighters have served lengthy terms in prison. But the list is more exclusive when limited to heavyweight champions who spent an extended period of time under lock and key. I'm not talking about John L. Sullivan, jailed on numerous occasions for public intoxication and fighting (both in and out of the ring). Nor am I referencing beltholders like Michael Moorer, Oliver McCall, and Hasim Rahman, each of whom had brushes with the law. I'm talking about heavyweight champions who served long hard time. Let's look at who they are.

* Jack Johnson: In 1913, Johnson was convicted of transporting two women across state lines for immoral purposes and, as the culmination of the legal campaign against him, sentenced to a year and a day in prison. He jumped bail, fled the country, and, after spending seven years in exile, returned to the United States and surrendered to federal agents to serve a ten-month prison term.
* Rocky Marciano: While stationed in England during World War II, Marciano and a fellow soldier robbed two Englishman, beating them up in the process. They were court-martialed and convicted, after which Marciano was dishonorably discharged from the Army and sentenced to three years in prison. He was released after twenty-two months and then allowed to rejoin the military for the duration of 1946 in order to receive an honorable discharge.
* Sonny Liston: Liston's résumé before he began boxing professionally included incarceration for a long string of violent offenses including armed robbery (28 months in prison) and assaulting a police officer (nine months). "Boxing," Jimmy Cannon later wrote, "gave Liston the opportunity to meet bigtime hoodlums instead of small ones."
* Michael Dokes: After serving two years' probation following a plea bargain on charges of cocaine trafficking. Dokes spent eight years in prison subsequent to pleading guilty in 2000 to charges of attempted murder, kidnapping, and battery with intent to commit sexual assault on his girlfriend. Her injuries were so severe that,

according to the police, the victim could not be identified from her driver's license photograph.

* Trevor Berbick: Berbick spent fifteen months in prison in Florida after being convicted in 1992 of raping a woman who had worked as a babysitter for his family. At the time of the crime, he was on probation for assaulting a former business manager.
* Mike Tyson: Tyson spent three years in prison (March 26, 1992, through March 25, 1995) in Indiana after being convicted of rape and deviate sexual conduct. In 1999, he returned to prison—this time in Maryland—for 108 days after assaulting two motorists following a minor traffic accident.
* Riddick Bowe: Bowe was convicted in 1998 of kidnapping his estranged wife and children at knifepoint in the belief that it would lead to a marital reconciliation. Pursuant to a plea bargain, he served seventeen months in prison.

And one who was saved by Lady Justice . . .

In 1967, Muhammad Ali was convicted of refusing induction into the United States Armed Forces and sentenced to five years in prison. Ultimately, his conviction was overturned by the United States Supreme Court. But while Ali's appeal was pending, he was sentenced to ten days incarceration in Dade County, Florida, for driving without a valid license.

"Jail is a bad place," Ali said years later. "I was there for about a week until they let us out for Christmas, and it was terrible. You're all locked up. You can't get out. The food is bad and there's nothing good to do. You look out the window at cars and people, and everyone else seems so free. Little things you take for granted like sleeping good or walking down the street, you can't do them no more. A man's got to be real serious about what he believes to say he'll do that for five years. But I was ready if I had to go."

★ ★ ★

Manny Pacquiao's July 20, 2019, victory over Keith Thurman at age forty has raised the question: Why are so many old fighters successful today?

Boxing has traditionally been a young man's sport. Archie Moore defied expectations in the late 1950s and early '60s by competing into his forties at a high level. In 1994, George Foreman captured lightning in a bottle against Michael Moorer at age forty-five. But Rocky Marciano retired at age thirty-two. And other ring greats were long past their prime at that age.

In other sports, the stars are getting younger. In boxing, the contrary is true. Look at the success enjoyed in recent years by Bernard Hopkins and the Klitschkos. Look at today's elite fighters. Vasyl Lomachenko, Terence Crawford, Gennady Golovkin, Oleksandr Usyk, Mikey Garcia, Deontay Wilder, and Tyson Fury are all in their thirties.

"I'll tell you why it's happening," veteran trainer Don Turner says. "For starters, young fighters aren't being taught the right way. In every other sport, the teaching has gotten better. In boxing, it keeps getting worse so fighters aren't learning how to fight until they're old, if they ever learn. Number two, doctors can do things now for injuries and other things that used to end a fighter's career. And the biggest reason is that fighters used to fight ten or fifteen times a year. Now they fight once or twice. You read about guys from the old days who had a hundred fights. Do you know what your body feels like after you've fought a hundred fights?"

★ ★ ★

It's often said that fighters are the most accessible athletes in professional sports. They might also be the most quotable.

- ★ Kevin Kelley: "When you're fighting, it's like an uncontrollable rage inside you that you have to control. And everything is happening so fast. It's like road-rage on the rollercoaster at Coney Island."
- ★ Roland LaStarza: "No matter what anybody says, you have to live with your own brains. Don't take any punch you don't have to."
- ★ Lamon Brewster: "A good fighter imposes his will on his opponent. It's like when you look at a lion and he's about to get you. It ain't about what you're thinking. It's what the lion is thinking."
- ★ Randy Neuman: "Hitting other people is easy. Getting hit in the face is hard."
- ★ James Scott: "When boxing finishes with you, it really finishes with you."

* Micky Ward: "Boxing is a tough business. Inside the ring and outside the ring, people get bruised."
* Nikolay Valuev: "If I feel sorry for my opponent, it will have bad results for me so I cannot allow that to happen. Every boxer will tell you, it's nothing personal."
* Wladimir Klitschko: "From nothing to everything is a very long road in boxing. But from everything to nothing is just one short step."
* Paulie Malignaggi: "Combat for a living is crazy in general. I don't think anybody who does combat for a living is all there all the time. To compete year in and year out and to have a professional career in combat sports is not only dangerous; you probably have to have a couple of screws loose."

★ ★ ★

On June 26, 2019, the World Boxing Council announced that it had created yet another category of "world champion" and designated Canelo Alvarez as its first "franchise champion." This paved the way for "interim champion" Jermall Charlo to become the regular WBC "world champion." As explained by the WBC, "A Franchise Champion shall enjoy special status with respect to his or her mandatory obligations, holding multiple titles, and competing for titles of other organizations as the WBC Board of Governors rules on a case-by-case basis."

Let's call this move for what it is—a shameless grab for more sanctioning fees. And worse.

In creating a loophole to exempt "franchise champions" from mandatory challenges, the WBC is coddling to big-money names who want to avoid certain fighters. For example, Dillian Whyte has been the #1-ranked WBC heavyweight contender for more than 600 days. But if the WBC labels Deontay Wilder a "franchise champion," Wilder won't have to fight Whyte. That would open the door for Whyte to fight for the WBC "world" championship, and the Whyte camp might be satisfied. But boxing would be further diminished in the process.

Carlos Acevedo has written, "Although the sanctioning bodies are nothing but corrupt, senseless, and avaricious, they do not operate in a vacuum. They are part of the boxing industry and are propped up by everybody involved in the fight racket from top to bottom."

So true.

★ ★ ★

I've watched a lot of documentaries about Muhammad Ali over the years and viewed a lot of additional film footage that wasn't incorporated in them. The images tend to blur. But there's one moment in *What's My Name / Muhammad Ali* (the two-part HBO documentary that premieres on May 14, 2019) that stands out in my mind.

"I thought Ali and I had a relationship as friends," Ernie Terrell told me years ago. "When you're a fighter coming up, you deal with lots of people, and for me Ali was one of them. In 1962, we sparred together in Miami. In fact, for about a week, we shared a room. I was getting ready to fight Herb Siler, and he was on the same card against Don Warner. Both of us won, and afterward I was getting ready to take a plane home to Chicago. He had this big red Cadillac and offered to drive me as far as Louisville, where I stayed overnight at his parents' house until I could catch a bus to Chicago in the morning."

But that was then. Four years later, as Ali was readying to fight Terrell in Houston, Muhammad's world had changed.

"The way the name thing started," Terrell told me, "I didn't consciously decide to call him 'Clay.' What happened was, when we signed to fight, the promoter told us, 'You'll both have to be in Houston two weeks ahead of time and complete your training there to help the promotion.' He asked me, 'Is that all right with you, Ernie?' And I said, 'It's all right with me if it's all right with Clay.' I wasn't trying to insult him. He'd been Cassius Clay to me all the time before when I knew him. I didn't mean no harm. But when I saw that calling him 'Clay' bugged him, I kept it going. To me, it was just part of building up the promotion."

To Ali, it wasn't "part of building up the promotion."

The exchange of words between Ali and Terrell in *What's My Name / Muhammad Ali* is fascinating because of the anger—even rage—visible in Muhammad's face and body language. Ali and Terrell are being interviewed by Howard Cosell six weeks before their heavyweight championship bout. Ali was known to voice angry words in those days. This was something more.

"I'd like to say something right here," Terrell said, "Cassius Clay has—"

"Why do you want to say 'Cassius Clay'?" Ali interrupted. "Why do you got to be the one of all people, who's colored, to keep saying 'Cassius Clay'?"

Things escalated from there.

Ali wasn't playing.

> Ali: You're making it really hard on yourself now. Why don't you keep the thing in the sport angle? Why don't you call me my name, man?
> Terrell: Well, what's your name? You told me your name was Cassius Clay a few years ago.
> Ali: My name is Muhammad Ali, and you will announce it right there in the center of the ring after the fight if you don't do it now.
> Terrell: For the benefit of this broadcast; him, all right?
> Ali: You're acting just like an old Uncle Tom. I'm going to punish you.

Now Terrell was angry and stepped forward into Ali's space. That sort of thing didn't happen when fighters were interviewed years ago.

> Terrell: Wait a minute. Let me say something. You ain't got—
> Ali: Back off of me.
> Terrell: Don't call me no Uncle Tom, man.
> Ali: That's what you are, an Uncle Tom.
> Terrell: Why you gonna call me an Uncle Tom?
> Ali: You heard me. Back off of me. Uncle Tom.

At that point, Ali gave Terrell a two-handed shove and the fighters had to be separated. For real.

The HBO documentary then moves to Ali and Terrell in the center of the ring with referee Harry Kessler giving them their final pre-fight instructions. Ali wasn't one for staredowns. But he gives Terrell one here, and not for purposes of intimidation or show. His anger is bubbling near the surface. This time, he's the one who leans forward into Terrell's space.

Both fighters decline Kessler's instruction to shake hands. Instead, Terrell reaches out with his left glove and pushes Ali away.

The bout that followed was ugly and brutal. In the early rounds, Terrell suffered a fractured bone under his left eye and swelling of the left retina. From the eighth round on, he was virtually helpless. From that point on, Ali taunted him mercilessly.

"Uncle Tom! What's my name! Uncle Tom! What's my name!"

"By the fourteenth round," Tex Maule wrote in *Sports Illustrated*, "Terrell could no longer control his tormented body. Instead of reacting normally to a feint, he flinched instinctively with his whole being, and when he ventured to lead with his left, his recovery into a protective crouch was exaggerated and somehow pitiful. It was a wonderful demonstration of boxing skill and a barbarous display of cruelty."

Jerry Izenberg, who was at ringside that night, later told me, "'What's my name!' It wasn't a question. It was a demand. Ali was determined to make Terrell say it, and the fight was absolutely horrible. If Ali was an evil person, that's the kind of person he would have been all the time. Somebody really pushed the wrong button that night because it was a side of him so out of character that, to this day, I find it hard to believe it was him. It was evil. Ali went out there to make it painful and embarrassing and humiliating for Ernie Terrell. It was a vicious ugly horrible fight."

What's My Name / Muhammad Ali captures the antecedents of that moment.

★ ★ ★

Anthony Joshua's loss to John Ruiz in his June 1, 2019, debut at Madison Square Garden brings back memories of a British invasion that began twenty-three years ago.

When Lennox Lewis fought at Madison Square Garden for the first time, he was widely regarded as damaged goods. After winning a gold medal at the 1988 Olympics, he'd advanced through the heavyweight ranks and annexed the WBC heavyweight crown by decision over Tony Tucker. Next, he'd defeated Frank Bruno and Phil Jackson. Then, shockingly, Lewis was knocked out by Oliver McCall in London.

The road back ran through Ray Mercer at Madison Square Garden on May 10, 1996. Mercer was a heavy-fisted brawler with an iron chin. And Lennox considered himself a "pugilistic specialist." The plan that night was for Lewis to outbox Mercer. Except the plan wasn't working. By the late rounds, Lennox's face looked as though someone had inserted a golf ball beneath his right eye. Sensing that the fight was slipping away, trainer Emanuel Steward told his charge, "Just fucking fight him." Lewis did as instructed and eked out a 96–94, 96–95, 95–95 decision win.

Nine months later in Las Vegas, Lennox avenged his loss to McCall and reclaimed the heavyweight crown. Victories over Henry Akinwande, Andrew Golota, Shannon Briggs, and Zeljko Mavrovic followed. That set the stage for a return to Madison Square Garden and a March 13, 1999, title unification bout against WBA champion Evander Holyfield. The widespread belief was that Lewis deserved the nod that night. But the judges ruled the contest a draw.

Eight months later, Lennox won a unanimous decision over Holyfield in Las Vegas. In his next bout—on April 29, 2000—he fought at Madison Square Garden for the third time and final time.

The opponent was Michael Grant; twenty-seven years old, undefeated in 31 outings, six feet, seven inches tall, 250 pounds. Some observers called Grant the best pure athlete ever to come into boxing. More than a few insiders considered him the heir apparent to the heavyweight throne.

Lewis knocked Grant down three times in the first round and ended matters in the second stanza. That was Lennox's most impressive performance at Madison Square Garden. It won over the doubters and solidified his position as the dominant heavyweight in the world.

I have vivid memories of all three Lennox Lewis fights at Madison Square Garden, some of them more personal than others.

When Lewis and Mercer fought in 1996, I was a book writer, not a journalist. I'd authored *The Black Lights* and *Muhammad Ali: His Life and Times* but written only a handful of articles. That night, I was on assignment for a magazine called *Boxing Illustrated*.

Three years later, Holyfield–Lewis I (as the promotion was styled) marked a step forward in my journey as a boxing writer. I was on assignment for a nascent website run by HBO Sports. My article would be posted on a burgeoning medium called the internet. It was the first time I

was ever seated in the ringside press section for a major fight—the corner
seat in the last row. When I picked up my credential, a BBC producer
whose credential request had been denied offered me a thousand dollars
for my seat. That seemed like a good way to be banned for life from the
press section at Madison Square Garden. I turned him down.

Lewis–Grant was another turning point in my evolution as a boxing
writer. Grant's team invited me to spend the hours before and after the
fight in Michael's dressing room. It's an experience that I've shared with
dozens of fighters since then and a wonderful way to write a fight.

* * *

There was a time when the heavyweight championship of the world was
the most coveted title in sports. No more. Major sports have true champions. Boxing has world champions, super world champions, interim world
champions, world champions in recess, and other designations that have
reduced the term "champion" to a marketing tool.

It's in vogue now—particularly on ESPN—to talk about Tyson Fury
as the "lineal" heavyweight champion of the world. No one that I'm
aware of talks about "lineal" champions in any other weight division. But
let's put Fury's "lineal" crown in perspective.

Boxing's line of lineal kings began with John L. Sullivan, who annexed
the bareknuckle crown by bludgeoning Paddy Ryan senseless in 1882 and
became boxing's first modern gloved champion in 1885. Sullivan was
dethroned by James Corbett who lost to Bob Fitzsimmons who lost to
James Jeffries.

So far, so good.

Then things got messy. In 1905, Jeffries announced his retirement,
ending the lineal chain. Marvin Hart was matched against Jack Root
and a new king was crowned. But the new king (Hart) lost his first title
defense to Tommy Burns who was separated from the crown by (gasp!)
Jack Johnson. In 1910, Jeffries came out of retirement and was beaten to
a pulp by Johnson, thus reinstating the lineal chain. Things went along
lineally from there through Jess Willard, Jack Dempsey, and Gene Tunney.

Then there was an oops! Tunney retired and stayed retired. No more
lineal champion.

In 1930, Max Schmeling was matched against Jack Sharkey and claimed the heavyweight title on a foul. An inglorious procession of champions followed. Sharkey defeated Schmeling in a rematch and was succeeded by Primo Carnera, Max Baer, and James Braddock. Then Joe Louis seized the crown and reigned for twelve years.

Louis retired in 1949, ending of the House of Louis lineal line. Ezzard Charles beat Jersey Joe Walcott (new line). Louis came out of retirement and lost to Charles (old line restored but now headed by Charles). Charles then lost to Jersey Joe Walcott. Walcott lost to Rocky Marciano. And Marciano retired undefeated in 1956 (end of line).

Next line: Floyd Patterson, Ingemar Johansson, Patterson redux, Sonny Liston, Cassius Clay, Muhammad Ali, Joe Frazier, George Foreman, and the return of Ali (who reestablished himself as the rightful king). Claims to the throne by Ernie Terrell and Jimmy Ellis during that era can be disregarded. Then Ali lost to Leon Spinks and the age of stripping began.

In recent decades, boxing has had a head-spinning number of claimants to the heavyweight throne. Various sanctioning body champions have included Gerrie Coetzee, Francesco Damiani, Michael Bentt, Herbie Hide, Bruce Seldon, Francois Botha, Henry Akinwande, Sergei Liakhovich, Oleg Maskaev, Ruslan Chagaev, Sultan Ibragimov, Bermane Stiverne, and Charles Martin.

On occasion, a fighter achieves widespread acceptance as the best heavyweight in the world. Larry Holmes, Mike Tyson, Evander Holyfield, Riddick Bowe, Lennox Lewis, and Wladimir Klitschko come to mind in that regard. In these instances, the man who beats the man (e.g. Michael Spinks beat Holmes, Buster Douglas beat Tyson) is widely accepted as the new heavyweight king. When Lewis retired as champion after defending his title successfully against Vitali Klitschko in 2003, it marked the end of another line.

Tyson Fury began his so-called lineal reign by beating Wladimir Klitschko in 2015. But even by the most ambitious calculations, Klitschko's reign only went as far back as his 2006 victory over Chris Byrd. And having been knocked out in previous title bouts by Corrie Sanders (ending Wladimir's first incarnation as a "champion") and Lamon Brewster (in a subsequent title challenge), Klitschko wasn't recognized as the true heavyweight king until well into his second reign.

Insofar as it pertains to today's heavyweight champions, the term "lineal" has been rendered meaningless.

★ ★ ★

The greatest officiating controversy in the history of the National Football League erupted in the NFC championship game on January 20, 2019, when Gary Cavaletto and Todd Prukop (two on-field officials with an apparently clear view of Los Angeles Rams cornerback Nickell Robey-Coleman's illegal hit on New Orleans Saints receiver Tommylee Lewis) failed to call pass interference. The non-call cost the Saints an almost-certain trip to the Super Bowl and has been widely condemned as one of the worst blunders in the history of sports officiating.

The men and women who officiate sports events carry a heavy responsibility. And mistakes can be magnified by the circumstances of the moment. Baseball umpires erroneously called runners safe at first base for a hundred years without significant consequences. Then, on June 2, 2010, first base umpire Jim Joyce (one of the best in the game) blew a seemingly easy call and cost Detroit Tigers pitcher Armando Galarraga a perfect game.

But let's keep things in perspective. Yes, these calls were important and had significant repercussions. But compare them to the burden that a referee in boxing carries. In the sweet science, the failure to make the right call and end a fight can cost a fighter his life.

★ ★ ★

Claressa Shields won gold medals at the 2012 and 2016 Olympics and has amassed more than her share of professional titles. Earlier this year, she told TMZ, "I spar with men. I drop men. I bust [men's] noses. I beat men up all the time. They may be stronger than me, but their boxing ability isn't like mine. I think I can beat up Keith Thurman. I really do. GGG, he's older now. I could give GGG a run for his money. Power for power isn't a question because what is boxing? Boxing is the sweet science. It's not about strength."

About Claressa's statement that she drops men. To date, Shields has compiled a 9-and-0 record in the professional ranks. And while she has scored two stoppages, she has never knocked down an opponent. Good luck against Thurman and Golovkin.

★ ★ ★

The World Boxing Association is well known for creating phony belts that are fought over by fighters of dubious merit. Its female championship bouts are even less credible than the men's.

Consider the case of Schemelle Baldwin. When Ms. Baldwin woke up on the morning of August 29, 2019, her record was listed by BoxRec.com as 3 wins, 0 losses, and 1 draw. Her opponents as of that date had a composite ring record of 0 wins against 21 defeats. In other words, Baldwin had never faced an opponent who had won a professional fight. Yet according to the WBA, that qualified her to face Alicia Napoleon-Espinosa (11–1, 6 KOs) at Foxwoods Resort for the sanctioning body's world female super-middleweight title.

Think about that for a minute! Replay the numbers in your head. It's embarrassing to boxing and women's boxing. The only reason it isn't embarrassing to the WBA is that WBA is beneath shame.

To no one's surprise, Napoleon-Espinosa dominated Baldwin throughout the bout and knocked her out.

★ ★ ★

Some Thoughts from Fighters After They Lost:

* Jack Dempsey (on his "long-count" defeat to Gene Tunney in their 1927 rematch): "It was just one of the breaks. Tunney fought a smart fight."
* King Levinsky (after being knocked out by Joe Louis in 1935): "It's not the blows as much as they hurt. It's all them witnesses."
* Roberto Duran (after his 1972 loss to Esteban De Jesus): "I don't like him, mostly because he is the only man ever to beat me and he is the only man to ever knock me down. I don't like him for a lot of reasons, but I have to respect him for them."

★ ★ ★

There's a pattern that club fight cards tend to follow.

There were seven fights on the April 10, 2019, DiBella Entertainment fight card at Sony Hall in New York. The house fighters (coming out of the red corner in each instance) won all of them. There was never a moment when the outcome of any bout was in doubt. Out of forty-six scheduled rounds of boxing, the underdog won zero.

The room was filled to capacity before the first fight began. The crowd enjoyed the show. There was lots of action. Fighters threw clubbing blows against opponents who didn't know how to avoid them. The course of each bout was dictated by how much punishment the opponent was willing and able to take. The fights were fair in the sense that the same rules applied to each fighter. But kids in a schoolyard understand that, when the class bully beats up a nonathletic kid, it isn't a fair fight. Most of the underdogs tried to win. But inevitably, hope gave way to discouragement and defeat.

Two fights on the card showed boxing at its worst.

In the fifth bout of the evening, Alicia Napoleon beat up a woman named Eva Bajic. Napoleon entered the ring with a 10–1 record and a WBA belt. Bajic had sixteen defeats on her ring ledger including losses in her most recent five fights. The New York State Athletic Commission shouldn't have allowed the fight to happen. The conduct of the bout was worse. Napoleon knocked Bajic down twice in the second round. Each time, she appeared to punch Bajic after the knockdown, but the referee seemed to not notice. NYSAC chief medical officer Nitin Sethi intervened to stop the slaughter.

In the next bout, Bakhodir Jalolov faced Brendan Barrett. Jalolov, who represented Uzbekistan in the super-heavyweight division at the 2016 Olympics, came into the ring with five knockout victories in five outings. Barrett, a likeable man with a degree from Muhlenberg College, is a former mixed martial artist who was grossly overmatched and had no command of boxing fundamentals. Barrett visited the canvas twice en route to a first-round stoppage. Following the second knockdown, Jalolov punched Barrett when Barrett was on the canvas. Again, the referee let it pass. And again, Dr. Sethi intervened to stop the beating.

The powers that be at the New York State Athletic Commission should stop approving gross mismatches like Napoleon–Bajic and

Jalolov–Barrett. They should also sit down with the referee for each fight, watch a video of the fight together, and discuss what should happen when a fighter punches an opponent who's helpless on the ring canvas.

★ ★ ★

Bruce Trampler, Top Rank's Hall of Fame matchmaker, has been described as laconic. But he's rarely at a loss for words. That said; a fighter named Edgar "Mad Dog" Ross once left Trampler speechless.

Ross was born in Tuscaloosa, Alabama, in 1949. He did a lot of street fighting when he was young and turned pro in 1972.

"I picked him up in 1974," Trampler recalls. "I was matchmaking and managing fighters at the time and drove from Indiana to Alabama with a fighter named Jerry Evans to pick up a win. Edgar was 5-and-0. But he had no knockouts, two of his wins were by split decision, and the guys he'd beaten couldn't fight. So what happened, of course, was Edgar beat my guy. I kept in touch with him after that. Then I moved to Orlando and started using him."

In his first fight with Trampler, on February 11, 1975. Ross knocked out a fighter named Henry "Tiger" Hall. That brought his record to 9-and-0. Then he lost to Charlie Grimmett who was making his pro debut.

"At that point, I didn't see much of a future for Edgar," Trampler acknowledges. "But he kept getting better. He got down from 166 pounds to super-welterweight, which was his best weight. He fought the guy who'd beaten him two more times and beat him both times. Edgar was a tough guy. I liked him."

By 1979, Ross had 57 wins against that one loss and a draw.

"Then I brought him to Kansas City to fight Tony Chiaverini," Trampler remembers. "That's when the bubble burst. Chiaverini was a different class of fighter. He beat the crap out of Edgar and knocked him out in the tenth round. After the fight, I was taking Edgar's gloves off just outside the ring. He looked at me and, in a way that demanded an answer, said, 'Bruce; why didn't you tell me how bad I am?' I was speechless. I didn't know what to say. And Edgar never fought again."

One would like to think that the story has a happy ending. But it doesn't. In Ross's later years, he suffered from seizures and serious cognitive issues. For a while, he lived on the streets, eating out of dumpsters. Then a cousin who owned a trailer took him in and cared for him. He died on June 19, 2012, at age sixty-two.

"It was really kind of a blessing that the Lord came and got him," a friend of Ross's named Randy Frazier told a reporter for the *Tuscaloosa News*. "He really at that point didn't have much of a life."

★ ★ ★

The two most significant fights of 2018 were Canelo Alvarez's September 15 majority-decision triumph over Gennady Golovkin and the December 1 split-decision draw between Deontay Wilder and Tyson Fury. In each instance, a change in one round on the scorecard of one judge would have changed the outcome of the fight. And in each instance, tens—if not hundreds—of millions of dollars perched precariously on that round.

Canelo Alvarez and Golden Boy recently signed a contract with DAZN, the centerpiece of which calls for Canelo to fight his next eleven bouts on DAZN for a minimum of $365 million. The deal was predicated in significant measure on Alvarez's victory over Golovkin and the fact it earned him the WBC and WBA 160-pound titles.

Let's look at the scoring of the judges:

> Dave Moretti 115–113 for Canelo
> Steve Weisfeld 115–113 for Canelo
> Glenn Feldman 114–114 even

If Moretti or Weisfeld had changed one round on either of their cards from Alvarez to Golovkin, the result would have been a majority draw. In that instance, Gennady would still hold the WBC and WBA titles. And Canelo, while still a marketable elite fighter, wouldn't be a 365-million-dollar-man.

Moreover, that switch would have been well within the realm of reason. Moretti scored round seven for Golovkin while Weisfeld gave it to Alvarez. And Moretti scored round eight for Alvarez while Weisfeld gave it to Golovkin.

The scoring for Wilder–Fury was equally ambiguous.

Alejandro Rochin scored the bout 115–111 in favor of Wilder, which most observers agree is a good reason why Rochin should be retrained before judging again. Meanwhile, Robert Tepper's scorecard read 114–112 in favor of Fury while Phil Edwards saw matters as a 113–113 draw. If Edwards had flipped one round, the beneficiary of that flip—whether it was Wilder or Fury—would have won the fight.

Had Fury won, Wilder would now be beltless but contractually entitled to an immediate rematch. Had Wilder won, Fury would now be a man without either the "lineal" heavyweight crown or the incredible bargaining power he now has.

It's no secret that some boxing judges don't perform up to the standard that's expected of them. Canelo–Golovkin II and Wilder–Fury put the stakes in perspective and show the value of one round.

★ ★ ★

The New York State Athletic Commission has become known for erratic officiating. And it's getting worse. That was painfully evident at fight cards contested at boxing's showcase arena—Madison Square Garden—on June 1 and June 8, 2019.

In recent months, there have been egregious lapses in refereeing in New York. On these two nights, the judging was more problematic. The NYSAC could have pulled three knowledgeable fans out of the crowd on June 1, put them in judges' seats, and improved on the scoring in Katie Taylor vs. Delfine Persoon, Josh Kelly vs. Ray Robinson, and Anthony Joshua vs. Andy Ruiz. But these scorecards bore the imprint of Solomon when compared with the card turned in by Alan Rubenstein on June 8 while scoring Charles Conwell vs. Courtney Pennington.

Conwell clearly dominated the first half of the fight. Judge Ken Ezzo scored the first six rounds in his favor while judge Mark Consentino gave him six of the first seven. Rubenstein inexplicably scored the first four rounds for Pennington.

Multiple sources say that Rubenstein's scorecard was so off the mark that, after the fourth stanza, a deputy commissioner was dispatched to ask him if he'd confused which fighter was which. That's hard to confuse, since the cards filled out by judges after each round clearly designate a "red" and a "blue" corner. Rubenstein denied that he had confused the fighters.

But wait! There's more. Pennington rallied in the second half of the fight, winning three and two of the last four rounds on Ezzo's and Consentino's respective scorecards. But after being questioned about his scoring, Rubenstein scored all six of the final rounds in favor of Conwell.

In the end, the verdict was just. Ezzo and Consentino scored the fight 97–92 for Conwell. And Rubenstein's scorecard read 96–93 in Conwell's favor. But that doesn't negate the fact that Rubenstein's round-by-round scorecard ran counter to reality.

Asked for comment on Rubenstein's scorecard, Lee Park (a spokesperson for the Department of State which oversees the NYSAC) responded, "We have no comment."

This is not the way to run a state athletic commission.

★ ★ ★

Some Thoughts on the Underside of Boxing:

* Art Bayliss: "I'm tired of this bullshit. I'm not making money. I'm getting all beat up for nothing."
* Kevin Rooney: "Boxers have always been the prostitutes of the sport. Promoters and managers are the pimps."
* Jerry Izenberg: "Most people have a dark side. A fighter's dark side is darker than most."
* Andre Berto: "I don't know too many fighters that have retired satisfied."
* Larry Merchant: "Boxing is not about happy endings. At the end of a chapter, maybe. But not at the end of many books."

★ ★ ★

His face isn't as recognizable as Don King's. But he shows up in a boxing ring with far greater frequency these days than King does. And no; it's not Al Haymon. It's Sam Watson, who says, "Al is my best friend, but I'm not Al Haymon. I'm me."

Watson is the public face of Premier Boxing Champions. In that regard, he's an extension of Haymon but he has a very different background and persona.

Unlike Haymon, Watson didn't go to Harvard. Much of his early education came on the streets. He has good people skills and relates well to fighters because he knows the world that they come from. He's the Yin to Haymon's Yang. Al is a recluse who recoils from the camera. Sam is an extrovert who loves it.

Watson and Haymon met in the early 1980s when Al was in the music business. They've been friends ever since. When Haymon got into boxing as an advisor to Vernon Forrest, Watson began working with him in that arena. The job involves more than dealing with fighters. There are aspects of PBC's business that the world doesn't see. Sam has a hand in many behind-the-scenes endeavors. He stays in his lane, but it's a wide lane. He knows when to be quiet and rarely shows all of his cards.

Watson fits easily into the role of father, brother, and friend. People like him. His word is good. He's intensely loyal to Haymon, and vice versa. They'd go to war for each other.

Watson is reliable. He does what he says he'll do. He's a good ally. You wouldn't want him as an enemy.

★ ★ ★

A thought for today's troubled times. . . .

In 1996, Muhammad Ali and I co-authored a short book about bigotry and prejudice entitled *Healing*. Thereafter, we were honored by an organization called Givat Haviva at its annual gala dinner.

Givat Haviva is based in Israel. Its mission is to promote tolerance and understanding between Arabs and Jews. As part of its effort, it arranges for Arab and Jewish students to attend classes at each other's schools and at Givat Haviva campuses on an extended basis. These cross-cultural experiences foster the ideals of mutual responsibility, equality, and respect.

Sixteen students from Givat Haviva were among the guests at the dinner. There were eight Arabs and eight Jews; eight young men and eight young women. They were comparably dressed. Guests were encouraged to talk with them. The one prohibition was that we weren't allowed to ask whether an individual student was Arab or Jewish. At the end of the evening, after mingling with the students for several hours, virtually all of the guests had to acknowledge that we couldn't tell which were the Arab students and which were the Jewish students.

There's a message in that for anyone who's listening.

★ ★ ★

The University of Arkansas Press is affiliated with an important academic institution. So this digression from boxing seems appropriate.

When I was a senior in high school, the school offered a two-semester elective course. The first semester—called American Life and Problems—dealt with American politics. The second semester—International Life and Problems—was devoted to foreign policy.

I was politically interested and decided to take American Life and Problems. There were two teachers who taught the course independently of one another. The first—Thomas Rock—had a reputation for being exceptionally demanding. Lots of homework, rigorous questioning in class, a tough grader. The other was a soft touch.

I opted for the soft touch. I was a good student. The subject matter interested me. There were three grading periods in each semester and I breezed through them. But the teacher mumbled a lot, looked down at his hands when he spoke, and was really boring. So I switched to Thomas Rock's class when it was time to register for International Life and Problems.

If I recall correctly, the switch might also have been motivated by the fact that three of the prettiest girls in twelfth grade were enrolled in Mr. Rock's class.

Each individual grading period covered six weeks. Every week, Mr. Rock would assign a book for us to read. We'd read it, write a book report, and discuss the book in class. These reports were our tests. At that point in my life, I hadn't learned how to read and think analytically. I read everything like it was the sports section of the daily newspaper.

The first book that Mr. Rock assigned to us to read was *American Diplomacy* by George Kennan. I zipped through it and wrote my report. Then my paper came back with a grade of 65. Beneath the grade,

Thomas Rock had written "Your analysis is ridiculous." That was his only comment.

Shock !!! I'd never gotten a 65 on anything before.

On my next book report, I got a 70. Then 75. I was learning to read and think analytically. After that came an 80, an 85, and a 90.

Thomas Rock did something that no teacher I've had before or since did. At the end of each grading period, he would sit individually with each student and explain the basis for the grade that he was about to give us. Grades were assigned at five-point intervals from 65 to 90 and one-point intervals above that. The grades on my six book reports averaged out to 77.5. I approached Mr. Rock's desk prepared to lobby for an 80. That seemed fair given the upward trajectory of my work.

"Sit down," Mr. Rock instructed.

Then he peered at his ledger that listed each student's book report grades.

"When you came in here six weeks ago, you didn't know how to read carefully and analyze what you read. Or if you did, you didn't do it. But you've worked hard. You've turned yourself into a 90 student. So I'm giving you a 90."

Years later, I co-authored a book about public education entitled *For Our Children* with Frank Macchiarola. I met Frank when I was a sophomore in college. He was my dormitory counselor. Frank later became chancellor of the New York City public school system and president of St. Francis College in Brooklyn. He was one of my most important mentors.

In the dedication to *For Our Children*, Frank and I wrote, "Good educators make a difference. We dedicate this book to the following teachers, who taught us, cared about us, and gave us much of what we have today. Some are deceased. We've been long separated from others. They are heroes who set a standard we would wish for children in school everywhere."

One of the teachers we dedicated the book to was Thomas Rock.

In Sunshine or in Shadow

Each new book by Donald McRae is cause for anticipation. *In Sunshine or in Shadow* is his eighth—and fourth about boxing. Like the previous three, it explores themes that go far beyond the sweet science.

In Sunshine or in Shadow focuses on a thirteen-year period during the time when Northern Ireland was torn apart by sectarian violence spawned by hate that claimed thousands of lives.

McRae's telling begins on January 30, 1972 (a day known as "Bloody Sunday"), when fourteen unarmed demonstrators were shot to death by British soldiers during a civil rights march in Northern Ireland. The march had been organized by Derry MP Ivan Cooper to protest a policy of internment without trial that the British government had introduced on August 9, 1971. Thereafter, "Loyalists" and "Republicans" unleashed random violence—often against innocent civilians—for political ends. McRae tracks the saga up until the night of June 8, 1985, when Barry McGuigan (a symbol of unity throughout Ireland) defeated Eusebio Pedroza in London to claim the WBA featherweight crown.

"These were the very worst years of the Troubles," McRae writes. "The IRA were emphatic there should be a complete withdrawal of British troops from Northern Ireland. This demand was dismissed by the British government, and hopes of reconciliation had been replaced by increased intransigence on both sides. The Provisional wing of the IRA resolved to unleash an unprecedented campaign of terror. Yet I was drawn to them because, in this period, boxing saved lives and steered countless young men away from joining paramilitary groups."

In Sunshine or in Shadow views the Troubles through the prism of trainer Gerry Storey and four fighters—Charlie Nash, Davy Larmour, Hugh Russell, and Barry McGuigan—each of whom was trained by Storey at some point in his ring career. It explores the intersecting worlds of controlled violence in the ring and uncontrolled violence outside it at a time when life was often safer within the ropes than on the streets.

Storey, a Catholic, coached Ireland's boxing team at the 1972, 1976, and 1980 Olympics. More significantly, he trained both Catholic and Protestant fighters at the Holy Family Boxing Club located in the heart of what was essentially a war zone in Belfast. The respect and admiration felt for Storey by both sides of the conflict was such that he was given what amounted to a diplomatic pass by each warring faction. Recounting a meeting between Story and Loyalist paramilitary leaders, McRae writes, "It was incredible. Many of the men in that room were used to ordering the murder of a random Catholic or planning targeted attacks on Republican communities. Yet they were embracing a Catholic boxing trainer whose family was linked to the IRA."

Like Storey, Charlie Nash was Catholic. His brother was killed and his father was shot on Bloody Sunday. Over the course of his ring career, he held several regional titles and beat a faded Ken Buchanan in 1979 but lost in his next outing to WBC lightweight champion James Watt.

Davy Larmour (Protestant) and Hugh Russell (Catholic) fought two hellacious battles against one another in Belfast five months apart for regional titles. The first was contested on October 5, 1982. Describing the scene, McRae writes, "Catholics and Protestants were jammed against each other. The ongoing tension and violence between the two communities should have turned the beautiful old Ulster Hall into a tinderbox. Instead, it became a roaring sea of unity. People were bound together by boxing. There was no trouble outside the ring that night, no discord nor sectarian chanting, no blood was spilt and no lives were threatened. It was a shimmering miracle in the depths of the Troubles."

Russell won a twelve-round decision. After the fight, the two fighters shared an ambulance to the hospital where they needed dozens of stitches to close their facial wounds. They had endured the bloodiest fight of their lives.

On March 2, Larmour and Russell fought again in Belfast. This time, Larmour prevailed over twelve equally hard rounds. "The strangeness of a Protestant and a Catholic fighting in front of a crowd that mixed supporters from both sides of the divide rose up all over again," McRae writes.

"Gerry Storey had been right all those years. Boxing, for all its brutality and danger, was a force for good."

As for McGuigan (a Catholic from Northern Ireland married to a Protestant woman); no man did more to bridge the divide between the warring sectarian factions in Northern Ireland than this slight 126-pound boxer.

McGuigan hailed from Clones in Northern Ireland, on the border with the Republic of Ireland. His water came from a utility in the north; his electricity from the south.

"It was a horrible, terrifying time," McGuigan says of the Troubles. "You look back and think, 'Christ Almighty, did our neighbors and friends really do such barbaric things?' But they did. It happened."

"As a statement of neutrality," McRae writes, "McGuigan wore a dove of peace on his boxing trunks. He did not believe in terrorism, in the way in which both Republican and Loyalist paramilitaries bullied and intimidated their own communities. He was sick of the bombs and the balaclavas, of the kneecappings and the punishment shootings. He had had enough of people being told what they could or could not do by hooded men who sometimes seemed to him to be no better than gangsters. McGuigan could say none of this in dangerous times. He knew that they could kill him in an instant. Far worse, they could kill his family and other innocent people around him. So he listened in silence to the whispers around him. But in his head, he was thinking of the hardcore militants and saying 'fuck you' to every one of them. He had lived, along with everyone else, for too long in the pressure cooker of the Troubles."

"Boxing was accepted and given freedom of movement unlike any other activity because it had street credibility," McGuigan told McRae. "Boxing has a hardness and a coldness about it. Unlike any other sport, you risk your life in the ring. And to get to the top in boxing you have to endure immense pain. Boxers often come from very harsh backgrounds, and the way they deal with adversity and hurt wins them massive respect with the paramilitaries. Boxing is a violent sport and it connected with these very violent people."

Thus, McRae recounts, "The ragged cry echoed again and again when the sadness seemed unbearable: 'Leave the fighting to McGuigan!' Amid the kneecappings and the killings, people whispered this phrase to

themselves. They were sick of the sectarian hatred and the incessant violence and so they said it in Belfast and Derry, in every forsaken corner of
Northern Ireland: 'Leave the fighting to McGuigan!' The dove of peace
on McGuigan's boxing trunks could have been cloying. But instead, in a
time of brutality and war, it gleamed with hope. It meant that you could
support the Belfast-based featherweight from Clones whether you lived
in the North or the South, whether you were a Catholic or a Protestant,
a nun or a gangster, a man or a woman, young or old. McGuigan offered
reason to believe in a world beyond the Troubles."

"Why did I get such special support?" McGuigan says in confirmation. "The answer is simple. There was so much sadness and people were
fed up. Boxing was an olive branch. That was the paradox. Peace be with
you—and you were punching someone in the mouth."

In Sunshine or in Shadow showcases McRae's art of painting portraits
with words and recreating both time and place well. If there's a flaw in the
book, it's that he assumes too much knowledge on the part of his readers.

In the opening pages, McRae writes, "This book makes no attempt
to explore the roots of the conflict or to recount how the Troubles finally
ended. That task has been completed many times before."

But the Troubles ended more than two decades ago. Many readers
(particularly young ones) don't have a frame of reference to put McRae's
narrative in. At one point, I took a break from reading to go online for
a brief tutorial on the Troubles. It's a tribute to the intensity of McRae's
writing that I chose to do so. But I shouldn't have had to do it.

Beyond that, *In Sunshine or in Shadow* offers McRae's reliable brand
of thorough research blended with clear evocative writing. One particularly moving chapter describes how, in the aftermath of the 1981 hunger
strikes, Storey was invited into the infamous Maze prison to teach boxing
to Republican and Loyalist prisoners on separate nights each week.

Billy Hutchinson (a loyalist paramilitary prisoner in the Maze) later
told McRae, "We needed Gerry Storey. It did not matter that we were
Loyalist prisoners and that Gerry came from the Republican side. We
needed him to help our men exercise their minds and bodies. Gerry and
boxing lifted us up."

"There were no misgivings with Gerry," Hutchinson continued.
"There would have been if it had been someone else. But Gerry's narrative

came before him. We all knew his interest was boxing. But he was also interested in building people's characters. It was not just about being a world or Olympic champion. It was about finding the best character in everyone, how boxing could build their confidence. He stayed away from sectarianism and boxing politics. There was always infighting and backstabbing, but Gerry rose above it. We noticed this about him, how he offered hope to everyone he met. How do you measure the depth of that hope? How do you measure the way that Gerry and boxing changed society for the better? You can't. It's too difficult. All I know is what I saw with my own eyes, and I felt it with every fiber of my being. He showed us a better way to live. The impact on us was profound. The fact that he moved between the Loyalist and the Republican cages made me think at first that Gerry was either very stupid or brave. But I soon realized he was the opposite of stupid—and he was more than just courageous. He was a genuine human being, and the goodness shone out of him. He was entitled to have worked only with the Republicans, who were his people. But he didn't live life like that. He wanted to bring boxing to both sides. He never asked people about their religion or political affiliations. He just saw us as people. Other people came into the cages—politicians and the press. But they came with their own agenda. It was like they were visiting a zoo and they saw us as animals. But Gerry just saw us as people who belonged to his boxing club, which just happened to be in a prison."

And lest one think that the political nature of *In Sunshine or in Shadow* has led McRae to shortchange boxing in favor of political discourse, readers should take note of his description of Davy Larmour's corner after round nine of his second fight against Hugh Russell.

"On his stool between rounds" McRae writes, "there was discord in Larmour's head. He felt the sponges and swabs at work on his face as Maguire tended to his bloody skin, but he could not concentrate on his trainer's instructions. It was as if his skull had split his brain in two. On one side, he heard an insistent voice telling him that he could not go on, he needed to rest, and he would feel better if he just sat on his stool and closed his eyes. A second voice reminded him that, when the bell rang, he had to get up and start all over again."

Young men frequently take up boxing because the ring offers sanctuary from the violence that pervades their lives every day on the streets.

Nowhere was that more true than in Northern Ireland during the time of the Troubles.

"This book does not claim that boxing changed the political landscape," McRae acknowledges. "It would be a mistake to argue that boxing, or even Storey or McGuigan, altered the course of history."

But McRae goes on to observe, "Boxing inspired people in Northern Ireland, from all corners and sides, to believe that another way of living was possible. In the strict confines of the boxing ring and the gym, a man's religion and political persuasion did not matter when set against his courage, discipline, and skill. Boxing did not stem the Troubles or end the killings, but it offered shafts of light and hope. Fighters and trainers from opposite sides crossed borders and faced each other on equal terms. They respected and liked each other. And they were loved and even revered by both communities. They offered a template for the future. Men were killing each other senselessly while, inside the ring, boxers were able to find a purity of purpose in improving themselves and respecting their opponents. When people looked in amazement at how boxers ignored sectarian divisions, they saw acceptance and respect. It helped them believe peace and harmony would finally arrive."

12 Rounds in Lo's Gym

12 Rounds in Lo's Gym by Todd D. Snyder (West Virginia University Press) is a memoir about Snyder, his father, Appalachia, and boxing in coal country.

Snyder grew up in Cowen, West Virginia, and paints a grim picture of life there.

"There is only one stoplight in the entire county," he writes. "And that stoplight isn't even necessary. Nothing much happens and when something happens that looks like something, everyone talks about it. To be a man, for the younger version of myself, was to dunk basketballs, catch touchdowns, score knockouts, and have sex with beautiful women, all before finding your place in the coal mines."

The coal mines.

"When economic times get tough," Snyder recounts, "so do the coal company lawyers. They'd shut down the mine, file bankruptcy, and cheat the workers out of their retirement money." In 2015, Patriot Coal Corporation implemented a plan to divert money that had been set aside for health care benefits for 969 retired coal miners to pay bankruptcy lawyers and other costs. "Now you see them, now you don't," Snyder writes. "No more health care benefits. Life in Cowen is no fair fight. You work till you die, be it in the early or late rounds of life. Folks know the judges aren't gonna give them a fair shake when it goes to the scorecards. They know a fixed fight when they see one."

And there's one thing more to know about life in Cowen.

"Our heroes are defined by their ability to take punishment, their willingness to grit their teeth through pain. Even Jesus Christ with all his talk of peace, love, and forgiveness would have never made it big in my town if not for that long ring walk to Calvary. He had to prove that he was one tough son-of-a-bitch or nobody in Cowen would have taken him seriously."

Todd's father was Mike "Lo" Snyder. The nickname "Lo" came from his penchant as a star running back in high school to run low to the ground to hit holes that the offensive line opened for him and, when need be, open holes on his own.

"You can be a big fish in a small pond in a town like Cowen, West Virginia," Todd notes. "You can be the prettiest girl in school or the richest kid in town or the toughest guy on the block. That's what my father was—a big fish in a small trailer park."

After graduating from Webster County High School, Mike Snyder exchanged his helmet and shoulder pads for a miner's accessories.

"For years," Todd continues, "he and my grandfather worked side by side at the Smooth Coal Company. Most young men from Cowen dream of becoming something better than their fathers, but their fathers are what they eventually become. That's how cyclical poverty works."

The cycle gnawed at Mike Snyder's insides.

"My father was the kind of fellow who was always much happier in retrospect," Todd remembers. "Never quite enjoying the moment itself. By the time he turned thirty-five years old, my father resigned himself to the fact that he'd accomplished all that he was ever going to accomplish. Those touchdowns hadn't gotten him anywhere but right back to the place where folks had always told him he'd end up."

"My only fear of death," Mike Snyder once said, "is that hell might be coal powered. The devil will have a coal mine down there in hell heating things up, and I'll have to be a damn coal miner the rest of eternity."

Within that milieu, boxing was an important part of Mike Snyder's life.

"My father's childhood dream," Todd recounts, "was to climb through the ropes at Madison Square Garden to beat the hell out of some poor fellow on national television and score a symbolic victory for the town of Cowen, for all of Appalachia perhaps."

Several months after starting work at the Smooth Coal Company, Mike took up boxing. He had five amateur fights, winning all of them by knockout. Then marriage and the demands of coal mining ended his sojourn as a fighter. "If the right person would'a come along and paid some attention to me," he later lamented, "I could'a made something out of this boxing shit."

In 2000, Mike set up a makeshift boxing ring in a small room in the back of the Classic Curl Beauty Shop (a business run by his wife). It would be a ray of sunshine in an otherwise dreary life, he thought, to teach a few young men how to box. Four years later, the First Baptist Church of Cowen opened a community center and gave Mike the upstairs portion of the building for a gym as a way of enticing young men at risk into the church family. Then, in 2009 when it became clear that young men were coming to the gym to learn to box but not coming to Jesus, the church elders shut the gym down. Thereafter, Mike erected a small training facility in the yard behind his house.

"The second [Baptist church] reincarnation of Lo's Gym was a big deal in our small town," Todd recalls. "My father found himself with a gym full of thirty to forty kids a night, mostly teenagers. He'd work each kid three rounds on the hand pads, sometimes doing fifteen or twenty rounds in a row before taking a break. This after working a 4:00 a.m. to 5:00 p.m. shift in the coal mines each day."

Mike Snyder had to convince his charges that conditioning and technique were as important as strength and toughness.

He was cautious about sparring.

"A bad sparring match," Todd explains, "would run a kid off. He'd get whipped and you'd never see him again. My father wasn't in the business of running kids off or getting them hurt. He mostly viewed the gym as a safe haven for poor and troubled kids. He didn't care if any of the guys competed. Rarely would he let fighters take part in what trainers call live sparring."

"One of my father's biggest flaws as a trainer," Todd continues, "was that he almost completely focused on the positives, rarely getting on a kid and telling him what he was doing wrong. My father's formula was to build a kid up, give him as much confidence and self-respect as possible, occasionally nudging him about minor flaws in his technique."

"Fighters from West Virginia don't have many hometown heroes," Todd acknowledges. "West Virginia fight towns have never been fortunate enough to have a working-class champion, at least not in the same way Youngstown, Ohio, celebrates Ray Mancini. Our boys were always in the tune-up fights, the last-minute replacements, the underdogs. A few ol' boys from the Mountain State had the opportunity to get in the ring with boxing's elite. Our boys always came out on the wrong end of it. When you turn eighteen years old, you get to chew stuff, buy lottery tickets, and sign up for your first Toughman Contest. But the working-class man-boys from my town always had their carriages turned back into pumpkins. Everyone thinks they can box until they give it a try."

For the young men training in Lo's Gym, a "champion" was a fighter who won a minor regional amateur title. Or maybe a local toughman contest.

The three gyms saved Mike Snyder's life as much as they enhanced the lives of the young men who learned to box there. They gave him purpose. And ultimately, they brought him recognition. As word of "Lo's Gym" spread, he was honored by the Jefferson Awards Foundation in a ceremony at the state capital and later invited to attend the national awards ceremony in Washington, DC.

The Jefferson awards, Todd explains, were designed "to highlight the accomplishments of ordinary folks who did exceptional things in their communities without expectation of recognition. My father had never been to our nation's capital. I'm not sure if he had ever been to West Virginia's state capital. He hadn't been much of anywhere outside of the Tri-State Boxing Association. My grandmother bought my father a J. C. Penny suit for the award ceremony. It was probably the first suit he'd owned in his life."

Meanwhile, Todd's life had taken him away from Appalachia. Writing of his early years, he recalls, "I didn't fish. I didn't hunt. No turkey season. No deer camp. No tree stand. I didn't ride four-wheelers. I didn't drive a jacked-up Ford truck with a lift kit. I didn't chew Skoal or score touchdowns. I didn't fit."

Thus, the move away from home.

"My decision to ship off to college required a new identity, a new understanding of my own Appalachian manhood. We are born into communities and family work histories that demonstrate a very rigid pathway to becoming men. If we earn college degrees, we become The Other. We'll never be able to come back home."

He's now an associate professor of English at Siena College in Albany, New York, far removed from the coal mines of Appalachia.

Snyder is a good writer. He crafts well drawn portraits and moving vignettes about the dozens of young men and the occasional woman who filtered in and out of Lo's gym and became, however briefly, boxers.

"Stereotyped and stigmatized," he says in summary, "Appalachian folks are easy prey, socioeconomically bullied by privileged society, the by-product of a uniquely Appalachian socioeconomic system, one that lacks access to both economic and educational opportunity. Our stories are tragic and beautiful. In these parables of Lo's Gym's, I write the story of Appalachia. This is who we are—fighters. We fight like hell, knowing the other fellow has the advantage."

12 Rounds in Lo's Gym is as much about brawling in a boxing ring as boxing. It's about gym fights, toughman contests, and amateur bouts with a few low-level professional encounters thrown in. And it's a reminder of what boxing can do to lift up young men and women who have gone through life without much hope or self-esteem and have little else to celebrate in their lives.

Literary Notes

Lou Jenkins was born into poverty in 1916 and dropped out of school before reaching his teenage years. His hardscrabble adolescence in Depression-era Texas included countless carnival fights contested for thirty or forty cents an outing.

Jenkins rocketed from obscurity to fame at age twenty-three during a ten-month period that culminated in his seizing the world lightweight crown. He was the second Texas-born fighter to win a world championship in boxing (Jack Johnson was the first). Then Jenkins self-destructed as spectacularly as he had risen to prominence. *From Boxing Ring to Battlefield* by Gene Pantalone (Rowman & Littlefield) tells his story.

Jenkins fought from 1935 through 1950 and compiled a 73–41 (51 KOs, 12 KOs by) ring record. During his mercurial career, he defeated Lou Ambers (twice), Tippy Larkin, and Bob Montgomery, and lost to Montgomery, Henry Armstrong (twice), Fritzie Zivic, Freddie Cochrane, Sammy Angott, Carmen Basilio, and Beau Jack. He also fought to a draw against Zivic.

Jenkins made a name for himself when he won ten consecutive fights (nine of them in New York) between July 18, 1939 and March 8, 1940. At Madison Square Garden on May 10, 1940, at age twenty-three, he knocked out lightweight champion Lou Ambers in the third round to claim the crown.

"I've been hit by many other good punchers," Ambers said in his dressing room after the fight. "But this Jenkins kid punched harder than a lot of them put together. What's the use of trying to alibi? He did it, and he did it good."

Nineteen months later, Jenkins lost his title by decision to Sammy Angott. His best days as a fighter were over.

Jenkins is regarded as one of the hardest pound-for pound punchers ever. Arthur Donovan (who refereed fourteen heavyweight championship fights including the historic rematch between Lou Louis and Max Schmeling) said of him, "That Jenkins, what a puncher he was. He was skinny and he looked half-starved all the time. But he'd hit you, and you'd just cave in, crumble to your knees."

But Jenkins had lifestyle issues that destroyed him as a fighter. Legendary sportswriter W. C. Heinz called him "a guy who, when champion, didn't live or behave like one."

Jenkins was an alcoholic and smoked thirty cigarettes a day. Pantalone writes, "Lew had been drinking alcohol and smoking cigarettes since he was a kid. He hardly slept or trained. He just depended on the power of his right hand. After winning the title, his training consisted of running a short distance, sitting and smoking a cigarette, sparring while taking swigs from bottles of liquor in his corner, working five or six rounds, washing up, then making the rounds of the nightclubs. Even during matches, he would put whiskey in his water bottles and drink between rounds. He was seldom not under the influence of alcohol. Once, he was so drunk while climbing into the ring, he fell on his face."

"He achieved so much with so little effort," Pantalone continues, "that no one will ever know how great he could have been had he trained—or at least not abused himself. His boxing title, money, and new-found fame would lead to an endless stream of alcohol abuse, womanizing, sleep deprivation, high-speed vehicle crashes, barroom brawls, and prodigality. He had no self-control."

"I just drank myself down," Jenkins acknowledged in his later years. "I never did go to sleep, never did eat right, never trained at all hardly. I just completely wore myself out."

Along the way, Jenkins also found time to have an affair with Hannah Dempsey (Jack Dempsey's third wife) that figured prominently in Dempsey's 1943 divorce litigation.

Over the years, Jenkins served four stints in the military. At age nineteen, he'd joined the peacetime army. He was in the Coast Guard during World War II. Later, there were two tours of duty and bloody infantry service in Korea.

Pantalone accepts the version of events that characterizes Jenkins as a war hero. Not everyone who served with him in Korea shared that point of view. But it's clear that the military gave Jenkins at least a modicum of discipline and, at the same time, satisfied his lust for combat.

"Finding no meaning in life at the peak of his success," Pantalone writes, "he discovered values to which he could cling amid death during war. He shared the ring with many greats, but he found purpose in sharing the field of battle with comrades in arms."

Jenkins died in 1981 at age sixty-four. Late in life, he liked to refer to himself as "pound-for-pound, the hardest hitter and biggest drinker in boxing history" and proclaimed, "I enjoyed every drunken minute of it."

From Boxing Ring to Battlefield is an engaging read. Katie Jenkins—Lew's spitfire first wife and de facto manager for much of his ring career—comes across as a particularly interesting character. It's also worth noting that Jenkins met his second wife in 1947 and married her after two dates. "Either you do or you don't," he said of their abbreviated courtship.

But there's cause for concern with regard to *From Boxing Ring to Battlefield*. An "About the Author" note at the end of the book says that copies of an earlier book by Pantalone—*Madame Bey's: Home to Boxing Legends*—were given out at the Atlantic City Boxing Hall of Fame induction ceremony in 2017. Giving a book away isn't noteworthy one way or the other. But the note goes on to state that book recipients included Arturo Gatti and Bert Sugar. Gatti died in 2009. Sugar died in 2012. By definition, they couldn't have been given books in 2017. Why is this important? Because something that's so clearly inaccurate can lead a reader to question whether he or she can trust the rest of the book.

That said, I knew next to nothing about Lew Jenkins when I started reading *From Boxing Ring to Battlefield*. I feel as though I know him much better now.

★ ★ ★

Gerry Cooney's life is a cautionary tale that, with a lot of effort on his part, has taken a happy turn.

Beaten physically and emotionally in childhood by an abusive father, Cooney turned to boxing and was one of the hardest punching heavyweights of all time. At age twenty-five, he was on the cover of *Time Magazine*. On June 11, 1982, he took Larry Holmes into the thirteenth round on a night when Holmes was as good a fighter as he had ever been before or would be again.

If Cooney had beaten Holmes, he would have been the biggest sports superstar in America. But by then, the seeds of self-destruction had been sown. Alcohol and drug abuse were undermining his potential as a fighter and wreaking havoc on his personal life. He's happy now—a loving husband and father—and has been clean for more than thirty years.

Cooney's story is told in *Gentleman Gerry* (Rowman & Littlefield), a book co-authored with John Grady. Before discussing the book, I should make full disclosure. Gerry is a friend. We have lunch together on a regular basis. We sit together at fights. I know him as someone who's thoughtful, generous, and admirably self-aware with regard to the road he has traveled. That makes reading *Gentleman Gerry* frustrating because of the manner in which his journey is chronicled.

Famous people often collaborate with a third party to tell their story. But almost always, the story is recounted in the subject's voice. *Gentleman Gerry* is told in Grady's voice. "I" and "me" are used only in places where Grady inserts himself into the narrative. Thus, an intensely personal journey becomes less personal and its emotional impact is dulled. Thoughts that would have been powerful coming directly from Gerry's mouth are less so when filtered through Grady's retelling.

Too often, the writing lapses into stilted flowery prose. For example, writing about meeting Gerry for the first time to discuss working together on the book, Grady recounts, "The morning sun gently blanketed the dining establishment's well-maintained patio, providing a welcomed balance to the cool invigorating breeze that persistently greeted the diners."

That's accompanied by unnecessary hyperbole. Jimmy Young is referenced as one of "the greatest talents the [heavyweight] division ever produced." Sportscaster Len Berman is "legendary" and heavyweight contender Ron Lyle is a "legend."

Assertions such as the claim that Jack Johnson has been "largely unappreciated by history" lead one to wonder what history Grady has been reading. We're told that Mike Tyson experienced "a stable nurturing environment" when he lived with Cus D'Amato in Catskill. But we now know that was hardly the case. Grady calls Holmes–Cooney the first "authentic megafight" of the post-Ali era. This shortchanges Ray Leonard's encounters with Thomas Hearns and Roberto Duran. He also tells us that Cooney and Holmes were guaranteed $10 million each for their battle. But Holmes was in the clutches of Don King at the time. His purse was less than one-third of that amount.

We're never told what it felt like when Gerry was being punched in the face by his father. What could have been a fascinating window into Gerry's mind—an exchange of blows that resulted when a bullying high school football coach challenged him to a sparring session in the school wrestling room—is reduced to two paragraphs.

There are flashes of good writing. Referencing the euphoria in the moments after Gerry's 54-second demolition of Ken Norton, Grady writes, "There was no future nor past—just the moment."

But the night that Gerry beat Norton was the night that the good part of Gerry's career came to an end. That night, he tried cocaine for the first time.

Grady writes at length about the perils of substance abuse in an often clinical style.

Regarding alcohol: "Given his genetics and the power of his addiction symptoms, Gerry's addiction was activated upon his first introduction to chemicals. The first drink is a landmark one for an alcoholic. It is a time when experimentation—with the user unaware of the horrific consequences to be paid—unites genetics, social learning behaviors, and the brain-changing processes to manifest the disease of addiction. It is a self-activated illness."

And cocaine: "As people turn to substances, not only to deal with negative emotions but also to prolong and heighten positive ones, they develop tolerance. This leads to increased use to get the same high which only works for a while. In time, substances are required simply to feel 'normal' and, later, to avoid the horrors of physical withdrawal."

But Grady never tells us how Gerry experienced being high. Don't just tell me that he was snorting cocaine. Show me!

Gentleman Gerry is most satisfying when Gerry is allowed to speak for himself. "I want to talk about what happened and maybe change some things for today's fighters, hopefully help some people out along the way," he's quoted as saying. "I had a great career, had a lotta fun, a lot of troubles. I look back and it's tough to think about what could have been. But then I think I'm lucky as hell. There are guys of my generation walking on their heels, not able to enjoy life. If I became champion of the world, who knows, maybe I'd be one of those guys. I've had a lot of great times, met a lot of great people. I'm very fortunate. That's the bottom line. And I'm able to appreciate all of it."

In sum, Gerry Cooney looks back on his life with understanding. He's happy and satisfied with where he is today. But there's a tinge of regret that, with all the assets he had to work with, a good career as a fighter could have been better. That's how I feel about this book.

★ ★ ★

Randy Gordon (former chairman of the New York State Athletic Commission) has written a memoir entitled *Glove Affair* (Rowman & Littlefield) that references Nat Fleischer, who founded *The Ring* in 1922 and reigned supreme at the magazine until his death fifty years later.

Gordon holds Fleischer in high regard. But as boxing historian Craig Hamilton notes, "Too often, Fleischer represented his personal opinion as fact. And even when he was just reporting facts, there were too many things he got wrong. Also," Hamilton adds, "as Fleischer advanced through life, he held onto the belief that the fighters he saw and read about when he was young were the best ever. He idolized fighters like Stanley Ketchel and built them up to be more than they were. The magazine was less biased than his books because it had to appeal to contemporary fans. But even there, there were problems."

In 1969, Gordan, then a student at Long Island University, met Fleischer. "Here are the top ten heavyweights of all time," Fleischer told him. Then he handed Gordon a list:

1. Jack Johnson

2. James J. Jeffries

3. Bob Fitzsimmons

4. Jack Dempsey

5. James J. Corbett

6. Joe Louis

7. Sam Langford

8. Gene Tunney

9. Max Schmeling

10. Rocky Marciano

Joe Louis #6? No Muhammad Ali? No Sonny Liston? That's not a good list.

★ ★ ★

Adam Pollack lives in Iowa. By last count, according to BoxRec.com, he has refereed sixty-three professional fights and been a judge at ringside for fifty-eight more. He has never refereed a major bout. But he has a unique distinction that separates him from other third men in the ring. Pollack has written critically acclaimed biographies of every gloved champion from John. L. Sullivan through Jack Johnson.

Pollack is a graduate of the University of Iowa College of Law. After working as a prosecutor with the Johnson County Attorney's Office in Iowa City, he opened a private practice as a criminal defense attorney. He boxed as an amateur while in law school and began refereeing and judging amateur bouts in the 1990s. Then he took a hiatus from officiating to coach, manage, and promote. One of his fighters advanced to the semifinals of the men's National Golden Gloves. A female charge won multiple national and international amateur championships. These are good credentials considering the limited talent pool in Iowa.

The most noteworthy fight that Pollack has refereed to date was the July 20, 2018, contest between Thomas Mattice and Zhora Hamazaryan in Sloan, Iowa. Showtime televised the bout nationally. Mattice was awarded a dreadful decision that sparked widespread outrage. But no one complained about the refereeing.

Quite a few referees have written books. Almost always, it's one and done, and the books are memoirs that focus on the author. Pollack has chronicled the lives of John L. Sullivan, James Corbett, Bob Fitzsimmons, James Jeffries, Marvin Hart, Tommy Burns, and Jack Johnson in detail, scouring old newspapers and other primary sources for material to construct his narratives.

As for his philosophy of refereeing, Pollack says, "It's not about me. It's about the fighters. The best referees are the ones you almost never notice. If people walk out of the arena talking about the referee, chances are I've done something wrong."

"I try to be old-school in my officiating," Pollack continues. "You want to stay out of the way. But you have to position yourself so you can see what's happening and jump in to stop a fight on a moment's notice. My general style is hands off, let the fighters fight. I don't get involved unless I'm forced to. My biggest pet peeve in officiating is referees who don't allow boxers to work on the inside and break the fighters too soon. That has a greater impact on the outcome of a fight than many people realize. Clinching and infighting are part of the sport. If one boxer is holding incessantly with a vice grip, the fighters should be broken and, eventually, points should be taken if the tactic is creating an unfair advantage and ruining the flow of the fight. But there are times when you see a fighter do a lot of work to get inside. He gets held. And instead of allowing the aggressor to work free and land punches, the referee breaks them and physically pushes the aggressor back. That gives the fighter doing the holding a break and forces the infighter to have to work to get back inside again."

"And another complaint I have," Pollack notes, "is referees who take too much time to decide whether a fight should continue or be stopped after a knockdown. A good referee can make a determination within several seconds of concluding the count. You're supposed to be assessing the fighter during the count. Taking twenty seconds after a knockdown to make a decision gives one fighter extra recovery time and penalizes the opposing fighter who wants to finish off his opponent. And it can be used as an excuse to not stop a fight that needs to be stopped."

Have Pollack's different roles in boxing influenced his work as a writer?

"It's all intertwined," he acknowledges. "The fact that I've refereed, judged, coached, even fought a bit, helps me see things from a number of different perspectives."

And suppose he were able to go back in time and referee one of the early fights that he has written about?

"I'd love it," Pollack answers. "It would be great to be in the ring with John L. Sullivan, James Corbett, Bob Fitzsimmons, all of the early champions, to see how good they were and how hard they hit."

★ ★ ★

Stillman's Gym, located on Eighth Avenue in Manhattan between 54th and 55th Streets, opened in 1921 and closed in 1961. The three-story structure that housed it was then torn down and replaced by a nineteen-story apartment building. No physical reminder that Stillman's was there exists today, not even a plaque.

Stillman's was assured a place in boxing lore by virtue of an essay entitled *The University of Eighth Avenue* that A. J. Liebling wrote for the *New Yorker* in 1955. Since then, many writers have sought to follow in Liebling's footsteps and add their vision of Stillman's to the historical record. One of the better efforts is an essay by historian Mike Silver entitled *Boxing in Olde New York* that appears in *New York Sports* (edited by Stephen H. Norwood, University of Arkansas Press).

Liebling used Stillman's Gym as the starting point for an essay that wove in the history of boxing and ended with his oft' quoted observation, "The Sweet Science is joined onto the past like a man's arm to his shoulder."

Silver, by contrast, focuses on the scene at Stillman's in the late 1950s, recreating it in painstaking detail and introducing readers to some of the gym's more fascinating characters including its owner. Asked in 1987 about his perpetually dour expression, eighty-two-year-old Lou Stillman replied, "How long do you think a man with a happy face would have lasted running a boxing gym? Everybody called me a grouch, a crab, a cranky guy who never smiled. Well, that's what scared off the chiselers, moochers, and deadbeats."

"If boxing had a voice," Silver concludes, "it would be the sound of Stillman's on a busy afternoon. But don't bother trying to find anything like it today because you will search in vain. The unique confluence of circumstances that created and nurtured Stillman's Gym from the 1920s to the 1950s—a veritable golden age for the sport—no longer exists."

★ ★ ★

And a non-boxing literary note.

In 1965, when I was in college, one of my grandfather's cousins died. When her belongings were dispersed, I was given a fifteen-volume set of Charles Dickens's writings published at the dawn of the twentieth century by the Werner Company in Akron, Ohio. I put the books on a shelf and admired the way they looked from time to time.

In 2010, I decided to write a novel about Dickens. That meant I had to read all of his novels and more. Prior to 2010, I'd read *A Tale of Two Cities* (which was assigned reading in high school) and *A Christmas Carol.*

I decided to begin with *Oliver Twist,* took my copy from the Werner Company set off the shelf, and discovered that it had never been read. I had to slit the pages that had been joined together by the old-fashioned printing process. The same was true of the other fourteen Dickens volumes. Some of the most significant literature ever written had been on a shelf, unopened for more than a century.

I read all fifteen volumes of my Dickens set, bracketing passages and making notes in the margins. *The Final Recollections of Charles Dickens* was published in 2014. Then I wrote a sequel—*The Baker's Tale*—which was less keyed to Dickens but required reading all of his books a second time. By the time I finished, because of its age and condition, my Dickens set was falling apart. Pages were loose. The spines were separated in varying degree from the signatures. The books were essentially unreadable.

Recently, I decided on a whim to see if I could find an identical set. The same Werner Company books were for sale on ABE.books.com at a reasonable price. So I bought them. When the books arrived, I cannibalized my original set, removing the colored engraving from each volume (which wasn't hard to do since most of them were loose anyway), disposed of what was left, and put my new Dickens set on the shelf. But before I did, I leafed through the books. The pages hadn't been slit.

So I'm back where I started in 1965, with some of the most important writing the world has known in a fifteen-volume set that hasn't been read since it was published by the Werner Company more than a century ago.

It's not enough for people in power to say that they abhor domestic violence. They should act in accord with that expression of belief.

The Silence on Marcus Browne

Marcus Browne is a talented fighter who, at age twenty-eight, has built a 23–0 (16 KOs) record in the professional ranks. On January 19, 2019, he outpointed Badou Jack to win the "interim" World Boxing Association and "silver" World Boxing Council 175-pound titles. He's now scheduled to fight Jean Pascal at Barclays Center on August 3 in a bout that will be televised on Fox. But there's a dark underside to the story.

On December 28, 2017, an order of protection was issued against Browne at the request of his former girlfriend (and the mother of his child) after she alleged that he'd assaulted her twelve days earlier. On March 30, 2018, Browne allegedly violated the order of protection. Thereafter, he was charged with criminal contempt, criminal mischief, and harassment. The two cases were consolidated and Browne pled guilty to disorderly conduct, after which he was ordered to enroll in and complete a course on domestic violence.

Browne was arrested yet again following another incident involving the same woman (who told police that, on September 27, 2018, he tried to choke her). This time he was charged with criminal contempt, criminal obstruction of breathing and circulation, criminal mischief, and harassment On January 30, 2019, Browne pled guilty to criminal contempt in the second degree with regard to this third set of criminal charges. He was sentenced to twenty-six sessions in a batterer intervention program and a conditional discharge with a more stringent order of protection being issued against him.

Most recently, Browne was arrested on June 12 of this year. According to the criminal complaint, the latest incident took place on May 22 when Browne barged into the woman's apartment after a visitation session with their daughter and wouldn't leave. The woman called 911, and Browne was charged with felony counts of aggravated family offense and criminal contempt in addition to misdemeanor counts of criminal trespass and criminal contempt. He was arraigned in Criminal

Court on June 12 and released on $5,000 bond. His next court date is set for August 12.

I don't know what extenuating circumstances might exist with regard to Browne's conduct. Often, there are two sides to a story. I do know that, from the criminal docket, it appears as though Browne's conduct would have been unacceptable at any time and is particularly noteworthy in today's #MeToo era.

The sports establishment in America, like much of the country, has been slow to react to violence against women. But over time, the National Football League, National Basketball Association, Major League Baseball, and other entities have evolved and now impose significant suspensions for misconduct by athletes who are role models for impressionable children and young adults.

How have the powers that be in boxing reacted to the case of Marcus Browne?

In large measure by pretending that the issue doesn't exist.

Browne, as noted above, holds WBC and WBA titles. The WBC purports to have high moral standards for its fighters. It once suspended Chris Arreola from its rankings and precluded him from fighting for a WBC title for six months because he said "fuck" in an on-air interview after losing to Vitali Klitschko.

Jill Diamond is international secretary of the World Boxing Council. By virtue of this position, she's one of the most prominent women in boxing. When asked about Browne, Diamond (whose email address is at "neverhitalady.com") answered, "I'll pass on this one." Pressed for more, she added, "As a woman, as a human being, I deplore all forms of violence, domestic and otherwise. I send support and compassion for all parties involved and hope for a quick and healthy resolution."

WBC president Mauricio Sulaiman also declined comment other than to say that the situation involving Browne was "a delicate matter" and "we have begun the WBC due process with regards to this matter and I will be happy to contact you once we have a clear definition of our findings and course of action."

WBA president Gilberto Mendoza Jr. did not respond to inquiries regarding Browne.

Neither did Barclays Center. Questions about the matter addressed to Brett Yormark (CEO of BSE Global, which oversees Barclays Center) were responded to by director of communications Stuart Bryan who wrote, "We will not be commenting."

Lest one forget; Barclays Center hosted a stop on the misogynistic Floyd Mayweather vs. Conor McGregor promotional tour. Speaking at Barclays Center during the tour, McGregor thrust his pelvis back and forth with a microphone strategically placed between his legs to simulate sexual intercourse and proclaimed, "Here's a little present for my beautiful black female fans."

That brings us to the New York State Athletic Commission.

The world sanctioning organizations and Barclays Center have a vested economic interest in Marcus Browne fighting. As a government agency, the New York State Athletic Commission is charged, not with making a profit but with doing what's right.

Good character was once a requirement for a boxer to be licensed in New York. That requirement was removed when the NYSAC regulations were revised in 2016. But the commission has long taken the position that a license to box in New York is a privilege, not a right.

Should Marcus Browne be licensed to box in New York? At what point does the NYSAC say enough is enough?

In theory, NYSAC policies are set by its five commissioners and implemented by the executive director. But that's a fiction. By way of example, public records indicate that the current commissioners have never discussed illegal performance-enhancing drug use by fighters in depth.

Major decisions at the New York State Athletic Commission are now made by political overseers at the New York State Department of State. Almost everything of importance that occurs at the commission is approved at or above this level. Executive director Kim Sumbler can take small steps on her own but that's all.

This writer posed the following questions in writing to Sumbler, Dr. James Vosswinkel (the commissioner most involved in overseeing the NYSAC), and Lee Park (the Department of State spokesperson who handles media inquiries regarding the NYSAC):

(1) Are incidents of domestic violence and other criminal conduct factors in determining whether a fighter is granted a license to box in

New York? And if so, what specifically is the standard applied by the NYSAC?

(2) Are you aware of Marcus Browne's history of domestic violence, including his most recent arrest? If so, what are you aware of and when did you become aware of it?

(3) What steps, if any, does the NYSAC plan to take with regard to Mr. Browne's conduct?

To date, Sumbler, Vosswinkel, and Park have refused to answer—or even acknowledge receipt of—these questions. As a government agency, the NYSAC should adhere to a higher standard than this in responding to media inquiries.

The New York State Athletic Commission needs clear standards and needs to make a serious inquiry regarding the issues surrounding Marcus Browne. Instead it's running from its responsibilities.

Here, one might contrast the conduct of the NYSAC with that of the California State Athletic Commission.

On March 23, 2019, heavyweight contender Kubrat Pulev survived a gash above his left eye and rallied to knock out Dinu Bogdan in the seventh round of a fight in Costa Mesa. After the bout, while being interviewed by a website reporter named Jennifer Ravalo, Pulev kissed her.

Thereafter, Pulev apologized to Ravalo. Despite the apology, the California State Athletic Commission suspended Pulev for six months and ordered him to pay a $2,500 fine (the maximum that could be imposed by the commission). It also ordered Pulev to attend a state-approved course on sexual harassment.

The CSAC may well have overreacted in its suspension of Pulev. The kiss was inappropriate. But Ravalo and Pulev had met previously. Ravalo reached out and touched Pulev on camera several times before the interview. She also appears to have engaged in a lap dance with members of Pulev's team that same night after the interview and kiss.

So here we are. The California State Athletic Commission suspends and fines a fighter for kissing a woman without her consent. And the New York State Athletic Commission ignores four arrests and two guilty pleas in conjunction with charges that range from criminal obstruction of breathing and circulation to the repeated violation of a protective order.

New York governor Andrew Cuomo purports to support the creation of an environment in which women are protected against physical violence. Talk is cheap.

Various arguments are being made in support of allowing Marcus Browne to fight in New York. Mike Tyson was allowed to fight after being imprisoned for rape. But Tyson had served his time and wasn't accused of violence against women thereafter. Floyd Mayweather was granted a license to fight in Nevada after multiple convictions for physically abusing women and while his jail sentence was pending. But that was before the #MeToo movement raised awareness of the issues surrounding violence against women.

I'm not judging Marcus Browne. But don't sweep the issue under the rug and pretend that it doesn't exist. Let's have an honest inquiry and discussion about what happened.

The rematch between Anthony Joshua and Andy Ruiz was marketed as "Clash on the Dunes." It would have been a more honest promotion if the "l" had been removed from "Clash."

Ruiz–Joshua 2:
Cash on the Dunes

On August 9, 2019, promoter Eddie Hearn announced that the rematch between Anthony Joshua and Andy Ruiz would take place on December 7 in Saudi Arabia.

Three days later, Hearn hosted a two-man press conference in London with Omar Khalil, managing partner of Skill Challenge Entertainment (the Saudi Kingdom's "official event partner" that is putting up the money to bring the fight to Saudi Arabia). After Hearn's opening statement, he engaged in a dialogue with Khalil who told those in attendance, "We're a democracy of forty million people" and said that the event was part of a plan to "enhance the quality of life and overall well-being" of the Saudi people.

"We love what you're doing here for sports," Hearn responded. "This is how you grow the sport of boxing. The world will stand still to witness history in Saudi Arabia."

Matt Christie (editor of *Boxing News,* the world's longest running boxing publication) wrote of the announcement, "It's hard to remember confirmation of such a highly anticipated showdown being so poorly received."

Joshua's career has been built on the adoration of British boxing fans, most of whom (like members of the boxing media) have little desire to travel to Saudi Arabia. Some employees of Sky Sport (which televises Joshua's fights in the United Kingdom) and DAZN (which will stream the bout live in the United States) are also wary of going to Saudi Arabia.

More significantly, the choice of Saudi Arabia as the site for Ruiz–Joshua 2 has led to an outpouring of criticism from human rights groups and others who are concerned that the move plays into the Saudi Kingdom's efforts to "sportswash" its dismal record on human rights.

Let's start with some facts.

Saudi Arabia is not a democracy.

The National Democratic Institute (a nonprofit, nonpartisan, non-governmental organization founded in 1983) states, "The Kingdom of Saudi Arabia has one of the most tightly controlled political systems in the world . . . Ordinary Saudis lack protections for the exercise of basic civil rights, including speech and association, and have limited opportunity to participate in the political process at the national level."

The Economist's 2018 Democracy Index ranks the Saudi government as the ninth-most authoritarian regime in the world among 169 countries listed.

Reporters Without Borders has described the Saudi government as "relentless in its censorship of the Saudi media and the Internet." In 2019, it ranked Saudi Arabia 172nd out of 180 countries in its Press Freedom Index.

Saudi Arabia has played a troubling role in the ongoing war in Yemen.

Women in Saudi Arabia are relegated by law to second-class status.

Sexual activity between people of the same sex in Saudi Arabia is punishable by fines, imprisonment, and torture.

And the involvement of the Saudi government in the murder of *Washington Post* journalist Jamal Khashoggi in the Saudi Arabian consulate in Istanbul on October 2, 2018, is a matter of public record. It's particularly troubling that, at the September 5, 2019, press conference in New York for Ruiz–Joshua 2, Eddie Hearn acknowledged the presence of Prince Khalid bin Salman, who had traveled to the United States for a meeting with officials of the Trump Administration. Prince Khalid has been named in reliable intelligence reports as having been complicit in Khashoggi's murder.

Moreover, there are legitimate safety concerns related to holding Ruiz–Joshua 2 in Saudi Arabia.

The United States Department of State has four advisory levels for travelers:

Level 1: Exercise Normal Precautions
Level 2: Exercise Increased Caution
Level 3: Reconsider Travel
Level 4: Do Not Travel

As of November 24, 2019, the State Department website had a "level 2" advisory for Saudi Arabia with the notation, "Exercise increased caution in Saudi Arabia due to terrorism and the threat of missile and drone attacks on civilian targets . . . Terrorists have targeted both Saudi and Western government interests, mosques and other religious sites (both Sunni and Shia), and places frequented by US citizens and other Westerners."

The September 14 terrorist drone attacks on nineteen key Saudi Arabian oil facilities further undermined confidence in the safety of the Ruiz–Joshua 2 promotion.

But money talks. And the Saudi Kingdom has given the promotion a lot of money (estimates range from $40 million to $100 million) to bring the fight to Saudi Arabia. Eddie Hearn referenced this reality at the September 5 press conference in New York when he declared, "No other country can compete with the money that's available for boxing in the Middle East. If I don't do it, some other promoter would."

Hearn has also referenced two fight cards previously contested in Saudi Arabia—the September 28, 2018, World Boxing Super Series final between Callum Smith and George Groves (before the murder of Jamal Khashoggi) and the July 12, 2019, event headlined by Amir Khan vs. Billy Dib.

Other thoughts offered by Hearn have included:

* "We really wanted to go somewhere who believed in the sport of boxing, that had a vision. We have to realize that there is another world out there outside of Cardiff and Madison Square Garden, and we have an obligation to grow the sport of boxing to new areas, to new regions. This event could change boxing forever because, if Saudi Arabia are going to invest in these kind of fights with the population that they have, with the potential to grow the sport of boxing, you could be seeing a big change in the dynamics of the sport. That's something that really truly excites me."

* "The world will stop to watch this fight. I'm telling you, this is another Thrilla in Manila. This is another Rumble in the Jungle. Trust me when I say, this is one of the biggest heavyweight events of all time."

* "This [Saudi Arabia] is probably the safest place I've ever been to."

Tickets for Joshua–Ruiz 2 went on sale on September 13. The top ticket price was listed at approximately $13,500.

There are political and economic reasons why the United States and United Kingdom do business in Saudi Arabia. But that doesn't mean we should pretend that it's a democracy or has the entertainment value of Disneyland.

In March of this year, Endeavor (which owns UFC) returned a $400 million investment from Saudi Arabia's Public Investment Fund and severed ties with the Kingdom to protest the role that the Saudi government played in the murder of journalist Jamal Khashoggi.

The absence of democracy in Saudi Arabia, the murder of Jamal Khashoggi, Saudi Arabia's role in the ongoing war in Yemen, and other issues involving the Kingdom should be weighed by the media in determining how to report on, and whether or not to attend, Ruiz–Joshua 2.

British journalist Kevin Mitchell spoke for many when he wrote in the *Guardian*, "This is about money, not morals—because the business does not do all that well with morals. Human rights abuse, the slaughter of innocent people in Yemen and the murder of the journalist Jamal Khashoggi seem to have been no impediment to doing a deal with a regime so transparently desperate for international approval that 'sportswashing', as it has become known, is a central plank of their public relations platform."

When an elephant is lumbering downhill toward a tar pit, it takes time for the elephant to stop and turn around. But first the elephant has to try to stop.

What's Happening With DAZN?

Part One

On May 10, 2018, Eddie Hearn (managing director of Matchroom Boxing) and Simon Denyer (CEO of what was then Perform Group) announced a joint venture at a press conference in New York. Former ESPN president John Skipper, who had joined Perform Group as its executive chairman three days earlier, was also in attendance.

Speaking about what was touted as a one-billion-dollar, eight-year joint licensing agreement to provide content for DAZN, Hearn proclaimed, "We're here to change the game and elevate boxing to a new level for fight fans in America. We can televise the fights on the days we want at the time we want. We don't have to come on at ten o'clock after a movie. We have the dates, the money, and the platform. We were dangerous without this. But with this money and this platform, oh my god!"

Two months later, on July 17, Hearn met again with the media. This time, there were questions regarding what appeared to be a thin roster of American fighters who would be appearing on DAZN. Addressing the issue, Hearn declared, "We live in a world where people say, 'Ah, he didn't get Charlo or Spence.' Calm down. We've just had seven or eight weeks. We're getting so much resistance from advisers and networks which is really good news because it means they're concerned. We're out there actively talking to Mikey Garcia, talking to the Charlos. We can pay them more money than other promoters. There are contracts out with another dozen fighters. We've signed three world champions [Maurice Hooker, Daniel Roman, and Jesse Vargas]. We've signed a number one middleweight in Demetrius Andrade. We've signed a load of really good amateurs. We're going to cause nightmares. We are resilient. We are absolutely ruthless. We won't stop. And we've got a team of people behind us who have a bottomless pit of money who will back us to the heavens. We've got eight years to make it work."

A lot has happened in boxing in recent years. Al Haymon launched Premier Boxing Champions. HBO left the sport while ESPN, FOX, and DAZN came in. Streaming video is now seen by many as the wave of the future, and its foremost proponent insofar as boxing is concerned is DAZN.

DAZN launched in Germany, Japan, Austria, and Switzerland in 2016 and has since added Canada, Italy, Spain, Brazil, and the United States to its roster. It began streaming in the US on September 10, 2018, and distributed its first boxing card here on September 22 when Anthony Joshua defended his WBA, IBF, and WBO belts against Alexander Povetkin.

Initially, DAZN was priced in the United States at $9.99 per month for up to three devices. But the cost of its monthly offering soon increased to $19.99. Alternatively, subscribers can buy an annual subscription for $99.99, which averages out to $8.33 per month.

DAZN's ultimate goal is to become the dominant player worldwide in digital sports media.

"The world we're heading into," John Skipper said in an interview posted on *SportsProMedia* on October 7, 2019, "is going to be overwhelmingly about streamed content as opposed to linear networked content. I think sport will continue to be the most valuable video content in the world because of the level of passion people have for it."

DAZN has rights to stream National Football League games in Germany, Austria, Switzerland, Japan, Canada, and Italy. It streams Major League Baseball in four countries overseas and National Basketball Association games in three. But in the United States, DAZN is still a startup streaming service. It has money to spend on rights fees. But only a limited number of important properties are available for it to buy since all of the major sports are contractually bound to other networks.

Thus, DAZN is seeking to penetrate the US market and build a following through boxing. It offers other sports content to subscribers, including an MLB "wrap-around" show, which Skipper says is "a clear declaration of intent that we're going to expand." But boxing is a sport that DAZN thinks it can become preeminent in now—or at least, it thought that at the time of its launch.

"Boxing is an excellent entry point for us into the United States," Skipper explains, "because it's not tied up by the major media companies. We will be, relative to live events, overwhelmingly a fight channel throughout most of 2020 because there aren't a lot of other available rights that come up. The major sports rights begin to come up in 2021, and we'll be a player in trying to acquire some of those packages."

But DAZN's entry into boxing has been bumpy.

The powers that be at DAZN were impressed by the spectacle of Anthony Joshua's conquest of Wladimir Klitschko in London on April 23, 2017. It fired their imagination. Thereafter, Hearn convinced them that, with DAZN's money and his expertise, they could duplicate this success and become a dominant force in boxing in the United States. Their interests were further unified by an agreement that gives DAZN what multiple sources say is a 40 percent equity interest in Matchroom USA (Hearn's American promotional company).

Skipper is smart. But he rarely dealt with boxing when he was at ESPN. And there's a long, steep, arduous learning curve when it comes to understanding the business of boxing.

Hearn's interests are unified in some respects with DAZN's. But his first loyalty is to Matchroom. And one can question whether anyone currently at DAZN has the expertise to properly oversee the network's boxing program.

Skipper is comfortable with the team that he has in place. "It has been a learning process," he says, "But working with Eddie Hearn has been cordial and seamless. Between Eddie, Joe Markowski [DAZN executive vice president for North America], and myself, I don't see the need for what some people are calling another 'boxing guy.'"

But there have been times when DAZN's deal-making has been clumsy. The fact that the network signed Canelo Alvarez and Gennady Golovkin for close to $500 million and has been unable to get them in the ring with each other for a third fight suggests a lack of expertise. And a familiar refrain heard from boxing insiders is, "The people who run DAZN are very naive when it comes to the business of boxing . . . DAZN needs an experienced boxing guy whose only loyalty is to DAZN . . . People who know next-to-nothing about boxing are making high-level deals for DAZN, and the numbers aren't adding up for them on any rational basis."

More than a few individuals and corporate entities have sought to control boxing over the decades. No one has succeeded since Frankie Carbo and his friends seventy years ago. DAZN, like Premier Boxing Champions, mistakenly thought that it could control a majority of elite fighters in the United States with its checkbook. Indeed, Hearn's May 10, 2018, announcement seemed based on the premise that elite fighters would line up en masse to sign with Matchroom USA and that the entire boxing community (with the possible exception of Bob Arum, Al Haymon, and Stephen Espinoza) would dance the hora in joyful celebration of DAZN's bold, innovative, well-financed approach to boxing.

"We came in with a load of money and I expected loads of people to just sign for us," Hearn told British journalist Ron Lewis this past October, "It has been harder than I thought it would have been. ESPN and PBC have dug their heels in and we've had to overpay fighters to come to us or stay with us."

To fill out its boxing programming, DAZN has moved beyond Matchroom in pursuit of content.

On July 2, 2018, it announced that it would televise all seven fights in each of the three weight divisions in season two of the World Boxing Super Series and would also showcase mixed martial arts bouts promoted by Bellator and Combate Américas.

On October 17, 2018, it announced an agreement with Canelo Alvarez and Golden Boy (Alvarez's promoter) to stream Canelo's next eleven fights on DAZN platforms throughout the world with DAZN paying a minimum of $365 million for the honor. DAZN also agreed to stream an unspecified number of less prominent Golden Boy fight cards during the five-year contract term.

In early 2019, Gennady Golovkin came into the fold.

These signings coupled with Matchroom's offerings (including the fact that Hearn has brought Anthony Joshua into the DAZN orbit for three fights on a fight-by-fight basis) have enabled DAZN to deliver better boxing to fans in the United States this year than any other network. But DAZN's business model was predicated on the belief that it could sign the best fighters and match them against each other. And DAZN's content hasn't maintained the consistently high level that was expected when it began operation in the United States.

"We underestimated the difficulties we'd face and the time we'd need to pull together enough boxing to form a stable subscription base," Skipper admits.

In part, that's because PBC and ESPN fought back hard when DAZN was launched and adopted what some observers have called a "kill the baby in the crib" mentality. If DAZN was disrupting and distorting boxing economics by paying unusually large license fees, they would respond in kind.

The primary beneficiaries of this largesse have been a handful of promoters, managers, and fighters.

Canelo Alvarez and his team are being paid a minimum of $365 million for eleven fights. Another $100 million in cash and DAZN stock has been committed to Gennady Golovkin. The amount paid for Sergey Kovalev's participation in a November 2 light-heavyweight title defense against Canelo has been reported as being in the neighborhood of $12 million. That was multiples more than Kovalev's previous high purse, which was for his 2016 outing against Andre Ward.

Sergiy Derevyanchenko (a largely unknown fighter with thirteen victories on his ring ledger) received a $5.2 million purse to fight Golovkin on October 5. Devin Haney was paid $1,000,000 for a September 23, 2019, bout against Zaur Abdullaev.

Joe Markowski took note of this distortion in the marketplace and, looking ahead to 2020, told writer Sean Nam, "If you don't move the needle and you demand X amount of money, we're going to tell you no thanks. We're not a money tree that needs to be plucked out by fighters and their representatives."

But can DAZN stand by this pledge? If it does, ESPN and FOX (with huge corporate empires, multiple platforms, and access to pay-per-view revenue) might cut off the flow of talent to DAZN.

Fight fans were ecstatic when DAZN, Matchroom, ESPN, Top Rank, Showtime, FOX, and Premier Boxing Champions entered into their various alliances. The assumption was that the networks' commitment to boxing guaranteed that there would be a lot of high-quality free boxing on television. But as Ferdie Pacheco once noted, "There is nothing so misplaced as optimism in boxing."

DAZN, ESPN, FOX, and Showtime are now paying Tiffany prices for boxing. But they're getting Kay Jewelers diamonds.

"Programming boxing is messy and painful," Showtime Sports president Stephen Espinoza says.

John Skipper concurs, noting, "Boxing is not a sport that lends itself to being organized."

Thus, in addition to paying extraordinarily large, cost-ineffective purses to fighters, the networks are now often being pushed into matching name fighters against vastly inferior opponents.

Boxing owes its place in sports lore to fights between great fighters. Confrontations like Dempsey–Tunney, Louis–Schmeling, and Ali–Frazier have linked their participants forever in history's eye. Promoters used to make their money by putting together fights that the public wanted to see. One reason Ray Leonard, Thomas Hearns, Marvin Hagler, and Roberto Duran fought each other so often was, that's where the big money was.

Now fighters get seven and eight-figure paydays for going in soft. Why should Tyson Fury go in tough more than once every few years when he can make millions of dollars for fighting Tom Schwarz and Otto Wallin?

There's more boxing available in the United States on television and streaming video today than ever before. One might expect this to lead to competition to put on the best fights possible. But instead, networks and promoters are building their own empires, and fighters are going in soft in a quest for belts that are increasingly meaningless except as marketing tools. Fight fans see developmental fights, stay-busy fights, and sanctioning-body mandatory fights. But too few good fights.

All of the networks are rewriting boxing history to fit their narrative. As Carlos Acevedo observed, "When Tyson Fury signed a contract with ESPN, it sparked a company-wide effort to brand him as some sort of heavyweight supernova ready to dominate the American sporting scene. Except Fury is now a man known for having free tickets to his last fight outnumber those he actually sold."

In a remarkable sit-down with reporters on November 2, Stephen Espinoza declared, "There is no sport that exists that lies as regularly to its fans as boxing. The announcers lie. You know the promoters lie. And it's not healthy. College football doesn't sell every single game as Alabama–LSU. Not every NFL game is the Super Bowl. Sometimes it's just a game. And I think we do a disservice when we try to sell something as one thing when it's not. The goal here is building the sport and doing it in a way that rewards the fans. And one thing we have to do with fans is be honest."

But the beat goes on.

For the most part, boxing fans are now seeing generic boxing on television. Often, the fighters are fungible. And generic boxing—unlike generic football—doesn't attract a broad fan base. Fans won't watch a fight simply because it's on ESPN, FOX, Showtime, or DAZN.

Moreover, after all the talk about free boxing coming to network television, there's a disturbing trend toward putting what would have once been an *HBO Championship Boxing* or *Showtime Championship Boxing* fight on pay-per-view.

The November 23 bout between Deontay Wilder and Luis Ortiz was FOX's fourth pay-per-view fight of the year. FOX Sports executive vice president of programming Bill Wanger has already stated his network's intention to distribute four to five PPV bouts in each of the next three years. ESPN (which televised two pay-per-view boxing cards in 2019) is expected to follow suit in kind if not in number.

Fans of college football are rewarded because the game gives them the matchups they want. On December 28, LSU beat Oklahoma and Clemson defeated Ohio State. On January 13, 2020, the winners will play each other. If the powers that be who run boxing ran NCAA football, LSU would play Baylor on January 13 and it would be on pay-per-view.

DAZN is fighting the pay-per-view trend. But there's a question as to how long it can sustain its current business model.

For ESPN and FOX, boxing is relatively inexpensive sports programming that can fill scheduling gaps. DAZN is in a different situation. Boxing dominates its budget and is at the core of what the network is supposed to be about.

DAZN has delivered better fights to boxing fans in the United States this year than any other network. It showcased Canelo Alvarez vs. Danny Jacobs and Sergey Kovalev in addition to streaming Golovkin–Derevyanchenko and the second year of the World Boxing Super Series (highlighted by Josh Taylor vs. Regis Prograis). It got lucky with Anthony Joshua vs Andy Ruiz, which gave viewers an entertaining upset followed by a much-anticipated rematch. Srisaket Sor Rungvisai vs. Juan Francisco Estrada, Maurice Hooker vs. Jose Ramirez, and the continuing development of Devin Haney, Ryan Garcia, and Vergil Ortiz were solid programming content. KSI vs. Logan Paul was a bonus.

But to put matters in perspective; pick a year from the HBO Boxing calendar "when HBO was HBO" and compare it with what DAZN has offered in 2019. Think back forty years to September 28, 1979, when Don King promoted a show at Caesars Palace headlined by Larry Holmes vs. Earnie Shavers with Ray Leonard, Roberto Duran, and Wilfredo Gomez all on the undercard.

And there have been times this year when DAZN stumbled.

DAZN hoped that a string of high-profile fights in the last three months of 2019 would encourage viewers to renew their subscriptions on a regular basis or sign up for its one-year plan.

The "fall season" (as DAZN called it) started nicely with Golovkin–Derevyanchenko on October 5 and Taylor–Prograis on October 26. Then DAZN dropped the ball.

Canelo Alvarez is DAZN's flagship fighter. The $365 million in license fees that DAZN has committed to him (a number that doesn't even include the purses for his opponents) speaks to his importance.

On November 2, Canelo challenged Sergey Kovalev for the WBO light-heavyweight crown. That same night, UFC promoted a pay-per-view fight card in New York. Hoping to attract a few extra subscribers, DAZN made the unfortunate decision to delay the start of Canelo–Kovalev until UFC's main event ended. That meant Canelo and Kovalev had to sit in their respective dressing rooms fully gloved for well over an hour. DAZN's paying subscribers were subjected to what seemed like interminable filler. And the bell for round one didn't ring until 1:18 a.m. East Coast time.

Think about that for a minute! Canelo–Kovalev was one of the most important fights of the year—for boxing and for DAZN.

NFL playoff games don't start at 1:18 a.m. eastern time. World Series games don't start more than an hour after midnight. Imagine NBA commissioner Adam Silver announcing, "The seventh game of the NBA Championship series between the Los Angeles Lakers and Milwaukee Bucks will begin sometime after 1:00 a.m. eastern time. We want to make sure that fans who are watching the Los Angeles Dodgers baseball game that night have the opportunity to watch both games in their entirety."

Think back to DAZN's May 10, 2018, kickoff press conference in New York when Eddie Hearn took a jab at HBO and proclaimed, "We don't have to come on at ten o'clock after a movie." This was worse.

One can understand DAZN's motivation for delaying the start of Canelo–Kovalev until the wee small hours of the morning. As will be explored more fully in Part Two of this series, the network has had more trouble than anticipated in building a robust subscriber base. But it was the wrong call.

Imagine five friends sitting in front of a television on the East Coast, falling asleep before the sound of the opening bell. The impression DAZN left them with was, "You don't care about us." The network alienated its core demographic, the very subscribers who have supported it up until now.

John Skipper gets it. "It was well intentioned on our part," he says, "But we regret the way it played out. I don't think we'd do it again."

DAZN's next big fight—the December 7 rematch between Andy Ruiz and Anthony Joshua—was also problematic.

Eddie Hearn promotes Joshua and has licensed the right to stream AJ's fights in the United States to DAZN on a fight-by-fight basis. DAZN had hoped that Ruiz–Joshua 2 would take place in New York because the timing of the bell for round one would have fit nicely with its subscribers' viewing habits and a wave of publicity for the network would have emanated from The Big Apple. Instead, Hearn took the fight to Saudi Arabia.

Holding Ruiz–Joshua 2 in Saudi Arabia made financial sense from Hearn's point of view. The Saudis paid a substantial site fee and Matchroom was able to open a new market for itself. But it was a prime example of Hearn and DAZN sometimes having divergent interests.

The decision deprived DAZN of the media attention it would have received had Ruiz–Joshua 2 been in New York. The timing of the fight placed it directly opposite the SEC championship game between LSU and Georgia. And there were obvious moral issues inherent in DAZN becoming a tool for use by the Saudi Kingdom in its effort to "sportswash" its image after the brutal murder of journalist Jamal Khashoggi and other outrages.

Skipper declines to say whether he had moral qualms about Ruiz–Joshua 2 taking place in Saudi Arabia. He's forthright in saying that, from the perspective of DAZN's economic self-interest, he would have much preferred that the fight be contested in New York.

That said; the $4 million license fee that DAZN paid to stream Ruiz–Joshua 2 in the United States and the other countries in which it has platforms was a good investment. Owing to Ruiz's popularity in the Mexican American community and the shocking nature of his earlier upset, Ruiz–Joshua 2 had more viewers in the United States than any other DAZN stream to date. And the $4 million license fee was fraction of what DAZN has paid for other, less attractive boxing content.

The final highlighted boxing match on the schedule for DAZN's autumn 2019 season was the December 20 contest between Danny Jacobs and Julio Cesar Chavez Jr.

There was a farcical quality to the proceedings. First, Chavez refused to give a urine sample for a PED test ordered by the Nevada State Athletic Commission and the fight was forced to relocate from Las Vegas to Phoenix.

Next, the contest had been slated for 168 pounds. But Chavez came in 4.7 pounds over the contract weight and forfeited $1 million to Jacobs in order to change the contract weight to 173 pounds.

Then there was the fight itself. Chavez, a 12-to-1 underdog, came into the ring with his dark hair dyed whitish-blond with electric blue highlights. That was the only thing electric about his performance. By round four, he was tiring. By round five, his nose was broken and he was bleeding from a cut by the corner of his left eye. At the end of round five, he quit. The crowd was not happy and seized on the moment to litter the ring with whatever projectiles could be thrown into it. Noting their reaction, DAZN blow-by-blow commentator Brian Kenny observed, "They can't be stunned given [Chavez's] track record."

DAZN shouldn't have been stunned either. But a source says that it paid close to ten million dollars for the bout and might be locked into paying Chavez a seven-figure license fee for another fight.

So where does that leave us?

Let's start with the fact that DAZN has given subscribers their money's worth in 2019. A one-year subscription for what has been the best boxing content available on any one network this year cost less than what viewers were asked to pay for Errol Spence's two fights against Mikey Garcia and Shawn Porter.

Skipper exudes optimism when talking about DAZN. "Our first fight was fifteen months ago," he says, "I think we've done pretty well since then."

But while DAZN has been a good deal for subscribers, it might not be a good deal for investors. Everyone understood going in that there would be red ink at the start. But not as much red ink as there has been. Revenue has been low and shows little sign of increasing to a viable level. DAZN's business model might be unsustainable.

Part Two

Bill King is a senior writer for *Sports Business Journal* and has honed his journalistic skills over the course of three decades. He's more than able to ferret out the details of a story.

So . . . What does King have to say about the economics of DAZN's business model in the United States?

"Ask DAZN executives about numbers and they're very candid in telling you nothing," King answers.

DAZN's finances are shrouded in secrecy. It's a privately held corporation and exempt from most financial reporting requirements. It appears to be doing well in some countries but struggling in the United States.

DAZN has been funded largely by Len Blavatnik, a Ukrainian-born billionaire who has both UK and US citizenship and, according to the Bloomberg Billionaires Index, is worth approximately $25 billion.

In September 2018, Perform Group (which Blavatnik controlled) was divided into two divisions (1) DAZN Group for consumer content operations; and (2) Perform Content for business-to-business sports data services. Perform Content was then sold to Vista Equity Partners (with DAZN retaining a small equity stake) in an effort to help DAZN fund the acquisition of live sports rights.

In today's cord-cutting world, consumers make choices regarding what to buy. There's Netflix, Amazon Prime, AppleTV, YouTube TV, Hulu, Disney+, ESPN+, HBO Max (in 2020), and myriad other outlets. In sum, DAZN is one of many streaming services vying for viewer dollars. And boxing fans are becoming more selective in what they watch, let alone buy. It's not just the investment of $4.99 or $9.99 or $15.99 per month. It's the investment of time at a time when there's an overflow of product.

Within this environment, DAZN isn't getting enough subscribers. Its sales pitch is simple: If a boxing fan is willing to spent $79.95 for one pay-per-view fight, he or she should be willing to spend $19.99 for a full month or, better yet, $99.99 for a full year of DAZN.

One industry source says that an early DAZN financial model anticipated that the streaming service could have as many as 3.5 million subscribers in the United States by the end of 2019. Another well-placed source says that DAZN now has roughly eight million subscribers worldwide and approximately 800,000 of these are in the United States.

This 800,000 number is less than the estimated number of buys engendered by HBO Pay-Per-View for Canelo–Golovkin I (1,300,000), Canelo–Golovkin II (1,000,000), and Canelo–Cotto (900,000).

Also, the 800,000 subscribers number reflects a significant bump that came about as a consequence of DAZN's costly, high profile, end of year schedule. DAZN is starting off 2020 with less of a bang. And the network's retention rate among subscribers has been less than desired.

Many people who watch streaming video stagger their subscriptions. They subscribe, binge for a month, let their subscription lapse, and move on to another channel. Live sports doesn't lend itself to binge watching. But that doesn't mean viewers aren't selective in what they pay for. Many of them ask, "If Canelo fights twice a year, why should I subscribe for twelve months?"

DAZN has telecast three Canelo Alvarez fights: against Rocky Fielding on December 15, 2018, Danny Jacobs on May 4, 2019, and Sergey Kovalev on November 2, 2019. The retention rate for viewers who signed up for DAZN at the time of each of these fights has risen from fight to fight. DAZN ends 2019 with approximately twenty percent of its subscribers on an annual plan.

Canelo has moved the needle for DAZN. So did the December 7 rematch between Andy Ruiz and Anthony Joshua, which was DAZN's most-watched show in the United States to date. Canelo–Kovalev was the second most-watched. Canelo–Jacobs and the November 9 confrontation between KSI and Logan Paul were third and fourth depending on how the numbers are calculated (i.e. streams vs. unique accounts, with or without next-day viewing, etc). Nothing else DAZN has streamed so far has broken out of the pack.

Here, it should be noted that three of DAZN's top four shows for 2019 were streamed in the final two months of the year, an indication that the network finished strong. That said, if ESPN's third or fourth most-watched football game of the year was a pick-up game in which the opposing quarterbacks were Justin Bieber and PewDiePie, it would be a problem.

Meanwhile, in mid-December, it was announced that Mikey Garcia had signed with Matchroom and would be fighting on DAZN on February 29 against Jessie Vargas. The agreement with Garcia is for one fight with matching rights on his next bout. DAZN hopes that Mikey will appeal to Hispanic viewers who subscribed to see Canelo Alvarez and Andy Ruiz on the network. But Garcia comes with a high price tag. And some viewers were less than enthused by what they perceived as a lackluster effort on his part against Errol Spence last March.

DAZN's first two main events in 2020—Jaime Munguia vs. Spike O'Sullivan on January 11 and Demetrius Andrade vs. Luke Keeler on January 30—are perceived mismatches that won't move the needle in the right direction. A fight between YouTubers Jake Paul and AnEsonGib has been added to the January 30 undercard.

Meanwhile, it should be noted that Canelo and Golovkin were recruited by DAZN independently of Matchroom. And Ruiz is a Premier Boxing Champions fighter. With regard to Anthony Joshua, DAZN will find out how many viewers he can draw in the United States without Ruiz if and when he fights Kubrat Pulev and Oleksandr Usyk in 2020.

Advertising might be a source of revenue down the road for DAZN. But to sell advertising, a network needs viewers. DAZN sold a Vaseline sponsorship for Ruiz–Joshua 2, but it's hard to believe that it generated much revenue for either DAZN or Vaseline. Not many viewers are likely to have seen the Vaseline corner-cam in action and said to themselves, "I'm going out after the fight to buy some Vaseline."

It's common for a company to go into a business knowing that it will lose money while establishing itself. On July 8, 2019, Bloomberg.com reported that DAZN had lost $627 million worldwide in 2018. One can put a smile face on this number by noting that the negative cash flow for Netflix in 2019 is estimated at $3.5 billion. But Netflix has built a colossus. And at the moment, the DAZN brand in and of itself is worth relatively little.

Appearing with Perform Group CEO Simon Denyer and John Skipper in New York on May 18, 2018, to announce the launch of DAZN in America, Eddie Hearn declared, "We've got a team of people behind us who have a bottomless pit of money who will back us to the heavens."

That pit no longer seems bottomless. Midway through 2019, there was industry talk that Len Blavatnik was unwilling to put any more of his own money into DAZN. On October 24, Bloomberg.com reported that Goldman Sachs was trying to raise $500 million in private investment on DAZN's behalf. In November, the ante was upped to $1 billion.

Skipper came in with the idea that he could make DAZN the ESPN of streaming video. The network's plans were summarized by executive vice president for North America Joe Markowski who, in October of this year, told *Sports Business Journal*, "Our strategy in the United States is to use boxing as an entry point to establish ourselves in the market, make a lot of noise, and generate a transactional relationship with a large audience of boxing fans. If we're successful in doing that in the next twelve to eighteen months, we will put ourselves in a fantastic position to make aggressive plays for a domestic top-three rights package when they come back to market."

But can DAZN get to that point? It current business model appears to be flawed in several respects.

First, like Premier Boxing Champions several years ago, DAZN seems to have overestimated the size of the market for boxing in the United States. Most of the people who watch boxing today are longtime supporters. There are relatively few crossover fans, and the number of hardcore boxing fans is relatively small. Also, many fans who follow specific fighters don't follow boxing as a whole. ESPN+, which debuted in April 2018, has met with modest success. But boxing hasn't been a significant driver for subscriptions.

Look at it this way. On June 1, 2019, Andy Ruiz knocked out Anthony Joshua at Madison Square Garden to claim three of the four major heavyweight championship belts. Ruiz was the first Mexican

American to ascend to the heavyweight throne. Years ago, he would have been elevated to superstar status. But most sports fans in the United States (let alone members of the general public) wouldn't recognized Ruiz if he was standing on line in front of them at McDonald's.

Also, DAZN is selling a product (boxing) that appeals to an older demographic on a platform (streaming video) that's utilized primarily by young people. It's not a good fit. As John Skipper acknowledged in an October 7, 2019, interview with SportsPro, "We're now engaged with the consumer who, as you know, may or may not understand exactly what kind of broadband connection they have, may not understand that they're getting buffering because too many people in their neighborhood are overtaxing the last hundred feet of connection. If you've got a pay-TV subscription and you've been used to getting all this content by putting on channel 83 and suddenly you've got to download an app; you've got to educate people as to how to do it and why ultimately it's better value and a better product."

And most significantly, DAZN lacks the platform it needs to generate subscription buys, build its fighters, and promote its fights.

ESPN and FOX promote across multiple platforms. FOX is a major broadcast network with a huge built-in marketing machine. ESPN is wired into the brain of every sports fan in America and has the entire ESPN empire to advance its boxing franchise when it chooses to utilize it. Fights on both of these networks and their pay-per-view offerings benefit from shoulder programming, free promotional spots, and the like.

Showtime permeated the boxing market long ago, offers viewers a lot more than boxing and, in some instances, benefits from synergy with CBS.

DAZN has DAZN. It can't arrange for Canelo Alvarez to be interviewed on television during halftime of a National Football League game. There's no "Ray Donovan" or "Billions" to bolster DAZN subscription buys. Someone who's channel-surfing might come across boxing on FOX, ESPN, or Showtime. A viewer who's flipping from channel to channel doesn't make his way to DAZN.

"It makes things more difficult for us," Skipper acknowledges, "That's reality. We've spent tens of millions of dollars on marketing in the United States. But it's impossible to deny that this puts us at a disadvantage."

Boxing fans are aware of DAZN. Casual sports fans aren't. There were people who heard Canelo Alvarez was fighting on November 2 and were interested in watching the fight but had never heard of DAZN and couldn't find it. Michael Buffer—the best ring announcer ever and the voice of big fights for decades—has all but disappeared on DAZN.

Canelo Alvarez and Gennady Golovkin were built on HBO. How do you build fighter recognition on a streaming video network? How can you create a star? Devin Haney will be an interesting test case for DAZN's ability to build a fighter into a commercial attraction. He's enormously talented and willing to go in tough. But most casual boxing fans—let alone most sports fans—don't know who he is.

In the end, the bottom line will be the bottom line. DAZN can exist worldwide without a platform in the United States. It can cut back significantly on its ambitions and exist in the US as a niche streaming sports service. Or it can adapt its business model, find a way to balance its budget, and become a long-term bigtime player in America.

Some observers have speculated that DAZN might move to a hybrid business model pursuant to which its most attractive fights (such as Canelo Alvarez outings) would require a one-year subscription to watch or be on pay-per-view with a reduced rate for DAZN subscribers. By way of analogy; ESPN+ subscribers have access to a great deal of UFC content. But the biggest UFC events are on pay-per-view with a discount for ESPN+ subscribers.

"DAZN has no plans for that," Skipper says. "But we're constantly running models to see what we might do."

One thing DAZN might do—and is planning to do—is move into online sports betting.

A 2018 United States Supreme Court decision opened the way for sports betting in all fifty states. It's now legal or about to become legal in nineteen states with a dozen more states certain to follow in the next five years.

DAZN has built and is constantly improving upon an interactive platform that can be used to support various kinds of exchanges with its subscribers in real time. Sunjay Mathews joined DAZN in June 2018 and has been head of legal, North America for the company since November 2018. Prior to that, he was corporate counsel for FanDuel. Also, DAZN partnered with MGM Bet for a brief sports betting segment on its stream of Ruiz–Joshua 2.

"We're in discussions with several companies about allowing viewers to place bets online while sporting events on DAZN are in progress," Skipper acknowledges.

Over the next decade, in-game betting is likely to produce a new world order in the gaming industry. But first, there will be a period of disorder. The sports gambling business is brutal. It isn't an automatic win. Moreover, insofar as DAZN's positioning is concerned, FOX already has an online sports betting website called FOX Bet. There are rumblings that ESPN and William Hill USA are moving toward a joint venture. Most online sports betting sites don't require a subscription fee. And fans bet on football more than any other sport, Bets on baseball are minimal. Bets on boxing are negligible.

"We'd like to use the interactive platform we're building in a way that betting becomes an auxiliary revenue stream," Skipper says. "But we don't anticipate being the house. That's a line we don't want to cross. Subscriptions will continue to be our primary source of revenue. And we hope that advertising, which is nascent for us right now in the United States, will be our second most important revenue stream. We don't anticipate revenue from gambling approaching those numbers."

In the end then, fans should enjoy DAZN's boxing program while it lasts and hope that it lasts longer. DAZN is swimming in red ink in the United States. Its current business model appears to be unsustainable. But a thought in closing: Amazon went public in 1997. For years, there were economic analysts who wrote that the company didn't have a sustainable business model. It was losing money year after year. Critics surmised that not enough people would buy things online to make Amazon profitable because buyers want to see a product and hold it in their hand before they buy it. After Amazon expanded its inventory beyond books, the criticism grew louder. The company didn't report a full-year profit until 2004. As late as 2012, it was losing money. But the company stayed focused on long-term growth. Sales revenue totaled $14.8 billion in 2007. In 2018, that number was $232.8 billion. Meanwhile, Amazon stock has risen from $1.73 a share in 1997 to $1,789 a share as of Christmas 2019.

"Our ambition level at DAZN is high," Skipper says.

The ritual ten-count is a constant in boxing.

In Memoriam

The call came on April 24, 2019, from Khalilah Ali, better known to the world as Belinda Ali, Muhammad Ali's second wife.

"Abdul Rahaman just died," Khalilah told me.

Abdul Rahaman, whose birth name was Sam Saxon, was born in Atlanta in 1931 and is a footnote to history. In March 1961, he was selling copies of the Nation of Islam newspaper, *Muhammad Speaks*, on a Miami street when a young man approached and said, "Hello brother."

They started talking. Rahaman told him, "Hey, you're into the teaching." And the young man responded, "Well, I ain't been in the temple, but I know what you're talking about." Then he introduced himself.

"I'm Cassius Clay. I'm gonna be the next heavyweight champion of the world."

Rahaman was a captain in the Nation of Islam mosque in Miami at the time. He'd first heard the teaching of Elijah Muhammad in 1955.

"I was what you'd call a sportsman," he told me in 1989 while I was researching *Muhammad Ali: His Life and Times*. "A man who shot pool, played poker, and attended sporting events. That's the kind of life I was living. A brother named James, who Elijah Muhammad sent to Atlanta, taught me. The first time I heard the word of the Honorable Elijah Muhammad, I knew it was the truth. I was convinced God had sent us a Messenger."

At Elijah Muhammad's urging, Rahaman moved from Atlanta to Los Angeles and then Chicago. He and his wife lived in the Windy City until 1961 when The Messenger sent them to Miami. The minister in charge of the Miami temple was a man named Ishmael Sabakhan. Rahaman became his captain.

"That wasn't like being a military captain," Rahaman explained. "My job was to see that the men in the temple were trained to be good providers for their family, made physically fit, and taught how to live right. Once you become a Muslim, you have to study, and I was also in charge of helping everybody in the mosque with that. There weren't many members who attended regularly. Realistically, in Miami, we had about thirty. More than that believed but only about thirty came regularly."

To provide for his family, Rahaman worked at Hialeah Race Track, Gulfstream, and Tropical Park. "One track runs at a time in Miami," he recounted. "When the first closes, the next opens up. You know the men's rooms where you see those brothers in there with shaving lotion and Bromo Seltzer and the towels? I had those concessions and the shoeshine stands. There were three brothers working for me, one track after the next."

Rahaman knew who Cassius Clay was. He'd been aware of him since the 1960 Olympics. Clay asked Rahaman if he'd like to come to his hotel room and look at his scrapbook. Rahaman said yes. Things flowed from there.

"I went to his room," Rahaman told me. "He was sharing it with another fighter. The scrapbook was full of articles about himself, and I looked at it real good. He was interested in himself and he was interested in Islam, and we talked about both at the same time. He was familiar in passing with some of our teachings although he'd never studied or been taught. And I saw the cockiness in him. I knew, if I could put the truth to him, he'd be great. So I invited him to our next meeting at the mosque."

Eventually, Jeremiah Shabazz would move to Miami to oversee Clay's teaching. And Malcolm X played a crucial role in the process. But Rahaman remained involved.

"I taught him straight, like it really was," Rahaman reminisced. "The same way I'd teach anybody else. The only difference between him and the other brothers was, because of his profession, he didn't have the same duties in the temple. We used to eat together at the Famous Chef Café. When I first sat down with Cassius, no one had taught him about not eating pork. But it wasn't hard to get him to change. He didn't drink or smoke or do drugs, and he didn't mind changing what he ate at all. At the meetings, he never talked much. He just sat there, listening, wanting to learn. He was a beautiful young man. All he wanted was what was right for our people. The Messenger taught—and it's definitely true—that we're no greater than the least one of us. If we don't pull the little man that society rejects up out of the mud, then we as a people are nothing. And Cassius understood that."

Rahaman was in the corner for several of Ali's fights prior to

Muhammad's 1967 exile from boxing. One of those fights was the infamous "what's my name" beating of Ernie Terrell.

"There was me and Angelo and I don't remember who else," Rahaman recounted. "And I don't regret what Ali did to Terrell. Ernie knew us because I had tried to convert him in Miami when he and Ali sparred together. He knew what we stood for and still he gave comfort to our enemies by calling Ali 'Clay.' Before the fight, I had it in my mind that we were going to make him call Ali by his proper name. I told Ali that. Then, during the fight, I reminded him, 'Make him call your name.' You know the beating Terrell took for not answering, but I don't see no need for an apology. The referee had authority to stop the fight. The doctor had authority to stop the fight. Terrell's corner could have stopped it if it was so cruel."

★ ★ ★

A word of remembrance in honor of Hugh McIlvanney, who died on January 24, 2019, at age eighty-four.

When I began researching *The Black Lights* (my initial foray into serious boxing writing) in 1983, I was told that there were two books I should read. One was *The Sweet Science* by A. J. Liebling. The other was *McIlvanney on Boxing*.

In later years, I spent time with McIlvanney on several occasions. The most memorable of these came in 2001 when he took me to lunch at the Garrick Club in London. The club was founded in 1831 for the purpose of bringing patrons and practitioners of theatrical arts together so that actors and others in theatre might meet with men of education and wealth. A portrait of Charles Dickens (who was a guest at the club as a young man and later an esteemed member) was prominently displayed. During that trip to London, the seed for a novel I later wrote—*The Final Recollections of Charles Dickens*—was planted in my mind.

McIlvanney excelled as a boxing writer, sportswriter, and general news writer (the latter being his beat when he joined the staff of *The Scotsman* six decades ago). But these labels don't do him justice. He was a remarkable wordsmith and one of the best ever at his craft. Boxing is fortunate to have had him.

★ ★ ★

A quirky memory regarding Pernell Whitaker, who died after being hit by a car in Virginia Beach on July 14, 2019.

Whitaker was a great fighter in an era when greatness had to be earned in the ring, not bestowed by publicity and hype. After winning a gold medal at the 1984 Olympics, he won titles in four weight classes as a pro and stood atop boxing's pound-for-pound list until he was supplanted by Roy Jones.

Pernell was honored twice by the Boxing Writers Association of America as "Fighter of the Year." In spring 1994, I was at the second of those occasions. The pre-dinner VIP reception was underway. And a jagged fingernail was making me uncomfortable. I had a small emery board in my suit jacket pocket. But I didn't feel like leaving the reception, filing down the nail in a hallway, and having to make my way past security to get into the reception again. On the other hand, filing my nails in the middle of a room populated by the boxing elite didn't seem like a good idea. So I moved to a corner, took the emery board from my pocket, and began filing as unobtrusively as possible.

That was when Whitaker walked by; did a double take; and blurted out, "Oh, man. Can I use that? I got a fingernail that's driving me crazy."

Let others remember Pernell Whitaker in the ring working his magic against Julio Cesar Chavez, Azumah Nelson, and Buddy McGirt. I'll remember the night he borrowed my emery board.

★ ★ ★

Jim Bouton, the iconoclastic pitcher whose major league career peaked when he compiled a 21–7 record and 2.53 ERA for the New York Yankees in 1963, died on July 10, 2019, at age eighty.

Bouton had a social conscience and was outspoken about it. He played for the Yankees from 1962 through 1968 and briefly for the Seattle Pilots, Houston Astros, and Atlanta Braves afterward. But his most lasting contribution to the game was as the author of a memoir entitled *Ball Four*.

Ball Four chronicled Bouton's career in the major leagues through the end of the 1969 season. Much of the book was devoted to his years with the Yankees when the Bronx Bombers—led by Mickey Mantle, Yogi Berra, Roger Maris, and Whitey Ford—ruled the baseball world.

The book stripped away the carefully cultivated image of major league players as boy scouts. It recounted in detail more than a few sordid goings-on from profligate womanizing to players who took the field while hungover from a drinking binge the night before. It took aim at some not-very-bright managers and criticized a repressive economic structure that left players at the mercy of avaricious club owners. It was enlightening, poignant, and funny.

The baseball establishment and many of Bouton's fellow players viewed *Ball Four* as a betrayal of the code of silence characteristic of professional sports at that time. Dick Young (an old-school columnist for the *New York Daily News*) branded him a "social leper." The next time Pete Rose saw Bouton, he shouted out "Fuck you, Shakespeare."

But the public loved it. After a small first printing of 5,000 copies, *Ball Four* rocketed past the million mark in sales and became part of a revolution that changed sports writing. In 2002, *Sports Illustrated* ranked it in the number three slot on a list of the best sports books of all time.

All sports fans and sports writers—boxing fans and boxing writers included—owe Jim Bouton a debt of gratitude.

★ ★ ★

Each year, I'm charged with polling past winners of the Nat Fleischer Award for Career Excellence in Boxing Journalism to determine who the next honoree will be. The award differs from others given out by the Boxing Writers Association of America in that only past recipients are eligible to vote.

Most of the nomination process and final voting is conducted by email. But the emails lead to telephone calls and a chance to catch up with old friends. As 2019 drew to a close, I reached out to Jay Searcy for his vote and learned that he'd died four days after Christmas the previous year, shortly after our last conversation.

Searcy made his mark in boxing by writing for a wide range of publications and serving as sports editor for the *Philadelphia Inquirer*. "He was a great writer," Jerry Izenberg remembers. "He saw things in and out of the ring that not many people see."

Jay was also tied to a unique undertaking and the best-kept secret in the history of war.

In the early 1940s, a town not seen on civilian maps, whose residents were subject to strict censorship and ruled by military decree, was built virtually overnight in eastern Tennessee. It was created to serve as administrative headquarters for a team of scientists and military leaders charged with developing an atomic bomb.

Searcy's parents were part of that team. Jay, like other children of school age, attended a hastily constructed school. In a 2010 memoir entitled *The Last Reunion*, he recalled, "We lived in plywood homes, showered in community bathhouses, sat on chamber pots. We walked to school in construction mud, stood in lines for rationed goods. We lived the mystery—felt it, touched it, smelled it—though we didn't know what it was. And except for a few, neither did our parents. Then, on August 6, 1945, when the bomb destroyed sixty percent of Hiroshima, everybody knew."

Jay Searcy was a craftsman with words and a good man. A lot of people, myself included, will miss him.

★ ★ ★

I met Saoul Mamby in 1983. I'd just begun researching *The Black Lights*—my first book about boxing—and wanted to talk to some fighters. So I went to Ringside Gym, one of three gyms near Times Square in New York. Mamby had just finished working out. I asked if we could talk. He said "sure." I asked my first question. And Saoul answered, "Wait a minute. This is a serious interview. Let me shower and then we'll talk."

We talked for two hours that afternoon. He was the first fighter I ever interviewed as a boxing writer.

Mamby was born in the Bronx in 1947. He graduated from Bronx Vocational High School in 1965 and began boxing that year as an amateur. He turned pro in 1969 after a stint in Vietnam.

"I was in Nam for one year, six days, and four hours," he told me.

Had he seen combat?

"Yeah, enough. And boxing is easier."

During the early years of his ring career, Mamby worked at a variety of jobs. He was a stock clerk and washed windows on skyscrapers. "I drove a gypsy cab for a while," he told me. "But it got too dangerous so I quit."

He was a master of ring generalship and pacing. Not a big puncher. But he hit opponents with a lot of punches and, as the rounds went by, the damage added up. The most impressive thing about him as a fighter was his defense. He had an intuitive sense of when punches were coming and the ability to make opponents miss by a fraction of an inch. On the day we talked, in hundreds of rounds of boxing, no one—not even Roberto Duran—had knocked him off his feet.

But Mamby's career languished until he met Don King.

Talking about King, Saoul said, "We met and he asked me to sign a promotional contract, which I did, and a managerial contract with his son Carl, which I refused. So now I had a promoter but no fights. All I got was a walkout fight against Norman Goins. And I was a fighter who'd gone the distance with Antonio Cervantes and Roberto Duran. Finally in 1979, I signed with Carl King as my manager. I'd never met him in my life. And right away after I signed with Carl King, I was offered Marion Thomas in New York and Tom Tarantino in Atlantic City—both easy fights. One month after the Tarantino fight, I was in Seoul, Korea, fighting Sang-Hyun Kim for the [WBC 140-pound] world title."

Mamby beat Kim on a fourteenth-round knockout and successfully defended his title five times (including a knockout victory over Esteban de Jesus). On June 26, 1982, he lost by split decision to Leroy Haley. Then Haley was defeated by Bruce Curry who relinquished the crown to Billy Costello.

As my research on *The Black Lights* progressed, I decided to view the sport and business of boxing through the prism of Costello, his manager (Mike Jones), and trainer (Victor Valle). In a twist of fate, the book's climactic fight, contested fourteen months after I visited Ringside Gym, was Billy's November 3, 1984, title defense against Mamby.

I was in Costello's dressing room in the hours before and after the fight. He beat Mamby. Beat him badly. The judges' scorecards (119–109, 119–109, 118–110) didn't reveal the full hurt that he put on Saoul that afternoon.

"I never went through this before," Saoul told me when I visited him in his hotel room that night. "I've never been hurt like this in the ring."

Time passed. I finished writing *The Black Lights*. After it was published, I sent a copy to Mamby as a courtesy. It was unlikely that he'd enjoy reading about his getting beaten up, but it seemed like the right thing to do.

Several days later, my telephone rang. It was Saoul.

"I just finished reading your book," he told me. "It's the best book I've ever read."

That moved me. A lot.

In the years that followed, Saoul and I were in touch from time to time. He fought a lot of tough opponents as his career wound down (champions like Buddy McGirt, Maurice Blocker, Javier Castillejo, and Jorge Vaca) and lost to most of them. He was always willing to go in tough. Overall, he fought thirteen men who held world titles at one time or another and was stopped only once (at age forty-six, by Derrell Coley).

Then, on March 8, 2008, Saoul did something bizarre. At age sixty, he returned to the ring as an active fighter and lost a ten-round decision to a mediocre club fighter named Anthony Osbourne. By most reckonings, that made him the oldest combatant ever in a professional bout.

After the fight, I had lunch with Saoul and asked him why he'd taken the fight.

"It was good for me," he said. "I enjoyed it. I didn't get hurt or beat down. It's just that my tools weren't sharp. Putting guys in body bags in Vietnam, knowing that all their dreams had died with them; I vowed that, if I got out of there alive, I was going to do what I wanted to do with my life. Boxing makes me feel happy and complete, so I'm boxing. I risked my life in Vietnam and I can do what I want with it now."

Saoul Mamby fought some of the best fighters in the world when he was young. And there was a time when he was one of the best. He died this week [on December 17]. I feel very sad this evening. A nice man who was important to me is gone.

Harold Lederman at the fights was a happy man. "For most people in boxing, it's all about the money," he said. "For me, it's all about the boxing."

Saying Goodbye to Harold Lederman

Harold Lederman, one of boxing's most beloved figures, died on May 11, 2019, at the Joe Raso Hospice Residence in Rockland County after a long battle with cancer.

Lederman was born on January 26, 1940, and grew up in the Bronx. His father was a pharmacist who owned a small drug store.

"My father had two passions," Harold reminisced years ago. "Theater and boxing. Each year when I was growing up, we'd go out to the Rockaways and rent a house on the beach for the summer. The next town over was Long Beach, where they had fights every Friday night. My father would go with his friends. They'd throw me in the back of the car, and I saw some great fights. That's where my love of boxing started."

After graduating from high school, Lederman followed in the footsteps of his father, grandfather, and uncles on both sides of the family by entering a four-year pharmacy program at Columbia University. The school was located at Broadway and 68th Street in Manhattan, several miles from Columbia's main campus but only two blocks from boxing's famed St. Nicholas Arena.

Harold became a regular at the fights and always kept score.

How much did he love boxing?

The night before Harold's wedding in 1963, he and his bride-to-be went to the fights at Madison Square Garden. "Gaspar Ortega beat an Italian kid from the Bronx named Billy Bello in the main event," he later recounted. "Our honeymoon was in Miami, and we went to the fights there too. Tony Mammarelli was in the main event at that one."

In late 1963, Harold filed an application to work as a ring judge for the New York State Athletic Commission. Initially, he was assigned to amateur contests. The first pro fight he judged was an eight-round super-welterweight bout between Grey Gavin (22–2–1) and Juan Ramos (13–15–2) at Sunnyside Garden in Queens on November 8, 1967. Ramos pulled off the upset on a split decision with Harold's card providing the margin of victory.

Over the years, Harold scored more than a thousand fights as an official judge. Muhammad Ali, George Foreman, Larry Holmes, Evander Holyfield, Marvin Hagler, Sugar Ray Leonard, Thomas Hearns, Roberto Duran, Michael Spinks, Julio Cesar Chavez, Pernell Whitaker, Alexis Arguello, Emile Griffith, and Floyd Patterson fought under his watchful eye.

Then came the break of a lifetime. On January 17, 1986, Harold was at home watching Tim Witherspoon versus Tony Tubbs on HBO. "What the commentators were saying and what I was watching on the screen were two different things," he later recalled.

The next week, Harold telephoned Ross Greenburg (then the executive producer of HBO Sports) and told him that HBO needed someone to score the fights. Greenburg said he'd think about it. Harold figured that was the end of that. But several weeks later, Greenberg called back and offered him a trial run. Harold made his television debut on HBO's telecast of the March 22, 1986, WBC heavyweight title bout between Pinklon Thomas and Trevor Berbick. The rest is history.

For the next three decades, Harold lived every boxing fan's dream. When he began scoring fights for HBO, he was paired with Barry Tompkins, Larry Merchant, and Ray Leonard. "Ray was one of my heroes," he said, looking back on that time. "I kept pinching myself, saying, 'I can't believe it. I'm on television with Ray Leonard.'"

Sports commentators on television get jaded. For many, it's just a job. Harold loved every minute of it. His role as HBO's "unofficial ringside judge" gave him a ring's-edge view of the action at boxing's biggest fights. Over time, he earned a following of his own.

The key to Harold's success went far beyond his knowledge of boxing. There's a sense that something separates most television sports commentators from the rest of us. Jock credentials, fluent diction, good looks.

Harold was "everyman." Rotund and balding, he would not have been mistaken for Fred Astaire. His harsh nasal voice and distinctive high-pitched laugh were unmistakably his own.

And he loved going to fights. There was a time when he went to a hundred shows a year. Don Elbaum was promoting in Atlantic City. Russell Peltz was promoting in Philadelphia. "How could I not go to their shows?" Harold asked rhetorically before elaborating, "It was a three-hour drive each way. I'd go to the fights, get home at two o'clock in the morning, sleep for four hours, get back up, and go to work. Every one of those shows was worth it. I love club shows from the bottom of my heart. You see good fights; you see bad fights. You see good shows; you see bad shows. But I'm always happy when I'm at the fights."

Harold loved spending time with boxing people. "There's something special about them," he said. "Even the bad ones are fun to be around." He was unfailingly cheerful. Asked to recall the last time he'd gotten angry, Harold answered, "Who knows? There's not enough time in life to get angry."

He loved talking with people about boxing. His idea of Nirvana was walking through a hotel lobby and having total strangers stop him to talk about fights. HBO was an ideal platform for him. It enabled him to talk to millions of fans at once instead of one fan at a time.

Harold loved working for HBO and he was proud to work for HBO. He was a perfect goodwill ambassador for HBO and boxing.

The HBO commentating team of Jim Lampley, Larry Merchant, Emanuel Steward, and Harold is regarded by many as the best announcing team ever assembled for boxing and perhaps any sport. When HBO boxing programming was at its peak, the other three team members paid tribute to Harold:

★ Jim Lampley: "Harold is the mayor at ringside at every fight he goes to. He's a global ambassador for boxing. Nobody cares more; nobody has seen more; and nobody would go to the ends of the earth for a fight more willingly and joyously than Harold. His enthusiasm for boxing is a supernatural force."

★ Larry Merchant: "It's unusual for someone who has been part of boxing for as long as Harold to maintain a wide-eyed enthusiasm for the sport. Harold has a wide-eyed enthusiasm for boxing that's beyond compare. When we do a show at an arena away from the hotel we're staying in, HBO arranges for a car to take us to the arena. Harold never goes with us. That's because, without fail, he's at the arena hours ahead of us, watching every preliminary fight, saying hello to every judge, and shaking hands with virtually every fan in the arena. He'll go anywhere at any time for any fight, and he's filled with wonder for it all."

* Emanuel Steward: "Harold is the greatest boxing fan on the face of the earth. The joy that he has for even the most ordinary fights is like nothing I've ever known. There has never been anyone like Harold before, and there will never be anyone like Harold again. If you opened him up, boxing would pour out of his veins."

I don't remember when I first met Harold. I know that he was part of my life for decades. We spent countless hours together, talking in media centers, driving home from Atlantic City after fights, and at other boxing-related events. The last time I saw him was in an HBO studio on East 23rd Street in Manhattan on the night of November 24, 2018.

Harold's deteriorating physical condition had made travel and navigating arenas on fight night increasingly difficult. Earlier in the year, HBO had made the decision to prolong his announcing career by having him call fights from a TV studio off a monitor. On this particular night—the next-to-last telecast in HBO's historic reign as "the heart and soul of boxing"—the network was televising a doubleheader from Atlantic City. Murodjon Akhmadaliev vs. Isaac Zarate would be the opening bout followed by Dmitry Bivol vs. Jean Pascal.

The telecast was scheduled to begin at 10:00 p.m. Harold arrived at the studio at 7:45 p.m. He walked haltingly. Production assistant Kate Adriani and studio engineer Joe Pepe were there to greet him and led him to a tiny enclosure designated "Announce booth A."

For the next two hours, Harold and I talked boxing. He was sitting in a black leather chair opposite a wall-mounted TV monitor. Once HBO went on the air, he'd wear a headset with an attached microphone.

"I think you do a better job scoring fights if you're at ringside," Harold offered. "And I miss the action. Not just the fights, the whole fight-week atmosphere. But you do the best you can wherever you are. And this way, I see exactly what the fans at home are seeing."

What was his favorite fight as HBO's "unofficial ringside judge"?

"I really didn't have a favorite. I loved them all."

And his most memorable fight as an official ring judge?

"That's easy," he answered. "Muhammad Ali against Ken Norton at Yankee Stadium [on September 28, 1976]. Fights in New York were scored by rounds rather than points in those days. Barney Smith and I scored the fight eight rounds to seven for Ali. Back then, the referee also scored fights. Arthur Mercante—senior, not junior—had it 8–6–1 for Ali. I had it dead even going into the last round, and I gave the last round to Ali. I got a lot of criticism. My phone didn't stop ringing for a month. But I still think we were right."

A notebook, a large bottle of Diet Coke, and a mug filled with ice water were set out on a table in front of Harold. Also, a half-pound of fudge, pound cake, and a bag of taco chips that Harold would nosh on throughout the night. When the telecast began, Adriani and Pepe would monitor the proceedings from behind a large glass window separating the control room from the announce booth.

At 9:59:30, Pepe instructed, "Put your headset on, Harold. Thirty seconds to air."

The first fight began. Akhmadaliev (an Olympic bronze medal winner from Uzbekistan) vs. Zarate (a part-time brewery worker from San Pedro, California). It was, Jim Lampley acknowledged at the top of the telecast, "a formula for a potential mismatch."

Harold watched intently as the action unfolded on the monitor and listened to the audio on his headset. During the rounds that followed, his attention never wavered. After each round, he called out his score, which Kate recorded in a ledger and transmitted on an open line to the HBO truck in Atlantic City.

Fifteen seconds into round four, Jim Lampley spoke the magic words: "Let's check in with our unofficial scorer, Harold Lederman, to see how he has it so far."

"Okay, Jim," Harold responded. "I have it 2-to-1, 29–28, in favor of MA or however you pronounce it. In any case, I thought he did enough to win the first round. I also thought he won the third round. But I gave the second round to Isaac Zarate, whose name is a lot easier to pronounce."

After round six, Harold was brought into the telecast for the second time. Akhmadaliev ended matters on a ninth-round stoppage.

The main event—Bivol vs. Pascal—went the full twelve-round distance with Harold being called upon after round six and again at the end of the fight. His 119–109 scorecard in favor of Bivol matched the scores turned in by two of the three judges.

"I never get bored watching boxing," Harold said when the evening was over. "Never! Not even on television."

HBO had arranged for a car service to drive Harold home. It was pouring rain, and he offered to drop me off at my apartment; an offer I gladly accepted.

For most of the ride, Harold was quiet. The physical toll of a long night's work was catching up with him. Then a pensive look crossed his face. "I love this stuff," he told me. "HBO was boxing. I would have liked it to go on, even if it was without me. I hope, wherever I go next, they have boxing."